D0987112

NOV   2011

DATE DUE

Digital Discourse

DIGITAL DISCOURSE

Language in the New Media

—◈—

Edited by

CRISPIN THURLOW

KRISTINE MROCZEK

OXFORD
UNIVERSITY PRESS

OXFORD
UNIVERSITY PRESS

Oxford University Press, Inc. publishes works that further
Oxford University's objective of excellence
in research, scholarship and education.

Oxford   New York
Auckland   Cape Town   Dar es Salaam   Hong Kong   Karachi
Kuala Lumpur   Madrid   Melbourne   Mexico City   Nairobi
New Delhi   Shanghai   Taipei   Toronto

With offices in
Argentina   Austria   Brazil   Chile   Czech Republic   France   Greece
Guatemala   Hungary   Italy   Japan   Poland   Portugal
Singapore   South Korea   Switzerland   Thailand   Turkey   Ukraine   Vietnam

Published by Oxford University Press Inc.
198 Madison Avenue, New York, New York 10016
www.oup.com

Oxford is a registered trade mark of Oxford University Press

Library of Congress Cataloging-in-Publication Data
Digital discourse: language in the new media / edited by Crispin Thurlow and
Kristine Mroczek.
p. cm. — (Oxford studies in sociolinguistics)
Includes bibliographical references and index.
ISBN 978–0–19–979543–7 (hardcover : alk.paper) — ISBN 978–0–19–979544–4 (pbk. : alk.paper)
1. Sociolinguistics.   2. Social media.   3. Digital media   4. Technological innovations—Social aspects.
5. Discourse analysis—Social aspects.   I. Thurlow, Cripin.   II. Mroczek, Kristine R.
P107.D54 2011
306.44—dc22   2010049086

1 3 5 7 9 8 6 4 2

Printed in China
on acid-free paper

For Sally Johnson

Contents

Foreword
Naomi Baron

PREDICTING THE FUTURE of the written word is a tricky business. Just ask Johannes Trithemius, the Abbot of Spondheim, whose book *De Laude Scriptorum* (*In Praise of Scribes*) appeared in 1492. Trithemius railed against a modern invention of his time—the printing press—arguing that hand-copied manuscripts were superior to printed ones. Among the Abbot's complaints were that parchment would last longer than paper, that not all printed books were easily accessible or inexpensive, and that the scribe could be more accurate than the printer. At the time Trithemius was writing, he was perhaps correct. He noted, for example, that printed books were often deficient in spelling and appearance. But he also maintained that "Printed books will never be the equivalent of handwritten codices," a prediction that thankfully proved untrue.

New technologies can understandably be unnerving. Decades back, people were sometimes terrorized upon seeing their first automobile or airplane. In the 1970s and 80s, telephone answering machines produced similar fears. Many users hung up when they reached an answering machine, too tongue-tied to know what to say.

Today, it is new technologies such as computers and mobile phones that are commonly depicted as threats to both the social and the linguistic fabric. Regarding social issues, the concern has been that face-to-face encounters will diminish because we replace physical meetings with e-mail or text messages. Work by Barry Wellman, Anabel Quan-Haase, and others (e.g., Quan-Haase et al., 2002; Wang & Wellman, 2010) has challenged the contention that new media are reducing social capital.

The question of whether new media will compromise language standards is particularly vital in light of how much *Sturm und Drang* the issue has generated. Crispin Thurlow (2006) has provided an array of examples of the "moral panic" expressed in the popular press over lexical shortenings, random punctuation, and nonstandard spelling assumed to typify the text messaging of young people. These linguistic transgressions are seen as spelling doom for the English language. My own favorite from Thurlow's collection is this one from the *Observer*: "The English language

is being beaten up, civilization is in danger of crumbling" (March 7, 2004).
This rhetoric, as Thurlow (2011) has noted most recently, is surprisingly
persistent and sometimes even more sweeping: "Text messaging corrupts
all languages" (*Economist*, May 2008).

But is English actually being beaten up (much less civilization in danger of a swift demise)? The simple answer is "no", but the story behind that
verdict illustrates how important it is to substantiate off-the-cuff claims
about new media language with both empirical research and awareness of
the larger social context in which new media and language are used.

The English language has a far-reaching history of people being concerned that linguistic standards must be established—or maintained
(Baron, 2000; Crystal, 2008). Around 1200, an Augustinian canon named
Orm wrote a lengthy homiletic verse through which he illustrated his
proposed new spelling system. (Medieval English spelling was chaotic,
to say the least.) The eighteenth and nineteenth centuries were the hey-
day of prescriptive grammars, in which self-appointed authorities set out
normative rules, including the infamous "no prepositions at the ends of
sentences." Among the consumers of these handbooks were members
of the lower classes, for whom "proper" speech and writing were necessary steps to bettering one's station in life. The twentieth century brought
a new generation of language mavens, ranging from Henry Fowler (in
England) to John Simon or Edwin Newman (in the United States). By the
early twenty-first century, we had Lynne Truss (*Eats, Shoots & Leaves*), along
with the popular press.

However, this steady drumbeat of prescriptivism needs to be set in a
broader linguistic and social context. As I argued in *Alphabet to E-mail*
(Baron, 2000), the relationship between speech and writing has under-
gone major changes over the past 1200 years. From Old English times
to the Elizabethan era, writing largely served to record the formal spoken word or, in many cases, to be re-presented as speech. Chaucer read
his works aloud in court, and Shakespeare's plays were essentially created to be performed, not read in printed quartos. Then, for roughly three
centuries, writing emerged as a medium distinct from speech. Writing
became the platform for defining a standard language. However, by the
latter half of the twentieth century, the role of writing began to shift again,
commonly functioning as a medium for recording informal speech. As a
result of these transformations, today's "off-line" writing (for instance, the
writing of newspapers or magazines, as opposed to the language of e-mail
or texting) is far more casual than writing of half a century ago. (If you

doubt this generalization, simply compare a current front page of the *New York Times* with its counterpart around 1960.)

The most recent linguistic shift was the product of a cluster of social changes. And here I will speak principally of the USA as the context I know best. One such change was a growing sense of social informality, evidenced, for example, in forms of address (calling people you don't know by first name rather than by title and surname) or through wearing casual dress, regardless of the occasion (think of showing up in jeans at the opera). This informality was also reflected in American pedagogy. No longer was the teacher the center of many classrooms: The model of the "sage on the stage" was replaced by that of teacher as "guide on the side" (Baron, 2000, Chapter 5).

A second factor was the rise of American youth culture and the tendency among adults to emulate youthful behavior patterns (Baron, 2003). These days it is common to find baby boomers wearing trendy clothing designed for young people, and even saying "Awesome!", "What's up?", or "LOL."

Thirdly, there was multiculturalism. In the United States, struggles in the second half of the twentieth century to confront the evils of racism drew attention to the linguistic legitimacy of African-American Vernacular English. During this same period, America began actively promoting multiculturalism, entailing tolerance of people with nonmainstream identities or from different cultural (and linguistic) backgrounds. National rhetoric (and curricular design) reflects a legally and pedagogically structured acceptance of individual and group differences, including teaching children not to pass judgment on regional dialects or nonnative speakers. In the process, society loosens the grip of norms regarding linguistic correctness or consistency.

These social changes led, in turn, to relaxation of traditional notions concerning what students should be taught about English grammar. Today, grammar books are no longer part of many American schools' curricula. Students can hardly be expected to follow rules they have never learned—and that are not consistently evidenced in everyday speech (is it "between you and I" or "between you and me"?). In the world beyond the schoolroom, there is a growing sense that consistency of linguistic usage or knowledge of the rules being violated is not especially important. To use an American colloquialism, the attitude reflects a "Whatever!" approach toward language standards (Baron, 2008, Chapter 8). This attitude is evidenced in subtle but palpable ways: in the increasingly sloppy proofreading found in publications from respected presses or in costly print advertisements; in the laissez-faire attitude toward grammatical usage heard on mainstream television and radio broadcasting—and in the language used by university students. In my early years of teaching, students used to apologize for "incorrect" grammar. Today, they often don't know which usage is correct (is it *who* or *whom*? *he* or *him*?), and more significantly, commonly they don't believe the answer matters.

Combine together shifts in contemporary expectations regarding off-line writing with current social attitudes about informality, youth culture, and multiculturalism. The result is a sociolinguistic milieu in which speakers and writers feel they have considerable latitude in the language they use. These attitudes predate the profusion of computers and mobile phones. To the extent that laissez-faire approaches toward traditional linguistic conventions appear in e-mail, IMs, text messages, and the like, digital media are not to blame. Rather, we use electronic devices to perpetrate language patterns that were already in play.

The moral of this tale is that in thinking about language used with new technologies, the relationship between surface phenomena and root causes may be less than obvious. As with any scientific venture, the study of new media language demands both creative sleuthing and hard work.

It is just this kind of creativity and focus that characterizes *Digital Discourse*. Crispin Thurlow and Kristine Mroczek's welcome volume offers up a collection of fascinating—and methodologically rigorous—studies of the intersection between new media and the social use of language. Such research enables us to speak with authority (rather than from fear or bravado) about how new media may—or may not—be transforming the ways in which we use language with one another. The editors are also to applauded for following in the tradition of Brenda Danet and Susan Herrring (2007), whose book *The Multilingual Internet* offered a linguistically and culturally diverse perspective on how to think about "mediated" language. What is more, *Digital Discourse* casts a broad net regarding what constitutes "discourse," including not only the anticipated fare of texting, blogs, social networking sites, or online gaming, but also other social contexts that entail exchange of ideas or information, such as tourism or performance.

Thurlow and Mroczek have produced a collection that is at once timely but grounded in earlier research, theoretically driven but highly readable. While it's tricky business to predict the future, it's a safe bet that *Digital Discourse* will become part of the emerging cannon of trusted voices regarding communication in a digital world.

References

Baron, N.S. (2000). *Alphabet to E-mail: How Written English Evolved and Where It's Heading*. London: Routledge.

Baron, N.S. (2003). Why e-mail looks like speech: Proofreading, pedagogy, and public face. In J. Aitchison & D. Lewis (Eds.), *New Media Language*, (pp. 102–113). London: Routledge.

Baron, N.S. (2008). *Always On: Language in an Online and Mobile World*. New York: Oxford University Press.

Crystal, D. (2008). *The Fight for English*. New York: Oxford University Press.

Danet, B. & Herring, S. (Eds.). (2007). *The Multilingual Internet: Language, Culture, and Communication Online*. New York: Oxford University Press.

Quan-Haase, A., Wellman, B., Witte, J., & Hampton, K. (2002). Capitalizing on the Net: Social contact, civic engagement, and sense of community. In B. Wellman & C. Haythornthwaite (Eds.), *The Internet in Everyday Life*, (pp. 291–324). Malden, MA: Blackwell.

Trithemius, J. ([1492] 1974). *In Praise of Scribes (De Laude Scriptorum)*, K. Arnold (Ed.), R. Behrendt (Trans.). Lawrence, KS: Coronado Press.

Thurlow, C. (2006). From statistical panic to moral panic: The metadiscursive construction and popular exaggeration of new media language in the print media. *Journal of Computer-Mediated Communication* 11(3), 667–701.

Thurlow, C. (2011). Determined creativity: Language play, vernacular literacy and new media discourse. In R. Jones (Ed.), *Discourse and Creativity*. London: Pearson.

Wang, H., & Wellman, B. (2010). Social connectivity in America: Changes in adult friendship network size from 2002 to 2007. *American Behavioral Scientist* 53(8): 1148–1169.

List of Contributors

Jannis Androutsopoulos, Professor of German and Media Linguistics, University of Hamburg, Germany

Naomi S. Baron, Professor of Linguistics, Department of Language and Foreign Studies, American University, USA

Elaine Chun, Assistant Professor, English Department and Linguistics Program, University of South Carolina, USA

Christa Dürscheid, Professor of German Linguistics, University of Zurich, Switzerland

Susan S. Herring, Professor of Information Science and Linguistics, Indiana University Bloomington, USA

Alexandra Jaffe, Professor of Linguistics and Anthropology, California State University Long Beach, USA

Adam Jaworski, Professor, Centre for Language and Communication Research, Cardiff University, Wales

Graham M. Jones, Assistant Professor of Anthropology, Massachusetts Institute of Technology, USA

Rodney H. Jones, Associate Professor and Associate Head, English Department, City University of Hong Kong, Hong Kong

Carmen K. M. Lee, Assistant Professor, Department of English, Chinese University of Hong Kong, Hong Kong

Aoife Lenihan, Doctoral Researcher in Applied Language Studies, University of Limerick, Ireland

Kristine Mroczek, Doctoral Researcher, Department of Communication, University of Washington (Seattle), USA

Lisa Newon, Doctoral Researcher, Department of Anthropology, University of California Los Angeles, USA

Yukiko Nishimura, Professor, Faculty of Humanities, Toyo Gakuen University, Japan

Saija Peuronen, Doctoral Researcher, Department of Languages, University of Jyväskylä, Finland

Bambi B. Schieffelin, Professor of Anthropology, New York University, USA

Rachel E. Smith, Writing Consultant, New York University Abu Dhabi, UAE

Tereza Spilioti, Lecturer in English Language and Communication, Kingston University London, England

Lauren Squires, Assistant Professor of English, University of North Carolina, Wilmington

Elisabeth Stark, Professor of Romance Linguistics, University of Zurich, Switzerland

Crispin Thurlow, Associate Professor of Language and Communication, University of Washington (Bothell), USA

Carmel Vaisman, Postdoctoral Researcher, Smart Family Foundation Communication Institute at the Hebrew University of Jerusalem, Israel

Keith Walters, Professor and Chair, Department of Applied Linguistics, Portland State University, Portland, USA

Shana Walton, Assistant Professor, Department of Languages and Literature, Nicholls State University, Thibodaux, USA

Introduction

FRESH PERSPECTIVES ON NEW MEDIA SOCIOLINGUISTICS

Crispin Thurlow and Kristine Mroczek

OUR PRIORITY IN editing a collection such as *Digital Discourse* is to give precedence (and space) to the work of our contributors. Instead of providing a lengthy and probably tedious literature review, therefore, we offer only a brief meta-review of *some* of the most comprehensive, sociolinguistically relevant publications to have appeared in English. (See our comment below about language politics.) The kinds of sociolinguistic topics, trends, and directions that others in the field have already pinpointed, enable us to locate *Digital Discourse* in the field. They also help us to identify the four most important concepts or organizing principles that we think delineate (or should delineate) the field of new media sociolinguistics: *discourse, technology, multimodality, ideology*.

Since 1996, there have been only three edited volumes in English dedicated, at least in part, to providing an orchestrated perspective on new media language. Following Susan Herring's groundbreaking *Computer-Mediated Communication: Linguistic, Social and Cross-Cultural Perspectives* in 1996, came Brenda Danet and Susan Herring's *The Multilingual Internet: Language, Culture, and Communication Online* (2007) and then, in 2009, Charley Rowe and Eva Wyss's *Language and New Media: Linguistic, Cultural, and Technological Evolutions*. Of course, Naomi Baron's highly regarded and much-cited book *From Alphabet to E-mail* (2000) was another key moment for new media sociolinguistics; her *Always on: Language in an Online and Mobile World* (2008) is already proving to be similarly influential. Although less grounded in first-hand empirical research, David Crystal's *Language and the Internet* (2001) and *Txting: The Gr8 Db8* (2008) have been hugely popular and undoubtedly raised public awareness about the role of language in new media.

In this time, there have also been three journal special issues offering coordinated accounts of language/discourse and the new media. Two of these appeared in the *Journal of Computer-Mediated Communication*: Brenda Danet and Susan Herring's (2003) issue on new media multilingualism, a precursor to their edited volume; and our own issue on young people's new media discourse (Thurlow, 2009). Arguably the most significant special issue was Jannis Androutsopoulos' (2006a) on computer-mediated communication for the *Journal of Sociolinguistics*.

Without a doubt, the work presented by our contributors (and our selection of their work for the volume) is heavily informed by these various scholarly "distillations" in the English-language literature and, of course, by a wealth of research published in other languages. We can tease things out a little further, however, by listing some of the specific topics, trends, and directions identified by scholars like those just mentioned.

Arguably the best known—internationally speaking—scholar of new media language, Susan Herring (e.g., 1996, 2001a, 2004) characterizes her own work as *computer-mediated discourse analysis*, which she organizes around a series of analytic priorities that continue to direct a lot of research in the field; these are

- *technological variables* such as synchronicity, size of message buffer, anonymous messaging, persistence of transcript, channels of communication (e.g., text, audio, video), automatic filtering;
- *situational variables* such as participation structure (e.g., public/private, number of participants), demographics, setting, purpose, topic, tone, norms of participation, linguistic code; and
- *linguistic variables* (or discourse features) such as structure (e.g., typography, spelling, word choice, sentence structure), meaning (i.e., of symbols, words, utterances, exchanges), interaction (e.g., turn taking, topic development, back-channels, repairs), and social function (e.g., identity markers, humor and play, face management, conflict).

This basic framework—a shopping list of new media discourse variables—informs and grounds a great deal of sociolinguistic research in the field, and reference is made to them throughout *Digital Discourse*. Others have, however, wanted to push the field a little further and suggested a more refined and perhaps also up-to-date research agenda for sociolinguists interested in new media—or what is often referred to as computer-mediated communication (cf. Thurlow et al., 2004). In the introduction to his special issue of the *Journal of Sociolinguistics*, for example, Jannis Androutsopoulos (2006b) offers some specific suggestions; for example:

- the need to challenge exaggerated assumptions about the distinctiveness of new media language;
- the need to move beyond early (i.e., 1990s) computer-mediated communication's simplistic characterization of—and concern for—asynchronous and synchronous technologies;
- the need to shift away from an undue emphasis on the linguistic (or orthographic) features of new media language and, related to this, the hybrid nature of new media genres;
- the need also to shift from "medium-related" to more ethnographically grounded "user-related" approaches.

In more recent work (e.g., 2010), Androutsopoulos has continued to promote the value of research shaped by this type of *discourse-ethnographic* rather than variationist approach, something he also addresses in his contribution to the current volume (Chapter 13). In this regard, Androutsopoulos' driving concern is that scholars move beyond a one-track interest in the formal features of new media language (e.g., spelling and orthography) and a preoccupation with delineating individual discourse genres; instead, greater attention should be paid to the *situated* practices of new media users (i.e., communicators) and the intertexuality and *heteroglossia* inherent in new media convergence (i.e., people's use of multiple media and often in the same new media format, as in social networking profiles).

Along much the same vein, and in both an earlier article for the journal *Pragmatics* and in a commentary for the Androutsopoulos special issue, Alexandra Georgakopoulou (2003, 2006) summarizes and problematizes recurrent linguistic topics in the broader field of computer-mediated communication. She also offers her own recommendations for future research, which parallel many of Androutsopoulos's concerns and include:

- the need to accept as read the way new media blend spoken and written language (this is no longer news);
- the importance of attending less to the "informational" functions of computer-mediated communication and more to the playful identity performances for which it is used;
- ensuring that the study of language is grounded in a concern for the broader sociocultural practices and inequalities of communities (or social networks);
- always considering the connections between online and offline practices, and between different technologies;

- a general move toward emphasizing the contextual and particularistic nature of new media language;
- relying on the combination of *both* quantitative and qualitative (particularly ethnographic) research methods.

Once again, we see in Georgakopoulou's "manifesto" for new media language studies a call for research that is altogether more committed to the social meanings of technology and its particular (hence "particularistic") significance for specific users, groups, or communities.

One persistent problem in new media scholarship (sociolinguistic or otherwise) has been the apparent dominance of English—as both the medium of publication and, more importantly, as the subject of analysis. This has certainly been a central criticism in the reviews by European colleagues like Androutsopoulos and Georgakopoulou. In their groundbreaking collection *The Multilingual Internet*, Brenda Danet and Susan Herring (2007) made a concerted effort to rectify the situation, drawing together a wide range of work about the use of languages other than English on the internet, work that was written largely by scholars whose first/preferred language was not English. In the introduction to their book, Danet and Herring set out the following list of topics for organizing its chapters; this is a list that likewise helps set a more multilingual/multicultural agenda for new media sociolinguistics:

- language and culture (e.g., speech communities, context, and performance);
- writing systems (e.g., the restrictions of ASCII encoding, ad hoc improvisations by users;
- linguistic and discourse features (e.g., orthography and typography);
- gender and language (e.g., politeness, turn taking, social change);
- language choice and code switching (e.g., language use in diasporic online communities);
- linguistic diversity (e.g., small and endangered languages, the status of English).   .

In addition to elevating these topics for consideration by researchers, Danet and Herring's book also gave space to a world of non-English-language scholarship. The fact remains that, for all sorts of problematic institutional and geopolitical reasons, valuable research by scholars such as Michael Beißwenger, Chiaki Kishimoto, or Silvia Betti, to name only three, is still too easily overlooked. This is something that we were certainly very mindful of when putting together *Digital Discourse*, and we are pleased to be able to offer a collection that engages with multiple languages (specifically, Irish, Hebrew, Chinese, Finnish, Japanese, German, Greek, Arabic, and French), as well as a number of other important nonstandard and/or nonofficial ways of speaking.

Delineating New Media Sociolinguistics

All the work represented in *Digital Discourse* responds either directly or indirectly to the kinds of issues and recommendations proposed by prominent scholars like Herring, Androutsopoulos, Danet, and Georgakopoulou. And, as we say, they are certainly the ones best known in the English-language literature. Inspired by the same run of priorities, we want now to set out four organizing principles that we think could/should define the work of new media sociolinguistics; they are certainly the ones that ground *Digital Discourse*. For a field with such an interdisciplinary authorship and readership, these types of conceptual clarifications have the added benefit of making our disciplinary stance a little more transparent and hopefully understandable. The four principles are quite apparently interrelated and only separated for rhetorical convenience; they are also presented here as deliberately short, only loosely mapped statements.

Discourse: Language, Mediation, and Technologization

Putting "language" in its place, we establish from the outset that the object of this volume—and also for the field as a whole—is the study of language insofar as it illuminates social and cultural processes (cf. Bucholtz & Hall, 2008; Georgakopoulou, 2006). In other words, our primary concern is not with the abstract, "grammatical" language of linguistics, but rather the everyday life of *language in use*—or just *discourse*.

Whatever theoretical variations and methodological styles they encompass (see Jaworski & Coupland, 2006), sociolinguistics and linguistically oriented discourse analysis are grounded in a shared commitment to the following: the social function of language, the interactional accomplishment of meaning, the significance of communicator intent, and the relevance of social/cultural *context* (cf. Duranti & Goodwin, 1992). This has two specific implications for new media sociolinguistics. First, we should accept the inherently *mediated* nature of all communication (cf. Norris & Jones, 2005;

Scollon, 2001) and not just in the case of so-called computer-mediated communication; communication is always contextualized (i.e., mediated, embodied, emplaced) by, for example, relationships, setting, layout, gesture, accent, and typography. Sometimes, the medium (i.e., "technology") is the least of the mediators. Along these lines, we might also usefully draw a distinction between mediation and *mediatization* (cf. Couldry, 2008) for instances where language is mass-produced or broadcast in, say, newpapers, magazines, or websites.

The second implication of a strictly social-cultural approach to language is a need to think about its *technologization* (cf. Fairclough, 1999), before, that is, we even get to thinking about literal technologies for communication (Thurlow & Bell, 2009). In other words, we should engage with the particular historical-political context of contemporary language use: its commodification and its recontextualized use as a lifestyle resource or marketing strategy to be sold back to us, or as a workplace tool used to "manage" us (cf. Cameron, 2000; Heller, 2003). This is the real stuff of *symbolic power* (cf. Bourdieu, 1991) and an important part of the way new media language is nowadays also being organized, talked about, and (re-) valued (Thurlow, 2011a). In many ways, new media language simply adds another dimension (or domain) to these larger cultural shifts.

Technology: From Spectacular to Banal, from Digital to Linguistic

Technology is not a straightforward matter. People readily think of computers, telephones, fax machines, and perhaps also of washing machines, hearing aids, and rockets. But what of paper clips, pencils and paper, or writing? It is not only the machinery of clocks that is designed to enhance our basic human capacities, but also the mechanism of time itself (Thurlow et al., 2004). New media sociolinguistics needs an altogether more critical, carefully theorized take on technology before even contemplating its role in human communication.

Against the backdrop of technological determinism and extreme social constructionism, we should accept a certain *materiality* to communication technologies; undeniably, they *afford* certain communicative possibilities and not others (cf. Hutchby, 2001). Technologies—even "new" communication technologies—are, however, often not as spectacular or revolutionary as many would have us believe (cf. Thurlow, 2006). Indeed, they are usually *embedded* in complex ways into the banal practices of everyday life (cf. Herring, 2004). Technologies are thus best understood as *prosthetic extensions* of people's abilities and lives, rather like the hearing aid and the paperclip (Keating, 2005; cf. McLuhan, 2005 [1964]).

It is for this reason—the embedded, prosthetic nature of technologies—that we have privileged the notion of *media* over that of technology (cf. Buckingham, 2007; Kress, 2003; also Livingstone, 2002). For us, speaking of "new media" is a way to debunk—and reflexively acknowledge—the tendency for popular and scholarly writing to fetishize technology at the expense of its social meanings and cultural practices (cf. Herring, 2008; Thurlow, 2006). Mark Nelson (2006, p. 72) puts it rather nicely: "Power tools do not necessarily a carpenter make." Just as we are interested in language for its social uses, so, too, are we interested in technology for its cultural meanings. As sociolinguists and discourse analysts, we are also mainly concerned with what technology tells us about language.

To complicate the relationship between language and technology a little further, we might even consider drawing a distinction between mechanical or *digital technologies* and between semiotic or *linguistic technologies* (cf. Leupin, 2000; Nusselder, 2009). Although not everyone would agree (see Pinker, 1994), language is, at heart, a cultural construction (cf. Pennycook, 2004). In other words, it is a technology just like, well, "technology." Working with the idea of language as a technology forces an ongoing consideration of the constant interplay of the message and the medium (cf. McLuhan, 2005 [1964]; see also Hutchby, 2001) and of any overly neat or artificial separation between language *and* technology.

Multimodality: Beyond Language and into the Bedroom

Multimodality is—or at least should be—a "taken-for-granted" in new media studies. It is increasingly regarded as a core concept in sociolinguistics and discourse analysis more generally (e.g. Jewitt, 2009; Kress & van Leeuwen, 2001; Scollon, 2001; Scollon & Scollon, 2003). In this regard, something new media scholars outside of discourse analysis seldom do is follow a clearly articulated line on the difference between *medium* and *mode* (see Jewitt, 2004; cf. Kress & van Leeuwen, 2001) and the interplay of the two. This is especially germane given the growing complexity of the *multimedia* formats of newer new media, brought about by the inevitable *convergence* of old and new media (Jenkins, 2006) and the *layering* of new media with other new media (cf. Androutsopoulos, 2010; Myers, 2010).

In their efforts to redress the relative absence of the linguistic in computer-mediated communication, scholars often overlook the fact that it is only ever one of many communicative resources being used. All texts, all communicative events, are always achieved by means of *multiple semiotic resources*, even so-called text-based new media like instant- and text messaging. Herein lies much of the potential in new media for *invention and creativity*; time and again, research shows how users overcome apparent semiotic limitations, reworking and combining—often playfully—the resources at their disposal (cf. Burgess, 2010; Danet, 2001; and Thurlow, 2011b). New media sociolinguistics is going to need advanced analytical equipment if it is to keep track of the changing significance (in both common senses of the word) of language in the synaesthetic (Kress, 2003) and *heteroglossic* (cf. Androutsopoulos, 2010) spaces of new media.

Speaking of space, Gunther Kress and Theo van Leeuwen (2001, p. 11) use the bedroom for demonstrating the inherent multimodality of texts as well as the "orchestration" of multiple semiotic modes. For our purposes, another telling invocation of "bedroom" is Rodney Jones' (2010) more literal reference to bedroom as a common location of new media practice/access for young people (cf. also Holloway & Valentine, 2003). It is the situated, *spatialized* (which is not to say static) experiences of new media that are also crucial to an understanding of their meaning.

Ideology: The Disciplining of Technology and Language

Linguistically oriented discourse studies, especially those falling under the rubric of critical discourse analysis, often also orient to the notion of Foucauldian *discourses*—what we dub *F-discourse* as opposed to *L-discourse* ("language in use"; cf. Gee, 2010, on d-discourse and D-discourse). In practice, what this means is that scholars are interested both in the ways microlevel interactional and textual practices constitute our social worlds and in the ways that our everyday communicative/representational practices are structured by the social order, by larger systems of belief, and by hierarchies of knowledge. Insofar as Foucault (e.g., 1980, 1981) thought about the normative, naturalizing, and "neutralizing" qualities of discourses, they are not far removed in their effect from Marxist *ideologies* or Barthesian *mythologies*.

To start, digital technologies are themselves inherently ideological, both in terms of their political economies of access and control (see below), and also in terms of their potential as mechanisms or resources for both *normative* and *resistive* representation (cf. Kress, 2003; Thurlow, 2011b). This is quite apparent when one thinks of the symbolic power of the news and broadcast media (see Durham & Kellner, 2001); no less is true, however, of any number of seemingly mundane mechanical, medical, or digital technologies (cf. Headrick, 1981; Feenburg & Hannay, 1995). Technology or not, language, too, is fully ideological.

Online or offline, spoken or typed, face-to-face or digitally "mediated," what people do with language has material consequence (cf. Foucault, 1981), and language is instrumental in establishing categories of difference, relations of inequality, or at the very least, the social norms by which we all feel obliged to live our lives (see Thurlow, 2011c). Whether it is done by academics, journalists, teachers, or "nonexperts", talk about language (or *metalanguage*—cf. Jaworski et al., 2004) always exposes the vagaries of the symbolic marketplace (cf. Bourdieu, 1991): competing standards of "correct," "good," or "normal" language; debates about literacy and occupational training; the social categorization and disciplining of speakers; and the performative construction of language itself (cf. Cameron, 1995; Pennycook, 2004). And some people's ways of speaking inevitably come out better than others; some are voices of authority and reason, some speak "street talk," "pidgin," or a "subcultural antilanguage." Needless to say, as work on *language ideology* (Blommaert, 1999; Schieffelin et al., 1998; Woolard, 1998) reminds us, talk about language is usually, at root, a matter of disciplining the bodies of speakers rather than the niceties of their speech.

Concerning the "New" in New Media (and the "Global" in Global Media)

To these four organizing principles, we also want to add one obvious but no less important caveat about the supposed newness of "new media sociolinguistics." There is a contradiction inherent in any book such as the one we have put together here. On the one hand, its existence is predicated on and justified by a claim to novelty—to reporting something new (as in "new media" and "fresh sociolinguistic perspectives"). On the other hand, by the time the book has been published, disseminated, and more widely read, the digital technologies/media will have moved on, will have already started to mature, and will have embedded themselves deeper and/or differently into people's lives. Inevitably, the sociolinguistic and sociocultural practices of which these technologies are a part will also have changed.

None of this precludes scholars from wanting to keep up to date as best they can. There is much to be gained from simply tracking and recording developments and changes. Nonetheless, it is important to think twice before making overextended claims and wild predictions about the stability or endurability of the technolinguistic changes of the moment. It is also important to keep in check our academic enthusiasm for the *newness* of "new media" and any undue *presentism* (cf. Sterne, 2005) by which technological change is regarded as somehow removed from its historical or "developmental" context. For the most part, technologies unfold gradually out of previous technologies and emerge into broader, complex systems of technological practice. Besides, moderating our own uptake of in-the-moment buzz phrases like "Web 2.0" can help us stay one step ahead/above of the excitable rhetoric of corporate discourse that is deeply and unavoidably invested in obsolescence and the marketing of newness (or the rebranding of oldness). It behooves us to remember, for example, that *Facebook* profiles bear a strong formal and functional resemblance to personal home pages, and that interactivity, user comments, and online collaboration existed *before* the so-called Web 2.0. In the early 1990s, we also heard many of the same hopeful/ idealistic claims for the liberatory/participatory ("global-conversational") potential of the internet that circulate in the 2010s about social networking sites, wikis, folksonomies, and so on.

In this regard, it is equally important that scholars keep a constant check on their enthusiasm for, and very real investment in, the new media and acknowledge how it all continues to be structured by entrenched— albeit variable and slowly changing—inequalities of access, control, and opportunity (cf. Alzouma, 2005; Castells, 2009; Rodino-Colocino, 2006). While we appreciate the excitement (and genuine hope) that underpins sweeping visions for a "global communication network," the fact remains that so-called global flows of wealth, information, and technology are also marked by stoppages, blockages, trickles, and any number of nonflow metaphors. The opportunities of new media may span the globe, but they certainly do not cover it, nor do they span it in equal measure (Herring, 2001b; cf. also Thurlow & Jaworski, 2010). Closer to home, these same political-economic realities are such that much of the academic work on new media studies is also done by rich-country scholars writing about the experiences of their own people—with the occasional dabbling in other people's places. Just as sociolinguists are coming to terms with the utterly local and tightly bounded realities of some people under globalization (e.g. Block, 2004; Blommaert, 2005; Jaworski & Thurlow, 2010a), so too must new media scholars see through the presumptions of phrases like "global networks" and "global media."

Digital Discourse: *Background and Overview*

In September 2009, we co-organized at the University of Washington in Seattle, USA, the third in a series of international conferences on the role of the media in the representation, construction, and/or production of language. The first two conferences were organized by Sally Johnson at Leeds University in 2005 ("Language in the Media: Representations, Identities, Ideologies") and 2007 ("Language Ideologies and Media Discourse: Texts, Practices, Policies"). Both of these conferences have resulted in the publication of edited collections (see Johnson & Ensslin, 2007; Johnson and Milani, 2010), books concerned with the way the conventional media commonly depicts language-related issues and also how the media's use of language is central to the construction of what people think language is or should be. As we have already indicated, *Digital Discourse* shares a similar interest in issues of metalanguage and language ideology; however, with its focus on contemporary *new* media (rather than broadcast or news media per se), our volume is more broadly concerned with the situated language practices of ordinary communicators and *relatively* less concerned with issues of policy and "old" media depictions of language use.

We do want to be clear about one thing: while *Digital Discourse* comprises a careful selection of some of the best work presented at the 2009 conference in Seattle, there are also number of invited chapters, and the book is by no means simply conference proceedings. With an invited foreword and commentary from two of the most internationally recognized scholars of new media language, *Digital Discourse* brings together the work of some well-established scholars in sociolinguistics and/or new media sociolinguistics; it also showcases the work of several newer scholars whose research represents the cutting edge of new media studies, a truly interdisciplinary field that has always—and for obvious reasons—been driven in large part by younger/junior scholars.

The Organization of Digital Discourse

We have organized the volume around a series of key analytic concepts in contemporary sociolinguistics and discourse studies, most notably, the bread-and-butter concepts of *discourse* (i.e., language in use and linguistic ways of representing), *style* (identities and linguistic ways of being), and *genre* (text types and linguistic ways of [inter]acting) (cf., for example, Fairclough, 2003). This tripartite system of discursive, stylistic, and generic meanings in language is clearly also akin to Halliday's (1994) core communicative metafunctions of language (i.e., ideational, interpersonal, and textual), which also serve as a useful way to frame new media generally and to structure the analysis of new media language in particular. The chapters in each section privilege discourse, genre, or style for special consideration, although every chapter in our book is necessarily concerned with all three. Each contributor is likewise, in one way or another, just as interested in the identificational, interpersonal, and ideological possibilities of new media language. In this regard, we also have a section dedicated to *stance*, a topic of growing interest in sociolinguistics (see Du Bois, 2007; Jaffe, 2009a), as well as a concluding section on issues of *methodology*, which new media have to some extent turned upside down (see Levine & Scollon, 2004; Norris & Jones, 2005). For now, we offer the following short overviews of each section.

Part 1 – Metadiscursive Framings of New Media Language

The three chapters in this section open the book by looking at three different ways new media language is represented and reflexively attended to; in other words, its existence as a metadiscursive or metalinguistic phenomenon (cf. Jaworski et al., 2004). Each chapter thus connects most directly with the broader *language-ideological* critique underpinning this volume (cf. Irvine & Gal, 2000; Woolard, 1998), which is to say our interest in the ways language and new media language are subject to the disciplining gaze (Foucault, 1973) of the news media, commerce, government and, of course, "users" themselves (cf. Johnson & Ensslin, 2007; Thurlow, 2007, 2011a, 2011b).

In one of the only studies to date to consider the text messaging practices of adults, Lauren Squires opens the chapter with her analysis of metadiscursive commentary in television news reports of a high-profile extramarital affair. Squires structures her detailed analysis around the *heteroglossic* renderings and institutional/ideological recastings of the original text messages. In this case of adult text messaging, not only are the news media's representations very inconsistent, but there is also an apparent investment in standardizing (or tidying up) the appearance of messages in stark contrast to the way the messages of young people are typically depicted.

In their chapter, Graham Jones, Bambi Schieffelin, and Rachel Smith address an even finer, more specific feature of everyday metalanguage. Returning to their previous work on the use of "polyphonic" reported speech—specifically, the quotative *be + like*—in young people's instant messaging (Jones & Schieffelin, 2009), they document the intertextual (or "metacommunicative") and multimodal (or "metasemiotic") co-construction of gossip by young people using both IM and *Facebook*. As before, Jones et al.'s work nicely refutes simplistic, negative stereotypes about new media language and perfectly demonstrates the interplay of online and offline discursive practices. In this chapter, we also see the emergent and/or convergent qualities of new media, developing out of previous media and in concert with others.

In the third chapter in Part 1, Aoife Lenihan, too, is concerned with the *production* (cf. Pennycook, 2004) and policing of language. Drawing on ethnographic-discourse data, she examines the metalinguistic practices of the self-appointed "community" of Irish-language translators for the social networking site *Facebook*. The elegance of Lenihan's argument lies in her added attention to the mechanical (i.e., application design) and institutional limitations imposed on translations by *Facebook* itself. In doing so, she takes on the poster child of Web 2.0 by showing that its idealizing rhetoric of inclusive linguistic diversity is rooted also in the self-promoting business of corporate reach. In this case, we see how *Facebook*, Inc. (the company) capitalizes on the political motivation and symbolic status anxieties of everyday speakers as unpaid translators.

Together, these three chapters set the stage for the ones that follow. From the outset, we have evidence that language is not only on the move but also under constant surveillance and invariably deployed as resource (or excuse) for social judgment and control. Of course, so too is language a resource for endless creativity, reflexive practice, social intervention, resistance, and play.

Part 2 – Creative Genres: Texting, Messaging, and Multimodality

A favorite preoccupation of linguistically oriented new media studies has been the identification and specification of emergent genres (e.g., e-mail, online chat, message boards)—an endeavor that typically "concludes" with the inevitable hybridity of the various text types (Herring, 2001). The chapters in Part 2 take their analysis of genre a little further, however: first, by bringing the technologies under consideration up to date (e.g., text messaging, mobile storytelling and microblogging); second, by taking hybridity as a given and attending instead to the inherent multimodality and cultural embeddedness of these different ways of (inter)acting with/through new media. Certainly, each contributor is careful to situate generic form and content in relation to both communicative function (cf. Myers, 2010; van Leeuwen, 2004) and the way users overcome (or capitalize on) the genre-defining affordances of the medium (cf. Hutchby, 2001; Norris & Jones, 2005). In each case, contributors are attentive to the emergent, variable nature of the features and practices they describe.

Tereza Spilioti sets the tone nicely in Chapter 4 by homing in on the pragmatic qualities of closings in an ethnographically grounded sample of Greek text messages. In doing so, she challenges two common assumptions about new media discourse: its impoliteness and its uniformity. What Spilioti in fact shows is how her texters make complex, situated decisions about how they close their messages with a view to relationship history and topical relevance (e.g., following a dispreferred response) as well as the sequential position of the message and the daily rhythm of interactions. Spilioti's analysis also complicates assumptions about new media synchronicity (or asynchronicity) as a mechanically determined trait rather than as something interactionally accomplished.

The second chapter in Part 2, is Yukiko Nishimura's study of the creative literacies of *keitai* ("mobile phone") novels in Japan (cf. Morrison et al., 2011, for more on mobile storytelling). Taking an innovative corpus–stylistics approach, she unravels public assumptions about *keitai* novels along two axes: ideologies of *literacy* and ideologies of *literary merit*. Nishimura examines *keitai* novels both in their own terms (e.g., orthography, literary style) and through a comparison with the readability of other conventional genres and canonical texts. Ultimately, Nishimura rather elegantly proves the creativity of new media language users and refutes the way so much new media discourse is dismissed as illiterate or as a kind of "dumbing down."

In the last chapter of Part 2, Carmen Lee offers a uniquely sociolinguistic account of one of the newest—and much talked about—new media covered in our volume: microblogging. Lee considers the emerging linguistic (or orthographic) literacies of Cantonese-English bilinguals' status updates on *Facebook* (a form of microblogging that rivals *Twitter* in its popularity). The small-scale, (auto)ethnographic approach Lee takes allows her to track carefully the dynamic nature of the genre in terms of not only its linguistic forms but also its deeply embedded, communicative function (cf. Thurlow & Poff, 2011). Following a content-analytic-style examination of the communicative functions typically served by status updates, Lee moves to a singular but no less compelling account of one woman's situated, convergent (as in multimedia) use of status updates.

Part 3 – Style and Stylization: Identity Play and Semiotic Invention

As with the chapters by, say, Jones et al. (Chapter 2) and Lee (Chapter 6), the identificational meanings and possibilities of new media are in evidence throughout this volume. In Part 3, however, chapters foreground style and stylization (cf. Coupland, 2007) by focusing on three particular social-cultural contexts and the ways users capitalize on the semiotic affordances of digital technologies. Where one chapter examines a less familiar group using a familiar medium (i.e., online discussion forums), the other two chapters profile hugely popular online media that are seldom—if ever—discussed by sociolinguists: blogging and role-playing games (although see Meyers, 2010, on blogs). What makes these three chapters particularly exciting is their ethnographically informed attention to three very different, perhaps even unusual (for many readers at least), communities of young people and their largely undocumented practices.

In this regard, we open Part 3 with Lisa Newon's rich participant observation study of a *guild* ("group" or "team") on *World of Warcraft*—the world's largest MMORPG ("massively multiplayer online role-playing game"). This mechanically and interactionally complex gaming environment provides Newon insight into the way players use spoken, written, and visual discourse *simultaneously* for game-focused collaboration and for social interaction. A key feature of MMORPGs is the discursive performance of (dis)embodied actions and the semiotic production of space (or *landscape*; cf. Jaworski & Thurlow, 2010b; Jones, 2010) in which the game takes place. Throughout, Newon pays particular attention to the co-construction and management of certain players' identities as leaders and expert gamers.

In Chapter 8, Saija Peuronen presents her ethnographic study of a Finnish online forum for Christian extreme sports enthusiasts. Members of this *translocal*, hybrid, heteroglossic community style themselves in a number of creative ways that combine the "expressive resources" of not just two linguacultures (i.e., Finnish and English) but also the globalizing discourses/styles of both extreme sports and Christianity. Through her careful analysis of discursive resources like code switching/mixing, orthographic invention, and in-group registers, Peuronen also tracks the role of global brands and the way members of this community slip effortlessly between standardized (often also globalized) and highly localized practices (cf. Coupland, 2010; Leppänen et al., 2009; Pennycook, 2010).

Following nicely from Peuronen's discussion of the interplay between new media styles and global cultural fashions, Carmel Vaisman rounds off Part 3 with her study of Israeli teenagers' Hebrew-language blogs. Her study is impressive not only for its multilingual perspective, but also because of its ethnographically informed gender critique of the styling practices used by a very particular subcultural group of bloggers (the "Girly Girls" known as *Fakatsa*). By homing in on the unique and highly complex orthographic practices of these young (often teenage) women, Vaisman demonstrates how their orthographic play often privileges the visual-aesthetic form of language—the look of the words—over its communicative function. New media language and/or typography is once again revealed to be a powerful identificational and cultural resource; it is also a means by which often disadvantaged groups like young people or women (cf. Nishimura's Chapter 5) assert themselves as cultural producers and especially vis-à-vis the negative stereotypes of others.

Part 4 – Stance: Ideological Position Taking and Social Categorization

No identity work happens outside of, or without a view to, relationships; acts of identity are also always acts of comparison, social distinction, and othering. For sociolinguists, a key linguistic manifestation (or, indeed, discursive accomplishment) of this process lies in stancetaking, the ways communicators position and align themselves vis-à-vis their speech/writing and those they are speaking/writing to/about (cf. Du Bois, 2007; Jaffe, 2009b). As such, this next section follows tightly on the previous one; like Section 1, however, it also attends more squarely to the matter of ideology since the evaluations that underpin stancetaking typically also hinge on the preservation of symbolic orders (J. Coupland & N. Coupland, 2009; Jaworski & Thurlow, 2009; cf. also Bourdieu, 1977). Each of the three chapters in this section is concerned with the ways that new media facilitate the micro-sociolinguistic accomplishment of larger, sociocultural structures of inequality—a nice corrective for the liberatory/participatory hype of Web 2.0 rhetoric.

In their opening chapter, Shana Walton and Alexandra Jaffe examine racialized and class-based stancetaking in the notorious (in the USA at least) blog *Stuff White People Like*. In considering the complex formation of stances expressed by the blog's author and those attributed to a presumed audience, Walton and Jaffe also show how this particular new medium (or genre) foregrounds the interactional, co-constructed nature of stancetaking (e.g., in reader commentaries). Like the other contributors in Part 4, Walton & Jaffe are left with mixed feelings about the ideological implications of blogging (or this particular blog, at least); while different people/positions are surely put into "conversation"—inducing what the authors call a "mild culture shock"—authorial control and preferred readings are no less prevalent.

Crispin Thurlow and Adam Jaworski take up a very similar line of investigation in their chapter, but this time turning to the use of online photo-sharing sites (in this case, *Flickr*) by tourists. In adopting a specifically *new media* perspective, Thurlow and Jaworski are forced to rethink the sociolinguistics of stance (e.g., its multimodality and complicated footing) but are also afforded new insights into tourism discourse. With regard the second of these "findings," *Flickr* confirms the circulation and ubiquity of tourist practices such as forced perspective shots of tourists interacting with monuments/sites. For Thurlow and Jaworski, processes of (re)embodiment and (re)mediation are also evidence of the ideology they call "banal globalization" for which photography, then digital photography, and now online photo sharing are key technologies.

In the last chapter in this section, Elaine Chun and Keith Walters shift to a yet another ("Web 2.0") new media: the video-sharing site *YouTube* and a particular video of a stand-up routine by Wonho Chung. Chun and Walters start with a critique of Chung's linguistic performance as/of a fluent Arabic speaker of Korean and Vietnamese parentage, which they follow with an analysis of multilingual, collaborative stancetaking in comments posted from 48 different countries. While this *YouTube* moment reveals the discursive "imagining" of a diasporic Arab community, Chun and Walters also recognize the limitations of the web's democratizing potential and how these media become tools (or resources) for maintaining the moral order and for shoring up privilege (cf. Hill, 2001, 2008). In this case, we see commenters and also Chung himself authenticating and reinscribing anachronistic notions of both Arab and Oriental. As they put it, "*YouTube* may be a space that inherently Orientalizes difference."

What each of the three chapters in Part 4 shows is how the kind of playful, entertainment or parodic frames that often occur on the web *may* well open up "safe" spaces (akin to "discursive licence" in Coupland & Jaworski, 2003) for public discussion and perhaps even deliberation, but they can, it seems, just as easily foreclose sustained, deeper engagement. Once again, we are reminded that the social meanings and influence of new media are seldom determined (sic) by the technologies themselves but rather by their users and the uses to which the technologies are put. Which brings us neatly to the last section in the volume.

Part 5 – New Practices, Emerging Methodologies

New technologies bring with them new social and cultural practices; these new practices in turn require that scholars rethink their investigative and analytic methods. As Erickson (1996) notes, whole new fields of research are sometimes made possible through the emergence of technologies that enable new ways of recording, organizing, storing, and disseminating data (see also Levine & Scollon, 2004). None of which suggests that older, better-established methods have nothing to offer still. In three quite different chapters, contributors in this final section of *Digital Discourse* explore some of the key challenges and solutions in researching new media language—and they do so from three very different but nonetheless complementary perspectives.

Returning to the notion of heteroglossia with which Lauren Squires started in Chapter 1, Jannis Androutsopoulos argues that a proper analysis of *contemporary* (for him, Web 2.0) digital discourse must move beyond the cataloguing of linguistic differences and sociolinguistic variations. (His chapter here thus extends his earlier critiques of new media sociolinguistics—see discussion above.) Instead, he argues, sociolinguists and discourse analysts should be engaging more holistically with the multi-authorship, translocality, multimodality, and "modularity" of more recent new media. A textual format like the social networking profile requires an analytic frame that can handle the different voices and styles by which it is "articulated" (we use this word for its meaning of expression and the joining of parts). With reference to social-networking and content-sharing sites—and with a specific case-study—Androutsopoulos demonstrates how his approach to *digital heteroglossia* better manages the complex layering and intertextuality (cf. Bauman, 2004) of many new media texts.

In Chapter 14, Christa Dürscheid and Elisabeth Stark turn the tables somewhat on the chapter by Androutsopoulos by presenting the basis for their large-scale, corpus-based study of text messaging in Switzerland.

In combination with the other chapters in this section, their work certainly demonstrates the continued value of quantitative approaches to the study of new media language (see also Georgakopoulou's promotion of combined methodologies discussed above). Dürscheid and Stark reveal some of the preliminary findings of their study that point to intriguing linguistic and sociolinguistic insights—not least of which is the power of their study to map the particular multilingual context of Switzerland.

We have deliberately chosen Rodney Jones' chapter to round off not only Part 5 but also the main run of chapters in *Digital Discourse* because he offers such a compelling example of the opportunities of new media as well as its methodological challenges. Informed by his approach to mediated discourse analysis (Norris & Jones, 2005; cf. also Scollon, 2001), Jones traces some of the special qualities of new media textualities (e.g., their deterritorialization, reproducibility, and mutability) in the online video footage crafted by young skaters ("skateboarders") in Hong Kong. In addition to this analytic framework, Jones also demonstrates the value of historicity for new media discourse studies, and of tracking the *convergence* and, most importantly, *emergence* of technologies from photography to digital photography to digital movie editing to online photo/film sharing. Ultimately, what Jones' chapter makes quite apparent is that distinctions between language and other modalities, between "virtual" and "real" or between "physical" and "symbolic" are only ever analytic conveniences.

Together with all the chapters in this volume, the three chapters in Part 5 leave little doubt that language is, as Noami Baron reminds us in her Foreword, clearly on the move, and that new media sociolinguists will be kept constantly on their toes. We hope that *Digital Discourse* makes some attempt to keep the field up to date. With this in mind, we are very pleased to leave the last word—as far as this book is concerned, at least—to Susan Herring as someone who has been working for over two decades to keep abreast of language in the new media.

Acknowledgments

Our very biggest thanks go to those new and old colleagues who generously agreed to contribute to this volume, who carefully reviewed each other's work, and who made the overall editorial process so smooth and enjoyable. We are also grateful to each of the external reviewers for their comments on individual chapters; those who agreed to be identified were Dieter Stein, Tim Shortis, Cornelius Puschmann, Allison Muri, Helen Kelly Holmes, Monica Heller, Alexandra Georgakopoulou, Astrid Ensslin, Marisol del-Teso-Craviotto, and David Barton. We are grateful to the series editors, Nik Coupland and Adam Jaworski, for supporting our proposal and agreeing to put it out for review (thanks to the anonymous reviewers, too, for their encouragement). We thank our University of Washington colleague and conference co-organizer Jamie Moshin (now Dr. Moshin), who, although not in a position to work with us on this volume, was instrumental in initially bringing many of the contributors together under one roof. Speaking of the conference, we want to offer a special thank you to the *Simpson Center for the Humanities*—the most amazing interdisciplinary refuge at the University of Washington—where we received nothing but material and collegial solidarity. We save our final, but very special thanks for Sally Johnson on whose coattails we rode. Sally was invited to give a plenary talk in Seattle but could not attend due to illness; she has since retired from academia, which is a huge sadness for so many of us working in sociolinguistics and discourse studies, and why we've chosen to dedicate this book to her.

References

Alzouma, G. (2005). Myths of digital technology in Africa: Leapfrogging development? *Global Media and Communication*, 1(3), 339–356.

Androutsopoulos, J., Ed. (2006a). Special issue of the *Journal of Sociolinguistics*, 10(4).

Androutsopoulos, J. (2006b). Introduction: Sociolinguistics and computer-mediated communication. *Journal of Sociolinguistics*, 10(4), 419–438.

Androutsopoulos, J. (2010). Localising the global on the participatory web: Vernacular spectacles as local responses to global media flows. In N. Coupland (Ed.), *Handbook of Language and Globalization*. Oxford: Wiley-Blackwell.

Baron, N. (2000). *From Alphabet to E-mail: How Written English Evolved and Where It's Headed*. London: Routledge.

Baron, N. (2008). *Always On: Language in an Online and Mobile World*. Oxford: OUP.

Bauman, R. (2004). *A World of Others' Words: Cross-Cultural Perspectives on Intertextuality*. Oxford: Blackwell.

Block, D. (2004). Globalization, transnational communication and the internet. *International Journal on Multicultural Societies*, 6(1), 13–28

Blommaert, J. (Ed.). (1999). *Language Ideological Debates*, Berlin / New York: Mouton de Gruyter.

Blommaert, J. (2005). Choice and determination. In *Discourse*, (pp. 98–124). Cambridge: Cambridge University Press.

Bourdieu, P. (1977). *Outline of a Theory of Practice*. Cambridge: Cambridge University Press.

Bourdieu, P. (1991). *Language and Symbolic Power* (J.B. Thompson, Trans.). Cambridge, MA: Harvard University Press.

Bucholtz, M., & Hall, K. (2008). All of the above: New coalitions in sociocultural linguistics. *Journal of Sociolinguistics*, 12(4), 401–431.

Buckingham, D. (2007). *Beyond Technology: Children's Learning in the Age of Digital Culture*. Cambridge: Polity.

Burgess, J. (2010). Remediating vernacular creativity: Photography and cultural citizenship in the Flickr photo-sharing network. In T. Edensor et al. (Eds.), *Spaces of Vernacular Creativity: Rethinking the Cultural Economy*, (pp. 116–125) London: Routledge.

Cameron, D. (1995). *Verbal Hygiene*. London: Routledge.

Cameron, D. (2000). *Good to Talk? Living and Working in a Communication Culture*. London: Sage.

Castells, M. (2009). *The Rise of the Networked Society* (2nd ed.). Malden, MA: Wiley-Blackwell.

Couldry, N. (2008). Mediatization or mediation? Alternative understandings of the emergent space of digital storytelling. *New Media and Society*, 10(3), 373–391.

Coupland, J. & Jaworski, A. (2003). Transgression and intimacy in recreational talk narratives. *Research on Language and Social Interaction*, 36(1), 85–106.

Coupland, N. (2007). *Style: Language Variation and Identity*. Cambridge: Cambridge University Press.

Coupland, J., & Coupland, N. (2009). Attributing stance in discourses of body shape and weight loss. In A. Jaffe (Ed.), *Stance: Sociolinguistic Perspectives*, (pp. 226–249). New York: Oxford University Press.

Coupland, N. (Ed.). (2010). *The Handbook of Language and Globalization*. Oxford: Wiley-Blackwell.

Crystal, D. (2001). *Language and the Internet*. Cambridge: Cambridge University Press.

Crystal, D. (2008). *Txting: The Gr8 Db8*. Oxford: Oxford University Press.

Danet, B. (2001) *Cyberpl@y: Communicating online*. Oxford and New York: Berg.

Danet, B., & Herring, S.C. (Eds.). (2003). Introduction: The multilingual internet. Special issue of the *Journal of Computer Mediated Communication*, 9(1). Available online at http://jcmc.indiana.edu/vol9/issue1/intro.html

Danet, B., & Herring, S.C. (Eds.). (2007). *The Multilingual Internet: Language, Culture, and Communication Online*. New York and Oxford: Oxford University Press.

Du Bois, J. (2007). The stance triangle. In R. Engelbretson (Ed.), *Stancetaking in Discourse: Subjectivity, Evaluation, Interaction*, (pp. 139–182). Amsterdam: John Benjamins.

Duranti, A., & Goodwin, C. (Eds.). (1992). *Rethinking Context: Language as an Interactive Phenomenon*. Cambridge: Cambridge University Press.

Durham, M.G., & Kellner, D.M. (Eds.). (2001). *Media and Cultural Studies: Keyworks*. Malden, MA: Blackwell.

Erickson, F. (1996). Ethnographic microanalysis. In S.L. McKay & N.H. Hornberger (Eds.), *Sociolinguistics and Language Teaching*, (pp. 283–306). Cambridge: Cambridge University Press.

Fairclough, N. (1999). Global capitalism and critical awareness of language. *Language Awareness*, 8(2), 71–83.

Fairclough, N. (2003). *Analysing Discourse: Textual Analysis for Social Research*. London: Routledge.

Feenburg, A., & Hannay, A. (1995). *Technology and the Politics of Knowledge*. Bloomington: Indiana University Press.

Foucault, M. (1973). *The Birth of the Clinic*. New York: Pantheon Books.

Foucault, M. (1980). *Power/Knowledge: Selected Interviews and Other Writings, 1972–1977* (C. Gordon, Ed.). New York: Pantheon.

Foucault, M. (1981). The order of discourse. In R. Young (Ed.), *Untying the Text: A Poststructuralist Reader*, (pp. 48–77). London: Roultedge & Keegan Paul.

Gee, P. (2010). *An Introduction to Discourse Analysis: Theory and Method* (3rd ed.). New York: Routledge.

Georgakopoulou, A. (2003). Computer-mediated communication. In J. Verschueren, J-O. Östman, J. Blommaert, & C. Bulcaen (Eds.), *Handbook of Pragmatics* (pp. 1–20). Amsterdam and Philadelphia: John Benjamins.

Georgakopoulou, A. (2006). Postscript: Computer-mediated communication in sociolinguistics. *Journal of Sociolinguistics*, 10(4), 548–557.

Halliday, M.A.K. (1994). *Introduction to Functional Grammar*. London: Arnold.

Headrick, D. R. (1981). *The Tools of Empire: Technology and European Imperialism in the Nineteenth Century*. London: OUP.

Heller, M. (2003). Globalization, the new economy and the commodification of language and identity. *Journal of Sociolinguistics*, 7(4), 473–498.

Herring, S.C. (Ed.). (1996). *Computer-Mediated Communication: Linguistic, Social and Cross-Cultural Perspectives. Pragmatics and Beyond* series. Amsterdam: John Benjamins.

Herring, S. (2001b). Foreword. In C. Ess & F. Sudweeks (Eds.), *Culture, Technology, Communication: Towards an Intercultural Global Village* (pp. vii–x). Albany: State University of New York.

Herring, S.C. (2001a). Computer-mediated discourse. In D. Schiffrin, D. Tannen, & H. E. Hamilton (Eds.), *The Handbook of Discourse Analysis*, (pp. 612–634). Malden, MA: Blackwell Publishers.

Herring, S.C. (2004). Slouching toward the ordinary: Current trends in computer-mediated communication. *New Media & Society*, 6(1), 26–36.

Herring, S.C. (2008). Questioning the generational divide: Technological exoticism and adult construction of online youth identity. In D. Buckingham (Ed.), *Youth, Identity, and Digital Media*, (pp. 71–94). Cambridge, MA: MIT Press.

Hill, J.H. (2001). Language, race, and white public space. In A. Duranti (Ed.), *Linguistic Anthropology: A Reader*, (pp. 450–664). Malden, MA: Blackwell.

Hill, J.H. (2008). *Everyday Language of White Racism*. Malden, MA: Blackwell Publishers.

Holloway, J., & Valentine, G. (2003). *Cyberkids: Children in the Information Age*. London: Routledge.

Hutchby, I. (2001). Technologies, texts, and affordances. *Sociology*, 35(2), 441–456.

Irvine, J.T., & Gal, S. (2000). Language ideology and linguistic differentiation. In P. Kroskrity (Ed.), *Regimes of language* (pp. 35–83). Santa Fe, NM: School of American Research Press.

Jaffe, A. (Ed.). (2009a). *Stance: Sociolinguistic Perspectives*. New York: Oxford University Press.

Jaffe, A. (2009b). Introduction: The sociolinguistics of stance. In A. Jaffe (Ed.), *Stance: Sociolinguistic Perspectives*, (pp. 3–28). New York: Oxford University Press.

Jaworski, A., & Coupland, N. (2006). Introduction. In A. Jaworski and N. Coupland (Eds.), *The Discourse Reader* (2nd ed.), (pp. 1–38). London: Routledge.

Jaworski, A., & Thurlow, C. (2009). Taking an elitist stance: Ideology and the discursive production of social distinction. In A. Jaffe (Ed.), *Stance: Sociolinguistic Perspectives*, (pp. 195–226). New York: Oxford University Press.

Jaworski, A., & Thurlow, C. (2010a). Language and the globalizing habitus of tourism: A sociolinguistics of fleeting relationships. In N. Coupland (Ed.), *The Handbook of Language and Globalisation*, (pp. 256–286). Oxford: Wiley-Blackwell.

Jaworski, A., & Thurlow, C. (Eds). (2010b). *Semiotic Landscapes: Language, Image, Space*. London & New York: Continuum.

Jaworski, A., Coupland, N., & Galasinski, D. (Eds). (2004). *Metalanguage: Social and Ideological Perspectives*. Berlin: Mouton de Gruyter.

Jenkins, H. (2006). *Convergence Culture: When Old and New Media Collide*. New York: NYU Press.

Jewitt, C. (2004). Multimodality and new communication technologies. In P. Levine & R. Scollon (Eds.), *Discourse and Technology: Multimodal Discourse Analysis*, (pp. 198–195). Washington, DC: Georgetown University Press.

Jewitt, C. (2009). *The Routledge Handbook of Multimodal Analysis*. London: Routledge.

Johnson, S., & Ensslin, A. (Eds). (2007). *Language in the Media*. London: Continuum Press.

Johnson, S., & Milani, T. (Eds.). (2010). *Language Ideologies and Media Discourse: Texts, Practices, Politics*. London: Continuum.

Jones, G. M., & Schieffelin, B. (2009). Enquoting voices, accomplishing talk: Uses of *be + like* in instant messaging. *Language & Communication*, 29(1), 77–113.

Jones, R.H. (2010). Cyberspace and physical space: Attention structures in computer mediated communication. In A. Jaworski & C. Thurlow (Eds.), *Semiotic Landscapes: Language, Image, Space*, (pp. 151–167). London: Continuum.

Keating, E. (2005). Homo prostheticus: Problematizing the notions of activity and computer-mediated interaction. *Discourse Studies*, 7(4–5), 527–545.

Kress, G. (2003). *Literacy in the New Media Age*. London: Routledge.

Kress, G., & van Leeuwen, T.J. (2001). *Multimodal Discourse - The Modes and Media of Contemporary Communication*. London: Arnold.

Leppänen, S., Pitkänen-Huhta, A., Piirainen-Marsh, A., Nikula, T., & Peuronen, S. (2009). Young people's translocal new media uses: A multiperspective analysis of language choice and heteroglossia. *Journal of Computer Mediated Communication*, 14(4), 1080–1107.

Leupin, A. (2000). *The End of Sex*. Available online at http://rhizome.org/discuss/view/28778/#i624

Levine, P., & Scollon, R. (Eds.). (2004). *Discourse & Technology: Multimodal Discourse Analysis*. Washington, DC: Georgetown University Press.

Livingstone, S. (2002). *Young People and New Media: Childhood and the Changing Media Environment*. London: Sage.

McLuhan, M. (2005 [1964]). *Understanding Media: The Extensions of Man*. London: Routledge.

Morrison, A., Mainsah, H., Sem, I., & Havnør, M. (2011). 'Points of Interest': Investigating technologically mediated discourse through the co-design of mobile fiction. In R. Jones (Ed.), *Discourse and Creativity*. London: Pearson.

Myers, G. (2010). *The Discourse of Wikis and Blogs*. London: Continuum.

Nelson, M. E. (2006). Mode, meaning, and synaesthesia in multimedia L2 writing. *Language Learning & Technology*, 10(2), 56–76.

Norris, S., & Jones, R.H. (Eds.). (2005). *Discourse in Action: Introducing Mediated Discourse Analysis*. London: Routledge.

Nusselder, A. (2009). *Interface Fantasy: Lacanian Cyborg Ontology*. Cambridge, MA: MIT Press.

Pennycook, A. (2004). Performativity and language studies. *Critical Inquiry in Language Studies*, 1(1), 1–19.

Pennycook, A. (2010). *Language as Local Practice*. London: Routledge.

Pinker, S. (1994). *The Language Instinct: How the Mind Creates Language*. New York: HarperPerrenial.

Rodino-Colocino, M. (2006). Laboring under the digital divide. *New Media & Society*, 8(3), 487–511.

Rowe, C., & Wyss, E.L. (Eds.). (2009). *Language and New Media: Linguistic, Cultural, and Technological Evolutions*. Creskill, NJ: Hampton Press.

Schieffelin, B.B., Woolard, K.A., & Kroskrity, P.V. (Eds.). (1998). *Language Ideologies: Practice & Theory*. New York: Oxford University Press.

Scollon, R. (2001). *Mediated Discourse: The Nexus of Practice*. London: Routledge.

Scollon, R., & Scollon, S.W. (2003). *Discourses in Place: Language in the Material World*. London: Routledge.

Sterne, J. (2005). Book review of "The Audible Past: Cultural Origins of Sound Reproduction" (written by J. Sterne, 2003). *Resource Center for Cyberculture Studies*, available online at http://rccs.usfca.edu/bookinfo.asp?BookID=258&AuthorID=67

Thurlow, C. (2006). From statistical panic to moral panic: The metadiscursive construction and popular exaggeration of new media language in the print media. *Journal of Computer-Mediated Communication*, 11(3), 667–701.

Thurlow, C. (2007). Fabricating youth: New-media discourse and the technologization of young people. In S. Johnson & A. Ensslin (Eds.), *Language in the Media: Representations, Identities, Ideologies*, (pp. 213–233). London: Continuum.

Thurlow, C. (Ed.). (2009). Young people, mediated discourse and communication technologies. Special issue of the *Journal of Computer Mediated Communication*, 14(4), 1038–1282.

Thurlow, C. (2011a). *Fakebook: Synthetic Media, Pseudo-Sociality and the Rhetorics of Web 2.0*. Plenary paper presented at the Georgetown Roundtable on Language and Linguistics, Georgetown University, March 10-13.

Thurlow, C. (2011b). Determined creativity: Language play, vernacular literacy and new media discourse. In R. Jones (Ed.), *Discourse and Creativity*. London: Pearson.

Thurlow, C. (2011c). Speaking of difference: Language, inequality and interculturality. In R. Halualani & T. Nakayama (Eds.), *Handbook of Critical Intercultural Communication*. Oxford: Blackwell.

Thurlow, C., & Bell, K. (2009). Against technologization: Young people's new media discourse as creative cultural practice. *Journal of Computer-Mediated Communication*, 14(4), 1038–1049.

Thurlow, C., & Jaworski, A. (2010). *Tourism Discourse: Language and Global Mobility*. Basingstoke: Palgrave Macmillan.

Thurlow, C., Lengel, L., & Tomic, A. (2004). *Computer Mediated Communication: Social Interaction and the Internet*. London: Sage.

Thurlow, C., & Poff, M. (2011). Text-messaging. In S. C. Herring, D. Stein, & T. Virtanen (Eds.), *Handbook of the Pragmatics of CMC*. Berlin and New York: Mouton de Gruyter.

van Leeuwen, T. (2004). *Introducing Social Semiotics: An Introductory Textbook*. London: Routledge.

Woolard, K. A. (1998). Introduction: Language ideology as a field of inquiry. In B.B. Schieffelin, K.A. Woolard, & P.V. Kroskrity (Eds.), *Language ideologies: Practice and theory* (pp. 3–47). New York: Oxford University Press.

PART ONE

Metadiscursive Framings of New Media Language

Chapter 1

Voicing "Sexy Text":
Heteroglossia and Erasure in
TV News Representations of
Detroit's Text Message Scandal

Lauren Squires

ENGLISH-LANGUAGE MAINSTREAM news media tends to represent new media as the provenance of young people and contributes to moral panic about declines in literacy and the English language (Jones & Schieffelin, 2009; Thurlow, 2006, 2007). This chapter examines mass media representations of new media practices where the new media users are adult political figures, not young people, to understand how new media language is represented across media contexts. The data come from television news coverage of a political scandal involving text messages in Detroit, Michigan (USA). I first provide background information on this "text message scandal," theoretical background, and previous work on media portrayals of text messaging. I then describe my method, which analyzes five metadiscursive levels of TV news representations of text messages from the scandal, before presenting findings from these analyses. In the discussion, I relate my findings to notions of *heteroglossia* and *erasure*, proposing a framework that involves five axes of linguistic form for understanding how text messages are multiply voiced in the multimodal space of television.

Background

In 2008, thousands of text messages sent via city-issued mobile two-way pagers implicated Detroit Mayor Kwame Kilpatrick in a range of past indiscretions. At 31, Kilpatrick had been the youngest candidate ever elected mayor of Detroit, a predominantly African-American city where over a quarter of residents live in poverty (*Detroit Free Press*, 2008; U.S.

Census Bureau, 2010). The former mayor's misdeeds included having an extramarital affair with his chief of staff Christine Beatty, conspiring with her to fire the city's Deputy Police Chief, and improperly using city funds. Following a trial in which Kilpatrick and Beatty were found guilty of perjury, both resigned in the face of public outcry. Thousands of text messages sent to and from Kilpatrick's and Beatty's Motorola pagers were initially acquired by a lawyer from SkyTel, the messaging service provider, as part of a whistle-blower trial against Kilpatrick (*Detroit Free Press*, 2008). *Detroit Free Press* reporters later acquired the messages, which were soon publicized and widely circulated by multiple news outlets (Gallagher, 2009; for complete background, see http://freep.com/kwamekilpatrick).

Text messages played a central role in the legal details of the scandal, proving numerous allegations against Kilpatrick and Beatty. Both had denied their romantic involvement under oath, and the text messages' content invalidated their denials. The text messages played just as central a role in defining public discourse around the events, becoming the focal point for media investigation and local discussion. The scandal was referred to as "text message scandal," "text scandal," "sexy text scandal," and "textgate." The scandal compelled local mass media to discuss text messages in their reporting, and furthermore to portray the text messaging practices of adults—both Kilpatrick and Beatty were in their 30s at the time—who were engaged in "adult" activities in both the professional and sexual senses. The scandal provides a case study for media representation of an age and lifestyle cohort that public discourse rarely links to new media (though recently, U.S. President Barack Obama's text messaging has added to his persona as a tech-savvy President, and golf star Tiger Woods' texts to his mistresses have garnered him attention similar to Kilpatrick's). To explore these representations, I consider the Detroit scandal text messages as rendered in television news broadcasts, a mass medium wherein multimodal resources are available for metadiscursively constructing the texts—and language more generally.

As forms of direct reported speech (Coupland & Jaworski, 2004), these mediatized representations recontextualize the text messages' content and form in the public space of the mass media; the televisual medium also provides opportunities for recasting the messages' formal properties in various ways. Not only can *content* be omitted or added, but via screen and vocal channels, message *form* can also be altered in terms of grammar, spelling, capitalization, and so forth. These representations are heteroglossic (Androutsopoulos, 2009; also Jones, Chapter 15, this volume; Bakhtin, 1981) in two relevant senses. *Horizontally* across the messages' instantiations in

TV broadcasts, there seem to be no set conventions for message reproduction: there are different levels of faithfulness to the original texts across different messages. At the same time, *vertically* within any given message, a confluence of features reproduced or altered from the original messages serves to portray multiple voices. These voices include centrally those of the newscasters, who in Goffman's (1981) terms are the text *animators*, and the text *authors*—Kilpatrick, Beatty, and other scandal actors.

The authors' voices, conceived as the linguistic or pragmatic features present in their original messages, compete with the journalistic voices of their animators. In this reported speech context, the newscaster's voice (or the message's on-screen representation) is "a gloss on the ideational layer of meaning" (Coupland & Jaworski, 2004, p. 32) of a text message, reproducing the message's form in ways suffused with language ideology and social positioning. In particular, the *erasure* (Irvine & Gal, 2000) of features of the texts—from Kilpatrick's stylistic use of capital letters to instances of <LOL>—serves to privilege the voice of animator and alter the voice of author, at once downplaying the novelty of text messaging as a linguistic medium.

Such heteroglossic practices emerge from tension between the linguistic forms used by Kilpatrick et al., on the one hand, and the dominant media-typified voices of adults, on the other. That the authors of these texts are adults is one element that distinguishes this case from previous studies. In contexts focused on youth, newsmakers exaggerate "novel" features of text messaging, such as abbreviations and nonstandard capitalization and punctuation (Thurlow, 2006, 2007; Thurlow & Poff, 2011). But in the present case, these same features are often glossed over or erased by the animating newscasts, even when the features are used in the original texts. We can thus see how language and linguistic practices are represented when the "triple-whammy" panic about youth, technology, and language (Thurlow, 2006) is disaggregated. The Detroit text message scandal perhaps instantiates a different panic—one that commonly arises in the wake of a political scandal involving sex. This highlights a second element distinguishing my analysis: the representations under investigation come from a media context where linguistic form itself was not the central concern. Yet in publicizing the messages, the mass media nonetheless unavoidably metadiscursively constructed text messaging usage. Precisely because language is not the main point of interest for the reporting, their representations can illuminate cultural framings of texting.

To understand these framings, I consider here five levels of metadiscursive representation in the text messages' reconstruction, which pertain to both the language used within text messaging and the social practice of text messaging. Later, in my discussion, I will relate this to five axes of form relevant to (mass) media constructions of (new) media discourse: *nonstandard/ standard, interactive/unidirectional, spoken/written, conversational/formal,* and *novel/mundane.* In contexts of new media recontextualization, particularly multimodal ones such as television, these axes underlie the heteroglossic representations of language, social practice, and new media users.

Data and Methods

I collected 130 excerpts of text messages being read aloud by TV news broadcasters reporting on the Detroit mayoral scandal.[1] The data come from the websites of three local Detroit television stations: WXYZ-TV (ABC), WDIV-TV (NBC), and Fox 2 News. Sixteen broadcast segments are in the corpus, each with between 1 and 19 messages. Nine named message senders or recipients are included, though the bulk of messages were sent between Kilpatrick (the former mayor) and Beatty (his chief of staff). I paired each message with its original text transcript when these were available, allowing comparison between the original message form and the consequent media representation.[2] Altogether, there are 75 unique original messages represented.

Included in my data capture is the segmented audiovisual portion of the reading of the text message itself, along with the immediately preceding metadiscursive introduction to the text message. Thus, a typical excerpt, as I have captured it, consists of a brief segment of introductory speech spoken by the pictured newscaster, followed by a vocalization of the message, which is also printed on-screen. These segments are excerpted from larger broadcasts in which the newscasters usually offer disclaimers as to the "graphic" or "adult" nature of the messages. Isolating the audiovisual format for each message's vocalization enabled me to examine different modes of information simultaneously contributing to a representation, including what is on-screen at the time of the text's vocalization in addition to the vocalization itself.

The multimodal format of television enables a range of communicative resources to be deployed in constructing text messages. To understand these practices, I analyzed five levels of metadiscursivity:

1) Text-to-screen replication: Discrepancies in reproduction from the original text message form to the visually rendered text message on-screen.
2) Text-to-voice replication: Discrepancies in reproduction from the original text message form to the vocalized text message.

3) Verbal framing: Terms used to signal the act of text messaging.

4) Intonational framing: Intonation in the text vocalizations.

5) Sequential organization: Grouping of individual messages within the course of a broadcast segment.

Clearly, multiple layers of reproduction are involved in the movement of an original text message to its TV news representation, and Figure 1.1 provides a possible schema for these layers of textualization. Note that when I say "original" message, I refer to the transcript of the original as presented in the court documents—already itself a metadiscursive representation, of course.

With a message decontextualized from its original modality (text on a pager screen, in this case), its recontextualization in the multimodal space of TV forms a comment on language, technology, and social actors involved.[3] Asking, "How are these messages represented?" is to ask, "How are these representations interpretable through the ideological, generic, and stylistic contexts of this instance of media discourse?" The metadiscursive representations in the corpus combine multimodal semiotic resources (screen, voice, text, image) and link the represented material to language ideologies, particularly ideologies about standard language, which are often employed in representing new media as nonstandard and youth language as innovative or stigmatized (Shortis, 2007; Squires, 2010; Thurlow, 2003, 2006, 2007). We might expect newscasters, as language technicians, to conform to highly standard patterns. Yet each of these metadiscursive levels constitutes a space of reconstruction with its own possible ideological indices, so that a single representation of a single message that incorporates these different levels permits the combination of these indices—giving rise to heteroglossia, which is the focus of my discussion below.

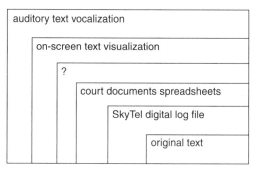

FIGURE 1.1: Layers of textualization of text messages ultimately read in television broadcasts.

Findings

Text-to-Screen Replication

In most news readings of texts, the viewer potentially both sees and hears the message's content, which is displayed as an image on the TV screen. Much new media representation focuses on orthographic form (Shortis, 2007; Thurlow & Poff, 2011), and this level of representation pertains to the metalinguistic construction of text messaging's formal properties. For each message, the on-screen text was compared to the original message transcript, and discrepancies between the two were marked. Table 1.1 summarizes the coding; 114 messages are included in this and the text-to-voice replication analyses.

Table 1.2 gives examples of the most frequent discrepancies: *omission, capitalization,* and *punctuation*. Less than half of the on-screen messages include these particular discrepancies; such inconsistency is a way in which horizontal heteroglossia across message representations emerges. However, it is illuminating to look at which *kinds* of discrepancies are more likely than others.

First, most *omitted* material is either message-initial or message-final (compare with Spilioti in Chapter 4, this volume). Often, however, discourse markers occur at the start of an original message; their omission reflects the focus of the newscasts on the messages' content. Also omitted are immediate responses to prior texts—second-pair parts of adjacency pairs (Sacks, Schegloff, & Jefferson, 1974). In several instances, this omitted message-initial content also includes a nonstandard linguistic feature, including <LOL> ("laugh out loud"; an acronym seen as emblematic of new media discourse).[4] For instance, Extract 1.1 shows Kilpatrick's exaggerated form of <LOL> in a response to a prior message, omitted in the on-screen image. In five messages, the originals include <LOL> both message-initially and message-finally but are omitted on-screen, such as in Extract 1.2.

Table 1.1 Text-to-screen replication coding scheme

Discrepancy Type	Description
Omission	Words or phrases present in original text but omitted on-screen
Addition	Words added to on-screen image
Capitalization	Differences from original capitalization
Punctuation	Differences from original punctuation
Spelling	Differences in word spellings
Word replacement	Differences in whole-word representations

Table 1.2 Examples of text-to-screen replication: most frequent discrepancies by type, number of messages exhibiting the type of discrepancy, original message feature, and on-screen rendering (my glosses in parentheses)

Discrepancy type	Occurrences (out of 114)	Examples	
		Original message feature	On-screen rendering
Omission	46	<LOL>	
		Acronyms	
		Profanity	
		Emphatic text	
Capitalization	44	ALL CAPS	Sentence case.
		midsentence Uppercase	midsentence lowercase
		<k>	<K> ("ok")
		<u>	<U> ("you")
		<mtg>	<MTG> ("meeting")
Punctuation	32	< ! >	< . >
		< >	< , >

Extract 1.1: Text-to-screen omission of <LOL> and turn-initial second pair-part (line breaks are represented as they appear in the on-screen image) (Mayor Kilpatrick to Christine Beatty; WXYZ)

Original text	On-screen visualization
LOLOLOLOLOL! That's BECAUSE IT MAKES ABSOLUTELY NO SENSE. I WILL FIGURE OUT WHEN AND HOW WE CAN SPEND THE REST OF OUR LIVES TOGETHER!	"I will figure out when and how we can spend the rest of our lives together."

Extract 1.2: Text-to-screen omission of <LOL> (Kilpatrick to Beatty; WDIV)

Original text	On-screen visualization
LOL! The might is on YOU! LOL	The "might" is on you!

As seen in Extract 1.1, on-screen renderings commonly set the text off with quotation marks. Not present in the original messages, these marks may give the feeling that the reported speech is faithful to the original, even when this is not the case.

In one case of message-medial content omission, the uppercase phrase <WITH MY COS> (probably "with my Chief of Staff") is omitted from a message from Kilpatrick; another omits the emotive form <(smile)> from one of Beatty's messages. In Extract 1.3, an on-screen instance omits a message-final sentence containing several nonstandard features used by Kilpatrick (<FINE>, <b4>, <:)>, <XOXO>; note that <u> is also changed from lowercase to uppercase letters, highlighting this phonetic substitution). In Extract 1.4, several presumably affective initialisms (possibly "soulmate, best friend, love of my life") are omitted.

Extract 1.3: Text-to-screen omission of nonstandard features (Kilpatrick to Unknown; Fox 2 News)

Original text	On-screen visualization
Hey sexy, hope u had a good day. By the way, meant 2 tell u that u look great-you've lost weight-not that u weren't FINE b4 :) XOXO	"Hey sexy, hope U had a good day. By the way, meant 2 tell U that U look great..."

Extract 1.4: Text-to-screen omission of acronyms (Beatty to Kilpatrick; WXYZ)

Original text	On-screen visualization
I will always be YOUR GIRL. I hope to one day be much more and get to show you and for me to experience the full depth of life as "your girl! Goodnight SM, BF, LOML! Talk to you tomorrow.	"I will always be YOUR GIRL. I hope to one day be much more and to get to show you and for me to experience the full depth of life as "your girl! Goodnight

In erasing some visually emblematic text message forms, these imaged transcripts represent text messaging as more like standard written English than as something especially novel, and as more standard than the original messages. This constructs Kilpatrick and Beatty's voices as perhaps more "adult" or more "official" than their original texts appear.

The modification of written text to be more standard-like is also seen in the alteration of capitalization and punctuation. A common capitalization change is from all capitals to sentence case (evident in Extract 1.1). Many of Kilpatrick's messages are written either wholly or predominantly in all capitals, and his automatic signature is in all capitals, so that original messages coming from Kilpatrick in reply to other messages read <Reply from THE MAYOR>. This is never shown on TV. Elsewhere, sentences written in title case are also changed to sentence case. And, sentence-initial lowercase letters are changed to uppercase. These holistic changes are moves toward standard print conventions.

Another capitalization alteration is nonstandard abbreviated forms changed from lowercase to uppercase, presumably to visibly mark them as abbreviations. This happens once for <mtg> to <MTG> ("meeting"), and twice each for <k> to <K> ("okay") and <u> to <U> ("you"). Occasionally, individual words presumably capitalized for emphasis in the original message are changed into lowercase in the on-screen transcripts, as in Extract 1.5.

Extract 1.5: Text-to-screen alteration of capitalization to sentence case (Kilpatrick to Beatty; WXYZ)

Original text	On-screen visualization
In this important and somewhat confusing time in your life, please know with all our heart and soul that I love you. And you will never, NEVER be alone. TBC	"Know with all our hearts and soul that I love you...and you will never, never be alone."

For punctuation, alterations are also in the direction of standard writing conventions. Several of the changes involve affective punctuation, where rather than exclamation marks <!> in the original, there are on-screen periods <.> sentence- or message-final, as in Extract 1.6, or no punctuation message-medial, as in Extract 1.7 (which also omits a period message-medially).

Extract 1.6: Text-to-screen alteration of punctuation, replacing <!> with <.> message-finally (Beatty to Kilpatrick; Fox 2 News)

Original text	On-screen visualization
LOL! YOUR GAME IS WAY ON BABY! "YOU HAD ME AT HELLO!" JERRY MCGUIRE 2000. LOL. I JUST DIDN'T WANT TO GET CAUGHT!	LOL! Your game is way on baby! "you had me at hello!" Jerry McGuire 2000. LOL. I just didn't want to get caught.

Extract 1.7: Text-to-screen alteration of punctuation, omitting <!> message-medially (Kilpatrick to Beatty; WXYZ)

Original text	On-screen visualization
LOLOLOL! RIGHT. You Are MY GIRL. You ALWAYS HAVE BEEN.	"LOLOLOL RIGHT You Are MY GIRL You ALWAYS HAVE BEEN.

There are also *additions* of punctuation to the message text where there is none in the original. Three messages add apostrophes, five commas, and two periods. These move the text in the direction of standard punctuation, as in Extract 1.8. (Note also the spelling out of the ampersand character from <&> to <and>, which makes Kilpatrick's usage consistent within the message.)

Extract 1.8: Text-to-screen alteration of punctuation, adding <,> (Kilpatrick to Beatty; Fox 2 News)

Original text	On-screen visualization
The tremendous bond of Parenthood. J,J & J's Mama. The Birth Experiences and the Dreams for our children.	"The tremendous bond of parenthood. J,J, and J's Mama. The birth experience and the dreams for our children."

To summarize, while no alterations at the level of a single variable occur in a majority of messages, most messages do contain some alteration. Extracts 1.6 and 1.7 show that the omission of nonstandard features like <LOL> is in no way categorical, that nonstandard features do sometimes remain in the screen visualizations—just not to the extent that they occur in the originals. The alterations pertaining to written form predominantly move the text toward standard print and away from the individual style of the message authors, yet at other points, Kilpatrick's style as playing with textual features and inserting affective markers comes through in the visual representation. This variation is what I mean by horizontal heteroglossia.

Text-to-Voice Replication

For the text-to-voice replication analysis, the vocal readings of the messages were compared with the original text. Most of the omissions present in the text-to-screen findings apply here as well, as typically newscasters spoke whichever words appeared on-screen. However, in some cases the auditory and visual content did not entirely match, as in Extract 1.9, where a message-final sentence is shown on-screen but not vocalized. This is one example of the production of *vertical* heteroglossia, where two modalities discrepantly represent one message.

In addition to these omissions, word forms are vocally altered in three ways (Table 1.3). First, in *glossing*, newscasters explicate the meaning of shortenings or abbreviations. A prime example is the reading of <LOL>. As discussed, <LOL> is often omitted on-screen, in which case it is also omitted in the vocal rendering. But when <LOL> *is* realized

Extract 1.9: Text-to-voice discrepancy, final sentence appears on screen but not read aloud (Misty Evans to Beatty; WDIV)

On-screen visualization	Message vocalization
Jermaine charged the Mayor's CC for $243.38 for his wife to go with him to Mackinac. I am asking him for it back today. Just an FYI on the reconcilation part, ok.	Jermaine charged the Mayor's CC for two-hundred forty-three thirty-eight dollars for his wife to go with him to Mackinac. I am asking him for it back today.

Table 1.3 Examples of text-to-voice word alteration by category, number of messages exhibiting the category, and examples from original messages and their vocalizations

Category of alteration	Occurrences (out of 114)	Examples	
		Original message	Vocalization
Gloss	19	<LOL>	*laugh out loud*
		<LOL>	*haha*
		<ck>	*check*
		<kk>	*Kwame Kilpatrick*
		<WV>	*West Virginia*
		<msgs>	*messages*
Standardization	11	<ain't>	*isn't*
		<bruh>	*bro*
		<sooooo>	*so*
		<she>	*she's*
		<nigga>	*n-word*
		<bitch>	*b-word*
		<want 2>	*wanna*
Contraction	9	<He is>	*he's*
		<I am>	*I'm*
		<want 2>	*wanna*
		<we will>	*we'll*

auditorily, it is either expanded ("laugh out loud") or enacted ("haha") (both somewhat ironic vocal approximations of a written utterance intended to approximate a vocal one). A few proper names are also glossed, as are other shortenings.

Second, *standardizations* move the text toward standard English, euphemistically replacing profanity and removing nonstandard features. For

Extract 1.10: Text-to-voice discrepancy, absence/presence of *has* in bold (Carlita Kilpatrick to Beatty; WDIV)

On-screen visualization	Message vocalization
Renee is going to be fired off of EPU! Found out **she been** talking to IA about things going on over here... But if she has said anything, she's GOTTA GO! It's the worst when you like someone and they don't do right. This is an issue I'm going to totally defer to God.	Renee is going to be fired off of EPU Carlita Kilpatrick wrote Found out **she's been** talking to IA about things going on over here But if she has said anything, she's gotta go It's the worst when you like someone and they don't do right This is an issue I'm going to totally defer to God.

example, in Extract 1.10, the present perfect progressive form <she been> omits *has*—a feature of African-American English—but in the vocalization is altered to contain *has*, rendered as a contraction (*she's*). Third and relatedly, *contractions* in the vocalizations combine two words into one, making the text exchanges sound more conversational.

These "translations" can make the texts "sound" more or less formal, written, or standard. The nature of these differences shows that inasmuch as formal properties of the original are altered, it is to "clean" the language—not necessarily to foster comprehension. While (possibly *because*) newscasters' focus in the messages is the content, changes made are to form. Especially when the on-screen and vocal renderings do not match, the medium of text messaging itself is framed as opaque and in need of translation.

Verbal Framing

When a newscaster is voicing a text message, the metadiscursivity of his or her reported speech is somewhat implicit. However, newscasters also give explicit metadiscursive framings to the messages through their message introductions, and these frames contribute to the representation of text messaging as social practice. To explore this, I examined the quotatives newscasters used to introduce individual messages. In particular, I coded the newscaster's speech immediately preceding each message, then categorized these into two types: phrases declaring the message sender or recipient, and quotative lemmas signaling the act of text message exchange. Table 1.4 shows how many times each form occurs across the corpus.

Table 1.4 Verbal framing by type, prototypical form, and number of messages exhibiting the form (italics indicates lemmas indexing writing, speaking, or texting)

Frame type	Prototypical form	Occurrences (out of 128)
Sender/Recipient	(from) Sender	25
	Sender (back) to Recipient	14
	to Recipient	1
Quotative lemmas	*write* (back)	20
	respond	16
	text (back)	14
	reply	13
	(message from device/ pager) *reads*	7
	say	7
	send *(text message; response; text)*	3
	ask	2
	receive text	2
	write + *say*	2
	assure	1
	tell	1

Naming the sender or recipient emphasizes the participant roles of those engaging in text messaging, reestablishing the actors and reascribing their authorship. These introductions remind the audience of Kilpatrick and Beatty and also affirm that these texts were produced as part of ongoing interaction, not in isolation. This also occurs with the use of the verbs *respond* or *reply*, which signal interactivity. Many more quotative verbs pertain to *writing, reading*, and/or *texting* than to *speaking* (italicized in Table 1.4). The message exchanges are framed primarily as written texts—though highly interactive—not speech.

Intonational Framing

Intonational framing, like verbal framing, is another level of representation that metadiscursively positions text messaging relative to other uses of language. In English, prosodic patterns tend to be different for speech that is read versus spontaneous; read speech contains more falling contours (e.g., Lieberman et al., 1985). Falling intonation is thus a cue to read, formal, or prepared speech. My intonational framing analysis explores whether the representations of text messages are aligned with written text (falling contours) or spoken conversation (rising contours). If the voices of the text message authors were subsumed by the journalistic practices of the newscasters' language norms, we would expect more falling contours, whereas if newscasters as animators wished to emphasize conversationality or the casual nature of the text messages, or if newscasters wanted to create symbolic distance between their informational speech and the texts or their authors, they might use rising intonation.

Using just the audio, I segmented each message into intonational phrases and coded each phrase's nuclear intonational contour as either rising or falling (see representative pitch tracks in Figure 1.2; cf. Podesva, forthcoming).[5] I also coded punctuation marks present in the on-screen transcript of the intonational phrase.

Newscasters predominantly use falling contours; as seen in Figure 1.3, the majority of contours in the text message reading are falling (296/321 or 92%). Of the 25 rising contours, all but 4 occur with punctuation—when rising contours are used, it is to convey the force of a punctuation mark (namely, a question mark).

Additionally, many falling contours occur message- or sentence-medially. McLemore (1991) argues that one of the functions of rising contours is to signal continuation of material; given this, we might expect message-medial intonational phrases to include rising contours, since they occur amid upcoming information. Instead, falling contours are the default intonational pattern in these readings, not just markers of the end of a sentence or the conclusion of a whole message.

The intonation here conforms to generic conventions of newscast reading. When reading the texts, newscasters are adding cues of spoken language to what is originally a written text. Intonation cannot be avoided, and it could be exploited as a stylistic resource to inflect message style. Yet

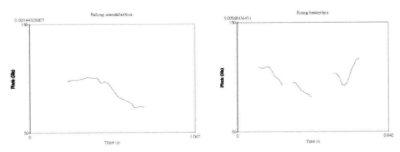

FIGURE 1.2: Falling (left) and rising (right) intonational contours in reported speech vocalization.

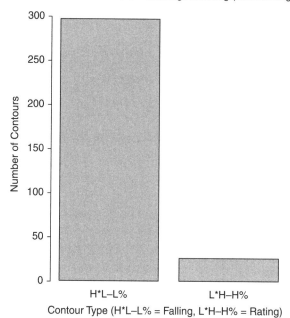

FIGURE 1.3 Total number of rising and falling contours in reported speech vocalization.

the newscasters' animating intonation is almost entirely that of "reading." Perhaps the impetus toward a formal style is so great that it subsumes the voices of the text authors, or perhaps text messages are thought of precisely *as* written texts, to be read, not enacted as speech.

Sequential Organization

Finally, I investigated the relation of individual messages to each other in the broadcasts, rather than properties of single messages. Message sequencing metadiscursively frames text messaging as social practice. Much computer-mediated communication research has investigated the constraints placed on interaction by the quasi-synchronous nature of new media (cf. Hutchby, 2001), and Thurlow (2006, 2007) has shown that news media representations of new media language disembed it from its everyday interactional use. My analysis of sequential organization explored the extent to which text messaging is represented by the newsmakers as interactive or unidirectional. To this end, I coded each broadcast segment for *conversational threads:* topically self-contained series of messages. Threads typically begin with the newscaster stating the date a message was sent

Extract 1.11: Excerpt from a broadcast demonstrating a one-turn thread followed by three-turn thread; text message vocalization follows introductory speech (Fox 2 News)

Thread Part	Introductory speech	Text message vocalization
1	on June eighth two thousand three, Kilpatrick received *this* text from an unidentified woman	I rented a cabana by the pool wow it's really sexy wish you could be here to chill with me oh well maybe soon
1	and on may ninth two thousand four *this* text also from an unidentified woman	I was saying should I extend my reservation to wait for you in Vegas?
2	he replies	yes if you can I will be sure tomorrow make sure I won't have company
3	she replies	ok baby I'll hit you tomorrow I'm on my way home now kisses

and/or a contextualizing note ("The mayor said many times he loved Christine, saying quote..."). Threads continue with one or more messages to their completion. I call each message a "turn," though the mechanics of turn taking in text messaging are of course more complex than this indicates. The sample transcript excerpt in (11) shows a one-turn thread followed by a three-turn thread.

Table 1.5 summarizes thread types in the whole corpus, showing how many turns the conversational threads contain (1 to 6), how many threads of this type occur across all segments, and how many broadcasts include this thread type. While the one-turn category has the highest raw frequency, only 38 messages out of the 130 in the corpus are presented as stand-alone threads. The majority of messages are presented as turns within conversational threads, related to other messages; texting is presented as consisting of interactive sending, receiving, and responding.

The TV news coverage of the Detroit scandal emphasizes the mutual exchange of messages between Kilpatrick and Beatty. Perhaps because what

Table 1.5 Occurrence of conversational thread types by number of turns

Turns	Occurrences	Broadcasts (out of 16)
1	38	12
2	23	9
3	9	5
4	2	2
5	1	1
6	1	1

is involved is a romantic affair, the representations center on interaction. Thus, one key feature of texting—its interactivity—is emphasized here and is *not* erased as it is in other contexts of representation.

Discussion

Across the five metadiscursive levels examined, the language of the Detroit scandal text messages is neither particularly exaggerated nor highlighted as especially novel; this is striking given the media's tendency to fetishize new media language produced by young people (Thurlow, 2006, 2007; Thurlow & Poff, 2011). Instead, in several examples shown above, features that might be considered emblematic of text messaging are suppressed. Yet representation of text messaging here is not monolithic or simplistic; rather, heteroglossia exists horizontally across the field of reported messages. Features are inconsistently included, omitted, or altered. Such heteroglossia reflects the ongoing negotiation of journalistic conventions for depicting text messaging—among other forms of new media—as a source for reported speech.

In the case of Detroit's mayoral scandal, text messaging became a central source of information in legal proceedings, for news reports, and for local discourse about the salacious happenings. As the news media work to convey informational content regarding the politicians and their actions, they sometimes erase aspects of linguistic form, other times leaving it intact. But their overt focus is not language: what is salient is its perception as a medium that facilitates the clandestine undertaking of extramarital affairs and questionable political deals—rather than as a medium for innovative or uncommon linguistic practice.

Yet heteroglossia also exists vertically *within* the representation of individual messages, where the voices of author and animator compete—the voice of author reformulated by animator. Here, I attempt to formalize the complexity behind this vertical heteroglossia by outlining five dimensions along which the text message representations differ. The multimodality of available symbolic resources enables TV broadcasts to characterize text messaging simultaneously along five sociolinguistic axes: *nonstandard/standard, interactive/unidirectional, spoken/written, conversational/formal,* and *novel/mundane.* Related and overlapping, these are conceptual schema for understanding sociolinguistic practice, and as the data here show, different representational levels contribute to the construction of form along different axes.

These axes are central to how new media forms are metadiscursively characterized by the mass media (Thurlow, 2006), new media users (Squires, 2010), and scholars (Androutsopolous, 2006). The question of whether new media is "ruining" Standard English is perennial in mainstream media (Squires, 2010; Thurlow, 2006). The relative value of computer-mediated communication as occurring in spatial isolation versus face-to-face has been a ripe debate from the earliest days of research in the field (cf. Kiesler et al., 1984). Whether mediated communication is more speechlike or writing-like has been a central linguistic focus, too (Androutsopoulos, 2006; Baron, 2003; Tagliamonte & Denis, 2008), as has the related matter of how conversational new media are (Tagliamonte & Denis, 2008). And previous research shows that linguistic novelty tends to be exaggerated (Herring, 2003, 2004; Shortis, 2007; Thurlow, 2003, 2006). While I am not arguing that the extremes of my sociolinguistic axes are themselves met by text messaging practices, I am suggesting that the axes reflect dimensions along which contemporary language ideologies often construe English linguistic practice. As such, they are foundational to how new media language is conceived as carrying values (status, position, personality) and consequences (social change, language change, sociotechnological evolution). They also form a foundation for heteroglossia: they are the recognizable stylistic dimensions from which multiple voices emerge in the reproduction of a single text.

For a simple invented example of how these axes apply to text message representations, take the following set of facts for a single message as presented in a newscast:

    a. text on-screen includes <LOL>
    b. text vocalization omits <LOL>
    c. text sequenced as second pair-part in a conversational thread

d. text quoted via verb *texts*

e. text read with falling intonation

Rather than view each of these features working together to draw a *cohesive* portrayal of texting along any single dimension, we can appeal to the axes of form to see how each feature may index a different axis (or multiple axes). In this case, we might say that (a) indexes *nonstandard* and *novel*, (b) *standard*, (c) *interactive* and *conversational*, (d) *novel*, and (e) *written* and *formal*. There are no one-to-one correspondences between features and axes; rather, any feature might signal any axis or multiple axes. And, of course, these are matters of degree—the point is just that when multiple semiotic resources are available to do metadiscursive work, multiple meanings may attach to those resources. These five formal dimensions can serve as reference points for ideologized representations of language as used in new media.

Now take an actual set of features from Extract 1.12. For this representation, the following features are present:

a. text on-screen replaces <NO THANK YOU!> with <Thank you>

b. text in voice reads, "It gives me so much pleasure..."

c. text sequenced as first-pair part, immediately followed by a response from Beatty

Extract 1.12: Original text, on-screen visual representation, and transcript of vocalization of message from Kilpatrick (Mayor) to Beatty (Chief of Staff) (WXYZ)

Original text	On-screen transcript	Introductory speech and message vocalization
		in June two-thousand three former mayor Kwame Kilpatrick writes
NO THANK YOU! FOR LETTING ME MAKE YOU FEEL GOOD. IT GIVES ME SOOOOO MUCH PLEASURE TO SEE, FEEL AND EXPERIENCE YOU!	"Thank you for letting me make you feel good. It gives me soooo much pleasure to see, feel and experience you.!"	thank you for letting me make you feel good it gives me so much pleasure to see feel and experience you

d. text quoted via verb *writes*
e. text read with falling intonation

Here, (a) indexes *standard*, through its shift to sentence case; *formal*, through its removal of the exclamation mark and the affect it might otherwise carry; and *unidirectional* (as read, the message itself is not contextualized as a response, nor does it invite a response—which is an example of the misrepresentation of message sequencing occasionally occurring in the broadcasts). (b) indexes *written* and *formal* in its shortened voicing of <sooooo>. (c) indexes *interactive*. (d) indexes *written*, and (e) indexes *written* and *formal*. Inasmuch as none of the cues highlight the novelty of text messaging, they all functionally represent the practice as *mundane*.

I've conceived of these as axes of *form* because mass media metadiscourse often concentrates on form, and formal features become the locus for ideas about the "effects" of new media. These axes provide ideologically grounded categories of form that are relevant in both explicit and implicit metadiscursive representations of new media (and in many cases, language in general), and they provide the foundations for constructions of the voices present in the representations. For instance, again from Extract 1.12, when a newscaster vocally produces "so" instead of a lengthened vowel in "sooooo," they index the text as written and formal, and by doing so, they represent the author (Kilpatrick) as *a user* of written formal language. However, the presence on-screen of <sooooo> reveals the author's practice as somewhat more speechlike. With the transcript on-screen taken as Kilpatrick's own, the animator's vocalization can maintain gravitas and professional convention. Layered linguistic resources enable both voices to emerge.

The potential for heteroglossia is especially significant when one takes into consideration the breadth of features Kilpatrick (the mayor) indeed used in his original texts, including all capital letters as a common format for whole messages, acronyms, and exclamation marks (which are often ideologized as feminine). As author, Kilpatrick does not fit what a typical "adult" texter might do according to common language ideology, and in fact, he uses many features commonly attributed to young texters. As his texts are animated, however, they use more standard formats, and the extent to which he draws upon the linguistic affordances of text as a medium is erased. Interestingly, in erasing many of these features, novel properties of the medium itself are erased, and the mass media metadiscursively construct adult texters as exempt from the stylistic resourcefulness portrayed for young people.

What I hope to have shown in my analysis here is that text-based linguistic practice in new media is not always represented as unique, nonstandard, or disembedded (cf. Thurlow, 2003, 2006). Rather, "novel" features of the medium may be erased when transferred to other media contexts, with stereotypical properties omitted, obscured, or translated. When television media report on and represent text messaging, text messages are transferred from private to public, from source to representation, from one mode to a different multimodal space. In the case of the mayoral scandal in Detroit, the context of the original text messages concerns adult actors engaged in what are typically construed as adult activities (from professional duties to sexual endeavors). The context of their metadiscursive representation is also "adult," television news being produced and presented by working professionals whose audience is adult viewers.

With a focus on adults, the erasure of novelty in the context of this particular scandal can be linked to the same language ideologies that might in other contexts lead to its exaggeration. That is, in altering adults' linguistic forms in new media to be more standard, these representations align with ideologies that stigmatize youth speech as novel in comparison with adult speech. While the Detroit officials' *use* of text messaging as the preferred mode of communication is highlighted as notable through the deployment of terms like "text message scandal," the *language* used within this text messaging is not in itself presented as striking. And whereas public discourse about youth-based new media focuses on nonstandard features that are not in actuality present to a great extent, this public discourse about adult-based new media language erases some nonstandard features that *are* actually present in the adults' text messages. The ideological, naturalized connections between youth and new media language on the one hand, and adults and standard language on the other, are thus reinscribed.

Acknowledgments

I'm extremely grateful to the organizers, audience, and other attendees at the Language in the (New) Media Conference, especially Crispin Thurlow and Jannis Androutsopoulos; the chapter reviewers and volume coeditors; the SocioDiscourse group at the University of Michigan; and Eric Brown.

Notes

1. I used the program SnapzPro to screen capture the broadcast segments and QuickTime Pro to edit them.
2. Original texts were obtained from two court documents available at http:// www2.wxyz.com/dpp/news/local_news/BREAKING:-New-Text-Messages-

Released (dated July 7, 2008) and http://media.freep.com/documents/ stefanio42908/0429stefani.pdf (dated April 29, 2008). In the former, texts are in their digital form as obtained by lawyers from SkyTel; in the latter, texts are reproduced but appear to maintain the orthographic styles of the original texts. Neither court documents nor news reports say precisely which pagers were used, though a photograph in court documents seems to show a Motorola T900 with a full QWERTY keypad. It is unclear what the character limit was; the original messages read in this corpus had a high of 253 characters.

3. Obviously, it would be useful to know what material newscasters referred to when reading the messages from the press releases, the original spreadsheet of the text messages, and so forth, and what editorial selection and editing took place prior. I can only acknowledge that I am unable to account for this information.

4. I use angled bracket notation for orthographic form.

5. I extracted audio from the video clips using MPEG Streamclip and used Praat to investigate pitch.

References

Androutsopoulos, J. (2006). Introduction: Sociolinguistics and computer-mediated communication. *Journal of Sociolinguistics*, 10, 419–438.

Androutsopoulos, J. (2009). Policing practices in heteroglossic mediascapes: A commentary on interfaces. *Language Policy*, 8, 285–290.

Bakhtin, M.M. (1981). *The Dialogic Imagination* (M.J. Holquist, Trans.). Austin: University of Texas Press.

Baron, N.S. (2003). Why e-mail looks like speech: Proofreading, pedagogy, and public face. In J. Aitchison & D. Lewis (Eds.), *New Media Language*, (pp. 102–113). London: Routledge.

Coupland, N., & Jaworski, A. (2004). Sociolinguistic approaches to metalanguage: Reflexivity, evaluation and ideology. In A. Jaworski, N. Coupland, & D. Galasinski (Eds.), *Metalanguage: Social and Ideological Perspectives*, (pp. 15–52). Berlin: Mouton de Gruyter.

Detroit Free Press (2008). The chain of events. Retrieved from http://www.freep.com/article/20080124/NEWS05/801240419/0/NEWS01/The-chain-of-events (July 16, 2010).

Gallagher, J. (2009). Free press wins Pulitzer for coverage of mayoral scandal. *Detroit Free Press*, April 20. Retrieved from http://www.freep.com/article/20090420/NEWS01/90420047/Free-Press-wins-Pulitzer-for-coverage-of-mayoral-scandal (August 7, 2009).

Goffman, E. (1981). *Forms of Talk*. Philadelphia: University of Pennsylvania Press.

Herring, S.C. (2003). Media and language change: Introduction. *Journal of Historical Pragmatics*, 4, 1–17.

Herring, S.C. (2004). Slouching toward the ordinary: Current trends in computer-mediated communication. *New Media & Society*, 6(1), 26–36.

Hutchby, I. (2001). *Conversation and Technology: From the Telephone to the Internet.* Cambridge, UK: Polity.

Irvine, J., & Gal, S. (2000). Language ideology and linguistic differentiation. In P. V. Kroskrity (Ed.), *Regimes of Language: Ideologies, Polities, and Identities,* (pp. 35–84). Santa Fe, NM: School of American Research Press.

Jones, G.M., & Schieffelin, B.B. (2009). Talking text and talking back: "My BFF Jill" from boob tube to YouTube. *Journal of Computer-Mediated Communication,* 14, 1050–1079.

Kiesler, S., Siegel, J., & McGuire, T.W. (1984). Social psychological aspects of computer-mediated communication. *American Psychologist,* 39, 1123–1134.

Lieberman, P., Katz, W., Jongman, A., Zimmerman, R., & Miller, M. (1985). Measures of the sentence intonation of read and spontaneous speech in American English. *Journal of the Acoustical Society of America,* 77, 649–657.

McLemore, C.A. (1991). The pragmatic interpretation of English intonation: Sorority speech. The University of Texas at Austin: Ph.D. Dissertation.

Podesva, R.J. (Forthcoming). Salience and the social meaning of declarative contours. *Journal of English Linguistics.*

Sacks, H., Schegloff, E.A., & Jefferson, G. (1974). A simplest systematics for the organization of turn-taking for conversation. *Language,* 50, 696–735.

Shortis, T. (2007). Gr8 txtpectations: The creativity of text spelling. *English Drama Media.* June: 21–26.

Squires, L. (2010). Enregistering internet language. *Language in Society,* 39(4), 1–36.

Tagliamonte, S.A., & Denis, D. (2008). Linguistic ruin? Lol! Instant messaging and teen language. *American Speech,* 83, 3–34.

Thurlow, C. (2003). Generation txt? The sociolinguistics of young people's text-messaging. *Discourse Analysis Online.* Available at http://extra.shu.ac.uk/daol/articles/v1/n1/a3/thurlow2002003-t.html

Thurlow, C. (2006). From statistical panic to moral panic: The metadiscursive construction and popular exaggeration of new media language in the print media. *Journal of Computer-Mediated Communication,* 11(3). Available at http://jcmc.indiana.edu/vol11/issue3/thurlow.html

Thurlow, C. (2007). Fabricating youth: New-media discourse and the technologization of young people. In S. Johnson & A. Ensslin (Eds.), *Language in the Media: Representations, Identities, Ideologies,* (pp. 213–233). London: Continuum.

Thurlow, C., & Poff, M. (2011). Text messaging. In S.C. Herring, D. Stein, & T. Virtanen (Eds.), *Handbook of the Pragmatics of CMC.* Berlin/New York: Mouton de Gruyter.

U.S. Census Bureau (2010). State & County QuickFacts: Detroit (city), MI. http://quickfacts.census.gov/qfd/states/26/2622000.html (July 16, 2010).

Chapter 2

When Friends Who Talk Together Stalk Together: Online Gossip as Metacommunication

Graham M. Jones, Bambi B. Schieffelin, and Rachel E. Smith

AT A TIME in their lives when friendships, relationships, and broader questions of identity are especially significant, it is no surprise that teenagers discuss their own and others' behavior, reporting interactions and circulating accounts of what has been said and done in social settings. Young people across cultures actively embrace tools of communication, from literacy and the telephone to the internet and cell phone, in order to enhance projects constituting self and society. These technologies of semiotic mediation provide resources for elaborating media-specific message forms and create channels for extending communication in space and time. They also offer users opportunities for communicating about communication, and specialized forms of communication for communicating about.

Researchers have found that adult metadiscourses often misconstrue young people's new media practices (Herring, 2008; Jones and Schieffelin, 2009a; Thurlow, 2006, 2007). In our chapter here, however, we focus on teenagers' own normative assessments of peers' online practices. The assessments we consider do not take the form of reflexively elaborated metadiscourses but, rather, emerge through and within metacommunicative gossip, that is, morally motivated stories about others' online communication. In particular, we concentrate on gossip conducted via Instant Messaging (IM) about communications on the social networking site (SNS) *Facebook*. Such gossip is not only metacommunicative; it is also metasemiotic insofar as participants incorporate materials from one new media channel into another through circulatory processes of decontextualization and recontextualization (Bauman and Briggs, 1990). To understand how they accomplish this, we begin by describing the communicative resources of IM. We then discuss *Facebook* as a catalyst for and subject of gossip, considering how users collect information about others through the site. In the final section, we analyze several examples in which IM partners collaboratively access and assess *Facebook* content, constituting online gossip as a "situated activity system" (Goodwin, 2000).

"Social media mirror, magnify, and extend everyday social worlds," writes danah boyd (2010, p. 84). "By and large, teens use social media to do what they have been doing—socialize with friends, negotiate peer groups, flirt, share stories, and simply hang out. At the same time, networked publics provide opportunities for always-on access to peer communication, new kinds of authoring of public identities, public display of connectedness, and access to information about others" (pp. 84–85). Indeed, we find that the very public forms of self-display within peer groups connected through *Facebook* can create "storyable" (Sacks, 1984, p. 417) incidents that friends discuss and assess—in this case via the relatively private channel of IM. *Facebook* offers its users myriad ways of expressing views, conveying affinities, and establishing connections. Gossiping about these online activities of absent others, the teens in our study use IM to establish and affirm shared moral stances (Georgakopoulou, 2007; Jaworski and Coupland, 2005). While stance is a dimension of virtually any form of communication (Englebretson, 2007; Jaffe, 2009; see also Chapters 10, 11, & 12, this volume), we argue that the culture of *Facebook* emphasizes stance by encouraging public expressions of personal views that can provoke moral reactions in the form of gossip.

Background

IM is a form of synchronous, typewritten communication in which pairs of users exchange short messages (Baron, 2008; Tagliamonte and Denis, 2008). In this study, we consider how teenagers use IM to sustain joint attention, accomplish shared stance, and empathize with each other. This kind of successful communication requires mutually understood conventions. In this section, we briefly survey some conventionalized features that emerge from our data, namely: metalinguistic classifications, turn-taking features, affective keys, and stylistic features including reported speech. After reviewing salient conventions, we look in greater detail at how teens deploy them creatively in the activity of IM gossip.

In an earlier article, two of the present authors compared face-to-face and IM conversations among American young adults (aged 18–22) at a large

East Coast university, collected in 2003 and 2006 (Jones and Schieffelin, 2009b). We refer to these data as the Young Adult Corpus. Here, we seek to extend these analyses with more recent IM data collected between 2006 and 2009 from college freshman (age ~18) at the same institution and middle-class high schoolers (age 15–17) residing in the Northeast (USA). We refer to the totality of this newer data as the Teen Corpus. Collected from 11 focal users, it comprises 719 IM conversations between 96 individuals (or 107 different dyads), for a total of 508,186 words. We employ an inductive, speaker-centered, approach to analyze these data ethnographically (Coleman, 2010) and have selected the most succinct examples with the highest number of concentrated features for illustrative purposes. Unless otherwise specified, all examples reproduced in this paper are from the Teen Corpus and have been anonymized for both content and speakers' screen names.

Comparing data spanning 2003 to 2009, from users ranging from 15 to 22, reveals that IM has a number of relatively stable conventionalized features that distinguish it as a genre. In both the Young Adult and Teen Corpora, people consistently construe IM as a form of *talk*. The metalinguistic verbs they use to describe the activity of IMing—*talk, yell, say, speak*—make this construal explicit, as the following representative example suggests:

Example 2.1
1   blueIz408: no im not like putting myself down.
2   im just saying...
3   Guppy215: i dont wanna hear this kind of talk

Here blueIz408 uses the verb "say" to describe to her typewritten messages, and Guppy215, in turn, refers to those messages as "talk" that she can "hear."

As one would expect for any form of talk (Sacks et al., 1974), a set of turn-taking conventions in IM has proven relatively stable across time. We quantify these observations in terms of utterances and turns. We define an *utterance* as an individual message sent with a stroke of the return key (in our transcripts, as in IM talk, a speaker's screen name appears at the beginning of each utterance), and a *turn* as a series of uninterrupted utterances by one speaker. In the Young Adult Corpus, IM conversations averaged 5.8 words/utterance and 1.6 utterances/turn in 2003, and 5.7 words/utterance and 1.9 utterances/turn in 2006. Similarly, Baron (2004) reports that IM conversations in her corpus averaged 5.4 words/utterance and 1.7 utterances/turn. An analysis of the 42 IM conversations between the 23 high schoolers in the 2006–2009 Teen Corpus found averages of 6.1 words/ utterance and 1.9 utterances/turn. The stability of this particular configuration of turn-taking characteristics may have to do with recipient design insofar as a relatively small ratio of words to utterance and a relatively high ratio of utterances to turn helps a speaker hold the floor and thereby maintain joint attention to a specific topic in a medium of synchronous communication in which a message only becomes legible once it is sent. Thus, if an IMer spends too much time composing a message before sending it, his or her partner might break in and change the topic (as often happens).

In the Young Adult Corpus, IMers repeatedly discussed the challenges of conveying affect in a typewritten medium. IMers explicitly acknowledged this problem when miscommunications arose or when struggling to convey subtle nuances of tone, particularly sarcasm. They also developed resources for keying affect, and creatively using emoticons, punctuation, capitalization, and codified abbreviations to establish shared structures of feeling. One novel means of expressing affect (or lack thereof) that emerges as significant in the Teen Corpus is the interjection *meh*. A recent article in the London *Guardian* called *meh*, "the word that's sweeping the internet" and explained that it "means rubbish. It means boring. It means not worth the effort, who cares, so-so, whatever. It is the all-purpose dismissive shrug of the blogger and messageboarder. And it is ubiquitous" (Hann, 2007). This description largely coheres with the function *meh* seems to serve in the IM conversations we analyze, as in the following examples.

Example 2.2
1   AmyDayNow: he's cute
2   blueIz408: meh.

Example 2.3
1   blueIz408: med school? you want to go to med
2   school?
3   AmyDayNow: meh maybe

As an interjection expressing indifference or apathy, *meh* adds to the panoply of resources IMers have at their disposal for conveying affect, responding to assessments, and establishing stance.[1]

Analyzing the Young Adult Corpus, Jones and Schieffelin (2009b, p. 99) use Bakhtin's notion of *polyphony* "to characterize narrative or discursive style deliberately and distinctively infused with multiple, often opposing, voices" (see also Squires' discussion of heteroglossia in Chapter 1, this volume). Comparing talk in two different channels—face-to-face and IM conversations—they find male and female speakers creating polyphonic narratives by voicing their own and others' speech and thought using the verbal formula *be + like*, as occurs twice in the following IM example from the Young Adult Corpus:

Example 2.4
1   wandawoman: I kinda thought I would ;-)[2] but
2   my dad was like "OH GOOD I'M SO GLAD YOU
3   WANT TO PAY YOUR OWN RENT!" and I was like
4   oh... okay. :-P[3]

Jones and Schieffelin determine that polyphony is a preferred feature "of informal talk and oral narrative" among the young adults, "which fore-grounds morally and affectively charged voicings overwhelmingly produced through the use of quotative *like*, and which is itself iconic of their cohort." In both face-to-face and IM conversation, quotative *be + like* allows interac-tants to create "constructed dialogues" (Tannen, 1986) in which they demon-strate the stance, aspect, and demeanor of themselves and others. Overall, polyphonic style was found to reflect a preoccupation with assessments and value judgments, and an interactional climate of moral scrutiny.

As with the Young Adult Corpus, IMers in the Teen Corpus strive to create a polyphonic style of typewritten communication, infusing their IM sessions with narratives, accounts, and imagined scenarios that fea-ture constructed dialog. Consider the following example, in which a young woman in her late teens complains to another about a relationship that she ended because her boyfriend was insufficiently interested in sex. In presenting her complaint, she contrastively demonstrates her ex's attitude towards sex and her own, using quotative *be + like* to introduce representa-tive remarks from both parties (lines 1 and 5).

Example 2.5
1   chicachevere123: cause he was like
2   chicachevere123: i can live without sex
3   chicachevere123: i don't need it
4   chicachevere123: hahaha
5   chicachevere123: i was like
6   dreamalittledream: whaaaaat

7   chicachevere123: yeah if we're dating
8   chicachevere123: that's gonna cause problems
9   dreamalittledream: that's a new one
10   chicachevere123: i know
11   chicachevere123: whatever

In the 2006 IM data, Young Adult speakers widely used *be* + *like* to introduce quoted material and deployed a variety of graphic resources to punc-
tuate quotation (viz., quotation marks, commas, and ellipses). However,
we did not find examples of these speakers using a stroke of the return
key to separate quotative *like* and the quoted material, as occurs twice in
this example (lines 1 and 5). Following the terminology of poetry, we call
these intentional and meaningful line breaks *enjambment*. As in a poem,
enjambment can serve to heighten expressive properties of language—
such as dramatic tension—within an instant message. It is also an efficient means of punctuation. Consistent with the ecology of turn-taking
characteristics we describe above, each stroke of the return key not only
initiates a new utterance, but it also can serve to replace intrasentential
punctuation such as commas or quotation marks with enjambment. In
the example above, chicachevere123 uses enjambment to establish the
frame of reported speech, where standard conventions of written English
would demand a comma and quotation marks. This choice is stylistically
coherent and allows her to maintain a preferentially low ratio of symbols
to utterance.

IMers in the Young Adult Corpus allude to multitasking (doing homework, talking on the phone, consulting social networking sites) in their
IM talk (Jones and Schieffelin, 2009b, p. 83). Still, we were surprised by
the extent to which IMers in the Teen Corpus actively and collaboratively
synchronize IM talk with communication in other channels—particularly
Facebook. These kinds of joint IM–*Facebook* sessions have been documented elsewhere (Baron, 2008, p. 95); here we examine the intertextuality of
such conversation as an extension and elaboration of the polyphonic style
that emerged as so important in the Young Adult data. The interface of IM
and *Facebook* produces a kind of polyphony that is not just metalinguistic,
but metasemiotic, spanning multiple new media and incorporating verbal
and nonverbal materials. In the rest of this chapter, we explore these issues, with particular attention to the way IM talk is constituted as a means
for coordinating selective attention to *Facebook* content and assessing the
presentation of oneself and others on the site.

Facebook and Moral Assessment

Chayko (2008, p. 174) notes that online communities offer "windows into others' lives, lifestyles, and interests—windows into which many of us peek from time to time. Widely accessible and available social networking sites, blogs, discussion boards, and any number of sociomental spaces encourage both the creativity of their makers and the curiosity of their audiences. It is easy to become intrigued by the sheer amount of identity offerings displayed." The IM conversations we analyze clearly indicate that those in the Teen Corpus are acutely attuned to what Chayko calls the "voyeuristic" dimensions of *Facebook*. They describe their own efforts to project favorable images of themselves in light of often very specific social projects, and an awareness that these self-projections open them up to scrutiny.[4] They also closely surveil the self-presentation and general activities of others on the site.

While it is just one of many SNS options, *Facebook* was by far the most popular choice for the IMers in our Teen Corpus. Here we give a heuristic description of the essential features of the site; boyd (2008, 2010) offers a more extended discussion (see also Lee, Chapter 6, this volume). Briefly, *Facebook* allows registered users to create a profile with photographs and personal information concerning family and friends, hobbies and interests, relationship status, sexual orientation, political views, religious affiliation, and so on. They can then send friend requests to users they wish to include in their network (which they refer to as "friending" someone) and receive friend requests from others. A list (and a tally) of a user's friends appears on each profile page, which usually can be viewed by at least everyone in the network of friends, depending on the privacy settings one selects. Users can modify their profiles, upload photos, identify themselves and others in photos (called "tagging"), post links to other websites, and post "status updates," short messages that appear instantaneously on a "News Feeds" feature on their friends' homepages (again, see Lee, Chapter 6, this volume). They can post public comments on each other's "walls," which everyone in a friend network can read and comment on; a "wall-to-wall" feature makes it possible to see the history of "wall posts" between two people. There is also an option to send private messages to select users (which they refer to as "messaging" someone). This combination of features creates an environment in which people can selectively inform each other about their lives and inform themselves about the lives of others in a variety of ways. As Jacquemet (2010, p. 60) writes, "these virtual communities are sites for the expansion of the cultural, communicative, and subjective capacities of their users, who are engaged in an exponential expansion of discrete nodes of both affect and affinity." *Facebook* is dynamic, interactive, and emotionally laden, and we see strong evidence in our IM data that users find it intensely engrossing.[5]

The IM conversations we analyze suggest that, for these teen users, *Facebook* is an affectively—and sometimes sexually—charged arena of self-display and mutual scrutiny in which participants construct desire and build alliances through complementary strategies of concealment and revelation. By design, the site provides features that make it possible to monitor the social behavior of others. For instance, in the following example, blueIz408 describes how the "wall-to-wall" feature allows someone to find out what one's friends have been discussing through wall posts.

Example 2.6
1   blueIz408: you know what the worst is? when
2   you look on facebook and you see a wall to
3   wall and the people have been talking about
4   you.

As we have already discussed in connection with IM, note that blueIz408 uses the metalinguistic term "talking," pervasive throughout the Teen Corpus, to describe asynchronous interactions on *Facebook* walls that can unfold spasmodically over hours or days.

In many of the IM exchanges we consider, *Facebook* itself emerges as a topic of gossip. Of course, notions of what constitutes "gossip" vary across cultures (Besnier, 2009; Schieffelin, 2008). For the purposes of this discussion, we draw on the culturally appropriate definition of *gossip* that Cameron (1997, p. 51) proposes in an analysis of speech practices among American college students, that is, "discussion of several persons not present but known to the participants, with a strong focus on critically examining these individuals' appearance, dress, social behaviours and sexual mores." Such moral assessments run throughout the IM exchanges about *Facebook*, which we therefore classify as a kind of gossip.

In the following example, two teenage girls have an IM conversation about an incident that occurred on *Facebook*, construing the actions of an absent third party as prudish and socially inept.

Example 2.7
1   blueIz408: wait remember mdog?
2   xoxoxi2: ya

3 xoxox12: why

4 blueIz408: so he wrote on my wall

5 blueIz408: so i wrote back being like "come to

6   america so we can shower together"

7 blueIz408: and his GIRLFRIEND, Lilah, friended

8   me

9 blueIz408: and messaged me like "i think you

10   should stop with that whole shower thing.

11   its not really necessary" .. hahahhah

12 xoxox12: HAHAHA

13 xoxox12: its funnier if you say that in a

14   brittish accent

15 blueIz408: hahahhahha

16 blueIz408: i know

17 blueIz408: crazzay

18 xoxox12: thats great

19 blueIz408: i just wrote back like "chill, i

20   have a boyfriend. we were kidding"

21 xoxox12: haha

BlueIz408 opens the topic with a presequence ("wait remember mdog?"), signaling a break from the previous frame of talk. She tells xoxox12 that mdog (a British teen who the girls indicate they met the previous summer) contacted her on *Facebook* by posting a comment on her wall, viewable by everyone in her network. She says that she responded with the sexually charged wall post, "come to America so we can shower together." This publicly viewable comment prompted mdog's girlfriend, Lilah, to invite blueIz408 into her network of friends and issue an admonition, sent in a private message: "i think you should stop with that whole shower thing. its not really necessary."

Lilah is the object of gossip here. The two parties construe her reaction to blueIz408's sexually provocative remark as a laughable overreaction. BlueIz408 signals her bemused attitude toward Lilah's admonition with "hahahhah." Xoxox12 endorses this view, replicating blueIz408's assessment and elevating the level of risibility by switching to an emphatic uppercase: "HAHAHA." She then suggests that voicing Lilah's typewritten statement in her "brittish accent" further ridicules her overreaction, presumably by making her sound excessively prim. In the next two utterances, blueIz408 reacts favorably to xoxox12's suggested revoicing of Lilah's original utterance ("hahahhahha/ i know") and then summarizes her stance: "crazzay." Xoxox12 compliments blueIz408 for a rich story ("thats great"). In turn, blueIz408 reports her own response to Lilah, which makes it clear why the latter overreacted: "chill, i have a boyfriend. we were kidding." Interestingly, blueIz408 reports that she changes the subject of the activity Lilah construes as morally problematic from implicitly singular ("you should stop with that whole shower thing") to explicitly plural ("we were kidding").

After this section, the topic shifts. It is unclear whether Lilah accepted blueIz408's explanation of the public exchange of messages with mdog— nor is that the point of the story. In this strip of talk, the two girls collaboratively produce an assessment of an absent third party as prim and humorless. On a deeper level, they affirm an interpretation of blueIz408's own actions, defending her against Lilah's accusation of moral transgression. By ridiculing her accuser with support from xoxox12, blueIz408 neutralizes the force of what could be a morally damaging complaint.

We would particularly like to note the use of reported speech in this exchange. BlueIz408 relates the incident with Lilah in the form of a constructed dialog, using *like* as a complementizer to establish a quotative frame with the verbs *write back* and *message* (lines 5, 9, and 19). These relatively novel constructions index the migration of polyphonic style from spoken conversation to the typewritten online media. While blueIz408 would have had the option to cut and paste textual material from *Facebook* into her account of the incident, our transcript does not indicate whether or not she did. Jones and Schieffelin (2009b) found clear stylistic linkages between quotative form and the representational specificity of enquoted utterance, with users favoring *say* to establish factual matters and *be + like* to assert judgments and evaluations. BlueIz408's use of *be + like* suggests that, whether or not she is quoting her exchange with Lilah verbatim, her constructed dialogue is not intended to communicate factual information about what was actually said, but rather to convey the opposition between conflicting moral viewpoints and styles of interpersonal communication (playful and worldly, on the one hand; dour and inept, on the other).

"Gossip and rumors have played a role in teen struggles for status and attention since well before social media entered the scene," boyd (2010, p. 105) writes. "When teens gather with their friends and peers, they share stories about other friends and peers. New communications channels— including mobile phones, IM, and social networking sites—have all been used for the purposes of gossip" and as "a catalyst in teen drama." While some scholars explore the way the internet alienates gossip from settings of intimacy (Solove, 2007), boyd suggests a focus on ways social media might expand opportunities for gossip within peer groups. In the above example of IM gossip about a transatlantic *Facebook* contretemps, we are particularly interested the linguistic and paralinguistic strategies intimates use to domesticate technology to create both new contexts and concerns for conducting gossip. In this regard, we entirely agree with Elizabeth Keating's assertion that viewing new media as *prostheses* makes it apparent how subjects can "incorporate a technology which enhances their abilities" (2005, p. 542) within activities they already pursue.

Stalking, Creeping, and Lurking

The collectively constructed mosaic of *Facebook* offers a dynamic backdrop of personal and interpersonal information against which IM gossip unfolds. *Facebook* provides topics for gossip, as users scour the site for information of personal interest, which they in turn report and assess. In the Teen Corpus, IMers refer to activities related to searching for information on *Facebook* as *stalking, creeping,* and *lurking*. Note that these three terms depend on an analogy between a physical action of seeing without being seen projected into the virtual realm of *Facebook*. Furthermore, all three terms have sinister connotations, suggesting that the teens in our study view these activities as morally ambivalent. This terminology has been documented in previous SNS scholarship. For instance, Aléman and Wartman define *stalking* as "largely an innocent voyeuristic and information-getting process" that involves looking at users' profiles and tracking their activities, but which sometimes takes "unacceptable, obsessive" forms (2008, p. 53); Chayko explains that online voyeurism commonly takes the form of *lurking*, "posting rarely if ever, but still regularly reading the postings on an online site" (2008, p. 174); and Jacquemet defines *Facebook creeping* as "the act of constantly browsing through friends' pages, pictures, and walls, but doing so without posting a comment" (2010, p. 61). In this section, we present examples in which IMers categorize and assess *Facebook* behaviors, considering attributions of voyeurism to oneself, to addressees, and to third-party others.

Speakers sometimes classify their own activities in terms of creeping, stalking, and lurking, often playfully. For instance, speakers reported that they were concurrently browsing for information on the *Facebook* profile of a current IM partner.

Example 2.8

1   LeanGene14: right now i'm facebook creeping
2   youuu
3   avocado in space: haha

In the following example, one IMer playfully acknowledges that invoking information gleaned from a friend's wall could be construed as evidence of stalking, although she is presumably not (in this instance) engaging in voyeurism.

Example 2.9

1   blueIz408: yoo i jsut saw what tania eisner
2   wrote on your facebook.go to her house.
3   blueIz408: it sounds fun
4   bombdotcom22: woah
5   bombdotcom22: didnt even see that til right
6   now
7   blueIz408: haha it looks like i stalk you..
8   blueIz408: which i do
9   bombdotcom22: i stalk u too its ok

Both users agree that they "stalk" each other, reaffirming that they use *Facebook* to sustain a friendly interest in each other's lives.

Speakers sometimes accuse each other of stalking, more or less playfully. In the following example, LeanGene14 playfully indicates that she is "about to *facebook* stalk" someone in whom she is sexually interested. Ojosverdes laughs, but then calls her a "creeeeeeeper" and teases her about "stalking." In her defense, LeanGene14 says she is "not stalking/ just/ looking," which to us suggests that she doesn't actually want to be seen as stalking.

Example 2.10

1   LeanGene14: like. im about to facebook stalk
2   her.
3   LeanGene14: hahaha
4   ojosverdes: creeeeeeeper lmao[6]
5   LeanGene14: man so what
6   LeanGene14: haha
7   ojosverdes: lol[7]

8   ojosverdes: stalking is illegal in all 50
9   states :P[8]
10   LeanGene14: im not stalking
11   LeanGene14: just
12   LeanGene14: looking
13   ojosverdes: coughstalkingcough[9]

In the following example, Nodoz claims that he doesn't "check *Facebook* as compulsively as" ginncaliente. Ginncaliente counters that, while Nodoz might not maintain a visible presence on the site, he is nevertheless "lurky," gathering information without leaving a trace.

Example 2.11
1   Nodoz: although i don't check facebook as
2   compusively as you
3   ginncaliente: XD[10]
4   Nodoz: so i might miss something
5   ginncaliente: well, i'm avoiding homework
6   ginncaliente: you're just lurky

In both Examples 2.10 and 2.11, one user accuses the other of engaging in potentially ambivalent voyeurism.

When people feel themselves to be the objects of stalking, creeping, or lurking by third parties, they express annoyance or even moral outrage. In this example, flamingo615 tells a story about how she cleared up a misunderstanding with a boy who suspected her of stalking him the previous year.

Example 2.12
1   flamingo615: and adam anton messaged me cause
2   last year a bunch of the eastern hills girl
3   had my sn[11] somehow and they like gave it to
4   him and he thoguht i stlked him
5   blueIz408: um weird.
6   flamingo615: yea idk[12]
7   blueIz408: did he message you recently?
8   flamingo615: yea last night he was like is
9   this the girl who stalked me last year??
10   blueIz408: hahahha
11   blueIz408: i woulda been lke "YESS GET IN MAH

12	BAGINAAA"[13]
13	flamingo615: hahahahahahaha
14	blueIz408: haha yaaah
15	flamingo615: but we cleared up that i didnt
16	stalk him any more than anybody else so now
17	he wont hate me
18	blueIz408: haha kay

The differences between appropriate and inappropriate uses of *Facebook* are often open to interpretation, as the following example makes clear.

Example 2.13

1	flamingo615: haha people are so creepy
2	flamingo615: that preppy kid from Lakeside
3	wrote on my wall "re your status: there's a
4	packing list on the school website (you can
5	get there from a link in the blog)"
6	blueIz408: yeah i saw
7	flamingo615: dont stalk my status
8	blueIz408: he wrote to me too
9	flamingo615: lol

Here, flamingo615 supports her argument that "people are so creepy" with evidence of someone who she alleges has "stalked her status." Her report of the wall post from "that preppy kid" (lines 2–5) shows how the content of *Facebook* can enter IM talk in a directly quoted form. It is interesting that the wall post is construed as problematic, since the poster must be in the friend network of both flamingo615 and blueIz408 to be able to read their status updates and post on their walls. This suggests that people become "*Facebook* friends" with people whom they are not really friends with (Richardson and Hesey, 2008), and that failing to respect the boundaries appropriate for offline relationships can constitute a moral problem. Flamingo615 affirms this, issuing "that preppy kid" a hypothetical imperative: "don't stalk my status" (line 7).

As the examples in this section indicate, the young people in the Teen Corpus are actively engaged in activities of social monitoring using *Facebook*. They may refer to their own behaviors in terms of stalking, creeping, or lurking but generally construe what they themselves do as relatively harmless or playful. However, discovering evidence that third parties are engaging in activities of online surveillance or voyeurism can engender gossip and provoke disputes (as Examples 2.12 and 2.13 show). While IMers construe stalking-spectrum behaviors as largely solitary, in the following section, we examine situations in which social monitoring on *Facebook* becomes a collaborative enterprise between two IM partners. We consider several examples in which IMers refer to *Facebook*, collaboratively guide each other's attention, and coordinate selective attention to storyable content.

Stalking Together

We view *Facebook* as resembling what John Du Bois (2007, p. 151) calls a "stance-rich environment" (see chapters in Part 4 of this volume). Du Bois writes that "stance is a public act by a social actor, achieved dialogically through overt communicative means, of simultaneously evaluating objects, positioning subjects (self and others), and aligning with other subjects, with respect to any salient dimension of the sociocultural field" (p. 163). *Facebook* is stance rich insofar as it provides contexts in which users generate visual and verbal representations of identity, taste, affiliation, and membership for others to respond to. When partners in the Teen Corpus scrutinize personal representations and interpersonal relations on *Facebook*, they use IM to construct what Du Bois calls a "shared stance object," which binds "the subjectivities of dialogic co-actors together thereby articulating an intersubjective relation between them" (p. 168). In this section we examine the intertexual relationship between IM and *Facebook* in generating shared stance objects.

IMers establish intersubjective orientations to *Facebook* material in a variety of ways: (1) direct or indirect reports; (2) putatively verbatim citation through cut-and-pasted content; and, when both interactants have access to the relevant profiles, (3) directing each other to view specific *Facebook* content; or (4) providing links to specific *Facebook* content. Among users in the Teen Corpus, there seems to be a default assumption that IM partners, who are obviously already online, will be logged onto *Facebook* or can log into it quickly, and interactants mutually orient each other to features of their own and others' profiles (viz., status updates, changes to personal info, or new photographic content). This provides them with grist for conversation, often centering on evaluating and assessing people's online self-presentations.

In Example 2.14, blueIz408 and flamingo615 assess the friend networks of others, comparing *Facebook* profiles in order to establish evidence of asymmetries of friendship. As they monitor a momentary change in status, they engage in a joint activity of comparing the profiles of three mutual acquaintances, Annie, Sharon, and Tania.

Example 2.14

1   blueIz408: wait, i just saw annie sharon &
2   tania best friends. wtf.[14]
3   blueIz408: i dont even know if thats you or
4   sharon simmons haha
5   blueIz408: annie's infooo
6   flamingo615: in annie's profile?
7   blueIz408: ya
8   flamingo615: it says sharon simmons studpi.
9   blueIz408: oh
10   flamingo615: *stupid[15]
11   blueIz408: well i dont get it
12   blueIz408: theyre best frienzz?
13   blueIz408: the shit i miss.
14   flamingo615: yea idk
15   flamingo615: i think annie's more like into
16   that than they are
17   flamingo615: like i dont see it in sharon or
18   tania's profile
19   blueIz408: haha yeah...

BlueIz408 begins by announcing to flamingo615 that she has noticed on *Facebook* that Annie, Sharon, and Tania are now "best friends," although she isn't sure whether the Sharon in question is her interlocutor or someone else with the same first name, Sharon Simmons. She guides flamingo615 to Annie's *Facebook* profile, allowing them to determine that it is Sharon Simmons. Flamingo615 then consults the other two profiles and reports that neither Sharon nor Tania has listed Annie as a best friend, suggesting that "Annie's more like into that than they are." Through collaborative stalking, they arrive at a negative assessment of Annie's *Facebook* self-presentation as misleading.

    In the next example, AmyDayNow and blueIz408 use IM to constitute a shared stance object. AmyDayNow attempts to guide blueIz408 to the "interests" section of a third party's *Facebook* profile. Frustrated with the amount of time it takes for blueIz408 to find this material, AmyDayNow eventually copies the relevant text and pastes it into an IM utterance (lines 9–13).

Example 2.15
1 AmyDayNow: look at mike's facebook interests
2 AmyDayNow: hint: you're famous!
3 AmyDayNow: look at it
4 blueIz408: im checking
5 blueIz408: what are you talking about though?
6 AmyDayNow: these are his interests
7 blueIz408: should i be scared?
8 blueIz408: wait im looking
9 AmyDayNow: Running, Clouds, Guitar, Sports,
10   Sculpture. A certain person living in a
11   suburb of Baltimore of the female
12   persuasion, about 16 yrs old and with blue
13   eyes.
14 blueIz408: OH MY
15 blueIz408: \dsopk siopdj
16   sdfsdfjiosfdjisjidjiosdjiosfdjiosfd
17 AmyDayNow: UH HUH
18 blueIz408: oh . my lord.
19 AmyDayNow: i know!

AmyDayNow has already seen that Mike has expressed his infatuation with blueIz408 on his *Facebook* profile. Instead of simply telling her, AmyDayNow directs blueIz408 to his page, so that she can make the discovery for herself while the two IM together. When blueIz408 realizes that she herself figures among the items in Mike's list of interests, she produces a sequence of random letters, smashing the keyboard to convey a sense of shock—an artful performance of being speechless. AmyDayNow supports her reaction ("UH HUH"), indicating that a shared stance has been achieved.

While the stance object in the two previous examples is textual, in the following example, Alexander leads Lizz to locate a photograph that he believes is evidence of a failure to uphold online behavioral norms. They sync the pace of their talk with the activity of stalking, achieving mutual orientation to a shared visual referent, using the typewritten signals to guide each other's attention.

Example 2.16

  1 Alexander: i was just on facebook
  2 Alexander: randomly stalking
  3 Lizz: and?
  4 Alexander: BlueberryMuffin in a photo that
  5   violates the number one principle rule of
  6   facebook!
  7 Lizz: oh no?! alcohol?
  8 Alexander: :([16
  9 Alexander: yes.
 10 Lizz: i'm on fb right now
 11 Alexander: shes not breaking the rule
 12 Lizz: hold on, I'll comment
 13 Alexander: mind you
 14 Lizz: wait is it her photo?
 15 Lizz: or someone else's?
 16 Alexander: photos of BlueberryMuffin
 17 Alexander: first one tagged by someone else
 18 Lizz: hold on i need to check this out
 19 Lizz: wait i can't find it...
 20 Alexander:
 21   http://yale.facebook.com/photo.php?pid=3591
 22   06&op=1&view=all&subj=1239834780&id=5923537
 23   51&ref=mf
 24 Lizz: that's a diet coke
 25 Alexander: what.
 26 Alexander: shit

After a session of "randomly stalking," Alexander has a hypothesis that he is excited to share with Lizz, namely that a mutual friend, BlueberryMuffin, has been tagged in a photograph depicting underage drinking. As in the previous example, Alexander hints at the nature of the problem, building dramatic tension, and enticing Lizz to guess what the problem is. Alexander explains that BlueberryMuffin herself may not be the one drinking, but suspects someone else in the photograph has an alcoholic beverage. When Lizz cannot locate the photo, Alexander provides her with a link directly to it (lines 21–23). She quickly determines that the beverage in question is not alcohol, but a Diet Coke. Disappointed that his proposed topic of gossip has fallen flat, Alexander responds, "shit" (line 26).

In Examples 2.14–2.16, teens use the expressive resources of IM to orient to and collaboratively interpret *Facebook* content. "Stance is not something you have," Du Bois writes, "but something you do—something you take... To realize stance dialogically means to invoke a shared framework for co-action with others" (2007, p. 171). In realizing stances through the simultaneous and synergistic use of multiple new media channels, these teens constitute what Charles Goodwin (2000, p. 1490) defines as a "situated activity system" in which "actions are both assembled and understood through a process in which different kinds of sign phenomena instantiated in diverse media, what I call semiotic fields, are juxtaposed in a way that enables them to mutually elaborate each other." Using linguistic and paralinguistic resources of IM (which young people themselves are instrumental in developing and promulgating), the teenagers in the examples we consider construct intersubjectivity and coordinate mutual attention to shared stance objects, revealing shared values and beliefs. Synchronizing communication in the semiotic fields of IM and *Facebook*, they co-construct metacommunicative, metasemiotic gossip as a situated activity system.

Conclusion

In this paper, we have provided evidence of teens' appropriation of IM as a tool for coordinating *Facebook* stalking, and for conveying moral views about *Facebook* users—stalkers, creepers, lurkers, and everyone else. The way that teenagers in our study make *Facebook* and IM cohere in situated activities of online gossip points to the necessity of analyzing the role that new media play within heterogeneous ecologies of talk (cf. Horst et al., 2010). It also underscores a strong interest among this loosely representative sample of middle-class American teenagers in representing and evaluating the communicative practices of oneself and others. Whereas our earlier research found IM functioning to extend a polyphonic style of talk through reported speech and constructed dialogue, here we find it constituting a subtly different kind of polyphony, one constituted through the recontextualization of online communication across semiotic fields.

The picture that emerges from the metacommunicative gossip we consider is of a population that is both engaged in adapting new communicative resources for particular cultural ends and closely attuned to the social implications of online communicative practices. When teen IMers negatively assess peers for misconstruing the tenor of wall posts, making overly familiar wall posts, misrepresenting their friendships, or revealing things better left concealed from prying eyes, they affirm tacit norms of *Facebook* communication. More importantly, we argue, they establish connections between communication and morality, treating putative lapses in communicative norms as moral blemishes against which they define standards of sociality and social acceptance.

Notes

1. While, at the time of writing, hundreds of amateur lexicographers have posted definitions of *meh* on the user-generated reference site UrbanDictionary. com, and the term has been recently included in the Collins English Dictionary (Hoyle, 2008), its use remains controversial (Caro, 2009).
2. ";-)" is a winking emoticon, conveying irony.
3. ":-P" is a tongue-sticking-out emoticon, conveying playfulness.
4. Recent reports suggest that *Facebook* users between the ages of 18 and 29 are becoming increasingly concerned about their privacy (Holson, 2010).
5. Stout (2010) reports that there is increasing academic and public debate about whether online social networking enhances or restricts the development of social skills among adolescents.
6. "lmao" is an abbreviation for "laughing my ass off."
7. "lol" is an abbreviation for "laughing out loud."
8. ":P" is a tongue-sticking-out emoticon, conveying playfulness.
9. "coughstalkingcough" suggests a speaker masking an accusatory remark in an ostentatious cough.
10. "XD" is a laughing emoticon.
11. "sn" is an abbreviation for "screen name."
12. "idk" is an abbreviation for "I don't know."
13. Here, blueIz408 tells flamingo615 how she would respond to a boy who accused her of *Facebook* stalking: "i woulda been lke 'YESS GET IN MAH BAGINAAA'," that is, "I would have been like, 'yes, get inside of my vagina!'" Her unconventional spelling is reminiscent of LOLcat orthography (Brubaker, 2008), inviting her partner to imagine a particularly goofy voicing to this obviously facetious sexual imperative.
14. "wtf" is an abbreviation for "what the fuck?"
15. The asterisk denotes a self-repair, correcting a typographical error in flamingo615's previous turn.
16. ": (" is a sad face emoticon, conveying sorrow.

References

Alemán, A.M., & Wartman, K.L. (2008). *Online Social Networking on Campus: Understanding What Matters in Student Culture*. New York: Routledge.

Baron, N.S. (2004). See you online: Gender issues in college student use of instant messaging. *Journal of Language and Social Psychology*, 23 (4), 397–423.

Baron, N.S. (2008). *Always On: Language in an Online and Mobile World.* New York: Oxford University Press.

Bauman, R., & Briggs, C. (1990). Poetics and performances as critical perspectives on language and social life. Annual Review of Anthropology 19, 59–88.

Besnier, N. (2009). *Gossip and the Everyday Production of Politics.* Honolulu: University of Hawai'i Press.

boyd, d. (2008). Why youth ♥ social network sites: The role of networked publics in teenage social life. In D. Buckingham (Ed.), *Youth, Identity, and Digital Media*, (pp. 119–142). Cambridge, MA: MIT University Press.

boyd, d. (2010). Friendship. In M. Ito et al., *Hanging Out, Messing Around, and Geeking Out: Kids Living and Learning with New Media*, (pp. 79–115). Cambridge, MA: MIT Press.

Brubaker, J.B. (2008). wants moar: Visual media's use of text in LOLcats and silent film. *gnovis journal*, 8(2), 117–124.

Cameron, D. (1997). Performing gender identity: Young men's talk and the construction of heterosexual masculinity. In S. Johnson & U.H. Meinhof (Eds.), *Language and Masculinity*, (pp. 47–64). Oxford, UK: Blackwell.

Caro, M. (2009). A surprising brouhaha over the use of 'Meh'. *Chicago Tribune*, March 2.

Chayko, M. (2008). *Portable Communities: The Social Dynamics of Online and Mobile Connectedness.* Albany: State University of New York Press.

Coleman, E.G. (2010). Ethnographic approaches to digital media. *Annual Review of Anthropology*, 39, 1–19.

Du Bois, J.W. (2007). The stance triangle. In R. Englebretson (Ed.), *Stancetaking in Discourse*, (pp. 139–182). Philadelphia: John Benjamins.

Georgakopoulou, A. (2007). *Small Stories, Interaction and Identities.* Philadelphia: John Benjamins.

Goodwin, C. (2000). Action and embodiment within situated human interaction. *Journal of Pragmatics*, 31, 1489–1522.

Hann, M. (2007). G2: Shortcuts: Meh - The word that's sweeping the internet. *The Guardian*, March 5.

Herring, S. (2008). Questioning the generational divide: Technological exoticism and adult constructions of online youth identity. In D. Buckingham (Ed.), *Youth, Identity, and Digital Media*, (pp. 71–92). Cambridge, MA: MIT Press.

Holson, L.M. (2010). Tell-all generation learns to keep things offline. *The New York Times*, May 8.

Horst, H.A., Herr-Stephenson, B., & Robinson, L. (2010). Media ecologies. In M. Ito et al., *Hanging Out, Messing Around, and Geeking Out: Kids Living and Learning With New Media*, (pp. 29–78). Cambridge, MA: MIT Press.

Hoyle, B. (2008). Meh chosen for 30th anniversary of Collins English Dictionary. *The Times*, November 17.

Jacquemet, M. (2010). Language and transnational spaces. In P. Auer & J.E. Schmidt (Eds.), *Language and Space: An International Handbook of Linguistic Variation*, vol. 1 (pp. 50–69). New York: De Gruyter Mouton.

Jaffe, A. (Ed.). (2009). *Stance: Sociolinguistic Perspectives.* New York: Oxford University Press.

Jaworski, A., & Coupland, J. (2005). Othering in gossip: 'You go out you have a laugh and you can pull yeah okay but like...' *Language in Society*, 34(5), 667–694.

Jones, G.M., & Schieffelin, B.B. (2009a). Talking text and talking back: "My BFF Jill" from boob tube to YouTube. *Journal of Computer-Mediated Communication* 14(4), 1050–1079.

Jones, G.M., & Schieffelin, B.B. (2009b). Enquoting voices, accomplishing talk: uses of *be + like* in instant messaging. *Language & Communication*, 29(1), 77–113.

Keating, E. (2005). Homo prostheticus: Problematizing the notions of activity and computer-mediated interaction. *Discourse Studies*, 7(4–5), 527–545.

Richardson, K., & Hessey, S. (2008). Archiving the self? *Facebook* as biography of social and relational memory. *Journal of Information, Communication & Ethics in Society*, 7(1), 25–38.

Sacks, H. (1984). On doing 'bring ordinary'. In J.M. Atkinson & J. Heritage (Eds.), *Structures of Social Action: Studies in Conversation Analysis*, (pp. 413–429). New York: Cambridge University Press.

Sacks, H., Schegloff, E.A., & Jefferson, G. (1974). A simplest systematics for the organization of turn-taking for conversation. *Language* 50(4), 696–735.

Schieffelin, B.B. (2008). Speaking only your own mind: Reflections on confession, gossip, and intentionality in Bosavi (PNG). *Anthropological Quarterly* 81(2), 431–441.

Solove, D.J. (2007). *The Future of Reputation: Gossip, Rumor and Privacy on the Internet.* New Haven: Yale University Press.

Stout, H. (2010). Antisocial networking? *The New York Times*, April 30.

Tagliamonte, S.A., & Denis, D. (2008). Linguistic ruin? Lol! Instant messaging and teen language. *American Speech* 83(1), 3–34.

Tannen, D. (1986). Introducing constructed dialogue in Greek and American conversational and literary narrative. In F. Coulmas (Ed.), *Direct and Indirect Speech*, (pp. 311–332). New York: Mouton de Gruyter.

Thurlow, C. (2006). From statistical panic to moral panic: The metadiscursive construction and popular exaggeration of new media language in the print media. *Journal of Computer-Mediated Communication* 11(3), 667–701.

Thurlow, C. (2007). Fabricating youth: New-media discourse and the technologization of young people. In S. Johnson & A. Ensslin (Eds.) *Language in the Media: Representations, Identities, Ideologies* (pp. 213–233). London: Continuum.

Chapter 3

"Join Our Community of Translators":
Language Ideologies and/in Facebook

Aoife Lenihan

IN THIS CHAPTER, I am concerned with the language ideologies present in—and expressed through—the metalinguistic discourse of *Facebook*'s "translations" application and the metalinguistic commentary of the *Facebook* "translators" as a community of what can be termed "language mavens" (Cameron, 1996), "language brokers" (Blommaert, 1999), or just "language workers" (Thurlow, 2007). Metalanguage is often understood simply as language about language, but, as Jaworski et al. (2004, p. 4) suggest, this is too literal a characterization for what they prefer to describe more broadly as any "language in the context of linguistic representations and evaluations." Certainly, the individual "translators" of *Facebook* are engaged in policing language in the sense that Blommaert et al. (2009, p. 203) talk about the "production of 'order'—normatively organised and policed conduct." Metalanguage thus inevitably works at an ideological level, influencing people's actions and priorities in a number of often quite concrete ways. The case study I am presenting here offers an insight into the ways language ideologies are uniquely produced by the "community of translators" who are themselves also facilitated (and encouraged) by Facebook, Inc.

Theoretical Background

Headquartered in California, USA, *Facebook* was first launched in 2004 and was initially only available to American university students and faculty. Today, however, Facebook, Inc. estimates that approximately 70% of its users are from outside the USA (*Facebook*, 2010, *Press room statistics*). Until 2008, *Facebook* was also only available in English, at which time the "internationalization" of the site into other languages began. Facebook, Inc. has not employed translators on its staff, however; instead, developers created a "translations" application that enables users to translate the site themselves—into certain languages as decided by Facebook, Inc. At first, a Spanish-language version was launched, followed quickly by French and German and eventually a further 21 languages. As of May 2010, there are 108 languages fully available or in translation. This list includes European regional or minority languages (e.g., Irish and Catalan), other "national" varieties (e.g., Français Canada and Français France), as well as a host of other "ways of speaking" such as Esperanto, Klingon (from Star Trek), and Pirate English.

Like many others, Paffey (2007, p. 322, on Spanish) notes that "it seems most people – expert or lay – have an opinion (often quite strong) on language matters" (see also Cameron, 1997; Thurlow, 2011). This is very much the case in *Facebook*'s community-driven translation effort where language ideologies are expressed implicitly and explicitly on many issues. In this regard, I rely on Woolard's (1998, p. 3) definition of language ideologies as "representations ... that construe the intersection of language and human beings in a social world." As Woolard notes, language ideologies are seldom just about the language alone. (This is apparent when discussion occurs over whether a *Facebook* translator's name appears in Irish or English.) In her definition of language ideology, Meylaerts (2007, p. 298) specifically includes translation: "a constellation of beliefs, assumptions and expectations, held by groups of people in a certain geo-political and institutional context, about language use, language values, language users, but also about language contacts and translation."

Translation, as Bassnett (2007, pp. 5–6) writes, is "not just the transfer of texts from one language into another, it is now seen as a process of negotiation between texts and between cultures, a process during which all kinds of transactions take place mediated by the figure of the translator." And the context(s) of translation are rarely neutral; translation is always conducted within the context of existing language regimes and hierarchies with their inherently unequal power relations (Cronin, 1996). Cronin also remarks that the translation of minority languages is oftentimes polemical due to the unequal relationship(s) between majority and minority languages. In the case of *Facebook*, this is a two-fold struggle between the translators and their context: first, through the confines of the actual translations application designed by Facebook, Inc. and, second, between the community of translators.

Furthermore, it is important also to acknowledge the language-ideological implications of the medium itself. As Johnson and Ensslin

(2007, p. 4) write, media policy and practice in relation to language are "central to the very construction of what we all (experts or otherwise) think language is, could, or ought to be like." However, new media are not as top-down in their influence as more traditional media with their explicit language policies and style guides. *Facebook* is not a medium of communication in which knowledge is simply presented or mis-presented; like many new media, it allows knowledge to be presented from many sources, and then ignored and/or negotiated. New media are also spaces where multiple language ideologies—as well as individual and commercial interests—meet and influence language practices. Ultimately, what occurs is the construction not only of an Irish language translation of *Facebook* but also of the Irish language itself in the new media domain (see Johnson & Ensslin, 2007, p. 8).

In what follows, I will start by giving a brief overview of the status of the Irish language and its relationship with the new media. The *Facebook* translations application will be introduced as well as the motivations of both Facebook, Inc. in translating the website and those of the community translators themselves. Along the way, I will briefly explain my research design and data collection. I will then consider in more detail the range of language ideologies that shape the discourse of Facebook, Inc. itself and the metalinguistic commentary of the translators.

Gaeltacht *2.0: The Irish Language and New Media*

The Irish language is the first official language of the Republic of Ireland as declared in Article 8 of *Bunreacht na hÉireann*, the Irish constitution. The English language is designated as the second official language. Since 2007, Irish has also been an official language of the European Union (EU), although not on a par with other EU official languages (European Union, 2005). While 1.66 million of the 4.2 million resident Republic of Ireland population claim to be able to speak Irish, just over a million of these report either that they never speak the language or that they speak it less than weekly (Central Statistics Office, 2007). The Irish language can thus be seen as a "privileged minoritised language" (Kelly-Holmes, 2006) but one that is also classified as "definitely endangered" on the UNESCO (2009) vitality scale.

Acht na dTeangacha Oifigiúla 2003 (Official Languages Act 2003) promotes the use of Irish for official purposes in the state and provides for the availability of public services in the Irish language. Under the act public bodies must agree to a language scheme for that organization with the Minister for Community, Rural and Gaeltacht Affairs. Needless to say, the act does not make provisions in relation to websites of public bodies. However, a public body can include the provision of website services in Irish in its language scheme, which, if not provided according to the language scheme, can be investigated by *An Coimisinéir Teanga* (the Language Commissioner).

The Department of Community, Rural and Gaeltacht Affairs is the Irish government department with responsibility for the promotion and maintenance of the Irish language. In 2009, it published *Straitéis 20 Bliain don Ghaeilge 2010–2030 (Dréacht)* (20 Year Strategy for the Irish Language [Draft]). Significantly, one of the nine areas for action it sets out is media and technology. The report notes the "new directions" in which the Irish language is going and that developments in communications and media technologies have "immense potential" and "open up new channels for individuals and communities to increase their knowledge and regular use of Irish" (Department of Community, Rural and Gaeltacht Affairs, 2009, p. 84). Possible initiatives discussed include encouragement of writing in Irish by young people in a range of media formats, including blogging and also youth-focused internet radio broadcasting (Department of Community, Rural and Gaeltacht Affairs, 2009, pp. 85–86).

The Irish language does have a presence online in what has been colloquially described as *Gaeltacht* 2.0. (*Gaeltacht* refers to Irish-speaking areas designated by the Irish government.) In terms of language policy, however, there really are no legislative provisions for the Irish language in the new media, although there are moves like those just mentioned toward developing such a strategy. *Foras na Gaeilge,* the statutory body responsible for the promotion of Irish, published its own report in 2009, *Straitéis Idirlín don Óige (Dréacht)* (Internet Strategy for Young People [Draft]) The organization had carried out field research to ascertain what Irish language services online young people wanted, what services were already online in Irish, and the gaps between these needs and services. In relation to *Facebook*, the report simply noted that it has been "localised" (Foras na Gaeilge, 2009, p. 3). In fact, the Irish language has been available for translation on *Facebook* via the translations application since July 2008.

The Facebook *Translations Application*

The translations application is a *Facebook* application users can add to their personal profile (akin to a personal homepage). Once a *Facebook* user adds the translations application to their profile, they automatically become a de facto translator and join the community of translators for the language they have chosen. Individual translators submit translations via the application, which the rest of the community must approve via a voting system. In piloting the application, *Facebook* was translated into Spanish in less than a month by 1,500 translators (*Facebook*, 2008, February 7). At the time of writing, Facebook, Inc.'s own statistics show that 300,000 users have been involved in translating *Facebook*. This is a small percentage of the overall *Facebook* population, but it is a prolific community of informal and formal language workers nonetheless.

Facebook, Inc. describes the translations application as an innovative approach combining "the passion of *Facebook* users with technologies that are systematic and manageable" (*Facebook*, 2008, July 23). Facebook, Inc. has applied for a patent to the US Patent and Trademark Office for the translations application and its method of generating translations (cf. *Facebook*, 2009, August 6). The translations application works via three steps; Step 1 is "translate the glossary," which is the translation of a glossary of core *Facebook* terminology. Step 2 is "translate *Facebook*": this is the translation of all the language strings of the site. Finally, Step 3 is "voting and verification," which entails further translation, along with reviewing and further voting of the translations submitted in Steps 1 and 2. As of May 2010, the Irish language translations application was at Stage 3 and was 98% completed. Once everything has been finished, a language is officially "launched" and made available for use by any *Facebook* user.

The translations application can be seen to be based on a type of gift economy, where philanthropy is apparently the main motivation for contributing knowledge as opposed to monetary gain (Gentle, 2009, p. 101), as in the case of collaborative communities involved in wikis like *Wikipedia*. However, from my close observations, it seems that there is more than simply philanthropy at work on *Facebook*. In this case, the translators as language brokers stand to gain a significant amount of symbolic capital (Bourdieu, 1994) by submitting their translations and through their involvement in discussions. They are presenting their linguistic expertise and fluency for the rest of the community to see. In their design of the translation application, Facebook, Inc. also fosters the creation of a community of senior translators (I return to this point in a moment). Ultimately, therefore, Facebook, Inc. draws on the gift economy to create a "community" of good/political will and social prestige in order to benefit commercially. This is a clear reminder that *Facebook* the social networking site is also Facebook, Inc. the corporation.

The Web 2.0 business literature discusses what is called the "community model" whereby social networking sites—not to mention the internet as a whole—are seen as primarily economically driven businesses (see Vossen and Hagermann, 2007). With this in mind, we can see how language/s is/are used in/by *Facebook* for all sorts of strategic ends. To start, they are used to classify or categorize users into speech communities according to the language they are translating. Facebook, Inc. likewise involves individual translators in this "game of categorization" (Heller, 2007, p. 14)—in this case, the construction of an Irish identity around the translation of Irish. Facebook, Inc. therefore uses language/s as a meta-discursive resource for building a community, which in turn helps them to extend its corporate reach and to brand itself international/multilingual. Language is always a major identity resource (Heller, 2003), and, as Anderson (1993) writes, the spread of a standard language via the media is crucial to the imagining of the nation-state. By standardizing language practices and norms in *Facebook*, users are creating an "imagined community" themselves, both an online community and a national community.

The translators of the *Facebook* translations application constitute a formal and informal mixture of what Thurlow (2007) calls "language workers"; they are "ordinary" users of many ages and backgrounds who contribute for the common goal of having an Irish language version of *Facebook*, although as highlighted above, their reasons for doing so may be complex. They are self-appointed in their role as translator; as I mentioned above, anyone adding the application to their profile becomes a translator. No experience or qualifications are required and no one is vetted based on any grounds; linguistic competence in the language is not tested or queried. Only in the debates of the discussion board are their translations and their individual votes questioned, and this is done by other self-appointed translators. Translators are quite passionate about the Irish language and committed to realizing the translation. Having *Facebook* in your preferred language is of particular importance to minority and minoritized languages such as Irish and Welsh. I noticed one Welsh translator posting words of encouragement on the Irish language translations discussion board in the early days of the application.

While the translations application works through this community of translators, it must be acknowledged that the technical (or mechanical) design of the application certainly influences how translators use the application and how they are obliged to progress through the translation steps. For example, in creating a community of *senior* translators Facebook, Inc. inevitably fosters a hierarchy of expertise (see Newon in Chapter 7 of this volume) and of dominant language ideologies. The leaderboard section of the application shows translators who have translated and voted the most in three leaderboards: "weekly," "monthly," and "all time"; this adds to the motivation to translate and makes "senior translators" visible to the entire community. Beyond this—and in more functional terms—an official "style guide wiki" displays advice on translating and is also editable only by the top 20 "all-time" translators of the language. Facebook, Inc. has also implemented translator awards in three categories: voting participation, words published, and translations published. The three levels of awards vary based on the frequency and accuracy of translators' contributions in translation activities such as translating words and voting on the "best" translations—as determined by Facebook, Inc., which notes: "These new awards complement the leaderboard previously in place in the application to publicly spotlight top translators" (Kwan, 2009).

Undoubtedly, there is interplay between user's intention(s) and the technological affordances of the *Facebook* applications; translators carry out their work within the definite confines of Facebook, Inc.'s mechanical designs and institutional regulations. Difficulties or grievances in relation to the translation process and the constraints and rules of the translations application on a practical level are discussed by the translators, but this contribution is primarily concerned with the influence of the language ideologies of Facebook, Inc. on the "language community," the speakers and users of that language.

Research Design and Data

The data for my chapter were generated using virtual ethnographic methods, also known as internet or "guerrilla" ethnography (Androutsopoulos, 2006; McCreery, 2000), first developed by Hine (2000). Virtual ethnography involves "deep looking" in online environments, in my case paying careful attention to language content and interactions between users. Like Hine, I am ultimately interested in knowing what the internet has come to mean as both a cultural space and as a cultural artifact. To this end, since January 2009 I have been collecting material from *Facebook* and, specifically, the translations application with a particular focus on the Irish language translations application. During this time, I assumed the role of a "lurker," who, as Hine explains, is "someone who reads messages posed to a public forum such as a newsgroup but does not respond to the group" (Hine, 2000, p. 106). In other words, I have been observing the development of the *Facebook* translations application and the Irish translations community in a nonparticipatory manner. I am an invisible onlooker to the changes in the application and the discussions of the community of translators.

The textual data I have been collecting are necessarily multimodal and have been gathered from the many layers and features of the overall *Facebook* site and from the Irish language translations application in particular. I have also been collecting official Facebook, Inc. publications, such as those discussing the translations application, press releases, career publications, the *Facebook Blog*, and the *Facebook* translations application's main profile page. The patent application by Facebook, Inc. for the translations application on the U.S. Patent and Trademark Office website was also examined.

Any translator can start a "topic" (or thread) in the discussion board on any subject or post a reply to any existing topic. Each of the 96 topics I looked at on the Irish translations application discussion board at the time of the study were examined for evidence of language ideological themes. These were written in Irish and English or a mix of both. The topics analyzed ranged from those posted in July 2008, when the translations application was first released to Irish, to May 2010. The large number of topics gives the impression that the community of translators as an entity regards itself as knowledgeable about the language and its translation, with repeat contributors possibly seeing themselves as more senior translators and/or serving as gatekeepers in the translation process.

"Facebook *Available to Everyone, Everywhere, in All Languages*"

In the 2008 press release first announcing the translations application, Facebook, Inc. founder and CEO Mark Zuckerberg stated that the aim of the application was to facilitate users' access to *Facebook* in their "native language(s)" (*Facebook*, 2008, February 7). When discussing the translations application, Facebook, Inc. describe the languages in translation as their user's "native" languages, and native language speakers as translators are placed at the heart of the translations application. The *Facebook Blog* meanwhile views translations by native speakers as the ultimate goal of translation: "Quality is very high - as though the site had been written natively in Spanish" (Wong, 2008). This ideology of the native speaker reveals how Facebook, Inc. views users as speaking a language or variety corresponding to the country they live in; it is an ideology that echoes the territoriality principle in language planning by which "one language is the official language of a specific territory" (Beheygt, 1995, p. 48). Facebook, Inc. brought this notion of territoriality online as a means of promoting membership of the communities created by the translations application. Needless to say, it also serves their corporate agenda of multinational branding (cf. Heller, 2003; Kelly-Holmes, 2005; Thurlow & Jaworski, 2003). To follow Thurlow and Aiello's (2007) critique, what looks like the servicing of national pride is often really about the shoring up of global capital.

The overall goal of the application, Facebook, Inc. states, is to "make *Facebook* available to everyone, everywhere, in all languages" (Vera, 2009). This is a comprehensive statement, implying that *Facebook* is all inclusive, a space for all peoples and all languages. Every language, we must remember, is ultimately another market with consumers and monetary gain for Facebook, Inc. Minoritized languages (Little, 2008), language dialects, regional varieties (Linder, 2009), and right-to-left languages (Haddad, 2009) are all included in the application. The ultimate goal of the translations application according to Facebook, Inc. is: "to eventually translate *Facebook* into every language in the world" (*Facebook* Site Governance, 2009). Facebook, Inc. thus also employs an ideology of parallel monolingualism (Heller, 1999) whereby multilingualism is viewed as multiple, coexisting, but bounded languages. The language varieties of the translations application are separated from each other, and each language has its own translations application where translations and discussions remain distinct from other languages. The users of *Facebook* may well be bi-, multi- and plurilingual, but Facebook, Inc. structures and promotes each language as a separate entity and categorizes users accordingly.

In their work on "discourses of endangerment," Duchêne & Heller (2007) are concerned about the disappearance of languages, typically "small" languages, in the near future. Facebook, Inc. certainly appears to take up this discourse, too; through their translations application, they are "saving" language(s) from extinction or, in the case of Latin, bringing it back from the dead. A *Facebook Blog* post, "Latin Becomes a Living Language on *Facebook*," goes on to say that "beginning today, Latin – the staid and reliable language – springs to life on *Facebook*." (Linder, 2009). The same post also refers to Latin as a "venerable language" and talks about students of "living languages." The Latin translators have, we are told, "meticulously translated the site into a 'dead' language. Cobwebs may accumulate on the stones that bear Latin phrases, but they will never conceal its distinguished past, nor stand in the way of people's desire to keep the language alive - even on the web" (ibid). They are very much the same discourses of endangerment that Facebook, Inc. applies elsewhere, subscribing to a kind of linguistic diversity that aligns with biodiversity, whereby the preservation of languages is seen as good for the global cultural environment—and, of course, the gateway to new markets for Facebook, Inc.

As I've explained already, the translations application is automatically open to all users who added it to their personal *Facebook* profile, which does potentially make the site and, consequently, the web more multilingual (cf. Danet and Herring, 2007). However, the default language of the translations application is always English; translations must be submitted from the original U.S. English, and the application interface is, at least initially, only available in English. Although unlikely to be a problem for most Irish speakers, this has the effect of excluding any non-English-speaker from the translation effort. Also, when corresponding with Facebook, Inc., even in relation to issues of translation, Facebook, Inc. demands English only. It is for this reason, that Facebook, Inc.'s translation mission reveals itself as another example of what Kelly-Holmes (2005) calls "fake multilingualism". Sure, *Facebook* and Facebook, Inc. are multilingual in 108 languages, but only on the face of it—or, in the case of new media, on the *interface* of it. It is hard not to conclude that multilingualism is something of a marketing strategy for Facebook, Inc. (See also Piller, 2001, and Thurlow & Jaworski, 2003, for similar cases of "fake multilingualism" in advertising.)

The Irish and English languages have a tense diglossic relationship in today's Ireland—a relationship that is often a topic on the translation discussion board. Typically, translators advocate a move away from reliance on and use of the English language as a starting point for translation. One translator, for example, talked about how Irish should look to other languages when dealing with new technology terminology rather than simply try to replicate the English term. Another translator, sharing this point of view on the "distancing" of Irish from English, commented that English terminology does not have to be literally translated into a number of Irish words if the meaning is clear in the use of one word in Irish for the English language term. These moments illustrate nicely how an additional ideology of "parallel monolingualism" (Heller, 1999) is also at play—the idea that Irish and English should coexist as separate, bounded entities. This marks a clear overlap with the previous "endangerment" ideology, insofar as code mixing and switching are seen as a threat to a minoritized language and evidence of its imminent demise (see Duchêne & Heller, 2007).

Another example of the mixing of these ideologies within the community of translators is to be found in discussions about *béarlachas*. This term is used to describe Irish words that are seen to be too influenced by the English language; in other words, Anglicism's. Although, as one translator makes clear, the term "Anglicism" is itself not without polemic:

> 'béarlachas' (the modern translation of which is 'Anglicism', while 'bastardisation' (the process of corruption or evolution of the meaning of linguistic terms) would be more accurate. (translator 1, 2008).

Ultimately, what is at stake here is an ideology of "linguistic purism" (Thomas, 1991) by which, in this case, translators seek to clear the Irish language of any English influence. Indeed, I have found *béarlachas* to be the most frequently occurring issue in discussions. As I indicated above, the issue arises in particular during discussions about new technological terminology, such as "mobile phone" and *Facebook* "profile." For example, in one translation of *mobile phone* as *fón póca* (literally, "pocket phone"), the use of *fón* is considered too Anglicized, too close to the English *phone*. In contrast, another translation of *mobile phone* is *guthán soghluaiste*, which is regarded as more "traditional" as it uses the official Irish word for telephone, *guthán*. This moment quickly sparked an explicit language ideological "debate" (cf. Blommaert, 1999), as in these two posts:

> mobile phone should either be guthán soghluaiste or guthán póca (I would argue that 'fón póca' is a straight-up english calque and should be avoided in this case) (translator 2, 2008)

> Can we decide once and for all that we are using the term Fón póca for mobile phone, as was decided at the glossary stage ... Regardless of whether guthán póca, etc. is 'more correct' - Fón póca was chosen in the first stage - will people stop using terms other than those from the glossary. (translator 3, 2008)

Another locus of discussions where language ideologies are apparent are those concerning which variety of Irish should be used: *an Chaighdeáin Oifigiúil* or a dialect of Irish, and if the second, *which* dialect.

An Chaighdeáin Oifigiúil is the official standard variety of Irish taught in schools, but there are also three main dialects of Irish corresponding to the geographical areas within which they are spoken: Munster, Connacht, and Ulster. In one discussion, a translator stated how the translation of "I am" should follow *an Chaighdeáin Oifigiúil*. However, fellow translators were quick to point out that *an Chaighdeáin Oifigiúil* is itself influenced by Munster Irish and that those using Connacht and Ulster Irish do not use or write "I am" in the same way. This eventually led into a discussion of standardness (i.e., standard versus nonstandard) and the politics of translation, with some believing that the standard (Irish) should be for office use and that nonstandard varieties (the dialects) ought to be acceptable, too. Here again, we can see the familiar tensions in endangerment discourses between preserving linguistic diversity in the form of the different dialects and the need to adopt monolingualism, in the form of one official standard, in order to bring a minoritized language to a new mode of use, that of new media.

A final example of the language ideologies involved in the community of translators is the debate over the translator's choice of language to write in on the discussion board. The majority of the topics and posts on the discussion board are in Irish, but there are some in English, with code switching also evident. On one occasion, a translator took exception to a thread written in English and challenged other translators about their use of English instead of Irish, saying they "should be ashamed." This purist ideology is also a clear attempt at policing the boundaries of translation and of language (cf. Blommaert et al., 2009). Other translators did disagree with this point of view, however, arguing instead that they did translation because they loved Irish and not because they hated English. One translator also pointed out that they were not ashamed because they speak both Irish and English and that there was nothing inherently wrong with English or being able to make the choice of which language to use. Language policing clearly takes place in the community but not without contestation.

Conclusion

In the specific context of *Facebook*'s translations application and of the Irish-language translation in particular, we find new media opening up a world of multilingual possibility (cf. Danet and Herring, 2007) but one that is inevitably structured by language policing, verbal hygiene, and a range of language ideological debates about endangerment, purism, parallelism, and so on. Unlike most other bureaucratic sites or processes of translation, however, *Facebook* translators are not experts chosen by a "top-down" authority to oversee a language according to certain parameters; instead, they come from many different background as students, academics, public representatives, and indeed, professional translators. From the offline world, they bring a combination of expert and lay knowledge about language and about the language they are translating. They also come with their own histories, priorities, and ideologies.

Lurking in the background, but clearly shaping everything, are the language ideologies of Facebook, Inc. itself. The new media are both *producers* of media texts such as online newspapers and also *facilitators* of user-driven content such as discussion boards or forums. In my case study, the language ideologies of Facebook, Inc. are part of the metalinguistic discourse/s of *Facebook* and must be taken into account. Facebook, Inc. is just as implicated in replicating ideologies of endangerment, purism, parallel monolingualism, and of course, monolingualism (fake or not). To some extent, theirs is a metadiscourse that conceals (or not) an obviously corporate agenda.

As I write this conclusion, *Facebook* has just announced that it has 500 million users. As someone in the mainstream news media explained it that means that one in every thirteen people in the world is on *Facebook*. I cannot help but wonder if languages like Walmajarri, Huitotot, Livonian, or Inupiaq will ever be elevated from profile pages to fully fledged "translations." For all of its self-proclaimed rhetoric, *Facebook* is a long way from the aspiration, expressed by one employee, to make it "available to everyone, everywhere, in all languages," just as the "multilingual internet" (cf. Danet & Herring, 2007) is yet to realize itself as a truly universal network. At the end of the day, the language ideologies of both *Facebook* and the internet itself are inevitably rooted in complex geopolitical realities and historical inequalities.

Acknowledgments

I would like to thank Helen Kelly-Holmes for commenting on earlier versions of this chapter. Many thanks also to my anonymous reviewers for their suggestions and comments, and to Crispin Thurlow for his generous editorial attention to my final version.

I also wish to acknowledge the support of the Irish Social Sciences Platform (ISSP) (Funded under the Programme for Research in Third

Level Institutions, administered by the HEA and co-funded under the European Regional Development Fund [ERDF]), which is providing a doctoral scholarship for my research.

References

Anderson, B. (1993). *Imagined Communities*. London: Verso.

Androutsopoulos, J. (2006). Introduction: Sociolinguistics and computer-mediated communication. *Journal of Sociolinguistics*, 10(4), 419–438.

Bassnett, S. (2007). *Translation Studies, New Accents*. 3rd ed. London: Routledge.

Beheydt, L. (1995). The linguistic situation in the new Belgium. In S. Wright (Ed.), *Languages in Contact and Conflict*. Clevedon: Multilingual Matters Ltd.

Bourdieu, P. (1994). *Language and Symbolic Power* (G. Raymond & M. Adamson, Trans.). 2nd ed. Cornwall: Polity Press.

Blommaert, J. (1999). The debate is open. In J. Blommaert (Ed.), *Language Ideological Debates*. Berlin / New York: Mouton de Gruyter.

Blommaert, J., Kelly-Holmes, H., Lane, P., Leppanen, S., Moriarty, M., Pietikainen, S. & Piirainen-Marsh, A. (2009). Media, multilingualism and language policing: An introduction. *Language Policy*, 8(3), 203–207.

Cameron, D. (1996). *Verbal Hygiene*. 2nd ed. London: Routledge.

Cameron, D. (1997). Demythologizing sociolinguistics. In N. Coupland & A. Jaworski (Eds.), *Sociolinguistics: A Reader and Coursebook*. Basingstoke: Macmillan.

Central Statistics Office. (2007). *2006 Census of Population Volume 9 – Irish Language* [press release]. Retrieved February 1, 2010, from http://www.cso.ie/census/census2006results/volume_9/volume_9_press_release.pdf

Cronin, M. (1996). *Translating Ireland: Translation, Languages, Cultures*. Cork: Cork University Press.

Danet, B., & Herring, S.C. (Eds.). (2007). *The Multilingual Internet: Language, Culture, and Communication Online*. New York & Oxford: Oxford University Press.

Department of Community, Rural & Gaeltacht Affairs. (2009). *Straitéis 20 Bliain don Ghaeilge 2010–2030 (Dréacht) / 20 Year Strategy for the Irish Language (Draft)*. Retrieved February 1, 2010, from http://www.pobail.ie/ie/AnGhaeilge/file,10094,ie.doc

Duchêne, A., & Heller, M. (Eds.). (2007). *Discourses of Endangerment*. London: Continuum.

European Union. (2005). *Council Regulation (EC) No 920/2005 of 13 June 2005 amending Regulation No 1 of 15 April 1958 determining the language to be used by the European Economic Community and Regulation No 1 of 15 April 1958 determining the language to be used by the European Atomic Energy Community and introducing temporary derogation measures from those Regulations*. Retrieved

February 1, 2010, from http://eur-lex.europa.eu/LexUriServ/LexUriServ. do?uri=CELEX:32005R0920:EN:NOT

Foras na Gaeilge. (2009). *Straitéis 20 Bliain Don Ghaeilge 2010–2030 Dréacht / Draft 20 Year Strategy for the Irish Language.* Retrieved February 1, 2010, from http://gaelport.arobis40.com/uploads/documents/Dréachtstraitéis_Idirlín_ don_Óige.pdf

Gentle, A. (2009). *Conversation and Community: The Social Web for Documentation.* Fort Collins, CO: XML Press.

Heller, M. (1999). *Linguistic Minorities and Modernity: A Sociolinguistic Ethnography.* London: Longman.

Heller, M. (2003). Globalization, the new economy, and the commodification of language and identity. *Journal of Sociolinguistics, 7*(4), 473–492.

Heller, M. (2007). Bilingualism as ideology and practice. In M. Heller (Ed.), *Bilingualism: A Social Approach.* Hampshire: Palgrave Macmillan.

Hine, C. (2000). *Virtual Ethnography.* London: Sage.

Jaworski, A., Coupland, N., & Galasinsiki, D. (2004). Metalanguage: Why now? In A. Jaworski, N. Coupland, & D. Galasinsiki (Eds.), *Metalanguage: Social and Ideological Perspectives.* Berlin: Mouton de Gruyter.

Johnson, S., & Ensslin, A. (2007). Language in the media: Theory and practice. In S. Johnson & A. Ensslin (Eds.), *Language in the Media: Theory and Practice.* London: Continuum.

Kelly-Holmes, H. (2005). *Advertising as Multilingual Communication.* Basingstoke: Palgrave Macmillan.

Kelly-Holmes, H. (2006). Irish on the World Wide Web: Searches and sites. *Journal of Language and Politics, 5*(2), 217–238.

McCreery, J. (2000). *From Worker Bees to Wary Shoppers.* Richmond, UK: Curzon Press.

Meylaerts, R. (2007). "La Belgique vivra-t-elle?" Language and translation ideological debates in Belgium (1919–1940). *The Translator, 13*(2), 297–319.

Paffey, D. (2007). Policing the Spanish language debate: Verbal hygiene and the Spanish language academy (Real Academia Española). *Language Policy, 6*(3/4), 313–332.

Piller, I. (2001). Identity constructions in multilingual advertising. *Language in Society, 30,* 153–186.

Thomas, G. (1991). *Linguistic Purism.* London: Longman.

Thurlow, C. (2007). Fabricating youth: New-media discourse and the technologization of young people. In S. Johnson & A. Ensslin (Eds.), *Language in the Media: Representations, Identities, Ideologies,* (pp. 213–233). London: Continuum.

Thurlow, C. (2011). Speaking of difference: Language, inequality and interculturality. In R. Halualani & T. Nakayama (Eds.), *Handbook of Critical Intercultural Communication.* Oxford: Blackwell.

Thurlow, C., & Aiello, G. (2007). National pride, global capital: A social semiotic analysis of transnational visual branding in the airline industry. *Visual Communication, 6*(3), 305–344.

Thurlow, C., and Jaworski, A. (2003). Communicating a global reach: Inflight magazines as a globalizing genre in tourism. *Journal of Sociolinguistics, 7*(4), 581–608.

UNESCO. (2009). *UNESCO Interactive Atlas of the World's Languages in Danger 2009.* Retrieved February 1, 2010, from http://www.unesco.org/culture/ich/index.php?pg=00206

Vossen, G., & Hagemann, S. (2007). *Unleashing Web 2.0: From Concepts to Creativity.* Burlington: Elsevier / Morgan Kaufmann.

Woolard, K.A. (1998). Introduction: Language ideology as a field of enquiry. In B. B. Schieffelin, K.A. Woolard, & P.V. Kroskrity (Eds.), *Language Ideologies: Practice & Theory.* New York: Oxford University Press.

Data Sources (some sources/links are accessible by subscribers only)

Facebook. (2008, February 7). *Facebook Releases Site in Spanish; German and French to Follow.* Retrieved February 19, 2010, from http://www.facebook.com/press/releases.php?p=16446

Facebook. (2008, July 23). *Facebook Expands Power of Platform Across the Web and Around the World.* Retrieved May 11, 2011, from https://www.facebook.com/press/releases.php?p=48242

Facebook. (2009, August 6). *U. S. Patent Application No. 20090198487.* Retrieved February 19, 2010, from http://appft.uspto.gov/netacgi/nph-Parser?Sect1=PTO2&Sect2=HITOFF&p=1&u=/netahtml/PTO/search-bool.html&r=1&f=G&l=50&co1=AND&d=PG01&s1=*Facebook*.AS.&s2=translation.AB.&OS=AN/*Facebook*+AND+ABST/translation&RS=AN/*Facebook*+AND+ABST/translation

Facebook. (2010). *Press Room Statistics.* Retrieved February 19, 2010, from http://www.*Facebook*.com/press/info.php?statistics

Facebook Site Governance. (2009, April 15). *Response to Comments on Facebook Principles.* Retrieved February 19, 2010, from http://www.*Facebook*.com/note.php?note_id=183540865300#/note.php?note_id=183535615300

Haddad, G. (2009). *Facebook Blog: Facebook Now Available in Arabic and Hebrew.* Retrieved February 19, 2010, from http://blog.*Facebook*.com/blog.php?post=59043607130

Kwan, E. (2009). *Facebook Blog: The Award Goes to…Translators.* Retrieved February 19, 2010, from http://blog.*Facebook*.com/blog.php?post=204787062130&comments

Linder, E. (2009). *Facebook Blog: Latin Becomes a Living Language on Facebook.* Retrieved February 19, 2010, from http://blog.*Facebook*.com/blog.php?post=145923442130

Little, C. (2008). *Facebook Blog: Arrr, Avast All Ye Pirates!* Retrieved February 19, 2010, from http://blog.*Facebook*.com/blog.php?post=31137552130

Vera, N. (2009). *Life at Facebook: Nico Vera.* Retrieved February 19, 2010, from http://www.facebook.com/careers/story.php?story=6

Wong, Y. (2008). *Facebook Blog: Facebook Around the World.* Retrieved February 19, 2010, from http://blog.*Facebook*.com/blog.php?post=10056937130

PART TWO

Creative Genres:
Texting, Messaging, and Multimodality

Chapter 4

Beyond Genre: Closings and Relational Work in Text Messaging

Tereza Spilioti

THE THRUST OF current research on language and interaction in new media often lies in the need for revisiting and refining "old" and established theoretical concepts in light of "new" computer-mediated data derived from an array of emerging and volatile cultural settings (cf. Georgakopoulou, 2006). More specifically, the study of (socio)linguistic concepts, such as genre, turn taking, identity, and community, has gained new impetus in the context of new media discourse studies. Nevertheless, the cognate concept of politeness in new media has received relatively scant attention to date, despite the early focus of popular and academic discourse on instances of antisocial and hostile behavior online (e.g., "flaming," Herring, 2001, p. 622). A notable exception is Locher's (2010) special issue on "politeness and impoliteness in computer-mediated communication," which attempts to pave the way for reconceptualizing Brown and Levinson's (1987) politeness theory through contextualized and empirically driven research. In line with current advances in politeness research (cf. Locher & Watts, 2005; Spencer-Oatey, 2007), the focus of the papers in Locher's special issue moves beyond the study of mitigation strategies and brings to the fore the issue of "what constitutes im/politeness in a particular practice and what factors might play a role in assessing it" (Locher, 2010, p. 3). It is partly with this in mind that I have become interested in the particular use of closing rituals in new media contexts.

The end of any encounter (whether mediated or face-to-face) represents an interesting interactional juncture, as participants have to leave (or suspend) current participation frameworks, as well as any claims regarding their roles and relationships. As suggested by Goffman (1972, p. 41), such interactional strains can be alleviated by means of ritual forms of talk, like farewells and other parting formulae. More specifically, farewells can serve as an index of the relationship claims that participants have made during the encounter, and, at the same time, preclude any risk to the relationship caused by separation. The role of closing formulae as a social lubricant in interaction has also been foregrounded by Brown and Levinson (1987, pp. 235–236), who approached farewells and other parting rituals as politeness strategies, that is, as mitigating devices for saving the participants' public self-image (*face*) during a potentially face-threatening closure. Brown and Levinson's understanding of closings as politeness strategies is still echoed in current studies of e-mail communication (e.g., Waldwogel, 2007).

My chapter here considers how text messagers' perceptions of politeness and appropriateness appear to inform the use of closing formulae in their messages. The chapter is based on empirical data collected from three young peer groups in Athens, Greece. These case studies follow an ethnographic perspective and concern the recording of temporally ordered sequences of SMS interactions, together with participant observation and informal interviews. Rather than presuppose closing sections as a generic characteristic of the texts produced in an asynchronous medium (cf. Herring, 1996, p. 86), however, I explore whether (and when) participants consider the use of closings appropriate, as well as the types of closing formulae they deploy. Unlike other features of text messaging, such as its thematic content, lexical/orthographic features, code switching, and gender variation (see Thurlow & Poff, 2011, for an overview), the study of closings remains a relatively uncharted territory with only a handful of studies (Ito & Okabe, 2005; Laursen, 2005; Spagnolli & Gamberini, 2007) pointing to the relative infrequency of such formulaic conventions. In this chapter, the issue of closings and politeness is brought back into the picture, but it will be explored in light of the texters' expectations and norms of appropriateness, emerging in the relational work the specific participants engage in.

Closings, Politeness, and Relational Work

It is by now a truism that the intricacies of social interaction do not paint a "rosy picture" of friendly and equal individuals who communicate cooperatively in order to achieve mutually shared goals. In fact, critical moments in interaction, including the unavoidable end of a conversational encounter, may foreground the participants' different agendas and reveal verbal and nonverbal means for negotiating their assumed roles and relationships. Such roles and relationships are tailored to the self-image that participants claim for themselves in interaction. The idea of an "image of self" or "face" that appears "delineated in terms of approved social attributes" was introduced by Goffman (1972) in his seminal work on social interaction. According to Goffman (1972, p. 5), "face" is a construct of self that is attributed by others according to the line[1] they assume someone is taking in specific instances of interaction. Considering that the end of an interactional encounter may put such face claims at risk, "farewells sum up the effect of the encounter upon the relationship and show what the participants may expect of one another when they next meet" in an attempt to "compensate the relationship for the harm that is about to be done to it by separation" (Goffman, 1972, p. 41).

The notion of "face" has also been paramount in later studies of pragmatic meaning and politeness. In particular, Brown and Levinson (1987) developed their theory of politeness around the concept of "face," which they argue is realized either as "positive" or "negative" face: "positive face," meaning the face claims relevant to the individual's desire to be liked and approved of by others, and "negative face," meaning the face claims associated with one's desire to be free to act without being restricted or imposed upon by others. Everyday interaction, however, opens up an array of possibilities for "activities that by their nature run contrary to the face wants of the addressee and/or the speaker" (Brown & Levinson, 1987, p. 70). The idea of such "face-threatening acts" (FTAs) is central to Brown and Levinson's theory and provides a frame within which "politeness" is understood as one among different strategies for performing an FTA. Within this framework attempts to bring interaction to a halt are understood as FTAs that can be mitigated by means of closing rituals, providing "evidence of the great utility and face-cost benefit of having ready-made ways of dealing with potential face-loss situations" (Brown & Levinson, 1987, pp. 235–236).

Brown and Levinson's framework of politeness strategies has influenced subsequent studies of written communication, including Pilegaard's (1997) study of business letters. Considering the absence of prosodic or other paralinguistic cues in the written mode, the study of politeness concerned primarily the identification of verbal strategies and their anchoring in the generic structure of individual letters, including openings and closings (Pilegaard, 1997, p. 224). Research on asynchronous forms of mediated communication approached closings as the last structural part

of a generic schema (opening, main body, and closing), which was documented in a variety of genres, including answering machine messages
(Goutsos, 2001, p. 361), Usenet and LISTSERV messages (Herring, 1996),
and workplace e-mail (Waldvogel, 2007). Closings have been associated
with verbal strategies attending to the participants' interpersonal relations,
and in Waldvogel's (2007) work, they are explicitly framed as politeness
markers, "in as much as [they] pay attention to recipient and are oriented
to the addressee's face needs."

With respect to text messaging, closings have been discussed by a limited number of studies (Ito & Okabe, 2005; Laursen, 2005; Spagnolli &
Gamberini, 2007) with a primary focus on the conversational nature of
texting and its sequential organization in terms of turn taking. This line
of work was theoretically grounded on conversation analysis, also preoc-
cupied with what Schegloff & Sacks (1999, p. 263) frame as the "closing
problem," in other words, an issue that participants need to ponder and
jointly manage in the organization of interaction. More specifically, previous studies of telephone calls (see Cameron, 2001, pp. 99–100) revealed
the use of long sequences of closing moves, which contribute no new
content to the conversation but operate as the only signals for disengagement in a medium of reduced paralinguistic cues. On the other hand, evidence from synchronous computer-mediated communication (e.g., IRC
exchanges) suggests a more flexible pattern of closing, where the breaking
off of contact can occur at any point and is not necessarily jointly managed
or verbally signaled by relevant participants (Goutsos, 2005).

Although the focus of previous research on texting is not on politeness
per se, the analysis and interpretation of turn sequences take into consideration the participants' relationships. More specifically, relevant findings
bring to the fore the impact of social presence (Spagnolli & Gamberini,
2007)—or "ambient virtual co-presence" in Ito and Okabe's (2005,
p. 264) words—as well as the coparticipants' expectations of reciprocity and immediacy (Laursen, 2005), upon the organization of SMS
exchanges. Therefore, the relational aspect of communication appears to
play a paramount role in managing interaction in the specific medium.
At the same time, the term "relational" is recurrently found in studies of
text messaging: for instance, messages have been described as primarily
"relational" in their thematic orientation (Thurlow, 2003), with a predominantly solidary function as one of the genre-defining features of texting
(Thurlow & Poff, 2011; compare also with Chapters 1 and 14 of this volume
on text messaging). The following analysis will discuss and reveal norms

of appropriateness in texting, by looking at the use of closings as part of the participants' relational work, that is, " 'work' individuals invest in negotiating relationships with others [...], to pursue and realise their life goals and aspirations" (Locher & Watts, 2005, p. 10).

Closings in Practice: The Current Study

The empirical data under discussion here concerns the everyday exchanges of text messages among young Greek people between the ages of 15 and 25. My data collection (summer 2003–spring 2004) took place in Athens and combined two basic techniques: a questionnaire survey, which constitutes the main methodological tool in early studies of SMS (e.g., Ling, 2005; Thurlow, 2003; see Dürscheid & Stark, Chapter 14, this volume), and three case studies. In this chapter, I want to focus specifically on the text sequences exchanged between my participants.[2] Participants were asked to store in their phone memory the messages exchanged between them for a sustained period of time (i.e., several weeks). In turn, taking advantage of infrared technology, the saved messages were transferred to a portable computer. The collection of messages was also accompanied by participant observation and interviews with the participants regarding their practices of text messaging. Androutsopoulos (2008, p. 2) has pointed out the significance of a "discourse-centred online ethnography," which "combines the systematic observation of selected sites of online discourse with direct contact with its social actors." This chapter is informed by a similar commitment to move beyond the examination of SMS as log data (i.e., a corpus of randomly collected individual texts) and to probe more into their analysis as contributions to sequences embedded into the participants' web of face-to-face and mediated interactions (cf. Androutsopoulos's "blended ethnography," 2008). An ethnographic perspective to the collection and analysis of sociolinguistic data is also driven by the aims of this chapter, which sets out to explore the participants' perceptions of politeness and norms of appropriateness in their use of closings. Systematic observation and interviews, together with detailed linguistic analysis, can contribute to an emic understanding of texters' practices and categories.

My participants all live in Athens and regularly interact with each other both in face-to-face and mediated environments. In fact, their everyday SMS exchanges constitute only a snapshot of a long and sustained interaction over many years. However, my sample included no group-directed messages, revealing a type of interaction where two parties are primarily involved (cf. "texter" and "textee," Spilioti, 2007). Systematic observation and notes from fieldwork indicated that the specific groups of friends were further divided into participant pairs who exhibited a higher frequency of text exchanges and, more importantly, identified each other as κολλητές/-οί ("best buddies"—akin perhaps to "bff," best friends forever). The literal meaning of the term invokes the notion of contact between two entities; that is, the words κολλητές/-οί denote two or more entities (here, two female/male friends) that are fastened or connected together with glue. In the colloquial use of the term, the adhesive quality of this uniting substance foregrounds the strong ties established between the relevant members of the participant pairs. In my data, the close contact among the specific participants coincides with other contextual parameters, such as residential proximity, being members of a shared institutional community (i.e., university/college), or regional affiliation to a particular area of Greece. As a result, the term of address κολλητή/-ός, which recurs both in the participants' text messages and interviews, may operate as an important "emic" category in the following analysis of closings and relational work.

The Relational Work of Closings

Similar to closings in other forms of Greek mediated communication (e.g., answering machine messages, Goutsos 2001; telephone calls, Pavlidou 1997),[3] the following types of closing formulae were identified in my text message corpus (see Table 4.1 for relative frequencies of occurrence):

(a) "Sign-offs" concern the affective expression φιλάκια "kisses" or the name of the texter as a signature;

(b) "Call-offs" include the formulaic allusion to future interaction "see you," couched either in the English abbreviated form cu or in the Greek equivalent expressions να/θα τα πούμε or τα λέμε;

(c) "Closing greetings" are realized by formulaic utterances like καληνύχτα "good night" and γεια "bye."

To be clear, only 30.4% (n = 136) of the total messages gathered (n = 447) include one of the above closing formulae. This finding seems to challenge previous understandings of closings as an integral part of the "message schema" in asynchronous interaction (cf. Goutsos, 2001; Herring, 1996; Pilegaard, 1997; Waldvogel, 2007). In other words, the striking evidence of a high number of texts without closings urges us to

Table 4.1 Types of closing formulae

Types of Closings		Instances of occurrence	
		n = 170	%
Sign-off	φιλάκια/φιλιά "kisses"	103	60.6
	signature	4	2.4
Call-off	να/θα τα πούμε "see you"	17	10
	τα λέμε "see you"	14	8.2
	cu	6	3.5
Greeting	καληνύχτα "good night"	22	12.9
	γεια "bye"	4	2.4

avoid approaching closings as an a priori normative characteristic of text messaging. As mentioned above, previous studies of turn taking in SMS (cf. Laursen, 2005; Spagnolli & Gamberini, 2007) have also noticed the relative absence of openings and closings in Italian and Danish messages and associated this finding with the "conversational frame of texting" (Thurlow & Poff, 2011). Here, I want to follow up this line of research by exploring further how the participants' relational work is manifested in the use of closings, through the lens of what is considered appropriate and/or (im)polite in their interaction.

The study of participants' perceptions of what is appropriate presupposes that participants jointly accomplish and achieve closings in a manner that is manifest in their sequences of SMSs. As a result, my analysis focuses on text messages that appear not only as individual, de-contextualized messages, but also primarily as contributions to longer sequences, exchanged among specific participants who share a long interactional history. In line with Laursen's (2005, p. 54) study of Danish SMS communication, my data also exhibit "an alternating A-B sequence," where A (or initial text) stands for the first message initiating the sequence, and B indicates the text that is sent as a response from the other party (or a follow-up message by the initiator of the exchange, as will be discussed below). In the following sections, I will examine the use of closings in relation to the position of a text in the A-B sequence and will discuss the relevance of relational aspects, such as the participants' in-group relations, their daily interactional routines and perceptions of politeness, to the management of closings in texting.

Dropping Closings in Texts Initiating a Sequence

In light of the above, I start by looking at the use of closings in "initial texts" that do not appear to have been sent as a reply to another SMS. My analysis suggests that 85% (n = 108) of such initial messages do not include one of the aforementioned closing formulae and appear to incite a response from the other party or give the same participant an opportunity to recontribute to the sequence. Texters' expectations for the other party to reply to a message have also been noticed by Laursen (2005) and Hutchby and Tanna (2008), but this practice has not been explicitly explored in relation to the occurrence of closings.

Extract 4.1 illustrates this expectation, arguably enhanced by the absence of a closing formula, which becomes particularly prevalent when a follow-up message is sent by the texter to challenge the textee's failure to reply. The specific sequence is exchanged while the two female "best friends" (κολλητές), Fay and Nana (Case Study I), live in different cities due to their studies and communicate only through telephone and SMS.

Extract 4.1:

MSG	Fay	ΟΜΟΡΦΟΥΚΑ ΜΟΥ ΚΑΛΗΜΕΡΑ!Η
1.1	13/01/04,	*Good morning [my] sweetie (lit. beautiful)!*
	11:01	Η ΚΟΛΛΗΤΗ ΣΟΥ ΕΧΕΙ
		Your best friend[4] can feel
		ΣΤΡΙΜΩΧΤΕΙ ΤΩΡΑ ΚΑΙ ΔΙΑΒΑΖΕΙ ΚΑΙ
		the pressure now and she is studying, but
		ΠΡΟΣ ΤΟ ΠΑΡΟΝ ΧΑΖΕΥΕΙ!
		[rather] slacking right now!
		ΚΑΠΟΙΑ ΣΤΙΓΜΗ ΘΕΛΕΙΣ ΝΑ
		Fancy talking
		ΜΙΛΗΣΟΥΜΕ ΣΗΜΕΡΑ,
		[on the phone] later on today,
		ΠΡΟΣ ΤΟ ΒΡΑΔΥ?
		in the evening?
–	Nana	–
MSG	Fay	ΟΜΟΡΦΟΥΚΑ ΜΟΥ ΓΙΑΤΙ ΔΕΝ
1.2	13/01/04,	*[My] sweetie (lit. beautiful) why aren't you*
	17:00	ΑΠΑΝΤΑΣ?
		replying?

The initial text updates the other party about Fay's everyday life and current activities (feeling under pressure, studying, and "slacking") and ends with a request for arranging a future mediated interaction, that is, a phone call. Together with the overall lower frequency of closings in initial texts, the argument that the absence of a closing move indexes the texter's anticipation for a reply from the other party is further supported by MSG 1.2. This text is sent again by the same participant (i.e., Fay) and focuses on the textee's failure to provide a response. In fact, it topicalizes the other party's non-availability for contact in the specific medium by explicitly requesting an account for the lack of feedback ("why aren't you replying").[5] Previous studies (Laursen, 2005; Spagnolli & Gamberini, 2007) accounted for such norms of reciprocity in terms of a frame of "perpetual contact" (cf. Katz & Aakhus, 2002), which sets the expectation that the other party is available by default and should provide some kind of feedback within a specific time lag.

Although this social use of the perpetually mobile affordances of the medium is a plausible interpretation, a more detailed sequential analysis suggests that the conversational norms of adjacency and conditional relevance are also important in texting (cf. Hutchby & Tanna, 2008, p. 152). More specifically, such follow-up messages targeting the other party's non-availability have been found to appear not only after initial texts without closings but also, or primarily, after messages that end with a question—or, more generally, the first part of an adjacency pair, such as a request for further interaction in MSG 1.2. Failure by the other party to provide a conditionally relevant response (e.g., accepting or refusing the request) is understood as marked behavior, triggering more messages from the texter in an attempt to reestablish contact.

Closings as Markers of Relative Distance

Although closing formulae in initial texts are rare (n = 19), they are not altogether absent in my data. However, such instances appear in exchanges between participant pairs who are not κολλητές ("bffs"/ "best friends") and do not interact on a daily basis. For example, Nana and Dimitra are two of the five female friends (Case Study I) who met each other at a camping site while still in primary school, but they do not often see each other separately from the other girls of the group (as Nana does, for instance, with Fay, who is her "bff" κολλητή, see MSG 1.1). The sequence in Extract 4.2, for instance, illustrates an SMS exchange between Nana and Dimitra regarding an outing in which all five friends are involved.

Extract 4.2:

MSG	Dimitra	ΓΕΙΑ ΣΟΥ ΝΑΝΟΥΚΑ!
2.1	21/09/03,	*Hi [little] Nana!*
	20:28	ΤΙ ΚΑΝΕΙΣ?ΟΛΑ ΚΑΛΑ?
		How are you? All is well?
		ΛΕΜΕ ΝΑ ΠΑΜΕ ΑΥΡΙΟ ΓΙΑ ΨΩΝΙΑ
		We're thinking of going shopping
		ΣΤΗΝ ΕΡΜΟΥ!ΜΠΟΡΕΙΣ ΕΣΥ?ΑΝ ΝΑΙ
		tomorrow to Ermou [street]! Can you
		ΑΥΡΙΟ ΣΤΟ ΣΤΑΘΜΟ ΣΤΟ ΜΟΝΑΣΤΗΡΑΚΙ
		make it? If yes tomorrow at Monastiraki
		ΣΤΙΣ 11.10! **ΦΙΛΙΑΑ**
		station at 11.10! **Kissess [sic]**
MSG	Nana	ΓΕΙΑ ΣΟΥ ΔΗΜΗΤΡΟΥΛΑ ΜΟΥ!
2.2	21/09/03,	*Hi my [little] Dimitra!*
	20:37	ΑΥΡΙΟ ΠΡΕΠΕΙ ΝΑ ΔΙΑΒΑΣΩ Κ
		I have to study tomorrow [a]n[d]
		ΔΕΝ ΝΟΜΙΖΩ ΝΑ ΜΠΟΡΩ!
		I don't think I can!
		ΑΝ ΕΙΝΑΙ ΘΑ ΤΑ ΠΟΥΜΕ ΕΚΕΙ! ΦΙΛΑΚΙΑ...
		If I make it, I'll see you there! Kisses...

The use of the very common (see Table 4.1) closing formula *ΦΙΛΙΑΑ* "kisses" at the end of MSG 2.1 cannot be interpreted in relation to the text's position in the sequence and, at the same time, it does not fit very well with previous studies' emphasis on the conversational frame of texting, which allows users to dispense with openings and closings. In contrast, the specific text includes a rather elaborate opening, with recurrent use of greetings (e.g., "Hi Nana! How are you? All is well?"). At the same time, the second part of the "question–answer" adjacency pair is preempted by Dimitra in her message (i.e., "can you make it? If yes"). This practice suggests that participants orient, here, toward a more asynchronous (less conversation-like) use of texting. In fact, the overabundance of phatic elements at the beginning of a text has also been found to indicate an attempt to reestablish a frame of contact that has been inactive for a long time (see Spilioti, 2007). As a result, the use of a closing may be linked with the participants' (in)frequency of contact and indicates an asynchronous use of the medium, manifested in the realization of a message schema that includes openings and closings. However, this asynchronous use can only be understood if we take into account the relational work in which the specific participants engage. In other words, the use of closings is deemed appropriate in interaction between participants who wish to acknowledge relative distance within their in-group relations.

Closing or Suspending the Daily Frame of Contact

Evidence corroborating the claim that the participant pairs of best friends (κολλητές) dispense with closings is further provided by all such pairs in my data. Out of the 48 texts exchanged between the members of such a pair (i.e., Anna and Dimitra), there are only four messages that include a closing formula. As illustrated in Extract 4.3, MSG 3.2, they all appear in the final position of an SMS sequence.

Extract 4.3:

MSG 3.1	Anna 20/01/04, 19:43	EIPA ME TH MELINA NA VRE8UME OLES THN *We agreed with Melina that we should all get together on* PEMPTH MAZI! VRHKES TELIKA TO PASO SU *Thursday! Have you found your [student] card yet,* XAZO? *you dodo (lit. dumb)?*
MSG 3.2	Dimitra 20/01/04, 20:46	ΟΚΕΙΚΣ ΓΙΑ ΠΕΜΠΤΗ!ΡΕ ΔΕΝ ΕΙΝΑΙ *Ok for Thursday!* **PE**(untranslatable) *it's* ΠΟΥΘΕΝΑ ... ΕΧΩ ΦΡΙΚΑΡΕΙ, ΕΙΝΑΙ ΤΡΕΛΗ *nowhere ... I'm freaking out, it's a real* ΔΙΑΔΙΚΑΣΙΑ ΝΑ ΞΑΝΑΒΓΑΛΕΙΣ ΠΑΣΟ! *pain to get a new card!* **ΚΑΛΗΝΥΧΤΑ!** **Good night!**

Considering that most SMS sequences (81%, n = 13) between Anna and Dimitra end without a closing move, I suspect that the choice of this parting formula is not merely an indication of the end of a particular SMS exchange. On the basis of background information gathered during my fieldwork, it is evident that the specific participants interact on a daily basis through *different* media (recall Jones et al.'s discussion of multichannel IM–*Facebook* exchanges in Chapter 2 of this volume). Assuming that the temporal frame of their contact was organized in one-day (i.e., 24-hour) periods, I would argue that the use of the closing greeting ("good night") in MSG 3.2 does not only mark the end of a text sequence, but also—or, rather, primarily— the closure of a day's interaction. Evidence from the participants' use of openings has also foregrounded the interrelation between the organization of text messaging and the daily interactional routine. As such, openings and closings in text messaging do not only serve as a means of initiating and terminating a specific exchange of text messages, but they also—or, in some cases, primarily—operate as signals of reestablishing and/or (temporarily) disengaging from the daily frame of contact between close friends.

Closings and Politeness

Following Locher and Watts' (2005) model, which suggested a more restricted view of politeness than commonly used in previous literature, I will now consider how closing formulae may be used and understood as positively marked (and, thus, polite) behavior. In this case, rather than assume what constitutes a "marked" closing in SMS, we can attend to the affordances of the medium and draw on our knowledge of the interactional norms of the specific participants. As mentioned above, the frame of "perpetual contact" in mobile technologies creates an expectation of texts without closings in texting. As a result, the co-occurrence of multiple closing formulae may constitute marked behavior in a medium where participants seem to follow the principle of "maximum speed, minimum effort" (cf. Spilioti, 2007; Thurlow, 2003). To explore this further, I focus on the two sequences in Extracts 4.4 and 4.5, which concern two exchanges of messages between the same participants: Nikos and Kostas (Case Study III). In fact, these sequences have taken place on two subsequent days and share the same topic. In other words, the initial text of both sequences was sent to fulfill the same communicative purpose, namely, to ask the other party (Nikos) whether the texter (Kostas) can drop by Nikos' place for a cup of coffee and a chat.

Extract 4.4:

MSG	Kostas	ΕΙΜΑΙ ΣΤΗ ΣΟΛΩΝΟΣ ΝΑ ΠΕΡΑΣΩ?
4.1	10/09/04, 16:30	*I'm at Solonos [street] can I drop by?*
MSG	Nikos	ΕΛΑ.ΘΑ ΡΘΕΙ+Η ΚΑΤΕΡΙΝΑ ΑΡΓΟΤΕΡΑ
4.2	10/09/04, 16:32	*Come over. Katerina ll be here later too*

Extract 4.5:

MSG	Kostas	ΝΑ ΠΕΡΑΣΩ ΓΙΑ ΚΑΦΕ ΤΡΕΛΕ?ΟΥ ΟΥ!
5.1	11/09/04,	*Can I drop by for coffee nutter? Oi oi!*
	17:05	
MSG	Nikos	ΟΧΙ ΤΡΕΛΕ. ΕΧΩ ΔΙΑΒΑΣΕΙ ΤΗ ΜΙΑ ΑΠΟ ΤΙΣ
5.2	11/09/04,	*No nut case. I've only done one out of twelve*
	17:12	ΔΩΔΕΚΑ ΕΡΩΤΗΣΕΙΣ&ΤΩΡΑ ΚΟΙΜΑΜΑΙ!!
		questions& I've fallen asleep now!!
		ΤΑ ΛΕΜΕ man ;)
		See you man ;)

Notable in the above sequences are the different responses to the same request. More specifically, the request is accepted on the 10th of September, 2003 (Extract 4.4), but it is refused on the following day (Extract 4.5). In terms of the same participant's use of closings, the following difference is also noteworthy: closing formulae are included in the refusal (MSG 5.2) but are omitted altogether in MSG 4.2, which accepts the request and invites the other party home. During my fieldwork, I noticed that the two best friends (κολλητοί) met each other almost on a daily basis, and the activity of "chatting over a cup of coffee" is central to the type of relational work they accomplish offline. As a result, the act of refusing to participate in this activity undermines their role in the specific relationship and can be considered as a threat to their face. The fact that closing formulae are included in such face-threatening—or "dispreferred," in conversation analytic terms—replies (but omitted in more agreeable responses; see MSG 4.2) leads to the argument that closings here are perceived as politeness markers. In other words, they are employed in order to mitigate the potentially face-threatening act of refusing the specific request. The mitigating function of this closing is further enhanced by the co-occurrence of other relationship-building devices, such as the term of address "man" (in English) and the use of emoticons in a medium of reduced paralinguistic cues.

General Discussion: Revisiting Genre and Closings

The types of closings identified in my data reveal a number of closing formulae that draw on a variety of already existing modes of communication, including signatures of traditional letter writing, parting formulae of face-to-face (e.g., "see you") and mediated (e.g., φιλάκια "kisses") communication. In other words, these formulae originate in a variety of genres that span the range of a spoken–written continuum. As a result, evidence from

Greek texting further reinforces the widely held assumption regarding the "hybrid" nature of genres emerging in new media (cf. Herring et al., 2005, p. 160; Thurlow et al., 2004, pp. 124–126). What is nonetheless distinctive about texting is the flexibility in the patterns of use evidenced in my study. In terms of the generic structure of individual texts, texters can shift between asynchronous and synchronous uses of the same medium and use closings accordingly, to signal relevant expectations of reciprocity and immediacy. The rare use of metalinguistic comments in the actual texts, together with the absence of explicit etiquette rules we find in other new media (e.g., online forums; cf. Graham, 2007), may also encourage flexibility in use. The study of such texts resists the neat categorizations of traditional genres and invites an understanding of genre as a more "fluid" concept (cf. Giltrow & Stein, 2009, p. 2).

Current developments in new media sociolinguistics (e.g., Androutsopoulos, 2006) have already set the stage for exploring textual aspects of language use in new media, by orienting to the different ways of (inter)acting, as embedded in the locally situated context. Hanks' work (1996, p. 246), for example, has been paramount in inviting researchers to understand generic norms and expectations not as "rules of use," but as "schemes for practice," a set of dispositions that, through routine use and habituation, become so naturalized as to be taken for granted (cf. "habitus," Bourdieu, 1990). According to Locher and Watts (2005, p. 29), it is against such structures of expectation that "individuals evaluate certain utterances as (im)polite." In my own work, therefore, closings were thus explored not as inherently polite strategies but as interactional accomplishments that may be (a) carried out in line with established norms of interaction and constitute "appropriate (unmarked) behavior" or (b) realized as marked behavior, either positively evaluated (and, thus, polite) or negatively judged (and, thus, impolite or over-polite). To my knowledge, there has been no attempt yet to explore closings of text messaging in this way, that is, with a focus on the discursive negotiation of what constitutes appropriate and (im)polite in a particular medium.

More specifically, I have argued that the use of closings is conditioned according to the position of the text in the SMS sequence and, more importantly, to the participants' relational concerns. Like previous studies in Italian and Danish texting, initial messages have been found to dispense with closing formulae, capitalizing on the texters' expectation that the other party is available to respond immediately. Indeed, failure to respond to such texts becomes marked behavior, triggering follow-up texts that topicalize the other party's non-availability. Such behavior is all the more prevalent when the initial text makes a specific type of reply relevant next, suggesting the texters' orientation to a sequential organization akin to face-to-face conversation (cf. Hutchby & Tanna, 2008, p. 161). On the other hand, the use of closing formulae is deemed more appropriate in texts that appear at the end of an SMS sequence. However, the boundaries of such sequences are not fixed, especially since interaction moves across different media (mediated and face-to-face) in any day. Given the chapter's ethnographic perspective, I have argued that the participant pairs of best friends (κολλητοί/κολλητές) operate within a relational frame of contact that is perpetually open but, at the same time, appears suspended and renewed on a daily basis, as suggested by closings indicating the suspension or closure of a day's interaction.

As a result, closings in texting appear to differ significantly from similar stages in telephone conversations, where the beginning and end of the mediated activity are clearly signaled by features of the technological medium. Unlike callers who carefully negotiate the breaking off of contact by means of long closing sequences, engagement with mobile phones and/ or texting is treated as given among texters, affording the absence of closing formulae in the majority of texts. At the same time, closings in my data become relevant as signals of disengagement from the daily frame of overall interaction, rather than the medium-specific SMS sequence. This finding corroborates the pressing need to explore texting practices as being embedded in the texters' ongoing face-to-face and mediated interactions.

Having discussed what emerges as the texters' unmarked appropriate behavior in terms of closings in texting, it is easier to isolate and explore marked behavior, which is manifest in the co-occurrence of multiple closing formulae in certain messages. My data analysis suggests that closings can be used to mitigate texts perceived as face threatening and to indicate relative distance in the participants' relations. However, the difference between this study and previous work on closings and politeness lies in the suggestion that closings operate as politeness strategies only in instances where participants explicitly engage in relational work, either because they need to reaffirm relationships that have been inactive for a long period of time or because they perform an act that is considered face threatening in the specific context. Undoubtedly, Brown and Levinson's work has provided unique insights into politeness phenomena; the overextension of politeness, though, as a notion underpinning normative behavior has often been found to run counter to participants' perceptions of language use and interaction (see Watts, 2003, on "politeness1" and "politeness2"). This chapter has explored participants' face needs, by looking at the ongoing negotiation of their roles and relationships in line with interactionally emergent goals and aspirations. It is in this way again that the study of politeness in new media opens up a window into exploring further the interplay between the technological affordances of the medium and the users' relational work.

Acknowledgments

This chapter draws on a presentation at the 11th International Pragmatics Conference (Melbourne, Australia, July 12–17, 2009), which was made possible thanks to financial support from the School of Humanities at Kingston University. I would also like to thank Crispin Thurlow and Korina Giaxoglou for their invaluable comments on previous drafts of the chapter. I am grateful to Miriam Locher and Alexandra Georgakopoulou for their insightful and constructive feedback to earlier stages of my research. I am fully responsible for any remaining shortcomings.

Notes

1. In Goffman's (1972, p. 5) terms, "line" is "a pattern of verbal and nonverbal acts by which he expresses his view of the situation and through this his evaluation of the participants, especially himself."

2. The text exchanges between five female friends (18- to 20-year-olds) represent the main sample (200 text messages). The messages collected from the other two case studies have been employed as supplementary data (i.e., 45 messages exchanged between two 17-year-old female friends and 43 texts exchanged between three 20-year-old male friends). All participants have given their informed consent to take part in the study, and their real names are substituted by pseudonyms in the data.

3. The criteria for identifying closing formulae in the data relied on previous studies of Greek mediated communication and, at the same time, took into account the participants' use of punctuation and other graphemic signals as a resource for demarcating the relevant utterances as a separate discourse unit in the messages. Taking into account the participants' specific linguistic choices implies an analytic stance that approaches the structure of texts "as a construct of the interaction between discourse participants" (Georgakopoulou & Goutsos, 1997, p. 74).

4. It should be noted that Nana uses here the Greek colloquial term κολλητή to refer to herself: rather than speak about her activities in the first person "I,"

she presents herself as the addressee's "best friend," foregrounding the close friendship bonds that hold between them.

5. The practice of topicalizing the other party's availability for contact has also been documented in other forms of mobile telephony, for example, mobile phone calls (cf. Weilenmann, 2003).

References

Androutsopoulos, J. (2006). Introduction: Sociolinguistics and computer-mediated communication. *Journal of Sociolinguistics*, 10(4), 419–438.

Androutsopoulos, J. (2008). Potentials and limitations of discourse-centred online ethnography. *Language@Internet*, 5. Retrieved from http://www.languageatinternet.de/articles/2008/1610/androutsopoulos.pdf/

Bourdieu, P. (1990). *The Logic of Practice*. Cambridge: Polity Press.

Brown, P., & Levinson, S. (1987). *Politeness: Some Universals in Language Usage*. Cambridge: Cambridge University Press.

Cameron, D. (2001). *Working with Spoken Discourse*. London: Sage.

Georgakopoulou, A. (2006). Postscript: Computer-mediated communication in sociolinguistics. *Journal of Sociolinguistics*, 10(4), 548–557.

Georgakopoulou, A., & Goutsos, D. (1997). *Discourse Analysis: An Introduction*. Edinburgh: Edinburgh University Press.

Giltrow, J., & Stein, D. (2009). Genres in the Internet: Innovation, evolution and genre theory. In J. Giltrow & D. Stein (Eds.), *Genres in the Internet: Issues in the Theory of Genre*, (pp. 1–26). Amsterdam/Philadelphia: John Benjamins.

Goffman, E. (1972). *Interaction Ritual: Essays on Face-to-Face Behaviour*. London: Allen Lane.

Goutsos, D. (2001). Sequential and interpersonal aspects of English and Greek answering machine messages. *Pragmatics*, 11(4), 357–377.

Goutsos, D. (2005). The interaction of generic structure and interpersonal relations in two-party e-chat discourse. *Language@Internet*, 2. Retrieved from http://www.languageatinternet.de/articles/2005/188/Goutsos0308_DOULOS.rtf.pdf/

Graham, S. (2007). Disagreeing to agree: Conflict, (im)politeness and identity in a computer-mediated community. *Journal of Pragmatics*, 39(4), 742–759.

Hanks, W. (1996). *Language and Communicative Practices*. Boulder, CO: Westview.

Herring, S. (1996). Two variants of an electronic message schema. In S. Herring (Ed.), *Computer-Mediated Communication: Linguistic, Social and Cross-Cultural Perspectives*, (pp. 81–106). Amsterdam: John Benjamins.

Herring, S. (2001). Computer-mediated discourse. In D. Schiffrin, D. Tannen, & H. Hamilton (Eds.), *The Handbook of Discourse Analysis*, (pp. 612–634). Oxford: Blackwell.

Herring, S., Scheidt, L., Wright, E., & Bonus, S. (2005). Weblogs as a bridging genre. *Information Technology & People*, 18(2), 142–171.

Hutchby, I., & Tanna, V. (2008). Aspects of sequential organization in text message exchange. *Discourse & Communication*, 2(2), 143–164.

Ito, M., & Okabe, D. (2005). Technosocial situations: Emergent restricting of mobile e-mail use. In M. Ito, D. Okabe, & M. Matsuda (Eds.), *Personal, Portable and Pedestrian: Mobile Phones in Japanese Life*, (pp. 257–276). Cambridge, MA: MIT Press.

Katz, J., & Aakhus, M. (Eds.) (2002). *Perpetual Contact: Mobile Communication, Private Talk, Public Performance*. Cambridge: Cambridge University Press.

Laursen, D. (2005). Please reply! The replying norm in adolescent SMS communication. In R. Harper, L. Palen, & A. Taylor (Eds.), *The Inside Text: Social, Cultural and Design Perspectives on SMS*, (pp. 53–73). Dordrecht: Springer.

Ling, R. (2005). The sociolinguistics of SMS: An analysis of SMS use by a random sample of Norwegians. In R. Ling & P. Pendersen (Eds.), *Mobile Communications: Re-Negotiation of the Social Sphere*, (pp. 335–349). London: Springer-Verlag.

Locher, M. (2010). Introduction: Politeness and impoliteness in computer-mediated communication. *Journal of Politeness Research*, 6, 1–5.

Locher, M., & Watts, R. (2005). Politeness theory and relational work. *Journal of Politeness Research*, 1(1), 9–33.

Pavlidou, T. (1997). The last five turns: Preliminary remarks in closings in Greek and German telephone calls. *International Journal of the Sociology of Language*, 126, 145–162.

Pilegaard, M. (1997). Politeness in written business discourse: A textlinguistic perspective on requests. *Journal of Pragmatics*, 28(2), 223–244.

Schegloff, E., & Sacks, H. (1999). Opening up closings. In A. Jaworski & N. Coupland (Eds.), *The Discourse Reader*, (pp. 263–274). London: Routledge.

Spagnolli, A., & Gamberini, L. (2007). Interacting via SMS: Practices of social closeness and reciprocation. *British Journal of Social Psychology*, 46, 343–364.

Spencer-Oatey, H. (2007). Identity, face and (im)politeness. *Journal of Pragmatics*, 39(4), 635–638.

Spilioti, T. (2007). Text-messages and social interaction: Genre, norms and sociability in Greek SMS. King's College London, University of London. Unpublished Ph.D. Thesis.

Thurlow, C. (2003). Generation txt? Exposing the sociolinguistics of young people's text-messaging. *Discourse Analysis Online*, 1(1). Retrieved from http://www.shu.ac.uk/daol/articles/v1/n1/a3/thurlow2002003-paper.html

Thurlow, C., Lengel, L., & Tomic, A. (2004). *Computer-Mediated Communication: Social Interaction and the Internet*. London: Sage.

Thurlow, C., & Poff, M. (2011). Text messaging. In S. Herring, D. Stein, & A. Virtanen (Eds.), *Handbook of the Pragmatics of CMC*. Berlin & New York: Mouton de Gruyter.

Waldvogel, J. (2007). Greetings and closings in workplace e-mail. *Journal of Computer-Mediated Communication*, 12(2). Retrieved from http://jcmc.indiana. edu/vol12/issue2/waldvogel.html

Watts, R. (2003). *Politeness.* Cambridge: Cambridge University Press.

Weilenmann, A. (2003). "I can't talk now, I'm in a fitting room": Formulating availability and location in mobile phone conversations. In E. Laurier (Ed.), *Environment and Planning A, Special Issue on Mobile Technologies and Space*, 35(9), 1589–1605.

Chapter 5

Japanese Keitai *Novels and Ideologies of Literacy*

Yukiko Nishimura

THE IMPACT OF mobile communication technology on peoples' lives and behavior, and on society in general, has in recent years been a focus of research in a number of disciplines, including communication studies, cultural studies, and sociology. Katz and Aakhus (2002), for example, have edited a range of studies concerned with the social and cultural impact of mobile communication in eight nations. Some early mobile communication studies have also focused specifically on Japan (e.g., Rheingold, 2002). In their edited collection, Ito et al. (2005) provide a more dedicated picture of Japanese mobile communication research. In sociolinguistics, Miyake (2007) has studied mobile e-mail communication focusing on interpersonal relations, and Yamazaki (2006) has conducted conversation analyses of Japanese mobile communication media among college students. However, one important aspect of Japanese mobile communication has been overlooked in scholarly discussion: *keitai* novels, or novels written and distributed by cellular phones.

Keitai novels are a major phenomenon in Japan and often draw harsh criticism in the mainstream media and from public commentators. Constituting a new genre of new media discourse, *keitai* novels are also subject to a particular judgment against existing standards of not only literacy, but also *literary* criteria (see also Lee, Chapter 6, this volume). In fact, professional novelists and literary critics find *keitai* novels to be "literally immature" (*Kokubungaku*, 2008). *Keitai* novels may well be described as "pulp fiction," but without the pulp. In this chapter, I consider what lies behind such harsh criticisms, based on my quantitative analysis of linguistic and stylistic similarities and differences between *keitai* and conventional novels.

Drawing on the notion of language ideologies (e.g., Kroskrity, 1999), I will argue that particular ideologies of language, literacy, and the

Japanese literary society play an important role in the reception of *keitai* novels. To this end, I rely on Silverstein's (1979, p. 193) definition of language ideologies as "sets of beliefs about language articulated by users as a rationalization or justification of perceived language structure and use." Of course, the "issue" with *keitai* novels is also a matter of literacy, a concept closely associated with written language. I therefore consider ideologies of literacy as language users' beliefs and conceptualizations of what *written* language, in this case written Japanese, ought to be like. Finally, in exploring literacy ideologies, I employ Barton's (1994, p. 169) idea of a "literary view of literacy," which comes from the study of literature and upholds the notion of canonical texts. I will discuss the similarities and differences between *literacy* and *literary* ideologies in the Japanese context, drawing on Shirane's (2000a, 2000b, 2009) account of Japanese literary history. I also want to consider how the phenomenon of *keitai* novels in Japan relates to a broader scholarly discussion of the language in mobile digital media (see, for example, Tagliamonte and Denis, 2008; Thurlow, 2006).

Comparing *keitai* novels with conventional novels, I want specifically to examine parts of speech, sentence endings, and sentence lengths to reveal stylistic features and general readability. Based on these results, I then return to the current mainstream literacy and literary standards by which certain styles are deemed "immature," such as speechlike fragments with simpler vocabulary embodied by easier *kanji* (Chinese characters). I argue that the popularity of *keitai* novels may indicate emerging literacies *and* new literary sensibilities, but which favor a more speech-oriented style rather than written style.

Background of Keitai *Novels*

Keitai novels are quite simply those crafted and enjoyed on mobile technology. "*Keitai*" literally means "carrying with" and is similar to the vernacular term "handy" for cell phones in places like Germany and Switzerland. The handset resembles cell (or mobile) phones in Europe or the United States, as can be seen in Figure 5.1.

However, unlike cellular/mobile phones, which have the basic features of mobility, telephony, and short message service (SMS), Japanese *keitai* have an array of additional functions and are best understood as inexpensive smartphones. Japanese *keitai* users can exchange e-mail in addition to text messages, search for information, watch TV, listen to the radio, play games, read comics, download music, purchase goods, take photographs, and shoot video footage, as well as make phone calls. In fact,

FIGURE 5.1

94.2% of Japanese *keitai* are internet accessible, and there are web pages that specifically cater to *keitai* users. *Keitai* are particularly important for young Japanese people, who may not be able to afford a desktop/laptop computer. Indeed, over 90% of people between the ages of 20 and 40 and almost 90% of teenagers are *keitai* users (Ministry of Internal Affairs and Communications, 2009). As Ito (2005, p. 1) puts it, a *keitai* is in essence "a personal device supporting communications that are a constant, lightweight, and mundane presence in everyday life."

Young novelists use *keitai* because they are inexpensive, handy, and mobile. It is easy for them to write on *keitai* "without conventional pens and paper," says Mayu, the first prize winner of the 4th *Keitai* Novel Contest in 2010. Readers can access them easily, too. Users can read and write any time or place, including during free time such as train rides. Public transportation is the ideal place for handheld quiet communication, as voice calls are discouraged (Okabe and Ito, 2005). Most *keitai* novels are posted to dedicated websites such as *Maho no I rando* or "Magic I-land" (http://ip.tosp.co.jp/index.asp), which boasted six million registered users as of June 2008 (National Diet Library, 2009). This and other similar sites offer a free "library" space for writers to upload their novels and for readers to download them. As of March 2010, the *Maho no I rando* library housed 136,699 long, medium, and short titles in genres including romance, comedy, fantasy, mystery, and horror. *Keitai* novels ranked highly by fan votes have also been published in print form, and some have sold as many as three million copies. In a few cases, there have even been film, TV drama, and comic book adaptations.

Keitai novels first appeared in 2000 on the personal website of someone called Yoshi. His novel, *Deep Love*, was a hit among high school girls and young women. In 2002, the printed version sold 2.7 million copies. In 2007, 5 out of the top 10 best-selling novels originated on *keitai*, according to Tohan, Japan's major publication distributor. At this point, the established, mainstream media could not ignore their popularity. In 2007, a special feature program about this "boom" was aired nationwide on the most popular TV network, NHK (NHK, 2007). Beyond Japan, the Western media also picked up on the phenomenon (Galbraith, 2009; Goodyear, 2008; Katayama, 2007; Onishi, 2008). Two literary magazines, *Bungakukai* ("*Literary World*") and *Kokubungaku* ("*National Literature*"), published special feature issues on *keitai* novels in 2008, which indicates that in a sense they were legitimatized. *Keitai* novels are now part of contemporary youth culture (Hayamizu, 2008). Though sales of printed *keitai* novels are in decline, titles uploaded on *keitai* novel websites are on the rise. Megumi Noguchi (April 30, 2010, personal communication), a public relations official at *Maho no I rando*, has remarked that *keitai* novels enjoy a broad and stable readership online.

Despite their phenomenal success and popularity, *keitai* novels are not without critics. Arguments against them typically fall into one or more of the following broad themes: (a) the language is immature, featuring only easy *kanji*, and is produced by untrained, inexperienced writers; (b) most of the novels maintain clichéd plots and have a narrow repertoire of topics, including love, sex, violence, rape, incurable disease, drug use, and suicide; (c) stories are structurally too simple, progressing rapidly without elaborate descriptive details of characters or settings; and (d) their prose deviates from stylistic conventions of standard novels in a number of ways, such as insertion of blank spaces even when there is no "necessary" grammatical effect.

Who then writes and reads — who supports — *keitai* novels? With the exception of a very limited number of existing professional novelists, *keitai* writers are usually amateurs, who may not necessarily intend to become professional writers. Sasaki (2008) interviewed ten leading *keitai* novelists and noted that, in addition to their largely amateur status, they were mostly women in their late teens and early twenties. Readers, meanwhile, include anyone with internet access. A clue to the demographic is found in the following 2009 survey by *Mainichi Newspaper*. In collaboration with the Japan School Library Association, *Dokusyo Yoron Chôsa* (2009, p.116) reported that in 2008 75% of middle school girls and 86% of high school girls read *keitai* novels regardless of printed or online versions. One reason for their popularity among this section of the population may be the subject matter. According to Sasaki (2008), authors explained how their works were usually based on personal experiences in the everyday settings of family and school. Peer readers are likely familiar with this reality and so sympathize with characters. Even though it is doubtful whether the stories are actually based on authors' own "real" experiences (Hayamizu, 2008), readers nonetheless perceive the stories as real. Those impressed deeply by the novels purchase printed versions as a material memory, even though they can easily read the novels for free online (Sugiura, 2008).

It is also important to note that *keitai* novelists receive a lot of feedback from readers, much more than is usually the case for authors of traditional print media. In fact, as one of the basic functions of *keitai* is exchanging messages, it is not surprising that a similar interactivity is applied to novels, with peer readers sending messages full of praise to authors. Authors say they are encouraged by readers (Mayu, 2010), and sometimes they even change the plot as a result of reader demand. There is thus a close relationship between writers and readers, and this type of "coproduction" is a key characteristic of *keitai* novels. Another feature is that there is no "middleman" presence, such as an editor. Supervising agents, mostly adults, are not present and so do not edit out language, style, and subject matter that may seem inappropriate to them (Yoshida, 2008).

Differences between Keitai *and Conventional Novels: Language, Style, and Readability*

Based on the 130,000-plus *keitai* novels housed in the *Maho no I rando* library and on other similar sites, I have chosen to look closely at seven of the best known and most popular. Popularity is judged by awards, sales records, and fan votes. The criteria for these judgments are likely different from the standards applied to canonical literature, which will be explored later in the chapter. The seven titles, all by female authors, are shown in Table 5.1.[1]

These seven *keitai* novels were compared to a sample of 88 conventional (i.e., print) novels, selected from the partially released monitor version of the *Balanced Corpus of Contemporary Written Japanese* (*BCCWJ*)[2] compiled by the National Institute for Japanese Language and Linguistics (2009). These novels were chosen from works of fiction published between 2003 and 2005, written by authors of the same generation as the seven *keitai* novelists. When necessary, the data from *keitai* and conventional novels

Table 5.1 List of *Keitai* novels analyzed

	Author	Title	Year	Pages analyzed	Notes
1	Towa	Kuriyanesu "Clearness"	2006	269 (all)	First prize in the first *keitai* novel contest
2	Mika	Koi zora "Love Sky"	2006	1–200	Best seller, adapted as film, TV, comics
3	Mei	Akai Ito "Red Thread"	2006	1–200	Best seller, adapted as film
4	Kiki	Atashi Kanojo "I Girlfriend"	2008	430 (all)	First prize in third *keitai* novel contest
5	Yuu	Wairudo Biisuto "Wild Beast"	2008	1–200	First place in fan ranking
6	Purple	Ashita no Niji "Tomorrow's Rainbow"	2008	1–100	First place in fan ranking on another site
7	Mayu	Kaze ni kisu, Kimi ni Kisu "Kissing the Wind, Kissing You"	2009	309 (all)	First prize in fourth *keitai* novel contest

is also compared with a spoken corpus analyzed in Nishimura (2010), in which linguistic features were compared across nine registers: one from spoken language (casual conversation), four from new media discourse (including *keitai* novels), and four from written language (e.g., magazine articles) to reveal where each register lies in a spoken–written continuum.

My study differentiates between (re)created conversations or dialogues enclosed by some conventions, most typically quotation marks, from the rest of the text in which the author narrates the story. Novelists often incorporate "orality" in their creation of conversations among characters (Lakoff, 1982). This separation of quotation (typically conversation) and narration (the rest of the text) is employed as an analytical frame in the following analyses (except for string length in Table 5.7). Distinguishing quotations from narrations in novels is a method employed quite often in stylistic analyses (e.g., Kabashima and Jugaku, 1965), as the features in quotations and narrations are likely to be different.

Step 1: Linguistic Analyses

These novels were first analyzed in terms of parts-of-speech distribution for the entire novels, including both quotations and narrations. A Japanese morphological analyzer, MeCab, along with a computerized dictionary, Unidic, was used to determine the parts of speech of each morpheme, so that its frequency can be calculated.[3] Ten parts of speech categories were considered: nouns, verbs, auxiliary verbs, particles, pronouns, adjectives, adverbs, prenominals, conjunctions, and interjections.

In considering grammatical structures based on parts of speech (my first linguistic analysis), their distribution was not very different in general between *keitai* and conventional novels, as shown in Table 5.2.

However, one category, interjections, which often characterize conversational data, shows a marked difference. In particular, I found that the

Table 5.2 Parts-of-speech distribution for quotations and narrations of *keitai* and conventional novels

Parts of speech	*Keitai* novels		Conventional novels	
	Quotations	Narrations	Quotations	Narrations
Auxiliary verbs	14.6%	12.4%	13.7%	12.3%
Verbs	13.6%	16.2%	13.8%	16.5%
Adjectives	4.5%	4.4%	3.8%	3.8%
Particles	31.1%	33.0%	33.5%	33.2%
Nouns	23.5%	26.0%	24.5%	27.6%
Pronouns	4.7%	3.4%	4.1%	2.4%
Adverbs	3.1%	2.9%	3.1%	2.6%
Prenominals	0.8%	1.0%	1.2%	0.9%
Conjunctions	0.4%	0.3%	0.3%	0.4%
Interjections	3.6%	0.4%	1.9%	0.2%
Total	100%	100%	100%	100%
Number of morphemes	52,602	207,784	80,491	208,490
Quotation: Narration ratio	20.2%	79.8%	27.9%	72.1%

quotation section in *keitai* novels had close to twice the frequency of inter-jections (3.6%) as conventional novels (1.9%). (I would note at this point that my goal is to ascertain broad descriptive—rather than statistical—tendencies due to the relatively small corpus.)

The tendency of *keitai* novels toward conversational features is also seen in the particle subcategories. This general category includes par-ticles with different functions. The focus among these subcategories is on the sentence-final particle, which indicates the speaker's attitude toward the hearer/addressee. Table 5.3 gives distribution-of-particle sub-categories for both quotations and narrations in *keitai* and conventional novels.

The frequency of sentence-final particles in the quotation sections of *keitai* novels (23.6%) is much higher than that of conventional novels (14.3%), though both of them depict dialogues or (re)created conversa-tions. As I know from my own work elsewhere, the percentage (23.6%) for *keitai* novels is actually similar to that of face-to-face conversational discourse, 23.5% (see Nishimura, 2010). Furthermore, the *relatively* high frequency of sentence-final particles is also reflected even in narrations (4.1% for *keitai* novels as opposed to 1.7% for conventional novels). In all other respects, the differences between *keitai* and conventional novels were, relatively speaking, not so great.

Table 5.3 Distribution of particles in quotations and narrations of *keitai* and conventional novels

Particles	*Keitai* novels		Conventional novels	
	Quotations	Narrations	Quotations	Narrations
Case	30.8%	53.7%	40.4%	56.9%
Relational	12.2%	15.1%	14.4%	16.2%
Conjunctive	18.1%	17.3%	16.6%	16.9%
Pronominal	6.7%	3.7%	6.7%	3.6%
Adverbial	8.6%	6.1%	7.5%	4.7%
Sentence final	23.6%	4.1%	14.3%	1.7%
Total	100%	100%	100%	100%
Number of morphemes	16,373	68,546	26,966	69,290
Quotation: Narration ratio	19.3%	80.7%	28.0%	72.0%

An additional tendency that shows *keitai* novels being closer to conversational discourse was found in the frequency of auxiliary verb subcategories (see Table 5.4). The focus here is the durative auxiliaries, *-teru* and *-deru*.

Both *-teru* and *-deru* are auxiliary suffixes attached to verbs to show that an action is ongoing, for example: *tabe-teru*, "eat-ing," and *non-deru*, "drinking." These are shortened forms of *tabe-te-iru* and *non-de-iru*, respectively, in which the deleted *"i"* indexes a casual or informal register. In Table 5.4, the frequency of these contracted auxiliaries is 10.0% in the quotations of *keitai* novels, which is almost twice as high as that of conventional novels (5.5%), even though both are (re)created conversations. It is not surprising that *i*-deleted auxiliaries appear often in characters' casual conversation. What is surprising is the magnitude of difference between *keitai* and conventional novels. The frequency of *i*-deleted auxiliaries in *keitai* novel quotations is once again very close to the percentage (10.7%) observed in face-to-face casual conversation (Nishimura, 2010).

Notice also that these shortened auxiliaries appear even in narration sections of *keitai* novels (4.2%) at a far higher frequency than conventional novels (0.5%). This difference between *keitai* and conventional novels in narration sections is even greater than that in quotations. In narration sections, the expectation is for more features of written than spoken language because these sections do not represent conversation.

Table 5.4 Distribution of auxiliary verbs in quotations and narrations of *keitai* and conventional novels

Auxiliary verbs	*Keitai* novels		Conventional novels	
	Quotations	Narrations	Quotations	Narrations
Copula *-da*	35.8%	31.7%	36.5%	32.2%
Past *-ta*	24.4%	41.7%	22.4%	44.1%
Negative *-nai*	10.7%	10.2%	9.1%	7.1%
Polite copula *-desu*	5.1%	0.7%	8.9%	1.4%
Polite verbal suffix *-masu*	2.9%	0.4%	5.4%	2.4%
Potential/passive *-reru/rareru*	2.7%	4.9%	3.9%	6.5%
Durative *-teru/-deru*	10.0%	4.2%	5.5%	0.5%
All other auxiliary verbs	8.4%	6.2%	8.4%	5.8%
Total	100%	100%	100%	100%
Number of morphemes	7,690	25,754	11,063	25,642
Quotation: Narration ratio	19.3%	80.7%	28.0%	72.0%

Yet *keitai* novelists employ more spoken auxiliaries, while conventional authors do not. In fact, unlike *keitai* users, people writing on the computer using standard word-processing software get a warning from the preinstalled style-checking program that *i*-deletion is inappropriate for written language. From this it seems that authors of conventional novels mostly follow the standards of written language when they narrate stories by avoiding "inappropriate" *i*-deletion, while *keitai* novelists incorporate a casual, informal, spoken register when they narrate stories. *Keitai* novelists employ shortened auxiliaries for both quotations and narrations. The significance of this will be discussed later, along with the results of stylistic and readability analyses.

Step 2: Stylistic Analyses

In order to consider matters of style, I decided to look specifically at sentence ending forms and string lengths. Sentence ending forms are interesting because the presence or absence of predicates indicating tense at sentence-final positions demonstrates whether the sentence is complete or fragmentary. By the same token, string length (based on the number of characters up to the point when the "return" key is entered) also gives a sense of textual complexity. Two examples from *keitai* novels (one from *Koizora* and the other from *Akai ito*) illustrate a complete sentence in two strings with full predicates showing the tense in (1) and a fragmentary sentence (hereafter referred to as "fragment") in one string without a predicate in (2):

(1) a. 帰 り 道
    Kae ri michi
    Return way
    "On my way home"
  b. 電話 　が 　　　鳴った。
    Denwa ga   *natta.*
    Phone SUBJECT rang.
    "On my way home, my phone rang."
(2) 　時 　に 　は迷い、時 に 　は間違い な が ら……。
    Toki ni wa mayoi, toki ni wa machigai nagara ... .
    Sometimes wonder, sometimes make a mistake...
    "Sometimes wondering, other times making mistakes..."

Natta in Extract 1b is a predicate consisting of a verb (*naru*) and a past tense auxiliary (*-ta*) in the terminal conjugation form, occupying the final position of the sentence. On its own, Extract 1a could not be regarded as a fragment, because it does not have a punctuation mark indicating its end, and is continued to the second string to form a sentence. Extracts 1a and 1b together constitute one complete sentence of 10 characters including the full stop (。). Extract 1 has two strings, with the first being three characters long, and the second string seven. Extract 2, meanwhile, is a fragment in which the linguistic expression (as opposed to nonlinguistic symbols) ends with a continuative particle, *nagara*. It is considered a fragment because it does not have predicates, even though it has a full stop at the end. This fragment consists of one string and is counted as 18 characters long (the preinstalled word count system of Microsoft Word regards the three dots of the ellipsis as one character). A complete sentence and a fragment are thus differentiated and the length counted accordingly.

In tracking stylistic differences and similarities such as these, I also looked at how sentences ended, since sentence-final forms often convey stylistic information, such as whether a sentence gives a sense of completion or continuation, and how the writer/speaker presents the information (e.g., "I'm telling you what you may not know"). With only one exception, sentence endings were identified by punctuation marks (e.g., full stops) in both *keitai* and conventional novels. Complete sentences, which have full predicates with modalities indicating tense and aspect, appear typically in terminal conjugation forms of verbs, adjectives, and auxiliaries (as well as imperative forms). Fragments, on the other hand, end with nouns without predicates and with verbs, adjectives, and auxiliaries in other conjugation forms such as continuative. It is no surprise that quotations in general have more fragmentary endings, as they are in principle re-creations of face-to-face conversation, where interruptions and fragmentary utterances are likely to occur (Chafe, 1982). On this basis, I felt I could identify what style the novelist was using.

Table 5.5 shows that *keitai* novels in general contain more fragments than conventional novels. Narrations of conventional novels have a higher percentage of complete predicates (87.0%) than *keitai* novels (67.1%). Fragments that end with nouns alone were almost twice as common in *keitai* novel quotations (14.7%) compared with the quotations of conventional novels (8.2%). In narrations, the frequency of *keitai* novels was almost three times higher (12.8%) than that of conventional novels (4.4%). It seems clear that there is a tendency for *keitai* novels to be more fragmented, more conversational in style, and lacking in predicates that otherwise express modalities such as tense and aspect.

Table 5.5 Complete versus fragmentary sentence endings for quotations and narrations in *keitai* and conventional novels

Sentences endings	*Keitai* novels		Conventional novels	
	Quotations	Narrations	Quotations	Narrations
Complete endings	24.4%	67.1%	36.0%	87.0%
Fragmentary endings	75.6%	32.9%	64.0%	13.0%
(Nouns alone within fragmentary endings)	14.7%	12.8%	8.2%	4.4%
Total	100%	100%	100%	100%
Number of sentences	8,546	14,430	8,731	13,315
Quotation: Narration ratio	37.2%	62.8%	39.6%	60.4%

As I explained, sentence/fragment length was measured in terms of the number of characters up to a certain punctuation mark, most typically a full stop. The number of words was not used as a measure of sentence length because Japanese orthography comprises characters strung together with no space between words. What I found was that there was a sharp contrast between *keitai* and conventional novels with respect to "new line" patterns or "string" mentioned earlier. In conventional novels, a new line is typically marked by indention, which signifies the start of a new paragraph, often containing more than one sentence. The end of a paragraph is marked by another line change, which is achieved by entering the return key in computerized writing. In contrast, *keitai* novels have very frequent "new lines" that result in multiple lines, even within a single sentence. It is a structure somewhat like the stanzas of a poem, and much like the structure of instant messaging and the online chat (see, for example, Jones et al., Chapter 2 of this volume). I refer to the part of scripts bordered by new lines as strings, which are equivalent to paragraphs in a conventional novel. In *keitai* novels, it is sometimes a short sequence of characters that is often only a part of a complete sentence.

The number of characters per sentence/fragment was counted for both quotations and narrations in *keitai* and conventional novels. Also, the number of characters per string was compared between entire *keitai* and conventional novels. I did not differentiate quotations and narrations for measuring string length because some strings contain elements of both quotations and narrations. Table 5.6 shows the average sentence/ fragment length, and Table 5.7 shows the average string length in *keitai* and conventional novels.

In general, sentences/fragments were five characters shorter in *keitai* novels than conventional novels. While the difference between *keitai* and conventional novels in terms of sentence/fragments length given in Table 5.6 does not seem too great, Table 5.7 shows a striking difference. For each string, *keitai* novels employ far fewer characters, and even one sentence with normal predicates is often broken into two separate strings, as the example of Extract 1 on page 95. Conventional novels adopt traditional layout to form paragraphs rather than chop strings into many short lines. The average number of characters in one string (one paragraph) in conventional novels (49.0 characters) is more than twice that of *keitai* novels (18.2 characters). Together, Tables 5.6 and 5.7 show how in *keitai* novels the

Table 5.6 Length of sentences/fragments for quotations and narrations in *keitai* and conventional novels

	Keitai novels			Conventional novels		
	Quotations	Narrations	Total	Quotations	Narrations	Total
Total number of characters	98,670	333,445	432,115	152,831	372,307	525,138
Total number of sentences/ fragments	8,546	14,430	22,976	8,731	13,315	22,046
Average number of characters per sentence/ fragment	11.5	23.1	18.8	17.5	28	23.8

Table 5.7 Length of strings in *keitai* and conventional novels

	Keitai novels	Conventional novels
Total number of characters	432,115	525,138
Total number of strings	23,796	10,728
Average number of characters per string	18.2	49.0

average string length of about 18 characters is almost equal to the average sentence length.

Step 3: Readability Analysis

My readability analysis was conducted using the *Obi* software developed by Sato et al. (2008). Their measure, based on a corpus of Japanese textbooks, was used to identify what school grade level my sample *keitai* novels could be assigned to. This readability analyzer utilizes *kanji* to determine grade level, which is possible because the number and kind of *kanji* taught at each grade level in Japan is rigidly determined up to Grade 6, and to a lesser extent up to Grade 9 (Gottlieb, 1995). Japanese textbooks must meet government standards. By comparing the readability of *keitai* novels with that of conventional novels, it is possible to clarify whether or not *keitai* novels belong to a different—and, indeed, lower—grade level, which is certainly the kind of criticism leveled at them in the mainstream media and elsewhere.

A brief note on *kanji* in the Japanese writing system, and its position in education and society, might be helpful. The Japanese writing system has four different scripts: phonographic *hiragana* and *katakana*, logographic *kanji*, and Roman letters, *rômaji*. While the first two sound-based scripts are taught early in Japanese schools, Japanese writers learn (and struggle with) *kanji* throughout their schooling—and beyond. In 1981, the government issued guidelines for *kanji* use, establishing 1,945 general-use characters (Gottlieb, 1995, p. 194). Beyond the semicompulsory high school curriculum, some 3,000 to 6,000 *kanji* were selected by the Japan Kanji Aptitude Testing Foundation for broader societal use. Because *kanji* is linked to grade level and hence knowledge of vocabulary, *kanji* is often associated with literacy in Japan, in a similar way as spelling is in the West (Sebba, 2007). It is thus not surprising that critics of *keitai* novels refer to inferior *kanji* use.

Readability measures developed by Sato et al. (2008) were applied to both *keitai* and conventional novels, separating quotations and narrations. Table 5.8 gives the results.

The average readability for all the seven *keitai* novels including both quotations and narrations is grade 7.71, and that of the 88 conventional novels rate at grade 8.2. Table 5.8 shows that there is about half a grade level difference between *keitai* novels and conventional novels. In narrations, the difference is slightly greater. The results of readability analysis

Table 5.8 Average readability of *keitai* and conventional novels

School grade level	*Keitai* novels	Conventional novels
Overall	7.71	8.2
Narrations	7.71	8.7
Quotations	5.857	6.682

(by *kanji* use) show that *keitai* novels are not too greatly different from conventional novels.

The results of the analyses so far can be summarized as follows. Linguistic and stylistic analyses show that *keitai* and conventional novels are quantitatively not very different. However, *keitai* novels reveal a clear preference for conversational styles, while conventional novels have more in common with typical written language. The most noticeable stylistic difference lies in the string length. One string consists of 18 characters in *keitai* novels, while conventional novels use 49 characters. The readability analysis has also shown that *keitai* novels are not all that different from conventional novels, employing *kanji* that are only slightly easier.

General Discussion: Intertwined Ideologies of Literacy and the Literary

Negative evaluations of *keitai* are broadly derived from two different, yet intertwined, ideologies: literacy and the literary. What I mean by "intertwined" is that works of literature have been used in language education for the ruling class in Japan for over a thousand years (Shirane, 2000b). Even after the Pacific War, when education was available to everyone, there was still an emphasis on literary works in the school curriculum, though the selection of canonical works changed periodically, depending on the curriculum developers' decisions that accommodated political, social, and cultural situations (Shirane, 2009). This tradition continues to this day. *Keitai* novel critics who draw attention to "immature language with easy *kanji*" and "deviation from standard prose writing style" epitomize literacy ideologies, and the comments about "banal themes" and "rough story lines without detailed descriptions" are more related to literary standards.

Harsh comments toward *keitai* novels from critics and established writers are based on traditional notions of "good" writing. To examine this assessment, it is worth considering what contemporary "experts" have to say on the matter. Iwabuchi (1989, p. 50), for example, is a well-known linguist and lexicographer, and one-time director of the National Institute of Japanese Language and Linguistics. He argues that too many line changes (which he equates with nonexistent paragraph organization) is a key feature of bad writing. More recently, Honda (2004, p. 206), a journalist and author of writing guides, has also expressed his displeasure with sentences that end with unpredicated nouns. Specifically, he mentions that first-class writers do not like such sentences, implying that they are the product of poor writing. Finally, Ishiguro (2004), a writing teacher and author of composition manuals for both native and nonnative Japanese students, warns writers to be always conscious of the differences between spoken and written language and to avoid spoken features in writing. In fact, a noticeable gap between spoken and written language is often considered by linguists to be a distinctive characteristic of the Japanese language (e.g., Neustupny, 1981, p. 231). These remarks certainly provide solid support for popular criticisms of *keitai* novels. The language used in *keitai* novels has features that these experts regard as bad for writing: *keitai* language is evidently colloquial with frequent line changes, and many fragments end with nouns without predicates. Moreover, the use of easier *kanji*, which is perceived to be greater than it actually is, contributes to the "amateurish" image of these new media novels.

Why, then, do *keitai* novelists write in a language and style that is deemed poor? To start, *keitai* novelists prefer a generally more conversational style of writing, even in narrations. Clancy (1982) observes a tendency in written Japanese to efface interactional features such as sentence-final particles due to social remoteness. Writers and readers generally do not know one another. In contrast, in the production and consumption of *keitai* novels, this assumption of social remoteness may not hold. As seen in interviews, *keitai* novelists are often quite close to readers, who, in turn, act as peers and interact closely with writers. Perhaps the conversational style of *keitai* novels is a product of these close writer/reader relationships, or perhaps it is deployed as a resource to create these kinds of relationships.

Concerning their "bad" elements of style, recall also how *keitai* novels are created and circulated. These novels reach readers directly (via websites) without interference from intermediaries such as literary agents and publishing houses. They are posted and downloaded quickly and freely. Conventional novels published in print go through lengthy editing processes before reaching the readers/consumers. Hanai (2005) described her struggle with editors when she attempted to publish her novels in unconventional prose styles for teenagers. In a sense, amateur writers' works appear online without being "corrected" by a third party. They not only speak directly to readers but also directly express the author's ideas.

There is another fairly obvious technical factor (or affordance) that helps explain the particular style of *keitai* novels. In order to fit on the tiny *keitai* screens, long sentences, which would require scrolling, are altered in favor of short sentences and strings. The opening page of *Koizora* in Figure 5.2 illustrates that the 18-character string more or less fits the *keitai* display.

Frequent line changes, also observable in Figure 5.2, are similarly a result of adapting to small *keitai* displays, and making content more accessible. This also may be one reason why complex *kanji* are avoided. In short, language choice in *keitai* novels is intentionally based on user needs and technical limitations. Expression is both expanded and constrained by *keitai* technology.

I want now to consider briefly some of the literary ideologies that compound the public literacy critique of *keitai*. Shirane (2000a, p. 2), drawing on Guillory (1993), writes: "canon ... means those texts that are recognized by established or powerful institutions." In his exploration of how the Japanese literary canon was formed, Shirane clarifies that since the 8th century, works of Japanese and Chinese literature, along with religious and historical writings, have appeared and disappeared in the canon, depending on political and social factors. Not only individual literary works, but also literary genres such as poetry and novels, have been granted or denied canonical status. After the Meiji Restoration, Japan attempted to catch up with Western nations, and this had an impact on the Japanese literary canon. The genre of fiction, which had a lower status, was raised up to canonical literature. This tendency was reinforced after the Pacific War. Shirane states, "The most striking aspect of the postwar kokugo [national language, no italics in original] curriculum, however, was the dominance of modern, often European-based notions of literature, particularly the *shôsetsu* (novel), in shaping the canon" (Shirane, 2000b, p. 248). It is not surprising that established literary circles value novels as a canonical genre today and might feel as if the "important" territory they have cherished has been invaded by *keitai* authors, who are thought to have had no training or experience in literature. The antagonism might be fueled by the astonishing sales of print versions of *keitai* novels. If *keitai* novels appeared only online, and no printed versions were sold, the harsh

第一章❸笑顔❸

「あ〜！！超お腹減ったしっ♪♪」

待ちに待った昼休み。
美嘉はいつものように
机の上でお弁当を開く。

学校は面倒。

だけど同じクラスで仲良くなったｱﾔとﾕｶと一緒にお
弁当を食べるのが唯一の楽しみなのだ。

一田原美嘉一

今年の4月高校に入学したばかりの高校一年生。

入学してからまだ
三ヶ月足らず。

仲良しで気の合う友達も出来て結構楽しく過ごして
いた。

チビだし
バカだし
特別かわいいってわけでもないし
特技なんてないし
将来の夢なんてあるわけもない。

高校に入ってすぐに染めた明るい茶色のストレート
髪。
ほんのりと淡いメイクがまだあまり馴染んでいない
今日この頃。

FIGURE 5.2

comments might not have been voiced. People in established circles might not have felt threatened by digital literature. Yet both Shirane (2009) and Ensslin (2006) point out that canons are changeable over the course of gradual paradigm shifts or in favor of political, social, or cultural upheaval. Especially in the contemporary emergence of competing canons, in the face of rising popular culture that has been marginalized, we may some-day see digital literature canonized.

Conclusion: The Literacy of Keitai *Literature*

There are both similarities and departures between what I see happening here and the public debate concerning the language of text messaging (e.g., Carrington, 2005; Thurlow, 2006). What seems to be a common comment from the media is that the kind of language, as well as of communicative practices, is bad or inappropriate. One example of English texting cited in a number of public documents (beginning with "My smmr hos wr CWOT...") may be difficult to understand without "translation" into Standard English. This may be different in the case of the language used in *keitai* novels, which are perfectly understandable to the general public as well as peer readers. Criticisms of *keitai* novels are not about comprehension, but rather the inappropriateness of the language for "novels." Here again we observe the intertwined nature of ideologies about the literary and literacy.

On literary aspects of literacy (Barton, 1994), I maintain that literacy does not simply mean the ability to read and write; rather, literacy is situated in broader sociocultural contexts because "texts and the various ways of reading them are ... the social and historical inventions of various groups of people" (Gee, 2008, p. 48). As Street (1995, p. 1) has famously noted, literacy is thus "an ideological practice, implemented in power relations and embedded in specific cultural meanings and practices." Bearing this in mind, I regard the beliefs about "good" and "bad" writing articulated by authorities as rationalization or justification for criticism of the styles, structures, and uses revealed in *keitai* novels.

Criticizing *keitai* novels as "immature" illustrates ideologies of literacy held by established writers. For them, speech and writing are different, as the former contains fragments of incomplete thoughts and is unsuitable to use in writing. Their argument is that if *keitai* novels are "novels," they are expected to follow the conventions of prose: complete, well-formed sentences in organized paragraphs (at least in narrations). *Keitai* novels represent an approach to novels as conversational, something that, with the aid of technology, amateurs, young people, or anyone can do. Herein lies the challenge to conventional novels. Following Kress (2003), it seems that *keitai* novels have given less privileged groups access/rights to the creative powers and status of "authorship" that ordinarily belong only to the most educated, elite, and privileged in society.

Even with the vocabulary and *kanji* ability of a middle school student, *keitai* novelists still impress a wide range of readers. Thus, in spite of critical assumptions that novels should employ more sophisticated topics and styles, *keitai* novels appeal to audiences who might not want to read texts with apparently difficult *kanji*. In fact, one *keitai* novelist, Rin, says in an interview with Abe (2007) that difficult *kanji* discourages readers. Japanese *keitai* novelists, together with their audiences, implicitly challenge the dominant literacy and literary ideologies by saying, "What's wrong with easy *kanji*?" Besides, as my analysis here has shown, the essential readability of *keitai* novels is really not that different from conventional novels.

Acknowledgments

This work was supported by a Grant-in Aid for Scientific Research (c) No. 21520448 from the Japan Society for the Promotion of Science. Earlier versions were presented at the "Computers and Writing" conference held at the University of California, Davis, in June 2009, and the "Language in the (New) Media" conference held at the University of Washington, Seattle, in September 2009. I am grateful for comments on both occasions, especially from Naomi Baron at the Seattle conference. I thank Crispin Thurlow, Tim Shortis, an anonymous reviewer, Patrick W. Galbraith, and Keiko Nishimura for their valuable comments for improving this chapter. Any errors that may remain are my own.

Notes

1. These works are available from:

    1. http://no-ichigo.jp/read/book/book_id/219907
    2. http://ip.tosp.co.jp/BK/TosBK100.
       asp?I=hidamari_book&BookId=1&SPA=200
    3. http://de-view.net/book/novel.php?aid=1&f=chapter&tid=1&%20pos=1
    4. http://no-ichigo.jp/read/book/book_id/148920

5. http://ip.tosp.co.jp/bk/TosBK100.asp?I=WildBeast&BookId=1
6. http://pure.mainichi.co.jp/purple/ezweb/ashitanoniji/0.html
7. http://no-ichigo.jp/read/book/book_id/240186

2. See http://www.ninjal.ac.jp/english/products/kotonoha/ for information.
3. MeCab is downloadable from http://mecab.sourceforge.net/, developed jointly at Kyoto University and NTT Communication Science Laboratories. Other application programs, Chamame and UniDic, are downloadable from http://www.tokuteicorpus.jp/dist/index.php

References

Abe, H. (2007). Keitai shôsetsu wa bungaku no yume wo miru ka. [Do *keitai* novels dream of literature?]. *Shukan Asahi*. October 26, 38–39.

Barton, D. (1994). *Literacy: An Introduction to the Ecology of Written Language.* Oxford and Cambridge, MA: Blackwell.

Bungakukai. [Literary World] (2008). Teidan--: Keitai shôsetsu wa "sakka" wo korosu ka. [Tripartite discussion: Would keitai novels kill "authors"?] January, 190–208.

Carrington, V. (2005). Txting: The end of civilization (again)? *Cambridge Journal of Education*, 35(2), 161–175.

Chafe, W. (1982). Integration and involvement in speaking, writing, and oral literature. In Deborah Tannen (Ed.), *Spoken and Written Language: Exploring Orality and Literacy*, (pp. 35–53). Norwood, NJ: Ablex.

Clancy, P.M. (1982). Written and spoken style in Japanese narratives. In Deborah Tannen (Ed.), *Spoken and Written Language: Exploring Orality and Literacy*, (pp. 55–76). Norwood, NJ: Ablex.

Dokusyo Yoron Chôsa [Public-Opinion Survey on Reading]. (2009). The 62nd public opinion survey on reading and the 54th survey on school children's reading. 2009 version. Tokyo: Mainichi Newspaper Company.

Ensslin, A. (2006). Hypermedia and the question of canonicity. *dichtung-digital*, 36. Retrieved June 2010 from http://www.dichtung-digital.org/2006/1-Ensslin.htm

Galbraith, P.W. (2009). Screen dreams: A digital-age literary form has become a publishing powerhouse. *Metropolis Magazine*. July 23 (774). Retrieved February 2009 from http://metropolis.co.jp/tokyo/774/feature.asp

Gee, J.P. (2008). *Social Linguistics and Literacies: Ideologies in Discourses* (3rd ed.). London and New York: Routledge.

Goodyear, D. (2008). I ♥ Novels: Young women develop a genre for the cellular age. *The New Yorker*. December 22. Retrieved June 2009 from http://www.newyorker.com/reporting/2008/12/22/081222fa_fact_goodyear?currentPage

Gottlieb, N. (1995). *Kanji Politics: Language Policy and Japanese Script.* London and New York: Kegan Paul International.

Guillory, J. (1993). *Cultural Capital: The Problem of Literary Canon Formation*. Chicago: University of Chicago Press.

Hanai, A. (2005). *Tokimeki Ichigo Jidai: Tyiinzu Hâto no 1987–1997 [Exciting Strawberry Age: Teens' Heart from 1987 to 1997]*. Tokyo: Koudansha.

Hayamizu, K. (2008). *Keitai Shôsetsu Teki [Keitai Novels-Like]*. Tokyo: Hara Shobou.

Honda, K. (2004). *Chuugakusei Kara no Sakubun Gijutsu [Writing Techniques from Middle School Students]*. Tokyo: Asahi Newspaper Company.

Ishiguro, K. (2004). *Yoku Wakaru Bunsyou Hyougen no Gijutsu [Easy-to-Understand Techniques for Textual Expression]*.Tokyo: Meiji Shoin.

Ito, M. (2005). Introduction: Personal, portable, pedestrian. In Ito et al. (Eds.) *Personal, Portable, Pedestrian: Mobile Phones in Japanese Life* (pp. 1–16). Cambridge, MA: MIT Press.

Ito, M., Okabe, D., & Matsuda, M. (Eds.). (2005). *Personal, Portable, Pedestrian: Mobile Phones in Japanese Life*. Cambridge, MA: MIT Press.

Iwabuchi, E. (1989). *Akubun [Bad Prose]* (3rd ed.). Tokyo: Nihon Hyouronsha.

Kabashima, T., & Jugaku, A. (1965). *Buntai no Kagaku [Science of Styles]*. Kyoto: Sougeisha.

Katayama, L. (2007). Big books hit Japan's tiny phones. *Wired*. January 3. Retrieved June 13, 2009 from http://www.wired.com/culture/lifestyle/news/2007/01/72329

Katz, J.E., & Aakhus, M. (Eds.). (2002). *Perpetual Contact: Mobile Communication, Private Talk, Public Performance*. Cambridge: Cambridge University Press.

Kokubungaku [National Literature]. (2008). Tokusyû—Keitai sekai [Special Issue—Keitai World]. 53(5).

Kress, G. (2003). *Literacy in the New Media Age*. London and New York: Routledge.

Kroskrity, P.V. (1999). Regimenting languages: Language ideological perspectives. In P. Kroskrity (Ed.), *Regimes of Language* (pp. 1–34). Santa Fe, NM: School of American Research Press.

Lakoff, R.T. (1982). Some of my favorite writers are literate: The mingling of oral and literate strategies in written communication. In Deborah Tannen (Ed.), *Spoken and Written Language: Exploring Orality and Literacy*, (pp. 239–260). Norwood, NJ: Ablex.

Mayu. (2010). "First prize winner of the 4th Keitai Novel Contest." Interview Column. *Mainichi Newspaper*, January 9 Morning edition, p. 4.

Ministry of Internal Affairs and Communications. (2009). *Information and Communications in Japan*. 2009 white paper. Retrieved March 2010 from http://www.soumu.go.jp/johotsusintokei/whitepaper/eng/WP2009/2009-index.html

Miyake, K. (2007). Relationship management in the use of mobile phone messages by young Japanese. Paper delivered at the 10th International Pragmatics Conference, Gothenburg, Sweden.

National Diet Library. (2009). *Denshi shoseki no ryûtsû / riyô / hozon ni kansuru kenkyû chôsa. [Survey on Circulation, Use and Archiving of Electronic Books]*. NDL Research Report No.11. Kyoto: National Diet Library Kansai. Available from http:// www.current.ndl.go.jp/files/report/no11/lis_rr_11_rev_20090313.pdf

National Institute for Japanese Language and Linguistics. (2009). *Balanced Corpus of Contemporary Written Japanese*, (BCCWJ) monitor version. Search demonstration available from http://www.kotonoha.gr.jp/demo/

Neustupny, J.V. (1981). Nihongo no naka no kakikotoba no ichi [Position of written language in Japanese]. In O. Hayashi, S. Hayashi, & K. Morioka (Eds.) *Bunshou To Wa Nani Ka [What Is Writing]*, (pp. 213–250). Tokyo: Meiji Shoin.

NHK (Nihon Housou Kyoukai). (2007). Tegaru na bungaku? *Keitai* shousetsu [Easy literature? Keitai novels]. *Kuroozu Appu Gendai [Close-up Today]*. Aired September 27.

Nishimura, Y. (2010, March). Variation across speech, writing and language online: A pilot research toward an overall approach to Japanese. Paper presented at Open Workshop on "Japanese Corpus," at the National Institute for Japanese Language and Linguistics, Tokyo.

Okabe, D., & Ito, M. (2005). *Keitai* in public transportation. In Ito et al. (Eds.), *Personal, Portable, Pedestrian: Mobile Phones in Japanese Life* (pp. 205–217). Cambridge, MA: MIT Press.

Onishi, N. (2008). Thumbs race as Japan's best sellers go cellular. *New York Times*, January 20. Retrieved September 2008 from http://www.nytimes. com/2008/01/20/world/asia/20japan.html?_r=1

Rheingold, H. (2002). *Smart Mobs: The Next Social Revolution*. Cambridge, MA: Perseus.

Sasaki, T. (2008). *Keitai Shôsetsuka: Akogare No Sakka 10 Nin Ga Hajimete Kataru "Jibun" [Keitai Novelists: 10 Adored Novelists Talk About "Self" for the First Time]*. Tokyo: Shougakukan.

Sato, S., Matsuyoshi, S., & Kondoh, Y. (2008). Automatic assessment of Japanese text readability based on a textbook corpus. *LREC-08*. Retrieved March 2010 from http://kotoba.nuee.nagoya-u.ac.jp/sc/readability/obi.html

Sebba, M. (2007). *Spelling and Society: The Culture and Politics of Orthography around the World*. Cambridge: Cambridge University Press.

Shirane, H. (2000a). Introduction: Issues in canon formation. In H. Shirane & T. Suzuki (Eds.), *Inventing the Classics: Modernity, National Identity, and Japanese Literature*, (pp. 1–27). Stanford, CA: Stanford University Press.

Shirane, H. (2000b). Curriculum and competing canons. In H. Shirane & T. Suzuki (Eds.), *Inventing the Classics: Modernity, National Identity, and Japanese Literature*, (pp. 220–249). Stanford, CA: Stanford University Press.

Shirane, H. (Ed). (2009). *New Horizons of Japanese Literary Studies: Canon Formation, Gender and Media*. Tokyo: Bensey Publishing Inc.

Silverstein, M. (1979). Language structure and linguistic ideology. In P.R. Clyne, W.F. Hanks, & C.L. Hofbauer (Eds.), *The Elements: A Parasession on Linguistic Units and Levels*, (pp. 193–247). Chicago: Chicago Linguistic Society.

Street, B.V. (1995). *Social Literacies: Critical Approaches to Literacy in Development, Ethnography and Education*. London and New York: Longman.

Sugiura, Y. (2008). *Keitai Shousetu no Riaru [The Reality of Keitai Novels]*.Tokyo: Chuuou Kouron Shinsha.

Tagliamonte, S.A., & Denis, D. (2008). Linguistic ruin? LOL! Instant messaging and teen language. *American Speech*, 83(1), 3–34.

Thurlow, C. (2006). From statistical panic to moral panic: The metadiscursive construction and popular exaggeration of new media. *Journal of Computer-Mediated Communication* 11, 667–701.

Tohan. (2007). Literary section best sellers for 2007. Retrieved April 2010 from http://www.tohan.jp/cat2/year/2007_2/

Yamazaki, K. (Ed.). (2006). *Keitai Denwa no Kaiwa Bunseki [Conversation Analysis of Mobile Phone Communication]*. Tokyo: Taishuukan.

Yoshida, S. (2008). Keitai Shosetsu Ga Ukeru Riyuu *[The Reason Why Keitai Novels Work]*. Tokyo: Mainichi Communications.

Chapter 6

Micro-Blogging and Status Updates on Facebook: *Texts and Practices*

Carmen K. M. Lee

"Thanx to internet, my spelling sucks!!!"
"Facebook killed my grammar"
"You should have to take a literacy test before being able to join Facebook"

THESE ARE SOME of the titles of public, shared-interest "groups" on the social network site, *Facebook*. What is interesting about these titles is that such accusations concerning poor literacy skills have been with us for over a decade, especially in English-speaking contexts (see, for example, the media reports discussed in Thurlow, 2007, 2011). The negative correlation between technologies and people's lives has spread cross-culturally; for example, it has been reported that young children in Hong Kong who spend more than an hour a day on texting, instant messaging, discussion forums, and blogs have lower reading skills in both Chinese and English (*Singtao Daily*, 2008). Needless to say, what is missing in reports like this and public discussions is how new media and their associated practices are already deeply embedded in people's everyday lives, and, in the case of students, their out-of-school lives. An important characteristic of new media is that, despite their multimodal and multimedia possibilities, they still involve extensive use of the written word. In fact, a growing body of research now shows that young people's new media use may actually enhance their standard language practices (e.g., Plester & Wood, 2009; Plester et al., 2008). It is this interplay between conventional literacy and so-called "new literacies" that is the focus of my chapter.

The study I report here grows out of a broader program of research on the emerging literacy practices of Cantonese-English bilinguals in Hong Kong. In this case, however, my focus is on microblogging and specifically the status-updating feature of *Facebook*. (See also Jones et al., Chapter 2 of this volume.) While the group titles previously mentioned uphold a "deficit" view of writing and language use on the internet, they nonetheless reveal *Facebook* users' linguistic awareness and their abilities to reflect on what is happening to their written language. This is why my chapter is grounded in contemporary literacy studies (e.g., Barton, 2007; Gee, 1996; Street, 1984; see also Nishimura, Chapter 5 of this volume) as a way to explore the creative practice and social meanings of *Facebook*'s status updates feature. In particular, I have two research questions: (a) What primary communicative functions do status updates serve? And, perhaps more importantly, (b) how are status updates embedded meaningfully and creatively in the everyday lives of *Facebook* users?

Microblogging refers to the writing of short messages on the web designed for self-reporting about what one is doing, thinking, or feeling at any moment. This can be performed on stand-alone microblogging platforms like *Twitter* or on social network sites such as *Facebook*. As of April 2010, over 100 million user accounts had been created on *Twitter* (*The Economic Times*, 2010), attracting people from all over the world, including many parts of Asia and Europe (Semiocast, 2010). Participants microblog or "tweet" for various reasons, such as sharing information, interacting with friends, or discussing current affairs (Java et al., 2007; Zhao & Rosson, 2009). Lenhart and Fox (2009) report that 75% of active *Twitter* users in the USA update their status through their mobile phones, PDAs (personal digital assistants), or laptops. *Twitter* users are, it seems, always on the go. Or this is how they want to appear to others.

The status updates feature on *Facebook* is similar to that of *Twitter* in that it works mainly with a prompt ("What's on your mind?") and a text box ("Publisher box") that appear at the top of a user's homepage and personal profile ("wall"). When I first studied status updates in late 2007, the prompt was "What are you doing right now?", and users had to begin the post with their first name and then the verb "*is*" appeared automatically (e.g., "Carmen *is writing*"). Later, however, *Facebook* removed the "is" to offer greater flexibility; in March 2009, the prompt was also changed to "What's on your mind?" Unexpected design (or affordance) changes such as these pose real challenges for internet researchers (see Introduction to this volume), but they are also a perfect opportunity for tracing creative adaptations in people's new media textual practices.

In terms of modes of interaction, status updates combine the affordances of personal blogs, *Twitter*, IM, and texting. In this sense, they exemplify the generic hybridity of so many new media spaces/formats (see also Spilioti, Chapter 4 of this volume). Originally designed as a self-report technology, status updates have become increasingly interactive and dialogic, especially with the introduction of the "Comments" and the "Like" functions. In terms of length, a status update on *Facebook* can be as long as 420 alphanumeric characters, which is much longer than the limit on *Twitter* or SMS texting. Like *Twitter, Facebook* status messages can be posted, read, and responded to from a mobile device. The current version of *Facebook* also allows users to post various multimedia content such as web addresses, photos, and videos. Heralded as a quintessential Web 2.0 application, *Facebook* clearly demonstrates multimodality (cf. Kress & van Leeuwen, 2006), intertextuality and convergence (cf. Androutsopoulos, 2010), and mash-up (cf. O'Reilly, 2007)—the coexistence of various formerly separate web spaces and media in one single platform.

Microblogging as Literacy Practice

To date, compared with other short messaging systems such as texting and IM, microblogging, an activity in which the written word is central, has received little attention in new media discourse studies. What research there is on microblogging has focused largely on *Twitter*. One good example of this work is Honeycutt and Herring's (2009) quantitative study of the functions of the @ sign and the conversationality of *Twitter* messages. However, as Honeycutt and Herring themselves point out, "analyses of user-created content ... should be supplemented with ethnographic studies and interviews with *Twitter* and non-*Twitter* users" (p. 9). Certainly, if microblogging is to be understood in terms of (new) literacies, the focus needs to shift away from the technology per se toward an analysis of its use as a creative, cultural practice (cf. Thurlow & Bell, 2009).

In this regard, the field of "new literacies" (Coiro et al., 2008) or media literacy (Buckingham, 2007) has emerged in recent years to explore the ways in which technologies are shaping and changing the meanings and nature of text, reading, and writing. Kress and van Leeuwen (2006) show how modern texts, whether print-based or web-based, are increasingly multimodal, combining various modes of representation such as words, images, and sounds. My own understanding of new media texts is grounded in a social theory of literacy, or what is often referred to as New

Literacy Studies (Barton, 2007; Baynham, 1995; Gee, 1996; Street, 1984). One of the key units of analysis here is "literacy practice" as the particular "cultural ways of utilising literacy" (Barton & Hamilton, 1998, p. 7). Another important contribution of this area of research is its focus on people's "everyday" or "local" literacy practices that are not usually valued by dominant institutions such as education and government. This approach fits in well with research that focuses on young people's "out-of-school" digital lives (Buckingham, 2007; Ito et al., 2010). Methodologically, most work within new literacy studies is ethnographically oriented, aiming to understand practices from an insider's perspective, which also provides interesting insights for understanding new media writing.

With these conceptions and background in mind, it is not surprising that genre theorists and literacy researchers have begun to bring together these two approaches. A great deal has been done to understand the situated nature of academic literacies in higher education (Lea & Street, 1998), including academic writing (Hyland, 2007). In my own research, I started by offering largely descriptive accounts of generic features of e-mail and instant messaging (see Lee, 2007b) but later began thinking about what I call "text-making practices" as a subset of literacy practices that considers the ways in which people choose and transform resources for representing meanings in the form of texts for different purposes (Lee, 2007c). This notion better captures the situated nature of written texts and shifts attention more specifically to the production and representational aspects of texts. Understanding new media discourse this way means observing particular ways people create and use texts, and investigating the *how* and the *why* of their text making. In this way, people's perceptions, feelings, and values are also taken into consideration. This is the approach I mean to demonstrate in my chapter here, moving through a descriptive account of status updates as texts to a more ethnographic case study of status updates as situated practice. These two stages also align with the two main research questions I identified in this chapter.

My Research Design and Data

My study adopted a virtual ethnographic approach to data collection and analysis (Hine, 2005), involving a qualitative content analysis of status updates, online interviews, and observation of individual *Facebook* profiles. As a convenience sample, the study reported in this chapter involved 20 of my own *Facebook* contacts, all of whom were Cantonese-English bilinguals in Hong Kong. A total of 744 status messages were collected from these coparticipants—372 were collected over a period of three months before *Facebook* removed the obligatory "is" from the status updates prompt, and the rest were collected over the three months after the "is" was removed and the prompt changed. Some participants were frequent posters and updated their status at least a few times a week while some did not update for a week at a time or even longer. Informed consent was sought electronically (i.e., participants wrote to me to indicate that they agreed to take part in the study). Because of the expected nonanonymity of *Facebook* profiles, I also asked if they agreed to reveal their real names in my publications, and if not, they could pick their own pseudonyms.

The first step was to carry out a traditional content analysis of the status updates collected. For the purpose of this study, the coding scheme focused on the primary communicative functions and the language(s) of the messages, thus covering the two basic aspects of text-making practices—production and use. The coding scheme was partly "directed" by previous research findings, while new codes were also derived from the data in question. My initial observation of the texts suggested that status updates were highly similar to away messages in terms of their technological affordances (e.g., short, intended to be one-way and asynchronous) and functions (e.g., self-reporting of personal information) (cf. Baron et al., 2005). After several readings of the data, new themes emerged, and some of Baron et al.'s categories were modified to better suit the status updates context. Given the small sample size and the ethnographic orientation of the research, only basic counting of codes was performed. The figures presented in this chapter aim to offer some preliminary insights into the possible message types. Comparing the two sets of status updates also helped understand the extent to which people reappropriated their text-making practices in face of changing technological affordances as well as their changing conditions in life (e.g., studying abroad, starting a new job, and even pregnancy). Findings from this basic content analysis of texts also served as a basis for the follow-up online interviews—a more discourse-ethnographic approach like the one Androutsopoulos (2008) has advocated.

While the first stage of my research was structured "horizontally" (Barton & Hamilton, 1998) by analyzing *texts* produced by different users, the second stage was organized more "vertically" by examining individual users' localized *practices*. This second phase of the study observed specific participants' *Facebook* profiles and "walls," focusing on the ways in which status updates were connected to other areas of *Facebook* and beyond. This was then followed by e-mail interviews with 10 participants to better understand their insider's perspective of status updates and new media use. The participants were all interviewed via *Facebook*'s private e-mail function. At the participants' requests, further exchanges were possible via e-mail.

Status Updates as Texts: Communicative Function and Language Choice

Understanding text-making practices involves studying the *use* of texts, including the communicative functions that texts serve. The status updates I collected were categorized into 11 basic functions, some of which were developed from Baron et al.'s (2005) categories for away messages while some were inferred from the data (see Categories 1, 9, and 11 following this paragraph). In the following, I provide descriptions and examples for these functions to provide a snapshot of the possible ways of using status updates, followed by a summary of the distribution of each message type before and after the change of *Facebook* prompt:

1. ***"What are you doing right now?"***: This type of status update was a direct response to the original *Facebook* prompt, and messages were constrained by the technological affordances of *Facebook* (i.e., starting the message with "is" and speaking as a third person).

   - Claudia is listening to Chris Brown's With You...
   - Frances is struggling with the assignment, exam and final project.

2. ***Everyday life***: In this type of status update, the participants talked about activities in their day-to-day life, including domestic and work-related topics.

   - Bates had a lot of meetings this Monday.
   - Katy just received a nice call from a friend in U.A.E.

3. ***Opinion and judgment***: Messages of this type expressed and revealed the participants' beliefs about themselves and others.

   - Snow can't believe CZZ thinks that's a weird book!
   - Ariel thinks that no news is good news.

4. ***Reporting mood***: Mood messages expressed participants' inner feelings and emotions, whether positive or negative.

   - Peter is feeling so BAAAAAAAD!!!
   - Amy is in a good mood.

5. **Away message**: Away messages on *Facebook* were similar to those on IM (i.e., letting people know the user is momentarily not at their computer); but at the same time, "away" messages on *Facebook* seemed to have a lower degree of immediacy, with messages indicating the poster's absence in the past or future.

- Nelson <u>goes to China on Feb 21 & 22.</u>
- Angie <u>will fly to Seoul tomorrow morning.</u>

6. **Initiating discussion**: This type of message often consisted of open-ended questions with an aim of eliciting responses and comments elsewhere on the personal profile.

- Claudia: <u>Is there anything we could do for the Haitians? The whole country is RUINED now...</u>
- Peggy<u>: "點解我句　status msg 會自動消失?"</u> (*"Why has my status message disappeared?"*)

7. **Addressing target audience**: As the code suggests, this type of message was directed to a specific audience but not all *Facebook* contacts.

- Katy : <u>take care my love.....</u>
- Joey : <u>Just want to say Merry Christmas to all of my friends and your families here in facebook</u>!

8. **Quotation**: This category of messages shared quotes of songs and famous sayings.

- Amy: <u>'Learn from yesterday, serve for today and hope for tomorrow' What a meaningful and thoughtful saying from Rev. Stephen Leung's sharing meeting today afternoon!</u>)
- Snow is <u>"I've seen you in the shadow"</u>.

9. **Silence and interjection**: This type of playful message expressed "speechlessness" through punctuation marks such as a series of ellipsis or question marks.

- Peter : <u>...................</u>
- Katy : <u>?</u>

10. **Humor**: Humorous messages occurred when the user made jokes or used (visual) language play.

- Uranus is <u>Uranus is Uranus is Uranus is Uranus is Uranus is Uranus is Uranus is Uranus is Uranus is Uranus is Uranus is Uranus is Uranus is Uranus is Uranus.</u>
- Peter : <u>Security: XXXX 2882 or XXXX 2401 (hahaha)</u>

11. **Facebook-related discourse**: This last type of message often expressed opinions about *Facebook* and its technological affordances.

- Claudia <u>hates the new FB interface.</u>
- Kenneth <u>quitting facebook.</u>

Figure 6.1 offers an overview of the use of different communicative functions before and after the *Facebook* prompt "What are you doing right now?" and the obligatory "is" were removed. The relatively high percentage of messages expressing personal opinions, judgments, or beliefs about themselves, other people, or events (Category 3) suggests that the participants often ignored the mechanical constraints imposed by *Facebook*; in other words, only a handful of messages actually answered the *Facebook* prompt (Category 1). It is these messages about personal feelings and states of mind that allow users to project their identity on- and offline just as IM away messages might do (Baron et al., 2005). Another aspect of self-reporting was the sharing of everyday activities, which could range from what was eaten at lunch to short personal narratives of "breaking news" (cf. Page, 2010). This tendency to post messages about oneself continued even after the *Facebook* prompt was changed to "What's on your mind," although my sample is too small to know for certain whether this was the

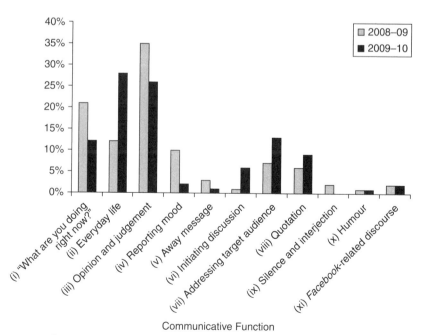

FIGURE 6.1

case in other instances of status updates. However, based on what is already known about texting (Thurlow, 2003; Thurlow & Poff, 2011) and away messages (Baron et al., 2005), communicating mundane and day-to-day topics does seem to be a persistent function of short new media messaging.

Facebook status updates are not as monologic as they seem; some can be highly interactive and relational in nature. The sharing of quotes and links was only one of many ways to relate to target readers. Some participants would use this space to communicate with one particular person, or a selected group of people (Category 7), while other messages were designed to elicit feedback (Category 6)—even if, as Knobel & Lankshear (2008) note, responses are seldom expected. The removal of the original prompt ("What are you doing right now?") definitely offered greater flexibility for the participants to write interactive messages, as indicated by the increased proportion of messages explicitly initiating discussions, addressing a target audience, and sharing quotes. Another way of relating to others was the use of humor. For example, Uranus played with *Facebook*'s affordance (the default "is") by repeating the first two words "Uranus is" 15 times (Category 10). Of course, playfulness is a core activity in many new media contexts (Danet, 2001; Thurlow, 2011), and verbal/visual play often serves phatic functions in short messaging. Perhaps in the relatively public environment of *Facebook*, users feel even more motivated to show off their wit and creativity, allowing target readers to display their own cyber literacy in comments and responses (Katsuno & Yano, 2007). I am well aware that the multifunctionality (or *polyphony*—see Jones et al., Chapter 2 of this volume) of language means that a message like "Kenneth *doesn't want to tell you what he is doing now*" not only may literally express the poster's feeling in the moment but also indicates his playful resisting of the conventional function of status updates by responding to the *Facebook* prompt negatively. As such, even though most messages were not classified primarily as "humor," they could still be perceived as jokes by the reader. Notwithstanding this, my preliminary findings offer a broad understanding of how status updates can be used to serve a wide range of communicative functions, and the extent to which the status updating has become a crucial aspect of everyday life.

In addition to these ways of *using* status updates, the language and style adopted in the *production* of the status messages are a crucial aspect of text-making practices. For example, one of the essential practices for bilingual online users is negotiating language choice (see Danet & Herring, 2007). About 60% of the status messages I collected before *Facebook* changed the prompt to "What's on your mind" were written predominantly in English.

However, more Chinese and mixed-code messages were identified in the more recent corpus (i.e., after the removal of the constraining "is"). This seems to suggest that the participants became more used to perceiving *Facebook* as a multilingual medium, partly because of the availability of *Facebook* in various languages and the easier processing of and access to non-Roman writing systems on the web. In Hong Kong–based new media discourse, a notable feature is code switching, especially in IM (Fung & Carter, 2007; Lee, 2007b), but this is less so in the data in the present study. One possible explanation is that code switching is more common in face-to-face oral communication than in writing (Li, 2002). Synchronous new media such as IM and online chat are designed to resemble the immediacy and interactivity of face-to-face talk, which motivates multilingual users to code-switch as they would do in a conversation. Status updating, however, is essentially a "delayed" mode of communication like e-mail and online forums, and thus bilingual users do not feel as strong a need to mix languages as they do in face-to-face talk or online chatting. All this also echoes recent findings about the reduced use of English on *Twitter* (Semiocasts, 2010).

With regard to the English posts collected, not so surprisingly, the sentence structures became more varied and creative since the prompt "What are you doing right now?" and the obligatory "is" were removed from *Facebook*. In the interviews, the participants frequently reflected upon their status-updating experiences by referring to linguistic terms as in "*It depends on the aspect of the verb and the tense*" (Peter) and "*I still keep saying things with a gerund after deleting the 'is' from the interface*" (Frances). Through such comments, the participants were reconstructing their own theories of "folk linguistics" (Niedzielski & Preston, 2000) or folk grammatical rules for their status updates. Such rules were often formulated according to *Facebook*'s technological affordances (e.g., the presence and absence of "is"). These metalinguistic views, together with language choice, gradually became part of the participants' resources for defining the "genre" of status updates.

Status Updates as Situated Practice: The Case of Peggy

While the previous section offered a snapshot of the wide-ranging communicative functions (and stylistic choices) of status updates as *texts*, I want now to consider just one of my participants, Peggy, in order to illustrate the social meanings of status updates as an integrated literacy *practice*.

Peggy was an experienced new media user, having regularly used e-mail and instant messaging (ICQ and MSN Messenger) since her high school days. She was also a regular informant in my research program. Our personal connection allowed me to situate her current online practices in her own new media history, which presents itself as one of the best examples of the embeddedness of new media in people's lives and of the "mash-up-ability" of new technologies. Peggy spends a great deal of time online every day with her computer at home and with her mobile phone. At work, she keeps in touch with friends and colleagues via IM and e-mail. At the time of writing, she had been an active blogger for almost 5 years, posting about a wide range of topics such as work and family events, her travel plans, and other random thoughts. Peggy joined *Facebook* in 2006 (the year it went fully public), but she used to be less active on *Facebook* than on her blog. When first asked to talk about how she used status updates, Peggy sounded rather indifferent and indicated that she generally ignored the prompt:

> *There are many places for writing on Facebook like the 'wall'.[...] I don't care what its intended function is. I just write whatever I want to say.*
>
> (Peggy, translated[1])

The convergence or collocation of different new media is, of course, a typical feature of social network sites such as *Facebook* where various tools or discursive opportunities exist side by side (see Androutsopoulos, 2010, and Chapter 13 of this volume for more on this). Elsewhere I suggest that technological affordances are not taken up automatically, however, but must be perceived by the users as worthwhile and meaningful (Lee, 2007a). For example, Peggy told me that she often wrote her status updates in Chinese because it was "more expressive." In looking at her posts myself, however, I noticed that many were, in fact, written in English, especially when posted from Peggy's mobile phone where typing Chinese would be more time consuming than typing in English.

Peggy often considered her blog to be the primary, public platform for sharing her thoughts and life, and she used to update her *Facebook* status messages only after updating her blog. What she wrote in her status updates were often summaries of selected blog entries. For example, her status update on October 8, 2008, "好嬲!!!!!!!!" ("*very angry!!!!!!*"), was actually the first line and the main subject of her blog entry on the same day. This is only one of many instances of her microblogging her main blog posts into short and concise status updates. (Occasionally, the same message might also be expressed in yet another way on her MSN "mood" message text box.) These cross-media practices demonstrate Peggy's ability to carefully and creatively deploy a "portfolio" of new media in ways that work with the different technological affordances of the media and that suit her own communicative needs.

A major turning point in Peggy's *Facebook* activities was the time when she found out that she was pregnant. Since then, much of what she posted on both *Facebook* and her blog was almost exclusively about her pregnancy, starting with the status update "*Peggy is pregnant!! =v=*" on November 25, 2008. It was then that Peggy also took up the multimodal affordances of the media. In addition to words, her pregnancy was represented through images, including ultrasound X-ray images of her baby (Figure 6.2), who was given the screen name YatYat before being given a "proper" name.[2] Posts also recorded Peggy's physical and emotional changes during her pregnancy, while regularly counting down to the due date ("*count down, 40 days left*"). As is often the case in other countries, traditional Chinese women do not reveal their pregnancy until the end of the first trimester (i.e., after three months). Peggy, however, broke this rule in her first month by posting ambiguous messages such as "4cm...you are so lovely" (which was later followed up with the ultrasound images). In this way, *Facebook* (and other new media) were never separable from Peggy's immediate, embodied experiences during her pregnancy.

When Peggy eventually went into labor at the hospital, she made the most of *Facebook* starting with the status update "@hospital." As the screenshot in Figure 6.3 shows, she then kept updating her status every few hours. (I have translated those status messages originally written in Cantonese and underlined them.) The mobile phone icon underneath the status message indicates that the updates were sent from a mobile device.

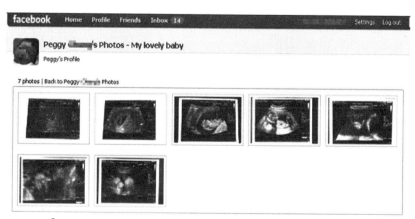

FIGURE 6.2

FIGURE 6.3

What becomes apparent is that each major phase of Peggy's labor was reported on *Facebook*. In wanting to keep her friends up to date on this long birth, it was clearly important for her to express an online presence and to have people be there (cf. Davies, 2007)—materialized (or textualized) in the large number of comments that she received within a few hours. This is how Peggy explained things herself:

I was so much in pain. I felt so miserable. I had to cheer myself up by talking to my husband and using my mobile phone to get in touch with friends on Facebook.

(Translated from Chinese.)

Just minutes after her long labor, Peggy announced on *Facebook*, "*After over 20 hours of labor, yatyat was born!*" This instantly attracted 25 comments congratulating Peggy and welcoming her new daughter. When Peggy returned home, she resorted to her blog in a post titled "A life of three has begun" and adding more details about what had happened in the hospital together with photos of her baby. Since then, she has gone back to blogging and posting summaries of her blog content regularly on *Facebook*.

Peggy's case illustrates at least two important issues in relation to new media use in contemporary life. First, Peggy's ability to move between media and text types (blogging and microblogging) demonstrates nicely what Thomas (2008) refers to as "transliteracies," the ability to travel seamlessly across different textual landscapes. In Peggy's case, this ability also involved employing different communicative practices in different media. Her online text-making practices were also "hypermodal" (Lemke, 2002) and intertextual, with words connecting to images and other texts within and beyond *Facebook* (cf. Androutsopoulos, 2010). The story of Peggy also makes the case for the domestication of new media (Berker et al., 2005; Silverstone & Haddon, 1996). Being "always on," as she was, certainly also blurred the boundary between Peggy's online and offline lives, and between her public and private personae.

Conclusion

While some *Facebook* users—perhaps prompted by external voices—may be worried about falling standards of grammar and spelling, many others seem quite prepared to resist the need to conform to standards: *"When I'm on Facebook, i dont give a shit about grammar"* and *"I like to spell it that way, stop trying to correct me Facebook chat!"*—both group titles on *Facebook*! In either case, what often gets overlooked are the emergent literacies (so-called "new literacies") in the practices of many new media users. From both the descriptive analysis and the more ethnographic account I have presented here, I hope to have drawn attention to a number of important characteristics about microblogging and status updates on *Facebook*.

Perhaps most importantly, status updates are hardly one coherent written genre, but a hybrid of genre features identified in different text types, from IM to texting and blogging. New media users seldom employ the same set of genre conventions in all instances. As Androutsopoulos (2010) suggests, new media users have become "intertextual operators" who regularly edit multimodal and multimedia materials across different online platforms and for different purposes. Such fluidity of genres and practices is further evidence of the emergent literacies in new media. Reading and writing are never simply a set of skills that people apply uniformly to all situations; instead, literacy is best understood as practices situated in everyday social contexts.

Barton and Hamilton (1998, p. 7) note that literacy practices "change, and new ones are frequently acquired through processes of informal learning and sense making." To a certain extent, using *Facebook* and other new media can be treated as an ongoing informal learning process through actively participating in a "friends-driven" networked public (Ito et al., 2010). New media users continuously make sense of various linguistic and nonlinguistic resources that they have created and come across on different platforms, and they generate suitable text-making practices for different purposes and audiences. Moreover, everyday online experiences are highly textually mediated (Barton, 2001), involving producing and using multimodal texts on multiple platforms. It is commonplace to see someone checking e-mail and text messages on a mobile phone, while playing a game on *Facebook*, chatting with friends on IM, and listening to music at the same time. Although these new literacies have become a crucial part of people's everyday activities, such private and self-generated practices are not always valued by dominant institutions. The ongoing "deficit" discourses about how illiterate people have become tend to focus on the possible impact of new technologies on the younger generation (as discussed in Thurlow, 2007). However, it has become obvious that new media are no longer owned by young people. Many of those teenage "victims" of the negative new media discourses we heard 10 years ago have grown up and continued to engage in various creative text-making activities and communicative practices. With the popularity of affordable mobile technologies, adults now constitute a large proportion of the "always on" generation. Recent research already reveals that there are more adult than teenage users on *Twitter* (Martin, 2009). Peggy is only one of many typical young adult media users in the contemporary world. At the same time, scholars have also acknowledged the importance of helping students to recognize new media language (Baron, 2005) and how social technologies may be incorporated into the classroom context (Castro, 2007; Kinzie et al., 2005). Nowadays, being able to deploy multimodal resources is also recognized as an important asset (Carrington, 2005).

Much of today's public discourse about technologies in mass media, and to a lesser extent, in academic research, tends to fall into the trap of the novelty of some underexplored technologies. However, people enjoy using *Facebook* not because it is new but because of the range of creative communicative practices it can afford to represent their lives. Likewise, while emphasizing the newness of technologies, new media researchers should also consider the actual discourses embedded in and associated with them and their relationship with other media. Researching media texts also involves connecting texts and the literacy practices, both of which are crucial in understanding the production and use of writing. Without looking closely at media texts, we would not be able to understand the actual linguistic "products" of technologies, and without observing users' authentic activities and beliefs about what they do online, we would not be able to see the dynamics of text-making practices.

Acknowledgments

I am very grateful to David Barton and two anonymous reviewers for their insightful comments on an earlier draft of this chapter, and to Crispin Thurlow for his editorial support with the final draft.

Notes

1. Participants answered my interview questions in either Chinese or English. "Translated" here indicates that Peggy's answer was written in Chinese and later translated by me.
2. All images in this section were sent to Peggy for approval. She made suggestions as to what should be blurred and what could be shown without editing (e.g., her baby's face). However, since I had no access to her friends' *Facebook* profiles, all of her friends' faces and names are also blurred in this chapter to preserve anonymity.

References

Androutsopoulos, J. (2008). Potentials and limitations of discourse-centred online ethnography, *Language@Internet 5*, article 9. Available at http://www.languageatinternet.de/articles/2008/1610/index_html/

Androutsopoulos, J. (2010). Localising the global on the participatory web. In N. Coupland (Ed.), *Handbook of Language and Globalisation*, (pp. 203–231). Oxford: Blackwell.

Baron, N. (2005). Instant messaging and the future of language. *Communication of the ACM 48*, (7), 29–31.

Baron, N. S., Squires, L., Tench, S., & Thompson, M. (2005). Tethered or mobile? Use of away messages in instant messaging by American college students. In R. Ling & P. Pedersen (Eds.), *Mobile Communications: Re-Negotiation of the Social Sphere*, (pp. 293–311). London: Springer-Verlag.

Barton, D. (2001). Directions for literacy research: Analyzing language and social practices in a textually mediated world. *Language and Education 15* (2–3), 92–104.

Barton, D. (2007). *Literacy: An Introduction to the Ecology of Written Language.* Oxford: Blackwell.

Barton, D., & Hamilton, M. (1998). *Local Literacies.* London: Routledge.

Baynham, M. (1995). *Literacy Practices.* London: Longman.

Berker, T., Hartmann, M., Punie, Y., & Ward, K. (Eds.). (2005). *Domestication of Media and Technology.* Maidenhead, UK: Open University Press.

Buckingham, D. (2007). Digital media literacies: Rethinking media education in the age of the internet. *Research in Comparative and International Education,* 2(1), 43–55.

Carrington, V. (2005). The uncanny, digital texts and literacy. *Language and Education,* 19(6), 467–482.

Castro, M. (2007). The use of microblogging in language education. *Proceedings of the third international wireless ready symposium.* Retrieved June 26, 2010, from http://opinion.nucba.ac.jp/~thomas/castro2009.pdf

Coiro, J., Knobel, M., Lankshear, C., & Leu. D. J. (Eds.). (2008). *Handbook of Research on New Literacies.* New York and Oxford: Lawrence Earlbaum Associates.

Danet, B. (2001). *Cyberpl@y: Communicating online.* Oxford: Berg Publishers. Companion website: http://pluto.huji.ac.il/~msdanet/cyberpl@y/

Danet, B., & Herring, S.C. (Eds.). (2007). *The Multilingual Internet: Language, Culture and Communication Online*: New York & Oxford: Oxford University Press.

Davies, J. (2007). Display, identity and the everyday: Self-presentation through online image sharing. *Discourse 28*(4), 549–564.

Economic Times. (2010). Twitter snags over 100 million users, eyes money-making. April 15. Retrieved on June 26, 2010, from http://economictimes. indiatimes.com/infotech/internet/Twitter-snags-over-100-million-users-eyes-money-making/articleshow/5808927.cms

Fung, L., & Carter, R. (2007). New varieties, new creativities: ICQ and English-Cantonese e-discourse. *Language and Literature 16*, 345–366.

Gee, J.P. (1996). *Social Linguistics and Literacies.* London: Routledge.

Hine, C. (2005). *Virtual Methods.* Oxford: Berg.

Honeycutt, C., & Herring, S.C. (2009). Beyond microblogging: Conversation and collaboration via Twitter, HICSS, pp.1–10, *Proceedings of the 42nd Hawaii International Conference on System Sciences.* Los Alamitos, CA: IEEE Press.

Hyland, K. (2007). Genre pedagogy: Language, literacy and L2 writing instruction. *Journal of Pragmatics,* 16(3), 148–164.

Ito, M., Baumer, S., Bittanti, M., Boyd, D., Cody, R., Herr, B., et al. (2010). *Hanging Out, Messing Around, Geeking Out: Living and Learning with New Media.* Cambridge, MA: MIT Press.

Java, A., Song, X., Finn, T., & Tseng, B. (2007). Why we twitter: Understanding microblogging usage and communities. *Proceedings of the Joint 9th WEBKDD and 1st SNA-KDD Workshop 2007,* (pp. 56–65). New York: ACM.

Katsuno, H., & Yano, C. (2007). *Kaomoji* and expressivity in a Japanese house-wives' chat room. In B. Danet & S.C. Herring. (Eds.). *The Multilingual Internet: Language, Culture, and Communication Online* (pp. 278–302), New York & Oxford: Oxford University Press.

Kinzie, M.B., Whitaker, S.D., & Hofer, M.J. (2005). Instructional uses of Instant Messaging (IM) during classroom lectures. *Educational Technology & Society*, 8(2), 150–160.

Knobel, M., & Lankshear, C. (2008). Digital literacy and participation in on-line social networking spaces. In C. Lankshear & M. Knobel (Eds.), *Digital Literacies*, (pp. 249–278). New York: Peter Lang.

Kress, G., & van Leeuwen, T. (2006). *Reading Images: The Grammar of Visual Design*. London: Routledge.

Lea, M., & Street, B.V. (1998). Student writing in higher education: An academic literacies approach. *Studies in Higher Education, 23*(2), 157–172.

Lee, C.K.M. (2007a). Affordances and text-making practices in online instant messaging. *Written Communication, 24*(3), 223–249.

Lee, C.K.M. (2007b). Linguistic features of e-mail and ICQ instant messaging in Hong Kong. In B. Danet & S.C. Herring (Eds.), *The Multilingual Internet: Language, Culture and Communication Online*, (pp. 184–208). New York & Oxford: Oxford University Press.

Lee, C.K.M. (2007c). Text-making practices beyond the classroom context: Private instant messaging in Hong Kong. *Computers and Composition, 24*(3), 285–301.

Lemke, J.L. (2002). Travels in hypermodality. *Visual Communication, 1*(3), 299–325.

Lenhart, A., & Fox, S. (2009). Twitter and status updating. *Pew Internet and American Life Project*, Retrieved on June 26, 2010, from http://fortysouth.com/wp-content/uploads/2009/05/Twitter-and-status-updating.pdf

Li, D.C.S. (2002). Cantonese-English code-switching research in Hong Kong: A survey of recent research. In K. Bolton (Ed.), *Hong Kong English: Autonomy and Creativity*, (pp. 79–99). Hong Kong: Hong Kong University Press.

Martin, D. (2009). Teens Don't Tweet: Twitter's Growth Not Fueled by Youth. Retrieved on June 26, 2010, from http://blog.nielsen.com/nielsenwire/online_mobile/teens-dont-tweet-twitters-growth-not-fueled-by-youth/

Niedzielski, N.A., & Preston, D.R. (2000). *Folk Linguistics*. Berlin: Mouton de Gruyter.

O'Reilly, T. (2007). What Is Web 2.0? Retrieved July 21, 2010, from http://mpra.ub.uni-muenchen.de/4578/

Page, R. (2010). Re-examining narrativity: Small stories in status updates. *Text & Talk, 30*(4), 423–444.

Plester, B., & Wood, C. (2009). Exploring relationships between traditional and new media literacies: British preteen texters at school. *Journal of Computer Mediated Communication, 14*(4), 1108–1129.

Plester, B., Wood, C., & Bell, V. (2008). Text msg in school literacy: Does texting and knowledge of text abbreviations adversely affect children's literacy attainment? *Literacy* 42(3), 137–144.

Semiocast (2010). Half of messages on Twitter are not in English Japanese is the second most used language. Retrieved on June 26, 2010, from http://semiocast.com/downloads/Semiocast_Half_of_messages_on_Twitter_are_not_in_English_20100224.pdf

Silverstone, R., & Haddon, L. (1996). Design and the domestication of information and communication technologies: Technical change and everyday life. In R. Mansell & R. Silverstone (Eds.), *Communication by Design: The Politics of Information and Communication Technologies*, (pp. 44–74). New York: Oxford University Press.

Singtao Daily. (2008). 小四生中英文閱讀有進步 (*Primary four students shown improvement in Chinese and English reading abilities*), July 10.

Street, B. V. (1984). *Literacy in Theory and Practice*. Cambridge: Cambridge University Press.

Thomas, S. (2008). Transliteracy and new media. In R. Adams, S. Gibson, & S. Arisona (Eds.), *Transdisciplinary Digital Art. Sound, Vision and the New Screen*, (pp. 101–109). Berlin: Springer.

Thurlow, C. (2003). Generation Txt? The sociolinguistics of young people's text-messaging. *Discourse Analysis Online* 1(1). Retrieved on June 26, 2010, from http://extra.shu.ac.uk/daol/articles/v1/n1/a3/thurlow2002003-paper.html

Thurlow, C. (2007). Fabricating youth: New media discourse and the technologization of young people. In S. Johnson & A. Ensslin (Eds.), *Language in the Media*, (pp. 213–233). London: Continuum.

Thurlow, C. (2011). Determined creativity: Language play, vernacular literacy and new media discourse. In R. Jones (Ed.), *Discourse and Creativity*. London: Pearson.

Thurlow, C., & Bell, K. (2009). Against technologization: Young people's new media discourse as creative cultural practice. *Journal of Computer-Mediated Communication*, 14(4), 1038–1049.

Thurlow, C., and Poff, M. (2011). Text messaging. In S.C. Herring, D. Stein, & T. Virtanen (Eds.), *Handbook of the Pragmatics of CMC*. Berlin: Mouton de Gruyter.

Zhao, D., & Rosson, M. B. (2009). How and why people Twitter: The role that micro-blogging plays in informal communication at work. *Proceedings of the ACM 2009 International Conference on Supporting Group Work*, (pp. 243–252). New York: ACM.

PART THREE

Style and Stylization:
Identity Play and Semiotic Invention

Chapter 7

Multimodal Creativity and Identities of Expertise in the Digital Ecology of a World of Warcraft Guild

Lisa Newon

RECREATIONAL INTERACTIVE GAMES are an increasingly popular genre of new media. The interactive entertainment industries of the United States, Japan, China, South Korea, Canada, and Western Europe produce thousands of video games annually, which are consumed by players globally. These games are broad in scope and include genres like action, shooter, role-playing, and simulation, across technologies like mobile phones, game consoles, and personal computers.

Roughly 12 million people subscribe to *World of Warcraft* (Blizzard Entertainment, 2004–2011), making it the most widely played massively multiplayer online role-playing game (MMORPG) on the global market. MMORPGs, developed for the personal computer, are set in fantasy worlds where players interact by assuming the roles of created avatar characters. Players progress through these games by completing game tasks that often require collaboration among several gamers. These games are described as "massively multiplayer" in that they are continuously populated and accessible to subscribers. Game servers host thousands of individual players who are situated throughout the world, and who together construct an online environment that is constantly awake and in motion (Yee, 2006).

The MMORPG is an interactive space where players initiate participation with considerable anonymity. Players design avatars (see Figure 7.1)—a virtual representation of themselves—by selectively combining character appearances, attributes, and skills that are often unrelated to their

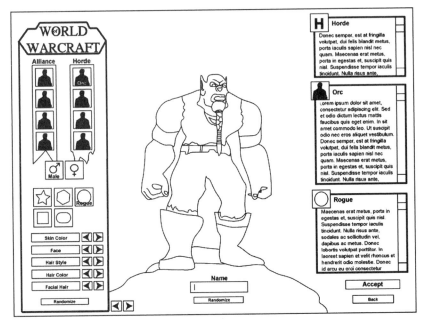

FIGURE 7.1

personas offline.[1] For example, a player may choose a male avatar belonging to the race of "Orc" and the stealth class of "rogue." Thus, the structural framework of the MMORPG requires players to actively engage in deliberate, self-conscious online identity construction.

Identity construction in online role-playing games, however, extends beyond the initial selection of individual character attributes. Players further create their online personas through dialogic talk and interaction with other local and geographically distant players. While individual character development is the ultimate goal of most MMORPGs (Sheldon, 2004, p. 40), high-level progression[2] is only achievable through multiplayer interaction and the formation of self-organized teams, or guilds (Williams et al., 2006). *World of Warcraft* guilds, ranging in size from three to several hundred people, designate individual roles that facilitate attainment of larger team goals. The relative success of a guild is determined by the

---

1. New players create their avatars by first selecting a faction: Alliance or Horde. They then choose an avatar race, class, and traits, such as gender, skin color, and facial features. A name is chosen or randomly assigned.

2. After players reach the highest level of the game, they continue to advance by what is referred to as "endgame" play. These players distinguish themselves through powerful status items (i.e., rare weapons and armor sets), which are found in high-level dungeons that require multiplayer collaboration.

group's ability to negotiate and coordinate the roles, actions, and hierarchical relationships of members during activity frameworks, such as "dungeon raiding."

Dungeon raiding is a competitive activity that typically requires 10 to 25 players in order to fight a series of game-generated monsters. Lasting several hours, dungeon raids are composed of fast-paced individual fights that must be completed in a limited amount of time. That is, each fight is a test of the coordination and skills of the group. As such, raids require participants to respond and perform quickly and under duress. Efficient player coordination is key to raiding success, which provides tangible game-specific rewards for all players in the form of coveted game objects, increased character power, and game currency. While some of these rewards are portioned equally, other objects are distributed at the discretion of guild's leadership. Novice players benefit from participating in these activities alongside expert players, as it gives them the opportunity to attain items that will allow them to reach higher levels of ability faster.

Within the activity framework of the raid, players negotiate and construct expert and novice identities through representation and multimodal interaction. Expert players are experienced players who have acquired the most cultural capital or sought-after game loot (e.g., armor, weapons, trade goods). As such, a player's visible gear functions as a marker of his or her ability, status, and commitment to the game (see Figure 7.2[3]). Players also display expert status through their ability to verbally direct and assess the group using technical explanations and gendered, masculine registers. Novice or less experienced players align to these directives using situated language and semiotic resources that are specific to the game world.

This chapter discusses the ways in which speakers and hearers in an online "community of practice" (Lave and Wenger, 1991) adapt to a semiotically restricted ecology for performing what I term "identities of expertise" (see also Peuronen, Chapter 8 of this volume). A community of practice is an aggregate of people who come together in some common endeavor (Eckert and McConnell-Ginet, 1992, pp. 464). In the community of the guild, particular ways of doing things emerge through the course of joint activity and mutual engagement. Members share a mutual orientation as well as a social sense of identity and place within

---

3. Items placed on this page are worn on the avatar's body. Items possess specific numerical values that determine the individual character's strength, agility, stamina, intellect, spirit, and armor protection. Items with high values increase the amount of damage an avatar is able to do while fighting.

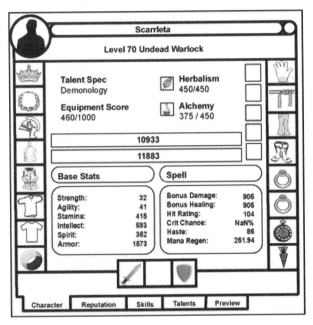

FIGURE 7.2

the community. Through their interactions with each other, players in the guild negotiate identities that correspond to core and peripheral memberships in the community. Players who hold core membership are those who display the most skill, dedication, and experience—qualities valued by competitive gamers. Experienced players perform these identities of expertise through specific styles or ways of speaking/being (Bell, 1984; Eckert & Rickford, 2001). Ultimately, expert styles are ways of performing authority and authenticity. This identity work is fully multimodal and occurs through overlapping, mutually elaborating semiotic tools (e.g., voice chat, text chat, visual displays). Through this multimodal enactment of style, players construct social meaning at the level of community (cf. Pennycook, 2010).

This material I am presenting here is drawn from 15 months of participant observation in a 40-person guild in the MMORPG *World of Warcraft*. The data include 60 hours of voice conversations recorded while dungeon raiding with an established guild of members who have been playing together nightly for three years. Audio data are synced to real-time video-capture, displaying simultaneous on-screen talk. As I will show, this kind of multimodal dataset allows for an examination of interaction that is informed by spatial practice and graphical representation.

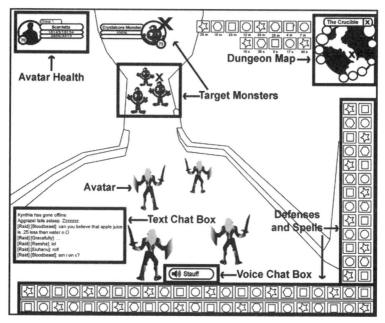

FIGURE 7.3

Building on Eckert and Rickford's (2001) discussion of the practice-based nature of style, my data show players linguistically and symbolically index different subgroups of game experience within the guild. The raid leader is typically an expert player, selected by the group to vocally direct the guild during dungeon raids. Although this position of authority operates on an event-rotating basis, allowing many expert players the chance to lead, specific men in the group regularly fill this role. (The guild has 40 active members: 34 men and 6 women. Only men were observed as raid leaders; women did not volunteer.) In particular, I illuminate the discursive complexity and creativity of interaction in this guild by paying attention to four key ways in which players use the multimodal resources (see Figure 7.3) at their disposal for both pragmatic and stylistic effect; these are: (1) vocal communication, (2) written communication, (3) avatar gestures, and (4) the built environment.

Resource 1: Vocal Communication for Decision Making and Solidarity

Guild members are required to download a free Voice Over Internet Protocol (VoIP) software program called *Ventrilo*. Although not compulsory to the structure of the game itself, this requirement is a standard expectation of most raiding guilds. Using this technology, players wear headsets with microphones to listen and respond to each other. Members log in to the chat channel in order to coordinate game strategies during dungeon raiding. Broadly speaking, two primary communicative functions are fulfilled through voice chat.

Directions and Decision Making

Raid leaders use spoken language for explanations/directions, decision making, and for game-focused collaboration. One way raid leaders accomplish this is through a specific kind of descriptive speech style, produced at the start of each new obstacle in the dungeon. These monologues negotiate compliance and promote team success. They typically unfold in three steps:

1. The raid leader begins with an explanation of the fight using technical, game-specific vocabulary.[4]
2. Next, the raid leader proposes directions to the group using directives constructed with auxiliary, deontic modal verbs.
3. Lastly, the leader concludes by describing the consequences of ignoring proposed directions: negative assessment of players.

Extract 7.1 typifies this type of monologue. The players are in "Serpentshrine Cavern," listening to directions issued by the expert player leading the guild. The raid leader explains the steps needed to collaboratively kill an overpowered, fishlike monster named "The Lurker Below." This monster alternates between fighting above and below water in Serpentshrine Cavern, requiring players to anticipate next moves and co-ordinate accordingly.

Extract 7.1:

Raid		
Leader	1	Ok basically the boss[5] is gonna have th:ree abilities. (.)
	2	Um one is called a geyser,

---

4. Leaders prepare for raids by referencing specific strategies on popular fan sites.

5. An elite monster that is very hard to defeat. Items of high value are found on the monster's corpse.

3 Which is basically a frostbolt.[6]

4 That he'll shoot at a random player fo:r,

5 For around three point five, ten, or three point five k[7],

6 Not that bad.

7 He does a s:pout, this is the big ability here, (.)

8 For everyone who's listening,

9 Uh, every forty five to fifty seconds: after he's spawned,[8]

10 He: will use a spout, which is, he will basically spin around,

11 Three hundred and sixty degrees and blow this spring of,

12 Or this jet of water at everyone.

13 Kinda like the uh high beam thing on uh::,

14 Whatever the last boss AQ40[9] is, I'm blanking on his name. (.)

15 Ye::ah, (.) so what needs to happen at that point,

16 Is we'll all kinda be standing on these platforms in a circle. (.)

17 When the beam gets kinda close to you,

18 You need to jump into the water,

19 And then jump back up on the platform=

20 =That's all you have to do.

21 If you get hit by the geyser you will probably die.

22 If you <u>don't</u> die,

23 You'll get knocked like three hundred yards into the water.

24 And then you'll die from fish or from boiling water,

25 Or from something like that.

26 <u>SO</u> ((breath)) you get hit, you <u>die</u>, we all call you a dumbass.

---

6. A mage spell that damages the target through a bolt of ice.

7. Damage to a player's health is shown visually and numerically through the decrease of "health points."

8. To appear or resurrect.

9. A no-longer-frequently played dungeon known as the Temple of Ahn'Qiraj, requiring 40 people.

The raid leader produces a narrative description of what the monster will do in the forthcoming attack (lines 1–14). Before issuing group directions, however, the leader positions himself by referencing his expert knowledge. He describes the fight and potential dangers in detail, using insider vocabulary and other culturally specific references. He also provides a complex explanation of the group's simulated *physical* game environment, describing the location and obstacles specific to situational contexts. (I return to this "built environment" below.) Speaking quickly and forcefully, he introduces the monster's first ability as a "geyser," explaining the skill by comparing it to a "frostbolt," a mage[10] ability that is familiar to most players (lines 2–3). This expert knowledge is again marked in lines 13–14, when he makes reference to a defunct game space. By referencing a dungeon that is obsolete, the raid leader marks himself as a player who has been playing the game competitively for a long time. Players who have spent less time playing the game may not understand this reference.

In lines 15–20, the raid leader gives organizational directions to the group, using the modal expressions "need to" and "have to." Deontic modality, described as "language of action," includes permission verbs like "may," obligation verbs like "should," and requirement verbs like "must." This type of language also includes quasi-auxiliary modal expressions like "have (got) to," "need to," and "had better." I observed these auxiliary modal expressions throughout my dataset. This choice of grammatical modality contributes to the construction of hierarchical relationships in the guild by setting up situational contexts of duty and obligation where players must follow the instructions of expert players. Here, mitigated forms of deontic verbs foster feelings of community solidarity by downplaying directives made by expert players. These modal forms are significant as they expand on Brown and Levinson's (1987) discussion of politeness theory (see Spilioti, Chapter 4 of this volume). Strategizing for efficiency, the raid leader uses a bald-on-record order to communicate his task-oriented requests. While the raid leader may be viewed as domineering or potentially offensive to some players, his simultaneous use of mitigated, quasi-auxiliary modal expressions seems to minimize face-threatening damage to hearers, making him an effective leader. Other players listen and follow.

The raid leader transitions from explaining the fight to giving directives to the group. The raid leader explains, "You need to jump into the

---

10. A magical avatar class that specializes in spell casting and causing damage to enemies from ranged distances.

water, and then jump back up on the platform" (lines 18–19). He then quickly states, "That's all you have to do" (line 20). A structure of duty and obligation frames the guild's modal interactions. Members of the guild are expected to perform specific tasks in ways that will maximize damage to the enemy. After the raid leader issues brief directions, he typically expresses the expectation and feasibility of the task described, further contributing to the construction of group hierarchy and relationships of power.

The raid leader then describes the potential negative consequences for diverging from his given instructions (lines 21–26), which include incurring significant individual damage and temporary death. Dying in raids affects the efficiency of the team and detracts from the strength of the guild as a combative force because resurrecting a player requires extra time, energy, and resources. Thus, players typically negatively assess individual and group failure.

According to Pomerantz (1984, p.57), people produce assessments when they engage in social activities. The activity of assessment positions certain players as evaluators and others as subjects to be evaluated. In line 21, the raid leader explains, "If you get hit by the geyser, you will probably die." He further poses, "If you don't die, you'll get knocked like 300 yards into the water, and then you'll die from fish or from boiling water or from something like that" (lines 22–25). The raid leader then produces the conditional evaluation: if "you get hit, you die, and we all call you a dumbass" (line 26). This example demonstrates how the raid leader uses evaluation to position himself and other experienced players above those who are unable to successfully maneuver their avatar in the way described. Although the raid leader selects the word "dumbass" in this example, other evaluative terms commonly used refer to players' experience and skill, such as "newbie" and "noob."[11] To some extent, of course, this playful, teasing key further mitigates the leader's talk, as it conceals the force of his directive.

Solidarity Maintenance

Brennan and Ohaeri (1999) argue that when people work together, they are invariably concerned not only with the task at hand but also with the manner in which they accomplish it. Within any group interaction, social

---

11. Terms referring to new players or players that lack skill. Usually used in contexts of playful insult.

needs must be observed, and players must not impose or threaten the face of others in interaction (Goffman, 1963). Brennan and Ohaeri (1999, p. 229) go on to note that, while electronic text communication may not display as many politeness hedges, the face management in online voice communication functions similarly to face management in offline, face-to-face communication. When making direct requests, the raid leader simultaneously makes use of specific politeness forms such as quasi-auxiliary modal verbs, hedges, and discourse markers.

According to Turnbull and Saxton (1997), speakers often use modality strategically to do the kind of facework that is so important in group interactions. This helps to explain why, as I have mentioned, raid leaders tend to choose certain modal verbs. Notably, strong modal verbs (e.g., "must" and "should") seldom appear in raid talk. While this may be because these particles are not regularly used in the everyday speech of the raid leaders, it may also be because they are understood to be too formal—too forceful—for casual gaming interactions. Instead, leaders choose weaker modal expressions (e.g., "need to" and "have to") for mitigating their positions as leaders. In this way, leaders are able to not only direct but also to maintain approachability and positive social regard. Speakers thus use modality as a resource for fostering feelings of solidarity within the group and for downplaying the impact of assertions made under duress or in the heat of the game.

In addition to this kind of modal styling, raid leaders utilize hedging. Hedges are linguistic mitigating devices, such as adjectives, adverbs, and clauses, which can either weaken or reinforce a statement (Clemen, 1997). Some scholars suggest that people use indirect speech, like hedging, as a strategy for interacting with higher status individuals in contexts of unequal power. More recently, scholars have come to recognize hedging as a mark of solidarity. As Clemen (ibid.) explains, speakers use hedging as a strategy to increase the likelihood of acceptance while minimizing the risk of rejection.

Using voice chat, raid leaders use hedging to achieve group cohesion and to successfully promote task progression. The hedge "I think" is used frequently by raid leaders before engaging in combat. In Extract 7.2, the group is continuing in "Serpentshrine Cavern." The raid leader is explaining a later part of the strategy designed to kill the gargantuan fish, "Lurker."

In addition to promoting solidarity, the raid leader repeatedly uses "I think" as a mitigating device (line 1), expressing uncertainty and limited confidence, to downgrade his assertion of expert knowledge. By keeping the assertions uncertain, via hedges, raid leaders are able to avoid criticism if their instructions cause the group to fail. This example demonstrates

Extract 7.2:

Raid

Leader

1   The other thing that he'll do, I think,

2   Is he will periodically dive under water,

3   And spawn th:ree groups of adds[12] I think,

4   No four groups of adds.

5   Um, well on each of the smaller outer platforms,

6   He'll spawn two:: um: ambushers[13], I think.

7   And he'll spawn 3 guardians in the middle.

8   And we'll basically have to kill all these guys,

9   Within I think it's a minute.

10   Otherwise, the lurker will come back up. ((breath))

11   And if he does his little spout thing,

12   And we kill him while he's doing his spout,

13   Then it will bug him out and bad things happen.

how leaders use hedging to destabilize their factual claims and disperse accountability for the potential failure of the group. Again, this is an ideal strategy for maintaining solidarity and promoting the successful completion of assigned tasks.

White (2003) argues that hedges and other resources of intersubjective stance are fundamentally dialogic and interactive. In monologic speech, performed by the raid leader as a single speaker, hedges are used to acknowledge the presence (and possible rival expertise-opinions) of other speakers and listeners, regardless of their verbal participation. Hedging thus works to maintain a "sense of community" by promoting a type of "imagined" dialogic engagement. In this context, hedging is a strategy of establishing group cohesiveness by deemphasizing or diffusing the hierarchical structure of the group.

In addition to modal styling and hedgework, raid leaders can also mitigate their talk by using a discourse marker such as "basically." Discourse markers, or lexical phrases used in conversation (e.g., "actually," "you know," "like," "I mean," "okay"), signal the speaker's intention to mark a boundary and achieve organization in texts. Returning to Extract 7.1 above,

---

12. Additional enemy targets.

13. A concealed enemy monster that launches a surprise attack.

notice the raid leader's repeated use of "basically" (lines 1, 3, and 10) as one example of the discourse markers used in this particular raid and elsewhere in gaming environments.

In her well-known work on discourse markers, Schiffrin (e.g., Schiffrin et al., 2001) discusses how they typically occur when speakers shift their orientation from one topic to another, alerting the listener that the speaker is pursuing a new subject for discussion. In this first extract, the raid leader initially uses "basically" (line 1) to mark that the raid is starting and that he will begin explaining the combat strategy. In addition to marking shifts in conversation topics, the discourse marker "basically" is used to introduce segments of the raid leader's explanation that he feels are particularly complicated. For example, he uses "basically," in line 3 to mark his intention to elaborate on what a "geyser" is, using the technical game term "frostbolt." He explains that the geyser will cause players enormous damage, making it a dangerous obstacle. Additionally, the raid leader uses the word "basically" before proceeding with a description that is not actually basic in order to frame the task-based directions as wholly accomplishable, regardless of skill and experience, through careful listening and execution. Given these various pragmatic interpretations or possibilities, the raid leader's use of "basically" ultimately functions to encourage and motivate the group. Raid leaders downplay the technical language used in raiding, stylistically deemphasizing the hierarchical structure of experts and novices, thus contributing to more cooperative teamwork and sentiments of solidarity.

I have discussed several discursive strategies leaders use in the spoken language mode to perform their identities of expertise in ways that sustain group solidarity and task focus. I now turn to another major channel of interaction, written communication, to examine the ways that this mode also constructs and lends itself to identities of expertise.

Resource 2: Written Communication

While the raid leader's spoken discourse dominates the voice channel, interactions occur concurrently by all members using text-based or written/typed chat, a phenomenon referred to as multilayered, platform-based code switching (Boellstorff, 2008). The causal, informal nature of texting creates an even more dialogic "sense of community," allowing for greater and more shared participation in spite of differences in players' ranks. In Extract 7.3, also taking place in the "Serpentshrine Cavern," both expert and novice players negotiate game tasks in the chat space.

This written communication simultaneously elaborates on and detracts from the raid leader's spoken conversation topics. In the following transcript, representing a multimodal exchange, voice chat is indicated in bold font, while conversations occurring through text are demarcated in italic font.

Extract 7.3:
Bold font: voice chat
Italic font: text chat

Novice A	1	*Does anyone have TS*
Raid Leader	2	**Because basically what's going to happen,**
	3	**When he spawns these adds,**
	4	**There's going to be 3 outer platforms,**
	5	**where these adds spawn. (.)**
Expert X	6	*I am summoning the souls[14] I have stolen.*
	7	*Please take a captured soul as a gift.*
Novice B	8	*I'll take a blue mushroom*
Raid Leader	9	**And we're gonna have the adds,**
	10	**that spawn in the middle,**
	11	**Be tanked[15] and polymorphed[16] or sheeped[17],**
	12	**Or whatever.**
Novice C	13	*I can tank[18] adds*
Expert Y	14	*Get your vent[19] fixed*
Raid Leader	15	**And the ones on the outer platforms,**
	16	**Kill those three groups of adds,**
Novice C	17	*If needed*

---

14. Referring to health stolen from slain enemies, manifested in the form of created health-imbued stones.

15. Referring to an avatar whose primary role in the raid is to absorb damage and prevent others from being attacked.

16. Referring to a mage spell that transforms the enemy into an animal, removing it temporarily from combat.

17. Referring to a type of polymorph spell that transforms the target into a sheep.

18. To initiate an attack on and to take maximum damage from a group of nearby monster(s).

19. Short for Ventrilo, the voice chat software used by the guild.

Expert Y	18	*Psh we have ferals[20] for that*
Raid Leader	19	**And then move on to the middle ones.**
Novice C	20	*Ok.*
Expert Z	21	*Yeah :p*
Raid Leader	22	**So we need roughly the same output[21],**
	23	**So we get done with those 3 groups at the same time.**
Expert Y	24	*Pull him*
	25	*(10 seconds)*
Raid Leader	26	**So that's one thing we need to figure out.**

While the raid leader speaks, five other topics of conversation are produced *visually* in print. In line 1, a low-ranking player asks the group if anyone has an alternative chat software system called "Team Speak (TS)," signifying that the player does not have the VoIP software used by the rest of the group. In line 14, a high-ranking player responds to his question with the written directive, "Get your vent fixed." In reply, the novice player drops the topic and does not respond.

Another topic is introduced when a senior member texts a player-created message that is programmed to automatically display when a specific action is performed (lines 6–7). This particular announcement notifies other players that they may obtain a special health stone[22] produced by the player. Players who raid frequently and who have specific, on-demand jobs within the group sometimes modify their text channel for sending automated messages such as this. These messages are stylized and are recognizable as belonging to particular players. While one warlock may use the message "I am summoning the souls I have stolen..." to signal his creation of health stones, another warlock performing the same action might use a message such as, "Health got you down? Stones in the back." These players use these messages repeatedly, requiring other players to recognize and understand the required action that goes along with this automated text.

---

20. Referring to feral druids, whose class-defining ability is shape-shifting into powerful animals for tanking.

21. The numerical amount of damage done to the target collectively, monitored through "add-on" software.

22. A stone created by warlocks that boosts avatar health when used.

Moreover, negotiations for low-status, less-sought-after, temporary items often occur through text (e.g., line 8). Players make requests for items, and unless contested, usually receive the loot desired. When high-status items "drop" from enemy monsters, negotiations typically occur through a combination of text and talk. When this happens, an expert player will first text a descriptive, informational link of the item to the rest of the guild. Using voice chat, the leader then invites all players who want to be entered in a drawing for the item to type, "/roll." Interested players enter this command into the text channel, and a winning player is generated at random. This interaction all happens very quickly and as a "sideline" activity.

Another topic is introduced in the chat channel when a junior player suggests that he can "tank" a fight (line 13). This request is refuted by a high-ranking player (line 18). The interaction ends with another high-ranking member responding "yeah" and then producing an emoticon sticking out its tongue (:P). This playful exchange is an example of how an expert identity may be skillfully negotiated through concurrent text-based interaction. The expert player rejects the novice player's request to fulfill a specific high-ranking role in the raid, implying that the novice player is not only unsuited for the role but is also foolish for not knowing the type of avatar class that fills the role most effectively.

In the last textual exchange, a high-ranking player writes, "pull him" (line 24). This player directs the group through text, as he tells his team-mates to start the "trash" fight, composed of a few low-powered monsters. The player gives these directions while the raid leader speaks concurrently about how the larger boss fight ought to be organized (see Extract 7.1 again). So, visual instructions issued by other expert players typically occur during the raid leader's spoken explanation, in order to move efficiently through the easier sections of the dungeon. Leadership tasks in the guild are shared only among players deemed to have high enough levels of experience and skill.

Extract 7.3 also demonstrates the complexity of concurrent modalities of communication. Speech turns in spoken raid talk are well defined. The leader speaks at length while high-ranking players occasionally make brief comments. In text-based or written conversation, however, turns are less clearly defined. Not only do typed messages of online chat require more time to produce than spoken utterances, players are not able to see each other's messages being produced incrementally. They receive messages only after the typist has hit carriage return. As Brennan and Ohaeri

(1999) explain, this delay means that two people may produce and send utterances in parallel, which can disrupt the relatedness between turns and the local coherence of the dialogue. (It is well known in new media studies that messagers become very skilled at reading/following complex conversational threads and turn-taking patterns—see Werry, 1996, for example.) The style that emerges in the text channel is, therefore, one that is mostly abbreviated and filled with game vocabulary and references. Players write messages that are short and always aligned with the immediate activity.

Resource 3: Avatar Gestures as (Re)embodied Action

A key feature of MMORPGs is the discursive performance of virtually embodied actions (i.e., the text-based expression of gestures and body movements). Dovey and Kennedy (2006, p. 108) describe how players become "inseparable" from the game through a sort of reembodiment into the virtual world. This entry into the world is mediated through the avatar, described as "cyborgian," or a "fusion of [...] wires, machines, code, and flesh" (p. 109). The avatar allows players to manipulate and explore objects and game space. In this way, the manipulation of the avatar is a sensory experience for the player, fusing disembodied consciousness and the embodied experience.

Building on this framework, "emotes" are pregenerated expressions, which simulate avatar-embodied actions (e.g., cheering, crying, hugging) and are activated when a player types in a short code. Some emotes include animations and some produce sayings that are voiced by the emoting character. Players use emotes to align, or orient to the talk, text, and actions of other players (cf. Jaffe, 2009). At the end of Extract 7.1, for instance, the raid leader in "Serpentshrine Cavern" produces his conditional negative assessment of players who diverge from his set of instructions (i.e., "So you get hit, you die, we all call you a dumbass"). This assessment, although playful, may be interpreted as offensive to some players. After the raid leader produces this assessment in the voice channel, several listening players visually produce emotes on screen in response to the harsh evaluation made by the raid leader. Appearing as a descriptive textual action and further demonstrated through animated gesture, players use emotes to comment on the raid leader's negative remarks, therefore indirectly evaluating the raid leader. The following list exemplifies the range of emotes used by guild members in response to the raid leader's commentary in the one instance described in Extract 7.1:

Command	Visual description	Visual animation
/cheer	You cheer at (Raid Leader).	Avatar raises arms in celebration.
/cry	You cry.	Avatar voices crying, hands used.
/laugh	You laugh.	Avatar throws back head, laughs.
/nervous	You look around nervously.	No animation.
/scared	You are scared!	No animation.
/shakefist	You shake your fist.	No animation.

Often when a player in the group uses an emote, other players will engage in a sort of format tying, by producing a structurally related or appropriate emote in response. For example, when one player types the emote "/cheer," often many others will respond with the same format, thus producing a number of avatars visually simulating the same actions (i.e., a group cheer). The following emote sequence occurs in response to the raid leader's conditional evaluation in Extract 7.1. Calydia and Aeraron are expert players who are in an offline romantic relationship and IronRogue is another novice player. The players type commands (left column below) in their own text-chat screens to in order to generate text descriptions (right column below) and corresponding avatar animations (when available) on all other guildmate's screens.

Command	Visual description
/cry	IronRogue cries.
/cry	Calydia cries.
/comfort	Aeraron comforts Calydia.
/laugh	IronRogue laughs at Aeraron.
/cry	Aeraron cries.
/hug	IronRogue hugs Aeraron.
/hug	Calydia hugs IronRogue.

This sort of dialogic participation also occurs in specific contexts of team celebration, like the conclusion of a successful enemy fight. Often in celebration, the entire guild will "/cheer" and then proceed to "/dance."

Players also use emotes in contexts of interaction with opposing players. In some areas of the game world, players are vulnerable to attack by other players associated with rival factions. After killing opposing avatars, for example, some players engage in "camping" the enemy's body. "Camping" refers to the act of hovering near a rival's body and reslaughtering this rival when the player attempts to resurrect. This act keeps targeted players from further game play. Emotes such as "/spit," "/dance," "/laugh," and "/sit" are used near or on top of the enemy's fallen body in a text-based exchange and are actions performed solely to antagonize the rival player. Using keyboard controls, players may also pace up and down over or jump on top of the opposing corpse. The reason players perform these taunting emotes is because other rival players can still view the play area where their corpse is after they die. As deceased players, however, they cannot respond with counter emotes. This antagonizing interaction exemplifies the performance of expert identities since only experienced players typically possess the skills needed to successfully and confidently "bully" and defend against other rival players.

The use of embodied avatar gestures enhance and extend players' concurrent spoken and written exchanges described above. While messages written during raids are typically brief, emotes allow players a creative, expressive range of parallel-track participation that is open to both expert and novice players alike. Virtual embodied actions, or (re)embodied actions, vivify avatars in a way that emulates face-to-face interaction but with players always producing context-appropriate gestures and sayings. Players also sometimes position their avatar's bodies to face other characters talking, much like "facing formations" in face-to-face interaction (cf. Kendon, 1990). While these formations are not always used, players will almost always move their avatar close in proximity to the avatar belonging to the player to which they are communicating. Sometimes this proximity is pragmatic and players move to exchange items, which can only be accomplished when positioned side by side. Other times, this phenomenon occurs for no specific purpose other than to allow the players to visually see the other avatar in conversation without obstruction. In this way, players sometimes mirror one of the ways in which attention is performed offline, further personifying their avatar bodies as extensions of their offline bodies. The next section expands on the way players orient to "virtual" space.

Resource 4: Deixis and Gesture as/for Built Environment

As I have already begun to show, players attend to the images on the computer screen as a new semiotic field and in ways that are specific to the ecology of the MMORPG. The dungeon is a fixed, temporal, and spatial locale, representing features in both offline and fantasy worlds. The online landscape, marked by enemy monsters, objects, and other referential environmental landmarks, provides a referential infrastructure for organizing interaction and discursive practice.

In her face-to-face work looking at play, Goodwin (2006) discusses the ways in which hopscotch players orient to the hopscotch grid as a physical, multimodal resource for meaning making. Girls use the hopscotch grid—otherwise just markings on the ground—as a tangible object, a three-dimensional space, to demonstrate appropriate actions and to contest wrong moves. Similarly, in the game world, players use the built environment as a referential grid, alongside talk and text. While the raid leader vocally produces spatial directions of where each player should be positioned during a specific fight, he or another expert player will often move their own avatar to the place described or a similar place outside the immediate location, using their "bodies" in conjunction with the built environment to demonstrate deictic reference. Once situated in the place of reference, the expert player moves his avatar up and down, in a jumping motion, signaling to others, while requesting joint attention. Figure 7.4 offers a static rendition of this type of situated action (note the box).

This style of referential interaction with the landscape extends the use of deictic terms in talk (Levinson, 1983). In my last extract (see Extract 7.4), the raid leader describes the future action of the guild as being situated in a specific game location. Words highlighted in bold represent deictic terms used. Words marked with * indicate when players "move to" and "jump" on specific places on the grid.

During raids, expert players direct novice players using both deictic terms (here, there, this, that) and deictic referential gestures performed by character representations. In this example, the raid leader talks about standing close to the monster on a specific platform. The words "here" and "there" are realized visually, even though each person is staring at the landscape from a different camera angle. In line 6, elaborating on the word "here," the raid leader moves to the spot described, using the keyboard to move his character up and down until players confirm notice

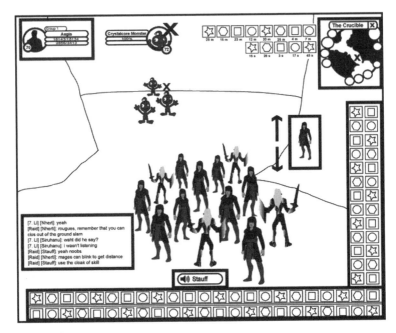

FIGURE 7.4

Extract 7.4:

* Deictic stomps

Raid Leader	1	So melee what we need to be doing, (.)
	2	Is on **this** platform **there**,
	3	That we're gonna be standing on,
	4	Picture **this** like big circular platform around **this** boss,
	5	Uhh we need to stand as close to it, (.)
	6	As close to it as possible, ***here**.
	7	Without being in the water, ***there**.
	8	Because he's gonna knock us back. (.)
	9	When he does that.
	10	And if you get knocked back into the water,
	11	You have to jump back on the platform ***here**.

through text. These "stomps" require avatars to move to a place of directed reference in the dungeon, "jumping" up and down on the pixilated grid until other players discursively confirm understanding.

This style of gesturing elaborates on the deictic speech of players, building on the semiotic resources available in the local, situated game ecology. While expert players use the environment as another tool for providing instruction to the group, novice players use the landscape to display competency and communicate readiness to proceed. Players move to the spaces referenced by experts and demonstrate attentiveness by "jumping" up and down as well. In this way, the players co-construct and maintain the space in which the game takes place (Jones, 2010). The simulated landscape of the game takes on meaning as a tangible object through practice, allowing players to define and make sense of their environment through negotiation and interaction. By referencing specific simulated "locations" in the game, these "places" become recognizable by all guild players as sites where specific and meaningful actions take place. This practice-based knowledge constructs notions of shared community and functions in a way that allows expert players to elaborate on technical "identities of experience."

Conclusion

As one of the first discourse ethnographies to examine new media gaming (cf. Keating & Sunakawa, 2010), this study illustrates some of the ways in which a self-organized community of gamers creatively uses the specific ecology of their MMPORG to perform identities informed by status and expert roles. In this complex digital environment, marked equally by its multimodality and by the multitasking of its members, we see how linguistic styles as ways of speaking/being specific to the community entail mutual and dialogic engagement in a common endeavor. As such, style is best understood as the dialogic co-construction of linguistic forms informed by shared beliefs, norms, and values giving meaning to the social world of the community—rather, that is, than seeing style as simply linguistic features that occur according to particular social distributions. The social function of style in the *World of Warcraft* guild serves to cohere the group as a particular community with a shared competitive identity, while also distinguishing members according to their experience and individual status as knowledgeable, expert players. Although these styles are not representative of all *World of Warcraft* players or all contexts of game, and variation may occur among other organized guilds, this study demonstrates how online game players use new media skillfully and creatively in the organization of their social worlds online.

Acknowledgments

My sincerest gratitude to Norma Mendoza-Denton and Marjorie Goodwin for their insightful contributions to this project. Thank you to my colleagues in Tucson and Los Angeles for their collaborative feedback and to Jennifer Newon Kos and Jeanne Arnold for help with revisions; to Saija Peuronen and one external reviewer for their suggestions; and to Crispin Thurlow for his generous editorial help. Additional appreciation to Paul Connor and Alethea Marti for media assistance. Lastly, thank you to the members of the "Bloody Reavers" guild, for graciously welcoming me into their community.

References

Bell, A. (1984). Language style as audience design. *Language in Society*, 13(2), 145–204.

Boellstorff, T. (2008). *Coming of Age in Second Life: An Anthropologist Explores the Virtually Human*. Princeton, NJ: Princeton University Press.

Brennan, S., & Ohaeri, J. (1999). Why do electronic conversations seem less polite? The costs and benefits of hedging. *Proceedings, International Joint Conference on Work Activities, Coordination, and Collaboration (WACC, '99)*, (227–235). San Francisco, CA.

Brown, P., & Levinson, S. (1987). *Politeness: Some Universals in Language Usage*. Cambridge: Cambridge University Press.

Clemen, G. (1997). The concept of hedging: Origins, approaches, and definitions. In R. Markkanen & H. Schröder (Eds.), *Hedging and Discourse: Approaches to the Analysis of a Pragmatic Phenomenon in Academic Texts*, (pp. 235–248). Berlin: Walter de Gruyter.

Dovey, J., & Kennedy, H. (2006). Bodies and machines: Cyborg subjectivity and gameplay. In *Game Cultures: Computer Games as New Media*, (pp. 104–122). Maidenhead, UK: Open University Press.

Eckert, P., & McConnell-Ginet, S. (1992). Think practically and look locally: Language and gender as community-based practice. *Annual Review of Anthropology*, 21, 461–490.

Eckert, P., & Rickford, J. (2001). *Style and Sociolinguistic Variation*. Cambridge: Cambridge University Press.

Goffman, E. (1963). *On Face-work: An Analysis of Ritual Elements of Social Interaction*. New York: Anchor.

Goodwin, M. (2006). *The Hidden Life of Girls: Games of Stance, Status, and Exclusion*. Malden, MA: Blackwell.

Jaffe, A. (2009). *Stance: Sociolinguistic Perspectives*. New York: Oxford University Press.

Jones, R. (2010). Cyberspace and physical space: Attention structures in computer mediated communication. In A. Jaworski & C. Thurlow (Eds.), *Semiotic Landscapes: Language, Image, Space*, (pp. 151–167). London: Continuum.

Keating, E., & Sunakawa, C. (2010). Participation cues: Coordinating activity and collaboration in complex online gaming worlds. *Language in Society*, 39(3), 331–356.

Kendon, A. (1990). Spatial organization in social encounters: The f-formation system. In A. Kendon (Ed.), *Conducting Interaction: Patterns of Behavior in Focused Encounters*, (pp. 209–238). Cambridge: Cambridge University Press.

Lave, J., & Wenger, E. (1991). *Situated Learning: Legitimate Peripheral Participation*. Cambridge: Cambridge University Press.

Levinson, S. (1983). *Pragmatics*. Cambridge: Cambridge University Press.

Pennycook, A. (2010). *Language as Local Practice*. London: Routledge.

Pomerantz, A. (1984). Agreeing and disagreeing with assessments: Some features of preferred/dispreferred turn shapes. In J. Atkinson & J. Heritage (Eds.), *Structures of Social Action: Studies in Conversation Analysis* (pp. 57–101). Cambridge: Cambridge University Press.

Schiffrin, D., Tannen, D., & Hamilton, H. (Eds.). (2001). *Handbook of Discourse Analysis*. Oxford: Blackwell.

Sheldon, L. (2004). *Character Development and Storytelling for Games*. Florence, KY: Thomson Course Technology.

Turnbull, W., & Saxton, K.L. (1997). Modal expression as facework in refusals to comply with requests: I think I should say 'no' right now. *Journal of Pragmatics*, 27, 145–181.

Werry, C. (1996). Linguistic and interactional features of Internet Relay Chat. In S. Herring, (Ed.), *Computer-Mediated Communication: Linguistic, Social and Cross-Cultural Perspectives*, (pp. 47–63). Amsterdam: John Benjamins.

White, P.R.R. (2003). Beyond modality and hedging: A dialogic view of the language of intersubjective stance. *Text*, 23(2), 259–284.

Williams, D., Ducheneaut, N., Xiong, L., Zhang, Y., Yee, N., & Nickell, E. (2006). From tree house to barracks: The social life of guilds in World of Warcraft. *Games and Culture*, 1(4), 338–361.

Yee, N. (2006). Demographics, motivations, and derived experiences of users of massively multi-user online graphical environments. *Presence: Teleoperators and Virtual Environments*, 15(3), 309–329.

Chapter 8

"Ride Hard, Live Forever": Translocal Identities in an Online Community of Extreme Sports Christians

Saija Peuronen

PEOPLE ENGAGING WITH digital communication technologies have various linguistic and discursive resources at their disposal. This also applies to internet users in Finland, the specific locus of my analysis. Having relatively easy access to these technologies, many Finns, the young educated generation in particular, are familiar with information, global language resources, and cultural practices that reach beyond their immediate locales (see Leppänen et al., 2011, for the results of a nationwide survey on the uses of English in Finland). Thus, from a sociolinguistic viewpoint, the realities of globalization may be manifested in a variety of ways, such as the ways in which people manage to make sense of and use mobile linguistic resources across contexts (Blommaert, 2010; Jaworski & Thurlow, 2010). Moreover, creative linguistic resources can be used for strategic styling, for representing certain identity aspects in specific situations, and for emphasizing what kinds of cultures or lifestyles one is willing to align oneself with (see especially Newon, Chapter 7, and Vaisman, Chapter 9, of this volume).

New media contexts, therefore, provide an important "field site" in which it is possible to examine how internet users, through their ways of communicating with one another, take up different positions toward specific topics, people, activities, communities, and also the medium of the communication itself. Furthermore, new media environments enable people to constitute their "communities of practice" (Lave & Wenger, 1991) also online. Existing offline communities can be transferred or expanded to online contexts, or the affordances of new media can be used to create completely new communities. For example, Lam (2004) discusses how two Chinese students in the United States found an internet chat room to be a space for social networking. In the chat room, the students were able to connect with other young people who shared a similar background. They began to use a mixed-code variety of English and Cantonese, which in turn contributed to the discovery of a shared identity related to the particular kind of English they were using. Hence, also within new media contexts, identifying oneself as a member of a specific community is largely achieved by showing competence in making appropriate linguistic, semiotic, and discursive choices across different communicative situations.

This chapter considers the use of bilingual language practices in styling new media discourse between members of one particular online community: Finnish Christians who participate in extreme sports. My aim is to examine the ways in which identity is negotiated through the use of a social-communicative style consisting of a variety of resources from two particular languages, Finnish and English. In this case, the community members have set up *Godspeed*, a network that has a dedicated website and online discussion forum (www.godspeed.fi). This online space serves as a place for community members to give information about their particular community activities, sharing their views, and creating networks within and between different extreme sports. Even though the community is Finland based, the members orient themselves to global contexts, cultures, and lifestyles by engaging in processes of borrowing and blending of cultural forms (Pennycook, 2007). They also draw on a variety of bilingual resources, which is one way for them to index communicative connectivity with different cultures and ideologies. Take for example, the community's English-language slogan—"Ride Hard, Live Forever"—which references the well-known expression "Live Fast, Die Young." Here, the phrase has been playfully but pointedly turned around to express the Christian worldview of the *Godspeed* community. Moreover, the choice of English is meaningful as the verb "to ride" offers a functional and dynamic concept for referencing a variety of action sports practiced by the community members.

I will begin by discussing briefly the general language context and some of the theoretical concepts that inform my research, before introducing the *Godspeed* community and the new media context. Next, my analysis will center on three specific communicative situations in the community's online forum. These are illustrative of the sociocultural frameworks prominent in the discussion forum data: Christianity, extreme sports, and youth culture. Finally, in the conclusion, I sum up my observations about how the members of this specific online community draw on a *heteroglossic* repertoire by making creative linguistic and discursive choices and how they can thus style their *translocal* identities as extreme sports Christians.

Finns as Users of English:
Style and Identity Construction in New Media Sites

Let us consider the linguistic repertoire of the average young Finn: he or she will have studied his or her mother tongue, and the other official language of Finland (either Finnish or Swedish) as well as one obligatory foreign language. Most pupils opt to study English as their mandatory foreign language. They usually begin their studies at age nine and continue for at least seven years for the duration of compulsory education. Many young people continue studying a foreign language for a further three years at the upper secondary school level (Taavitsainen & Pahta, 2003, p. 6).

Besides formal instruction given at school, there are many leisure activities in which young Finns encounter English and where they can learn the language (Nikula & Pitkänen-Huhta, 2008). Perhaps one of the most important everyday contexts for English is new media. Engaging in activities through different new media sites requires a knowledge of foreign languages (English in most cases) while also offering possibilities for learning and using foreign languages (see Piirainen-Marsh & Tainio, 2009, on language learning through playing computer and video games). In terms of both online and offline leisure time activities, sports are also a domain in which knowing English can be very useful. Due to the North American origins and the global nature of many extreme sports, people involved in them are even more likely to rely on English-derived terms. This is also because many of these newer sports are only now gaining ground in Finland and do not yet have an established Finnish terminology. Even in the case where a Finnish term exists, drawing on the "authentic" vocabulary is most likely preferred among devoted sports enthusiasts who wish to align themselves with a particular sports culture (cf. Heller, 2007b). However, the original English terms may and are also likely to undergo orthographic or morphologic changes when used by Finnish extreme sports devotees.

A diversity of language forms is constitutive of the Bakhtinian notion of *heteroglossia* (Lähteenmäki, 2010; see also Squires, Chapter 1, and Androutsopoulos, Chapter 13, of this volume). Bakhtin (1981) views heteroglossia from a social perspective and considers linguistic diversity, with different social dialects, jargons, and dynamic patterns of language use, characteristic of any national language (pp. 262–263). Heteroglossic discourse may, therefore, entail mixing of registers, genres, and codes. In comparison with theories of code switching, heteroglossia comprises a diversity of forms both in monolingual and multilingual discourse and, therefore, allows a more comprehensive analysis of social meanings, voices, and ideological positions created by language use (Bailey, 2007). Since particular language forms may be used across communities, cultures, or locales in which similar interests or values are shared, heteroglossia is also an important manifestation of *translocality*. In this chapter, my understanding of translocality is based on recent work focusing on the appropriation and use of globally available communicative and expressive resources in local activity spaces, and especially in the new media context (Hepp, 2009; Leppänen, forthcoming; Leppänen et al., 2009). By engaging in the dynamic processes of appropriation and creation of cultural and linguistic forms, translocal actors can index their sense of connectedness between different locales. The internet, in particular, enables users to move easily between different sites related to their interests, be it other community sites, online stores, or videos on *YouTube*, for instance. Because of their multilingual repertoires, young Finns are able to access and navigate a far wider range of sites and to find groups or communities with whom to align themselves and possibly also to connect.

In order to characterize global, technologized cultures today, Alim (2009) uses the concept of *translocal style communities*. He examines hip-hop culture as an example of one such community as it focuses on "sets of styles, aesthetics, knowledges, and ideologies that travel across localities and cross-cut modalities" (Alim, 2009, pp. 104–105). The view of style may simply refer to *ways of speaking* by which speakers create social meanings (Auer, 2007; Coupland, 2007). Here, this notion is applied to new media interactions between participants of the *Godspeed* online forum, by examining how they talk about certain topics and how this impacts the group members' identity construction. According to Auer (2007), social-communicative style may include language choice, linguistic variation, and pragmatic patterns (politeness, preference for certain genres). Thus, style can be crafted by using various heteroglossic resources. Moreover, the concept of style also includes aesthetic dimensions, both on a verbal and nonverbal level (see Vaisman, Chapter 9 of this volume).

In this way, participants in translocal communities can build identifications with certain cultures or lifestyles and align with their discourse practices. Bauman (2000) defines identity as "the situated outcome of a rhetorical and interpretive process in which interactants make situationally motivated selections from socially constituted repertoires of identificational and affiliational resources and craft these semiotic resources into identity claims for presentation to others" (p. 1). When members of a certain community of practice come together and engage in their shared activities, they may, therefore, by their ways of speaking, position themselves as similar or distinct from other groups (cf. Eckert, 2005). Along these lines, this paper takes a social perspective on bilingualism, viewing languages as not clearly definable, bounded systems but as sets of linguistic resources that speakers, or internet users, strategically draw on in specific social situations (Heller, 2007a).

Studying an Online Discussion Forum: Data from Finnish Christians Interested in Extreme Sports

As a medium, the online discussion forum is a well-established one and one that has received relatively substantial coverage in the academic literature (Androutsopoulos, 2007; Baym, 2000; Hinrichs, 2006; Kytölä, forthcoming; McLellan, 2005). In terms of its technological features, the kind of interaction that takes place in online discussion forums can be described as public, one-to-many, and asynchronous as users do not have to be logged on the system simultaneously to be able to read the messages posted to the forum (see Herring, 2007). Forums are created to address certain topics or themes, and therefore, discussion threads are thematically organized. In general, users identify themselves with nicknames and user profiles. However, the degree of anonymity varies; community members might be strangers to each other in both offline and online contexts, or they can include people who constitute an offline community but have decided to form an online community as well.

The *Godspeed* forum described in this chapter is focused on topics related to extreme sports and Christianity. The forum includes separate sections for different action sports such as snowboarding and other boarding activities, motor sports, biking, climbing, and parkour. There are also sections for discussing Bible passages and sermons. Additionally, forum participants talk about upcoming events, camps, and get-togethers. According to the *Godspeed* website, the community's main aim is to unite people engaged in different extreme sports activities, spread the gospel in the extreme sports community, and support people in their Christian faith. By updating their activities online, members also aim to create offline networks between different action sport groups and people involved in them. As a consequence, community members who interact in the online discussion forum often inform others of their offline identities by giving their names, ages, and places of residence, and of course their preferred sports activities.

The nature of online discussion forum interaction has been described as highly normative, for example, users may engage in boundary maintenance strategies such as making newcomers perform strict entrance rituals (Honeycutt, 2005) or expecting conformity in language use (Kytölä, forthcoming). In this respect, *Godspeed* differs from more conventional online forums in which participants might not otherwise know one another, and therefore, discriminatory discourses might arise. In the *Godspeed* forum, the tone of messages posted to the forum is in most cases highly cooperative. This might be because the community is small, the participants in the forum more or less know each other, and they might not want to create any unnecessary conflicts, and so they therefore also behave more politely than what is generally seen in regard to mediated behavior (see Spilioti, Chapter 4 of this volume). Based on her research, Georgakopoulou (1997, p. 144) has indicated that studying computer-mediated communication between intimates reflects the informants' everyday use of language better than in data collected from totally anonymous new media settings. Hence, it could be assumed that the language practices found in the *Godspeed* forum illustrate the participants' everyday, offline language use.

For the purposes of my research, I collected online discussion data from the community's web forum: a total of 205 discussion threads from the launching of the forum in August 2006 until March 2008. These threads comprise messages posted by 79 registered forum users. During the data collection period, online ethnographic observation was carried out in order to understand the lifestyles, specific cultural contexts, and fields of discourse with which the participants align themselves (cf. Androutsopoulos, 2008; Markham & Baym, 2009). With regard to my position as a researcher, I am not a member of the community, and during the data collection period I did not participate in the forum discussions. Since the forum is open and available for everyone, and reading the posts does not require a registration, I have considered the forum a public environment (Sveningsson Elm, 2009). That is why I have not sought an informed consent from every participant of the forum. However, in addition to the systematic observation, I have contacted community members on a few occasions, and thus I have incorporated the two levels of discourse-centered online ethnography (Androutsopoulos, 2008). First, I contacted the forum administrator to inform him about my research interest and, later on, I conducted a semistructured interview with another community member in order to gather information on the background and origin of the community. In these exchanges, I informed them about my research questions, the data collection, and how the data were to be used.

Styling Identities in an Online Community of Practice

In analyzing this new media discourse, I will show how the *Godspeed* community members construct a social-communicative style (Auer, 2007) through a variety of language resources at their disposal. I will analyze the kinds of identity aspects that the forum users construct throughout different communicative situations online. I will, therefore, pay particular attention to the kinds of online activities that the community members engage in, while also taking the purpose and the tone of the messages into account. As Herring (2007, p. 20) states, "each activity has associated conventional linguistic practices that signal when that activity is taking place." Consequently, the activities participants engage in require the mastery of certain discursive and linguistic resources as well as knowledge of the cultures with which they wish to associate themselves.

Playful Style in Constructing Community Membership

The first example illustrates how forum participants use a playful communicative style to construct membership in the community. Extract 8.1 deals with a post to a discussion thread about an upcoming Christian event that some of the community members had indicated their intention to attend. The thread comes from a forum section where participants announce and discuss upcoming events, camps, and get-togethers. The thread contains several posts in which community members have let others know about their individual plans (the post below is the 12th message in the thread). The overall aim of these exchanges is to match participants' schedules and to arrange some sports activities during the weekend in addition to simply attending the Christian event organized by one of the local churches. The message in Extract 8.1 is written by a young woman who wishes to inform others about her plans to participate in the event. My English translation of the example follows the extract. Any names of the participants have been omitted from the examples, and I mark in bold non-Finnish segments intended for discussion here.

Extract 8.1:

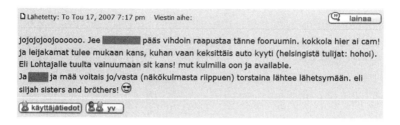

1 yeayeayeayeaayeaaaahh. Yeh [poster's first name] was finally able to write something here on the forum. **kokkola here I come!**

2 and the skysurfing gear will be coming too, as long as we are able to find a ride there (people from helsinki: ahoy).

3 So heading to Lohtaja to catch the wind! but I'll be in the hood and [I'll be] **available.**

4 And [first name] and I will be heading there already/only (depending on the viewpoint) on Thursday. so

5 **seeyah sisters and brothers!**

This example illustrates how a new member of the online community initiates her participation in the discussion forum. She uses various linguistic resources in order to construct a communicative style in her opening message. The overall style in her message is very informal, spoken Finnish; most of the words she uses are not written according to standard Finnish. By sending the message, she enters both this discussion thread and the forum as a whole. As she mentions at the beginning of her message (in line 1), this is the first time she has ever posted in the forum. However, her post is very direct and, as such, does not follow the self-deprecating style that is sometimes thought appropriate to newcomers in an online forum (see Honeycutt, 2005). Given her very casual way of using language and the in-group references to specific people and places (e.g., line 3 "Lohtaja"), one can conclude that she is already a member of the *Godspeed* community. For instance, she refers to herself and another girl by their first names, implying that others in the forum already know who they are. Hence, there is no need for her to introduce herself in a more detailed way.

The playful and creative use of language becomes evident right from the beginning of the post, which consists of affirmative exclamations such as *jojojojoojoooooo*, and *Jee* ("yeayeayeayeaayeaaaahh", "Yeh" in line 1). These lexical items can be considered similar to stylized orthographic practices common to new media users in general. For example, the first lexical entity, which reflects "joo," the Finnish equivalent for "yes," is illustrative of prosodic spelling, including repetition and vowel lengthening, also found in other types of (new) media genres, such as texting or subcultural magazines (see Androutsopoulos, 2000; Thurlow, 2003). With this playful introduction, the poster most likely characterizes her enthusiastic feelings toward the event and the possibility of meeting with other community members. The use of *jojojojoojoooooo* might also be understood as a reference to "yo," a greeting ritual in urban hip-hop slang (Pennycook, 2003), and therefore, it illustrates how linguistic forms may be given diverse interpretations in a translocal space. However it is interpreted, this lexical item functions similarly to "yo"—it can be seen as an informal, casual way of entering the discussion and greeting others.

After the greeting, the poster carries on with a similar, playful style of writing and uses English as a stylistic resource in her message. She draws on a particular "localized" way of writing a well-known English phrase as she informs others of her travels to the Finnish town, Kokkola, where the event takes place: *kokkola hier ai cam!* ("here I come!" in line 1). Androutsopoulos (2000, p. 521) describes "the phonetic spellings of loan-words according to native orthographic rules" as interlingual spellings. A similar process is taking place here. However, the poster's way of spelling the English words is not consistent throughout the message: on the one hand, she uses Finnish phonetic spelling of an English phrase (*hier ai cam!*), and on the other hand, she inserts an English lexical item into a Finnish phrase without any modification (*mut kulmilla oon ja available*: "but I'll be in the hood and [I'll be] available" in line 3). She explicitly uses the English word "available" for letting others know that she will be there and that she is interested in, and available for, going kite surfing. This language choice most likely fills an actual linguistic gap but also conforms to the playful style of the post. The use of English thus possibly mitigates any demands that she might otherwise impose on the participation of others.

At the end of her message, the poster once again draws on English, this time for leave-taking: *siijah sisters and bröthers!* ("see yah sisters and brothers!" in line 5). Again her writing practices vary as she partly adapts the English phrase according to Finnish phonetic spelling. Additionally, she uses some stylistic or aesthetic elements, such as attaching "h" to the end of the phrase *siijah* and replacing "o" with the Finnish letter "ö" in the word *bröthers*. It is notable that these modifications do not reflect Finnish pronunciation of the words but show the poster's willingness to play with language and orthography. By drawing on a variety of ways to style her discourse in a personal way and by calling the community members her sisters and brothers, the poster raises a sense of intimacy and solidarity in the discussion forum. My interpretation is that she also evokes the Christian register following the common use of "brothers and sisters" in biblical and church discourse. The phrase might also index a similar style of address used in hip-hop communities. From the viewpoint of heteroglossia and translocality, the poster manages to express multiple social and cultural meanings in her message and, thus, create a discourse that may be interpreted as multivoiced.

Overall, in the heteroglossic and playful deployment of different linguistic forms and socioideological voices, elements of humor, and thus informality, familiarity, and solidarity are created. By engaging in these processes of styling, the poster positions herself and others as insiders in the community and "members of the same family" who know each other even before entering the online space. In this way, she also contributes to the overall construction of their group identities as members of this community of practice.

Styling Religious Discourse

In the second example, the sociocultural frames (cf. Coupland, 2007) of Christianity and extreme sports are shown as interwoven in an intrinsic way. The style used in Extract 8.2 draws heavily on religious register, but it is incorporated into discourse about extreme sports. One of the most frequent users of the forum defines the ultimate purpose of this community by writing down a Bible verse as well as using Finnish and English to interpret its meaning in the context of their sports activities. This post comes from a section of the forum dedicated to recording Bible passages that the users find inspirational.

Extract 8.2:

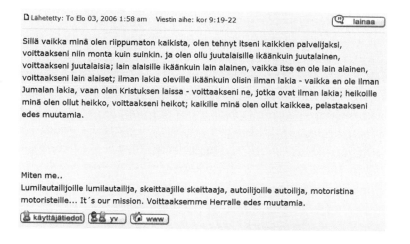

☐ Lähetetty: To Elo 03, 2006 1:58 am   Viestin aihe: kor 9:19-22   lainaa

Sillä vaikka minä olen riippumaton kaikista, olen tehnyt itseni kaikkien palvelijaksi, voittaakseni niin monta kuin suinkin. ja olen ollu juutalaisille ikäänkuin juutalainen, voittaakseni juutalaisia; lain alaisille ikäänkuin lain alainen, vaikka itse en ole lain alainen, voittaakseni lain alaiset; ilman lakia oleville ikäänkuin olisin ilman lakia - vaikka en ole ilman Jumalan lakia, vaan olen Kristuksen laissa - voittaakseni ne, jotka ovat ilman lakia; heikoille minä olen ollut heikko, voittaakseni heikot; kaikille minä olen ollut kaikkea, pelastaakseni edes muutamia.

Miten me..
Lumilautailijoille lumilautailija, skeittaajille skeittaaja, autoilijoille autoilija, motoristina motoristeille... It´s our mission. Voittaaksemme Herralle edes muutamia.

👤 käyttäjätiedot 👥 yv 🌐 www

1 Though I am free and belong to no man, I make myself a slave to everyone,

2 to win as many as possible. to the Jews I became like a Jew,

3 to win the Jews; to those under the law I became like one under the law, though I myself am not under the law,

4 so as to win those under the law; to those not having the law I became like one not having the law – though I am not free from

5 God's law but am under Christ's law – so as to win those not having the law; to the weak

6 I became weak, to win the weak; I have become all things to all men, so that by all possible means I might save

7 some.

8 How about us..

9 A snowboarder to snowboarders, a skater to skaters, a motorist to motorists, a motorbiker to

10 motorbikers... **It's our mission**. In order for us to win at least some to the Lord.

As with most of the previous messages posted to this forum section, this post begins with a passage from the Bible. The passage comes from the book of 1 Corinthians 9:19–22, and it has been written according to the 1938 edition of the Finnish Bible. (My English translation [lines 1–7] comes from the New International Version.) Unlike in the other messages in the forum section, this poster adopts a preacher-like role by presenting a mission statement for their group. He sets the Bible verse into a dialogue with the values of their community: after writing down the passage, he presents a question in line 8 to which he then provides an answer in lines 9–10. The poster crafts his message by drawing on different registers, codes, and patterns of language. He constructs the connection between the message of the Bible passage and the community members' everyday life as extreme sports enthusiasts by creating structural parallels in his text. He uses the rhetorical structure of the Bible passage when outlining the group's overall purpose in the extreme sports community. According to him, their "mission" is to be a snowboarder to snowboarders, a skater to skaters, and so forth, just as the Apostle Paul became like a Jew to the Jews, like one under the law to those under the law. At this point, he uses casual spoken language and adopts the extreme sports discourse. For instance, he uses the English-derived word *skeittaaja* for "a skateboarder" when the standard Finnish word would be "rullalautailija" (see the issue over Anglicans in Lenihan, Chapter 3 of this volume).

After drawing an analogy between the Bible verse and the different extreme sports activities, the poster verbalizes *Godspeed*'s shared goal of spreading the gospel to the wider extreme sports community when he points out in English that "It's our mission" (line 10). The switch into a different code is meaningful because, firstly, it adds emphasis to the communicative value of the argument he is making (Hinrichs, 2006, p. 4). Secondly, the use of the English phrase also has a translocal meaning: by using the word "mission," the poster associates their community with global missionary work. He is reminding the other members that missions can also be carried out locally. Thus, members align themselves with the community's sports activities and at the same time orient to Christian values and a global evangelistic mission. Overall, this identity work is carried out through the two codes: Finnish and English. The poster uses bilingual discourse to draw the community members together as a group. This is realized by the use of the personal pronoun "our" and also through the references to different activity groups (snowboarders, skateboarders, etc.) in the previous sentence.

In order to conclude and further argue for their shared goal, the poster then switches back to Finnish and employs a formal, specifically religious register when encouraging (himself and others): "In order for us to win at least some to the Lord" (*Voittaaksemme Herralle edes muutamia*). The first word in the Finnish phrase (*Voittaaksemme*, "In order for us to win") illustrates a verb structure (first infinitive, translative case, first-person plural) that is rarely used in everyday spoken language. Again, the choice of this structure reflects the verb structures in the Finnish Bible passage. In this way, the writer invokes a formal style of preaching.

In this post, the preacher-like discourse is achieved by the argumentative structure of the message and the use of formal religious register in Finnish. It is notable also that the inserted English phrase ("It's our mission") follows the *standard* spelling conventions and so does not include the kinds of adaptation or humorous language play in the orthographic level often seen, say, as described in this chapter. However, even though the tone of this message is somewhat serious and therefore different from the one in Extract 8.1, the heteroglossic style, including Finnish religious language and the use of English, makes this message distinct from conventional monolingual religious discourse. The alternating use of languages and registers creates a particular kind of religious discourse in this online context: a style that the poster uses to construct the community members' identities as extreme sports Christians.

Constructing Expertise

Extract 8.3 illustrates another aspect of the community members' identities and shows how *expertise* is constructed in the extreme sports community through bilingual language practices and cultural knowledge (see also Newon, Chapter 7 of this volume, on expert identities). A style used in this post draws on English extreme sports terminology, which is, nevertheless, adapted into the Finnish language. This post is part of a long discussion thread in a forum section called "other sports." The poster of this message (an experienced inline skater, "User B") initiated the thread and dedicated it to a discussion about inline skating/roller blading. During 2006–2007, he was very active in updating information about inline skating in this thread and, over time, constructed an image of himself as an expert inline skater. This was largely done through a style that included the use of an English or English-derived lexicon. His expert status was also other ascribed when other community members started asking him questions about roller-blading. This next extract is one such example of this, where a community member (User A) has asked for assistance in choosing roller blades from an online store that the expert member had recommended earlier.

The post is attached here first in its entirety in order to make its question-and-answer structure visible. The quoting possibilities of message boards enable posters to visually modify their messages. In this extract, User B positions himself in the role of an advisor by segmenting User A's questions into separate entities and systematically inserting his own answers immediately after each question. Hence, User B transforms computer-mediated discourse to reflect conversational turn taking (Georgakopoulou, 1997, p. 146). Later in this section, I will present my analysis of each question–answer segment.

User A's initial post is very casual as he has framed his request for help with a playful salutation (in line 1) and a humorous leave-taking (line 28). The salutation displays prosodic spelling (vowel lengthening), and the leave-taking illustrates "accent stylization" (Thurlow, 2003) in which dialectal Finnish is caricatured. Hence, the framing is done in Finnish, but the writer nevertheless uses heteroglossic, linguistic and

Extract 8.3:

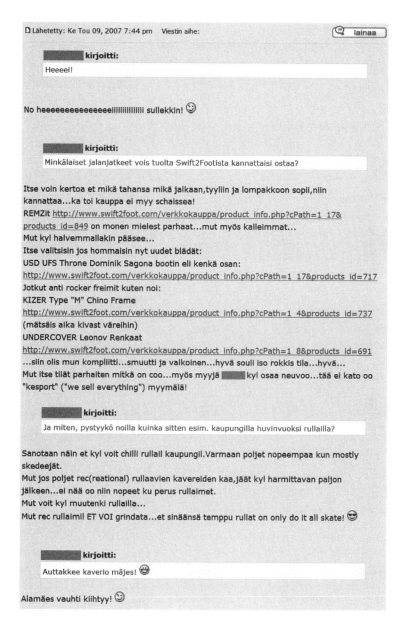

semiotic, resources, including orthographic creativity, emoticons, and a dialectical word play. User B responds to A by imitating, exaggerating, and elaborating on his style (but without conforming to the dialectal features drawn on by User A):

Salutation:

1   A: *Heeeei!*
      'Heeeey!'

2   B: *No heeeeeeeeeeeeeeeeiiiiiiiiiiiiiii sullekkin!* ☺
      'Well heeeeeeeeeeeeeeeeyyyyyyyyyyyyyyyy to you too! ☺'

Leave-taking:

28   A: *Auttakkee kaverio mäjes!* ☺
       'Please help me in my uphill battle! ☺'

29   B: *Alamäes vauhti kiihtyy!* ☺
       'You'll go faster downhill! ☺'

After the salutation, User B moves on to answer User A's two questions. First, User A wants to know what kinds of inline skates User B would recommend. User B adopts the role of expert by giving detailed information and commentary on what kinds of skates he himself would purchase. He accomplishes the construction of an expert role by using specialized sports jargon, referring to specific professional products, and evaluating different products, stores, and ways of practicing inline skating:

Extract 8.4:

> ██████ **kirjoitti:**
>
> Minkälaiset jalanjatkeet vois tuolta Swift2Footista kannattaisi ostaa?
>
> Itse voin kertoa et mikä tahansa mikä jalkaan,tyyliin ja lompakkoon sopii,niin kannattaa...ka toi kauppa ei myy schaissea!
> REMZit http://www.swift2foot.com/verkkokauppa/product_info.php?cPath=1_17&products_id=849 on monen mielest parhaat...mut myös kalleimmat...
> Mut kyl halvemmallakin pääsee...
> Itse valitsisin jos hommaisin nyt uudet blädät:
> USD UFS Throne Dominik Sagona bootin eli kenkä osan:
> http://www.swift2foot.com/verkkokauppa/product_info.php?cPath=1_17&products_id=717
> Jotkut anti rocker freimit kuten noi:
> KIZER Type "M" Chino Frame
> http://www.swift2foot.com/verkkokauppa/product_info.php?cPath=1_4&products_id=737
> (mätsäis aika kivast väreihin)
> UNDERCOVER Leonov Renkaat
> http://www.swift2foot.com/verkkokauppa/product_info.php?cPath=1_8&products_id=691
> ...siin olis mun kompliitti...smuutti ja valkoinen...hyvä souli iso rokkis tila...hyvä...
> Mut itse tilät parhaiten mitkä on coo...myös myyjä ██████ kyl osaa neuvoo...tää ei kato oo "kesport" ("we sell everything") myymälä!

3   [quote: What kind of footwear should one buy from this **Swift2Foot?**]

4   I can tell you that whatever suits your feet, style and wallet is

5   worth buying...see that store doesn't sell **Scheiße** [shit]!

6 For many **REMZs** [link to the product]
7 are the best...but also the most expensive ones...
8 But there are cheaper ones too...
9 If I purchased new roller **blades** I would pick:
10 a **USD UFS Throne Dominik Sagona boot** that is the shoe:
11 [link to the product]
12 Some of the **anti rocker frames** such as:
13 **KIZER Type "M" Chino Frame**
14 [link to the product]
15 (it **would match** the colors quite nicely)
16 **UNDERCOVER Leonov Wheels**
17 [link to the product]
18 ...this would be my **complete...smooth** and white...good soul plate big space for the rocker set up...good...
19 But you know best which are **coo**...also [first name] the salesperson can give you advice... see this isn't a
20 "kesport" (**"we sell everything"**) kind of store!

The product trade names of extreme sports equipment are a good illustration of global and translocal multilingual practices (Kelly-Holmes & Mautner, 2010). They exemplify how global brands shape the use of languages, and draw on certain linguistic resources by which they construct authenticity and legitimacy (Heller, 2007b, p. 543). Even though User B is rather careless in spelling words according to their standard spelling, he very rigorously follows the spelling of the product trade names. For example, this is evident when comparing how he describes the products in his own words and how he spells the actual product names:

12 *Jotkut **anti rocker freimit** kuten noi*:
    'Some of the **anti rocker frames** such as:'
13 **KIZER Type "M" Chino Frame**

The localized spelling of *anti rocker freimit* creates an interesting contrast with the spelling of the brand name. In *freimit* the Finnish vowel combination "ei" is used to phonetically reproduce the "a" in "frames," and the word ending is formed by using a Finnish inflectional vowel ('i) and the plural ending ("t"). This localized spelling reflects the writer's personal style (the way he would pronounce the word) whereas the product name becomes objectified by the use of the spelling most likely created by the producer of the brand.

Similarly, the poster uses a thoroughly modified word *blädät* to talk about (roller) blades, but, when referring to the actual product name, he more or less preserves the original spelling: *USD UFS Throne Dominik Sagona bootin.* He nonetheless chose to inflect the last part of the product name (*boot|in*) according to Finnish morphology by adding an inflectional vowel ("i") and an accusative case ending ("n"). Thus, in addition to the global market, this term, too, has been adapted to become part of a more localized Finnish extreme sports jargon. Despite this localization, the poster also provides a Finnish translation for the term "boot"—an act that further exemplifies his role as expert/advisor.

Later in line 16, the poster uses a Finnish term after the brand name: *UNDERCOVER Leonov Renkaat* ("UNDERCOVER Leonov Wheels"), but interestingly, he preserves the use of the initial capital letter in *Renkaat* ("Wheels") even though it is not a proper noun. According to conventional Finnish orthographic norms, common nouns in brand names should not be spelled with initial capital letters. These specific orthographic choices may therefore reflect the practices used on the online store website, which the poster is reproducing in this online forum.

After naming various products, the expert inline skater makes his comments about his preferences for the gear set:

> 18   *siin olis mun*   **kompliitti...smuutti** *ja valkoinen...*
>   'this would be my   **complete...smooth** and white...'

Here, he modifies the spelling of the original English adjectives to better reflect the Finnish pronunciation of the words. Used in the middle of a Finnish phrase *kompliitti* and *smuutti* are (to a local Finn) foreign lexical items, but after the modification their spelling (or, at least orthography) is more Finnish. The use of Finnish word endings also makes the words rhyme and thus creates a locally oriented instance of language play. In this kind of playful, informal, and creative linguistic environment in which mixing of codes is recurrent, localized words such as these may lose some of their foreignness (cf. Auer, 1999; also compare with Vaisman, Chapter 9 of this volume).

The author of this post positions himself as an expert, while at the same time positioning others as novices. In this way, he takes an epistemic stance, communicating that he has superior knowledge about different products and about inline skating; he also implies that he has the authority to evaluate, for instance, stores that sell sports products. Granted he gives others the authority to decide "what is cool," but nevertheless, he sets a norm in regard to the purchasing of sports equipment. According to his own explicit evaluation, the online store that he recommends "doesn't sell Scheiße [shit]" (line 5) whereas it is definitely not "cool" to buy skates from ordinary sports stores such as *Kesport*, which he dismissively characterizes with the English slogan "we sell everything" (line 20). By invoking this imaginary mass-marketing quote, he mimics the general concept of commercial practice in which the same products are sold to all customers with little attention to individual needs (Heller, 2007b). Overall, the poster invokes translocality and draws on heteroglossic resources as he incorporates multilingual extreme sports terminology, youth-cultural discourse with lexical adaptations (e.g. "schaissea" from the originally German word "Scheiße"), and diverse commercial voices into his message.

In Extract 8.5 (lines 22–27), the expert inline skater describes different ways of rollerblading in responding to User A's second question.

Extract 8.5:

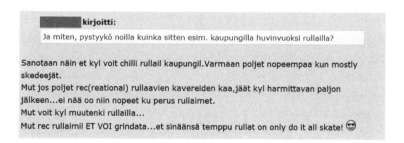

21 [quote: And how about, can you skate with those e.g. in town for fun?]

22 Let's say that you can **chill** skate in town. You'll probably go faster than

23 the **skateboarders mostly**.

24 But if you skate with **rec(reational)** skaters, you'll be annoyingly left

25 behind...these are not as fast as basic skates.

26 But there are other ways to skate too...

27 But with **rec** skates you CANNOT **grind**... so as such the trick skates are **only do it all skate!**

This exchange further illustrates how the poster shores up his epistemic stance by positioning himself in an expert role. For instance, he instructs User A in the correct use of English extreme sports vocabulary: when he first refers to "recreational skaters" he uses parentheses to imply that the abbreviation "rec" is generally used. Later on (in line 27), he refers to "rec skates," this time using only the abbreviation. This might be seen as a way to socialize the novice member into the professional jargon of inline skating (see, e.g., Lave & Wenger, 1991).

Another instance where English is drawn on is when User B inserts the phrase *only do it all skate!* This is a very casual way to mix the languages, and the English phrase does not seem to fit into the overall grammatical and semantic structure of the Finnish sentence. However, given that User B employs the phrase to describe trick skates in comparison with rec skates with which "you cannot grind," one can assume that he talks about a "do-it-all skate" and thus uses this term to refer to skates with all possible features. User B sums up his answer to User A with this English phrase; he prefers trick skates over recreational skates and considers them to be more legitimate in terms of the "true" nature of rollerblading.

Conclusion

In this chapter, I have attempted to show how translocality is an essential component of one specific online community. The analysis of just three instances of online interaction reveals that translocality is manifested by heteroglossic linguistic and discursive resources. For example, by styling their language use, forum users can localize a global language, make it a resource of their own, and thus construct their identities as Finnish users of the English language. Moreover, the members of the *Godspeed* community not only use English-language elements in their online discussions but they also create associations with other cultures by drawing on specific registers or displaying certain cultural knowledge. The sociocultural frames of Christianity, extreme sports, and youth culture structure the topics and ways of speaking in the online forum. For instance, topics related to extreme sports prompt the use of English-derived terminology, which in turn contributes to creating a style that is characterized by, for example, references to global products and ways of practicing sports. In the Christian framework, translocality is evoked in reference to the message of the Bible and the shared values and goals in the global community of Christians. English is also integrated into the Christian discourse but with a different meaning potential than the more playful and aesthetic appropriations of English in the discourse of extreme sports or youth culture. Overall, the members of the community are, by way of using a variety of linguistic and discursive resources, able to engage in a stylistic expression of their identities.

The extracts in this chapter can be seen to illustrate three different identity positions through which the community members style their interaction in the online discussion forum. Specifically, the resources for styling include language choice between Finnish and English, use of different registers, discourses and cultural references, and creative spelling practices. The analysis of the extracts showed how the members of the community can play with language, and hence, by drawing on and adapting English elements into the Finnish language, they are able to create a humorous way of communicating their message. By engaging in the playful use of language, the community members conveyed affiliation and solidarity and thus constructed a sense of shared community. Nevertheless, they can also associate themselves with global youth cultures that are often characterized by "[p]layful co-articulations of various social voices and cultural resources" (Androutsopoulos & Georgakopoulou, 2003, p. 5). By incorporating formal religious register into their talk about the community's sports activities, an evangelistic mission for the whole group was discursively constructed, and the Christian identity was explicitly evoked. Finally, consumer culture in extreme sports was highlighted through the use of specialized English extreme sports jargon. Expert identities were thus constructed through superior knowledge within the extreme sports culture.

On the whole, the three examples analyzed here illustrate how an online space can function as an authentic site for community construction. Shared interests, cultural identifications, and values as well as specific language practices may lead a particular group of people to form a community of practice online. Identifying oneself as a member of a group requires experiences, knowledge, or expertise both on relevant topics and the ways in which these topics are talked about. Current research on language practices in online communities, such as in communities for fan fiction writers or football enthusiasts, support these observations: specific ways of using language and discussing certain topics are drawn on and also expected by the participants when they construct and maintain their online community (Kytölä, forthcoming; Leppänen, forthcoming). This chapter, similarly, shed light on the mechanisms, or language practices, by which sociality is created online—both locally and translocally.

Acknowledgments

I would like to thank Crispin Thurlow for his helpful suggestions to improve my initial draft. I also wish to thank the internal and external readers, as well as my PhD supervisors Sirpa Leppänen and Päivi Pahta, for their valuable comments. I want to acknowledge the financial and moral support provided by the research team VARIENG in Jyväskylä. I am particularly grateful to my colleague Alicia Copp Jinkerson who proofread this chapter. Naturally, all remaining errors are mine. Lastly, I owe many thanks to Kane and Sami, active members of the *Godspeed* community, who have always generously answered my questions.

References

Alim, H.S. (2009). Translocal style communites: Hip hop youth as cultural theorists of style, language, and globalization, *Pragmatics*, 19(1), 103–127.

Androutsopoulos, J. (2000). Non-standard spellings in media texts: The case of German fanzines. *Journal of Sociolinguistics*, 4(4), 514–533.

Androutsopoulos, J. (2007). Language choice and code switching in German-based diasporic web forums. In B. Danet & S.C. Herring (Eds.), *The Multilingual Internet: Language, Culture, and Communication Online*, (pp. 340–361). Oxford: Oxford University Press.

Androutsopoulos, J. (2008). Potentials and limitations of discourse-centred online ethnography, *Language@internet* 5, article 8. Retrieved May 17, 2011, from http://www.languageatinternet.de/articles/2008

Androutsopoulos, J., & Georgakopoulou, A. (Eds.). (2003). *Discourse Constructions of Youth Identities*. Amsterdam: John Benjamins.

Auer, P. (1999). From codeswitching via language mixing to fused lects: Toward a dynamic typology of bilingual speech, *The International Journal of Bilingualism*, 3(4), 309–332.

Auer, P. (Ed.) (2007). *Style and Social Identities: Alternative Approaches to Linguistic Heterogeneity*. Berlin: Mouton de Gruyter.

Bailey, B. (2007). Heteroglossia and boundaries. In M. Heller (Ed.), *Bilingualism: A Social Approach*, (pp. 257–274). Basingstoke: Palgrave Macmillan.

Bakhtin, M.M. (1981). Discourse in the novel. In M. Holquist (Ed.), *The Dialogic Imagination: Four Essays by M.M. Bakhtin*, (pp. 259–422). Austin: University of Texas Press.

Bauman, R. (2000). Language, identity, performance. *Pragmatics*, 10(1), 1–5.

Baym, N. (2000). *Tune In, Log On: Soaps, Fandom, and Online Community*. Thousand Oaks, CA: Sage.

Blommaert, J. (2010). *The Sociolinguisctics of Globalization*. Cambridge: Cambridge University Press.

Coupland, N. (Ed.). (2007). *Style: Language Variation and Identity*. Cambridge: Cambridge University Press.

Eckert, P. (2005). Stylistic practice and the adolescent social order. In A. Williams & C. Thurlow (Eds.), *Talking Adolescence: Perspectives on Communication in the Teenage Years*, (pp. 93–110). New York: Peter Lang.

Georgakopoulou, A. (1997). Self-presentation and interactional alliances in e-mail discourse: The style- and code-switches of Greek messages. *International Journal of Applied Linguistics*, 7(2), 141–164.

Heller, M. (Ed.). (2007a). *Bilingualism: A Social Approach*. Basingstoke: Palgrave Macmillan.

Heller, M. (2007b). Multilingualism and transnationalism. In P. Auer & W. Li (Eds.), *Handbook of Multilingualism and Multilingual Communication*, (pp. 539–553). Berlin: Mouton de Gruyter.

Hepp, A. (2009). Transculturality as a perspective: Researching media cultures comparatively. *Forum: Qualitative Social Research*, 10(1), article 26. Retrieved May 17, 2011, from http://www.qualitative-research.net/index.php/fqs/article/view/1221/2657

Herring, S.C. (2007). A faceted classification scheme for computer-mediated discourse, *Language@internet* 4, article 1. Retrieved May 17, 2011, from http://www.languageatinternet.de/articles/2007

Hinrichs, L. (2006). *Codeswitching on the Web: English and Jamaican Creole in E-Mail Communication*. Amsterdam: John Benjamins.

Honeycutt, C. (2005). Hazing as a process of boundary maintenance in an online community. *Journal of Computer-Mediated Communication*, 10(2), article 3. Retrieved May 17, 2011, from http://jcmc.indiana.edu/vol10/issue2/honeycutt.html

Jaworski, A., & Thurlow, C. (2010). Language and the globalizing habitus of tourism: Toward a sociolinguistics of fleeting relationships. In N. Coupland (Ed.), *The Handbook of Language and Globalization*, (pp. 256–286). Oxford: Blackwell.

Kelly-Holmes, H., & Mautner, G. (2010). *Language and the Market*. Palgrave Macmillan.

Kytölä, S. (forthcoming). Language-ideological peer normativity of linguistic resources-in-use: Non-standard Englishes in Finnish online football forums. In J. Blommaert, S. Leppänen, P. Pahta, & T. Räisänen (Eds.), *Dangerous Multilingualism: Northern Perspectives to Order, Purity and Normality*. Basingstoke: Palgrave-Macmillan.

Lähteenmäki, M. (2010). Heteroglossia and voice: Conceptualising linguistic diversity from a Bakhtinian perspective. In M. Lähteenmäki & M. Vanhala-Aniszewski (Eds.), *Language Ideologies in Transition: Multilingualism in Finland and Russia*, (pp. 15–29). Hamburg: Peter Lange.

Lam, E. (2004). Second language socialization in a bilingual chat room: Global and local considerations. *Language Learning & Technology*, 8 (3), 44–65.

Lave, J., & Wenger, E. (1991). *Situated Learning: Legitimate Peripheral Participation.* Cambridge: Cambridge University Press.

Leppänen, S. (forthcoming). Linguistic and discursive heteroglossia on the translocal internet: The case of web writing. In M. Sebba, S. Mahootian, & C. Jonsson (Eds.), *Language Mixing and Code-switching in Writing: Approaches to Mixed-language Written Discourse.* London & New York: Routledge.

Leppänen, S., Pitkänen-Huhta, A., Piirainen-Marsh, A., Nikula, T., & Peuronen, S. (2009). Young people's translocal new media uses: A multiperspective analysis of language choice and heteroglossia, *Journal of Computer-Mediated Communication,* 14(4), 1080–1107.

Leppänen, S., et al. (2011). *National Survey on English in Finland: Uses, Meanings and Attitudes.* Studies in Variation, Contacts and Change in English. Retrieved May 17, 2011, from http://www.helsinki.fi/varieng/journal/volumes/05/

Markham, A., & Baym, N. (2009). *Internet Inquiry: Conversations about Method.* Los Angeles: Sage.

McLellan, J. (2005). Malay-English language alternation in two Brunei Darussalam on-line discussion forums. Retrieved March 25, 2011, from http://espace.library.curtin.edu.au:80/R?func=dbin-jump-full&local_base=gen01-era02&object_id=16277

Nikula, T., & Pitkänen-Huhta, A. (2008). Using photographs to access stories of learning English. In A.M.F. Barcelos, P. Kalaja, & V. Menezes (Eds.), *Narratives of Learning and Teaching EFL,* (pp. 171–185). Basingstoke: Palgrave-Macmillan.

Pennycook, A. (2003). Global Englishes, Rip Slyme, and performativity. *Journal of Sociolinguistics,* 7(4), 513–533.

Pennycook, A. (2007). *Global Englishes and Transcultural Flows.* London & New York: Routledge.

Piirainen-Marsh, A., & Tainio, L. (2009). Collaborative game-play as a site for participation and situated learning of a second language. *Scandinavian Journal of Educational Research,* 53(2), 167–183.

Sveningsson Elm, M. (2009). How do various notions of privacy influence decisions in qualitative internet research? In A.N. Markham & N.K. Baym (Eds.), *Internet Inquiry: Conversations about Method,* (pp. 69–87). Los Angeles: Sage.

Taavitsainen, I., & Pahta, P. (2003). English in Finland: Globalisation, language awareness and questions of identity. *English Today* 19(4), 3–15.

Thurlow, C. (2003). Generation Txt? The sociolinguistics of young people's text-messaging. *Discourse Analysis Online* 1(1). Retrieved May 17, 2011, from http://faculty.washington.edu/thurlow/papers/Thurlow(2003)DAOL.pdf

Chapter 9

Performing Girlhood through Typographic Play in Hebrew Blogs

Carmel Vaisman

THIS CHAPTER IS concerned with the ways girls employ discursive repertoires for styling their online gender identities. Specifically, I look at the playful use of Hebrew orthography and digital typography by Israeli teenage girls as part of a multimodal identity toolkit articulated through their blogging practices. The chapter emerges from a larger ethnography of girls' engagement with new media literacies in the Hebrew-language blogosphere. This study is based on posts sampled between 2004 and 2007, from the blogs of 140 Israeli girls aged 11–16 on *Israblog*, Israel's largest blog-hosting website and populated mainly by adolescent girls.

Research on language and gender emerged from a motivation to explore the reflection of social differences/inequalities between men and women (e.g., Lakoff, 1975) and initially was based upon an assumption of gender as a fixed category and on the sociolinguistic framework of speech communities. In the early nineties, however, the field was revolutionized

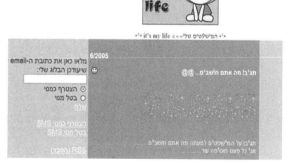

FIGURE 9.1

by two concepts that changed both the perception of gendered identity and the contexts in which it was analyzed. Judith Butler (1990) extended Goffman's identity performance concept in supporting her argument that gender was not simply a biological category but, rather, a set of performed rituals—something we do, not something we are. Research on language and gender then took a "performance turn" (Eckert & McConnell-Ginet, 2003), exploring the diversity *among* men and *among* women, who perform a variety of masculinities and femininities. One well-known example of this approach is Kira Hall's (1995) study of phone-sex service workers, which demonstrates how women (and one man) move between diverse feminine identities performed solely through their speech styles and other discursive resources. At the same time, the classic sociolinguistic framework of speech community was also being problematized and has now largely been replaced with the notion of "community of practice" (Bucholtz, 1999; Eckert & McConnell-Ginet, 1992; although see Rampton, 2009). The turn to practice theory has encouraged research on language and gender to take on more refined microanalyses of various linguistic practices involved in the performance and the struggle over gender identities. The focus is thus on language as local practice (cf. Pennycook, 2010) and on vernacular practice.

Much of the prominent research on gender and language is concerned with spoken discourse among groups of girls (e.g., Bucholtz, 1999; Coats, 1999; Goodwin, 2006), with less attention given to written discourse (mostly fictional, see Gilbert, 1993; Orellana, 1999). Indeed, the historical tendency of linguistics as a field is to focus mainly on spoken language, especially where nonstandard language is concerned (Sebba, 2003). This has, of course, changed with the advent of new media. The first wave of new media discourse research was mainly descriptive and criticized for its deterministic focus on listing formal features of new media genres (Androutsopoulos, 2006). Increasingly, it has been complemented by analyses that shed light on how different contextual parameters shape and are evoked in the discourse of various new media (see Thurlow & Mroczek's Introduction to this volume). In this way, we can trace the study of language and gender in new media in Susan Herring's pioneering research (e.g., Herring, 1993, 2000) through to more "doing gender" approaches (e.g., Rodino, 1997) and studies of multigender identity play (e.g., Danet, 1998; Turkle, 1997). All gender identities are produced through everyday communicators' discursive repertoires of which language is a key one (Eckert & McConnell-Ginet, 2003; Eckert & Rickford, 2001). Where in offline life this may also include clothing, gestures, hairstyles, and so on, gender performances online rely heavily on language.

New Media Orthography/Identity Play

Danet (2001) refers to the computer as a grand piano on our desktop. Indeed, in early online text-based communities, the use of keyboard was interpreted as voice and tones production. (For instance, the use of CAPS was interpreted as shouting.) In this way, digital texts could be regarded as objects to look *at* rather than to look *through* for their meaning; it is this that also invites aesthetic play (Lanham, 1993). Danet (2001) defines playfulness as playing *with* the rules as opposed to playing *by* the rules, a definition that applies for nonstandard orthography and typography (cf. also Thurlow, 2011). Typography is not to be looked at as an abstract sign system, but as a situated code choice, which is always part of a specific genre in a specific communicative situation (Androutsopoulos, 2004). Playful practices with orthography and typography demonstrate how people convey social meaning through form and not solely content (Sebba, 2003), signifying the discourse and text as sources of fascination apart from the semantic content they convey (Kataoka, 1997).

In this regard, vernacular forms of nonstandard orthography have been common throughout history (see Shortis, 2007); however, the first known example of online, English-language subcultural language play is *l33t*, a name given to the creative orthographic and typographic practices of (usually male) hackers (Raymond, 1991). A typographic play on "leet," *l33t* stands for "elite." To date, studies of orthographic and typographic practices in new media can be divided into two groups: studies on multilingualism, demonstrating Romanized vernacular literations interpreted in the context of globalization and identity (many of these are to be found in Danet & Herring, 2003, 2007), and studies on youth subculture discourse (e.g., Androutsopoulos, 2007; Sebba, 2003), where deviant orthography and misspelling are signifiers for speech styles and social identities. Few of these studies, however, emphasized linguistic creativity as means of performing feminine identities within online communities of practice. Having said which, the data I am presenting in this chapter does align with similar studies from the Japanese-speaking web (Kataoka, 1997; Katsuno & Yano, 2007).

Blogs have been conceptualized as a distinctive genre (Herring et al., 2005), but given the multiple variations of blogging software and the flexibility of user choices, others have suggested that the focus should instead be on the situated practices of bloggers (Schmidt, 2007; cf. also Androutsopoulos, Chapter 13 of this volume). While the majority of blogs were created by women and girls, they got little attention from either the mass media or academic research (Herring et al., 2004), where the attention was given to the journalism practices of male bloggers. Recently, there has been a growing body of research on girls and young women as active *producers* of culture in new media forms such as personal home pages and blogs (e.g., Bortree, 2005; Kearney, 2006; Mazzarella, 2005; Stern, 2002). These studies, however, typically don't emphasize the role of language. A few studies do look at identity performance through personal blog narrative (e.g., Langellier & Petterson, 2004; Page, 2008), while others dealing with the linguistic features of blogs (e.g., Huffaker & Calvert, 2005) focus on gender perceptions and linguistic differences rather than take a more performance approach.

In my own work, I have found girls' blogging styles and narrative practices to be clearly associated with the performance of their gendered and (sub)cultural identities. These identities are enacted and performed online through the design choices made on their blogs (e.g., *Freak* girls create black blogs with gothic iconography; *Anime* Girls create blogs with Manga iconography, etc.). One particular community of interest to me has been the *Fakatsa*, a girls-only community of practice that gained visibility through its unusual blogging style; specifically, their playful use of Hebrew orthography or digital typography.

Fakatsa: *Performing* "Girly Girl" *Online*

Fakatsa is the Hebrew abbreviation of "a little outlandish *Frecha*"—a popular Israeli stereotype often used similarly to the slang word "tart" in English. It was originally used as a derogatory name for Moroccan-Israeli women who rebelled against family tradition by identifying with American/global culture and fashion and were thus perceived as promiscuous and superficial. However, during the 1990s, as Israel was quickly globalizing, *Frecha* fashion became mainstream, and *Frecha* has now become a derogatory term for all women deemed to be noncritical early adopters of bold fashion trends. As before, and as a result of their prominence, these women are perceived to be "too loud"—both literally (i.e., in their speech) and metaphorically (e.g., in terms of their sexuality). Crispin Thurlow suggests that many Euro-Americans might recognize a *Frecha* quality in "celebutants" like Paris Hilton and in a combination of the somewhat outdated notions of "bimbo" and "girly girl."

In Japan, girls' engagement with American mainstream "global" culture has been met with similar opposition and is often interpreted as subversive to "authentic" or "traditional" Japanese culture (Hjorth, 2003). Similarly, despite the rapid spread of American/global culture in Israel since the 1990s, large portions of Israeli society are Orthodox Jews or at least consider themselves traditional Jews. Even among the secular portion of society, it seems that girls are still expected to conform to a Zionist gender stereotype rooted in a socialist ethos, which stresses communal values and natural beauty, while ridiculing vain preoccupations with outward appearance.

Young girls who overtly adopt global culture and consumerism and who zigzag between fashion trends, seemingly without criticism or reflexivity, are, therefore, labeled *Fakatsa*—the preadolescent version of the *Frecha* young women they are deemed to become. In short, the term has come to refer to any girl who is seen to care too much about her "style"—a spineless "fashion victim." In reaction to this moral/social judgment, many of these girls, usually preteen, have proudly adopted the derogatory term *Fakatsa*, giving it the positive meaning of being feminine and up to date with fashion. For them, this is precisely how a girl should be, not least because this is how the media messages they consume appear to regard girlhood. The *Fakatsa*, like the nerd girl (Bucholtz, 1999), isn't just a stigma but a purposefully chosen alternative, in this case to traditional Jewish and Zionist gender expectations, which is achieved and maintained through language and other social practices, drawing upon global media and new media cultures. (For an interesting comparison, see Peuronen, Chapter 8 of this volume.)

Starting in 2004, the front page of *Israblog* was filled with usernames, blog titles, and posted comments written in a very unusual, distinctive typography: mixing the standard Hebrew writing system with various ASCII signs. The style was described as "scribbled" and "meaningless" by veteran bloggers. At first sight, this typography, used solely by girls with pink blogs and blinking kitsch iconography, looked like digital strings produced by random strokes on a keyboard and was written off as disharmonic noise, an "environmental hazard contaminating the blogosphere," as one dismissive blogger put it.

Girls who used this typography and shared other similar blogging practices were commonly referred to as *Fakatzas* (plural) by other bloggers who created a new variation of the derogatory *Frecha*, applying the social judgment of girls' bodies to their blogs. A few popular male bloggers in their teens and twenties have satirized *Fakatsa* typography, for instance, by creating Microsoft Word *Fakatsa* fonts or introducing a designed image of a *Fakatsa* keyboard limited to a few ASCII signs and almost no letters, or even a funny web translator from standard Hebrew to the playful typography, which became known as *Fakatsa* language. Male hackers' typographic invention (l33t mentioned earlier) is typically perceived to be a sophisticated performance of linguistic skills (Danet, 2001) based on the assumption that one can only play with language when fluent in it and mastering it. By contrast, the Israeli media and adult bloggers have been quick to dismiss *Fakatsa* girls' no less inventive typography as illiterate and shallow.

Media representations of this playful typography either portray it as a silly code to amuse and challenge the readers, or express explicit concern for the deteriorating literacy and spelling skills of young girls, not even entertaining the possibility of linguistic creativity, nor appreciating the sophistication and the mastery of various scripts required for producing text in this typography. This attitude is consistent with public discourse about emergent technologies involving language change (Baron, 2000; Thurlow, 2006, 2007, 2011). Needless to say, it is only when one delves deeper into these supposedly "meaningless" keyboard strokes that a form of constancy becomes evident; vernacular orthographies may be nonstandard, but they are invariably rule based (Shortis, 2007). And this is precisely what a careful analysis of *Fakatsa* style reveals.

!!ה33פ *The Stylistic Conventions of* Fakatsa

As I say, the main orthographic/typographic principle of *Fakatsa* style is based on replacing Hebrew characters with ASCII characters—specifically, those that are graphically similar to the Hebrew script. The Hebrew alphabet consists only of consonants, written from right to left. It has 22 letters, 5 of which use different forms at the end of a word. It has no distinct capital or lowercase letters, but it has both typographic and cursive writing systems with various fonts and variations. During the three years I documented *Fakatsa* style, in as many as 140 girls' blogs, I found that ASCII signs were used as visual replacements for all but two Hebrew letters, including two extra forms used for the end of a word. Half of the letters had more than one possible replacement, and many of these signs were, in fact, similar to the respective cursive Hebrew letters, which vary from the shape of their typographic equivalents. Table 9.1 shows all documented variations, including rare replacements with extended ISO-ASCII signs, arranged by frequency of use. The typed letters are in *Times New Roman* Hebrew font, and the cursive letters are in *Guttman Yad*—a Microsoft Word font that represents cursive Hebrew in a standardized typographic version. One need not know Hebrew to assess the visual resemblance of Hebrew letters to their ASCII replacement signs. ASCII replacements are both case and font sensitive, as I will discuss presently.

Every sentence written using this creative typographic form is a unique performance of style, exercising different, often spontaneous choices that compel readers (ratified or unratified) to "decipher" them according to their specific context of use. Each letter has a number of possible replacements,

Table 9.1 *Fakatsa*-style ASCII replacements for Hebrew letters

Letter numbering	Hebrew typed letters	Hebrew cursive letters	ASCII replacements								
1	א		K	X	%	@	I<	I(	‡€	I€	IC
2	ב		2								
3	ג										
4	ד		T								
5	ה										
6	ו		1	!	I	‡	i	I			
7	ז		T								
8	ח		n	^							
9	ט		6	C							
10	י		*	^	'	+	1				
11	כ		<	[	{	¢					
12	ל		5	&							
13	מ		N	[\]	M	I\I					
13a	ם		][	][	0						
14	נ		J	[	)	{					
15	ס		0	O	()	§					
16	ע		y								
17	פ		9	F	g						
18	צ		3								
18a	ץ		Y								
19	ק		q								
20	ר		7								
21	ש		W	e	|/	(!)					
22	ת		)n								

and not all letters are replaced in every word; for example, the title of this section of my chapter contains a *Fakatsa* style literation of the word פצצה, which means "bomb," but is used as a slang word for a hot chick (as in "sex bomb") or a mind-blowing pleasure. This is one of the few words that is spelled the same way by all *Fakatsa* girls, replacing letter number 18 (in Table 9.1) with the numerical sign 3, which closely resembles the letter's cursive script; however, should a girl need to write the sentence "I am a mind-blowing hot chick" in Hebrew typed script ((אני פצצה פצצתית), she would have to decide which letters to replace and which of the ASCII signs to use as replacements. To list just a few of these possibilities, varying only in replacement choices of the first word from right to left, "I" (אני):

פ33ה פ33ה תית3K*נ
פ33ה פ33ה תית ^א|
פ33ה פ33ה תיתJX·
פ33ה פ33ה תית +%נ

From my careful analysis of the posts in my dataset, it appears that the choice of replacements is influenced by two main considerations:

1. *Accessibility and flow*

     a. An ASCII sign is more frequently used if it is easily accessible on the keyboard, making rapid and flowing writing possible in the new typography. For instance, on Israeli keyboards, numbers are more accessible than Roman letters, and so numbers are the most common replacements for letters.

     b. Letters tend to be replaced by a *single* ASCII sign whenever possible. Constructing a letter from two or more signs is clearly more complicated and slows down the writing.

     c. Despite genre and medium differences between text messages and blogs, they are both sites of spontaneous speechlike writing, and a similar concern for speed and flow influences typographic and orthographic choices in both cases (see Shortis, 2007; Thurlow, 2003).

2. *Visual proportion and design*

Many of the less common variations were preferred over the accessible ones when:

     a. The sign bore greater resemblance to the Hebrew letter. For instance, the cursive Hebrew letter numbered 14 in Table 9.1 can be represented by an easily accessible sign like], yet it is more commonly represented by the roman letter **J**, which has more pleasing, rounded proportions. For the same reason, girls are often sensitive to the use of capitalized letters or different Roman fonts. For instance, when the typed Hebrew letter ⅁ (17 in Table 9.1) is replaced with the Roman letter **g**, it is always in *Arial* font (**g**) since the *Times New Roman* **g** lacks the graphic proportions required for this replacement.

b. The sign or signs were proportional to the written Hebrew text in that segment. When using different sign systems in the same sentence, the width or height of the digital line is altered. In the example below (Extract 9.1), a girl uses the unique typography only in the title and signature, thus even for a non-Hebrew reader the digital field proportions of standard Hebrew typography versus the disturbed proportions of the unique typography are evident.

W!נ%ת תג!2!ת מגע⁺ל!ת

אז מה אם אני פאקצה? זה אומר שאין לי חיים? שאין לי תכלית?
אני פשוט ילדה שאוהבת וחד, בנים, מסיבות, שטויות, ולכתב עם סימנים.
הבלוג פה נעד כד׳ שאנשימוש יראו אותי אחרה, ולא ישפטו אותי רק לפי דעתם שאני פאקצה.
אני לאהוב אותכם הרבה, אזמה אם אתם לא מבינמוש?
ק!%ר⁺נה

In Extract 9.2, however, it is harder for a non-Hebrew reader to identify the replacements that are non-Hebrew script because of the careful proportions constructed by the use of less common ASCII replacement choices. In particular, notice that the first sign on the right is the Roman letter **c**; also notice the appearance of several **i** and **e** marks and the single use of **y**. The efforts put into proportion demonstrate a concern for the look (the design) of the typography, as part of what makes writing both creative and pleasurable.

There is an interesting paradox at play here. Playfulness with typography is, as I suggest, defined by striving for perfect proportions; however, things cannot be too perfect: if the act of replacement isn't slightly noticeable. then the effort of replacement is futile. The replacement has to be

very similar, but not so good that its readers will not spot it! This is the
reason why, for example, the Hebrew letter **o** numbered 15 in Table 9.1,
is so rarely replaced—in its cursive form it is merely a circle, and the
Roman letter **o** resembles it too much, making the replacement unre-
markable/unnoticeable. Replacing it with the number **0** is, therefore,
more common because it is slightly more noticeable due to the elliptical proportions of the sign. Occasionally, girls will use disproportional
sign replacements for aesthetic or phonetic emphasis, a point I return
to shortly.

In this playful typographic system, the graphic form—the *look*—of the
sign prevails over any other connotative meaning that it may carry (cf. van
Leeuwen, 2006). An extreme example (although a quite rare one) is the
replacement of the Hebrew letter ו numbered 6 in Table 9.1 with its most
rare replacement (the last sign on the right in Table 9.1), which is in fact
the cursive form of letter number 14 when appearing in the end of a word.
Both are from the same writing system, representing entirely different
letters and sounds, but they are graphically close (with one being a slightly
shorter line than the other) and are thus considered suitable replacements
for each other when proportions are altered and the word needs a shorter-
or longer-looking Hebrew sign. The reason this replacement isn't very
common is that it imposes hardship even on the reader familiar with the
Hebrew writing system, and it is also prone to be misjudged as a grammatical mistake (i.e., a question of poor standard literacy) rather than playful innovation.

Fakatsa style also favors the look over the phonology of the sign: girls
do not mind representing different Hebrew letters and sounds through
the same ASCII sign. For example, letters number 7 and 4 (ז, ד) or 11 and
14 (נ, כ) in Table 9.1 represent entirely different letters and sounds but are
graphically similar and often share some ASCII replacement signs. This
further forces the reader into a unique, context-based reading of each and
every written performance. Alternatively, of course, it serves the purpose of
excluding the outsider altogether, as users are sensitive to different audiences when making orthography and typography choices (Shortis, 2007;
Thurlow, 2007).

There are only two Hebrew letters, numbered 3 and 5 (ג and ה) that
have no evident replacements. For the girls there is a good reason for this.
What makes these letters unique is that they are made of two parts, one
below the other, making it impossible to represent them proportionally
with two signs in the same digital field, which allows room for only one

sign at a time. Meanwhile, some signs, although they might serve as letter replacements, are purely ornamental and used to decorate the sentence as a form of pencil art around written words, as in Extract 9.3.

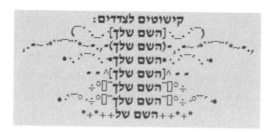

These are ornaments designed around nicknames on ICQ (i.e., instant messaging) that one blogger offers her friends. The writing in the middle says "your name" in standard typography; all other signs, including + ^ and], which are often letter replacements, serve as ASCII art decorations. This ornamental form of use is consistent with earlier documentations of ASCII art practices (Danet, 2001; Werry, 1996; see also Thurlow, 2011); however, the embedding of ASCII art practices around and in between words written in *Fakatsa* style further complicates its performance, challenging the reader to detect the function of the sign: Is it a visual-based letter replacement or an abstract ("meaningless") art decoration? To complicate matters, some ornamental signs can fulfill a communicative function of speech emphasis, signifying a certain slang/subcultural accent or pronunciation. This brings me nicely to another key expressive resource used by *Fakatsa* girls.

From Look to Sound: Phonetic Play in Fakatsa

In addition to the kinds of visual orthographic play that I have been discussing above, there is also another common type of sign play that *Fakatsa* girls like to engage in. The shaded signs in Table 9.1 stand for exceptions to the visual-form rule, involving a form of *phonetic* creativity. So, for example, **M** and **F** are not quite visually similar to the Hebrew letters they replace, but they do represent their sound. Some of these signs are thus double coded, requiring even more complex and, indeed, multilingual reading (or "deciphering") skills. For example: the ASCII asperand (@)often replaced the letter **a** in l33t, though it wasn't prominent in other vernacular literations mentioned earlier in the chapter. In Hebrew it is often used to represent the same sound (**ɑ:** in English phonetics). Understanding this therefore requires knowledge of two writing systems and additional familiarity with the conventions of English-language new media styles.

q and ¢, for instance, are graphic mirror images of the Hebrew cursive letters they often replace (numbers 11 and 19) and at the same time representations of their respective Hebrew phonetics. In yet another twist, bloggers' language play may often resonate with biblical Hebrew, which contains a set of written marks above the letters telling the reader how to pronounce the word or even how to sing it. Hebrew punctuation retains a trace of these vocal emphasis instructions, and my analysis of typography play revealed that some of the rare replacements are used as vocal signifiers for syllable emphasis and for expressing subcultural (or "slang") word pronunciation and accents. Take, for the example, Extract 9.4:

In this case, the ¢ signifies a deep-throat pronunciation of the letter c in English (phonetics: k) and כ in Hebrew (number 11 in Table 9.1), normally indicated in Hebrew punctuation by a dot in the middle of the letter (כּ). The § is a circle signifying the letter o (number 15 in Table 9.1) in the middle of the sign, but with "curled" edges. This letter's sound in Hebrew is like the English phonetic s, but in some Hebrew slang/subcultural styles the s sound is prolonged and "curled" with the voice (phonetics: ssssss), carrying various connotations of pleasure, teasing, or even threat, depending on the context of the performance. The graphic "curls" of this sign are a vocal signifier for such "curly" vocal playfulness with the word. Once again, these accent simulations are akin to those in other new media (Shortis, 2007; Thurlow, 2003).

The nickname in Extract 9.5 replaces only the Hebrew letter ו (number 6 in Table 9.1) that produces the sound u:, while the parenthesis around it {} is ornamental ASCII art; it serves, however, a phonetic function of stressing and prolonging the u: sound. The meaning of this word in Hebrew is "pampered," and the result of the prolonged u: is a pampered girly voice tone. Such practices could be interpreted as onomatopoeic forms, similar to some variations documented in text messages (Thurlow, 2003). In attempting to make the words look like they sound, girls bring it closer to what they actually mean (possibly in a Barthesian pursuit of the essence they stand for).

Another phonetic-based variation found in many of the blogs resembles the logic of letter-number homophones like the Gr8 (great), which are common in texting forms (Shortis, 2007). The number *100* is pronounced in Hebrew as *mea*; thus, many words that start with the syllable *mea* (and have nothing to do with the number) replace the syllable with the number. This variation appears mostly in adjectives, for instance: ממת100 (pronounced *mea-memet* and meaning "gorgeous" in the feminine grammatical form). Since the numbers *1* and *0* are common replacements on the basis of their visual form in *Fakatsa* style, this variation challenges the reader to switch quickly between different meaning-making systems: in other words, treating *100* as a number one minute and then having to attend to its phonetic value the next minute. Often *Fakatsa* girls create a one-off, context-based performance replacement principle that the reader also has to identify, as with the example in Extract 9.6.

קשה^*לה^*1 ת^*צנו^*עה^*כשאנ^*^*הט!2ה^*2^*!ר

The sign ^ in Extract 9.6, often used to replace either ' or ה (numbered 10 and 8 in Table 9.1) in Hebrew, is used here as a signifier for space between the words in the sentence. One can only figure out this temporarily established rule during the process of carefully deciphering the sentence.

General Discussion: New Media Language Play and/as Gender Performance

Like many varieties and styles that spread through imitation and evolve through continuous decentralized creativity, it is hard to trace the origin of the *Fakatsa* style. However, it seems that the development of the kind of language play I have been looking at here is multisourced. Some of its early uses were in instant messaging (ICQ) usernames, maintaining a girl's name through playful typography changes when her preferred nickname was already taken. Playful typography can be a convenient way for girls to avoid being "*Googled*" by their parents (i.e., checked up on by the parents). Indeed, I learned that most girl bloggers write their full name and other identifying details only in the blog frame that is a nonsearchable field in *Google*, while their posts, signatures, and self-mentions in the searchable blog text are almost always in playful typography or designed gif images.

Finally, some evidence suggests that *Fakatsa* style evolved from SMS "mistakes." Mobile phone keys represent both letters and numbers typically produced by a different number of keystrokes. On Hebrew mobile phones, the keys representing the letters ר, פ, ל, ט (numbered 20, 17, 12, 9 in Table 9.1) also represent their most frequent replacements in playful typography: 7, 9, 5, 6. These numbers are just one stroke away from the letters and are often mixed up when texting quickly, so it is possible that *Fakatsa* girls first noticed the graphic resemblance by mistake and later developed it intentionally. At the end of the day, it is also possible that girls are exposed to playful variations on the English-speaking web, might have wanted their own local version of it, and developed it intentionally according to similar principles.

Fakatsa style's communicative function is also consistent with research on new media vernacular literations, performing speechlike emphasis signifying subcultural/slang accents, punctuation, and pronunciation (see Nishimura, Chapter 5 of this volume). According to previous research, nonstandard orthography and typography signify subcultural speech styles related to music and graffiti practices (Androutsopoulos, 2007; Sebba, 2003) or in the case of Mandarin are used to express the Taiwanese accent (Su, 2003). However, *Fakatsa* style is more closely associated with the performance of a pampered, teasing, and girly "cute" identity, often resonating with a colloquial speech style associated with Tel Aviv's uptown girls. These findings run parallel to research on young Japanese women who perform their online gender identities and cuteness through playful orthography (Kataoka, 1997; Katsuno & Yano, 2007; Nishimura, 2010).

What makes *Fakatsa* style unique, however, is its added ornamental function for aesthetic emphasis of titles, prose, and quotes. This function could be interpreted as an attempt to dissolve the alienation of standardized digitized writing by bringing it closer to a brushstroke performing the calligraphy of personal handwriting (and then "drawing" some cute signs around it, as girls often do in their notebooks). The practice certainly brings orthography closer to ASCII art, corresponding with a reversed practice of ASCII calligraphy—letters "drawn" with ASCII signs (see Danet, 2001, for more on this). Along these lines, Katsuno and Yano (2007) also demonstrated a distinct feminine orthography based on motion and onomatopoeia inspired by Manga art and Japanese calligraphy tradition. They claim Japanese women have a tendency to artfully design handwriting and at the same time interpret online Kaomoji as a form of female embodiment online, facilitating emotional sharing within the respective community. It is in all these ways that I argue written words can be thought of as *avatars*, since they are a performative sign system facilitating both the ways girls appear *on* their blogs and appear *to* their blog readers.

As *Fakatsa* practices became prominent on *Israblog*, many other bloggers chose to mock it by, for example, opening a fictitious *Fakatsa* blog and blogging for a short while in the visual and linguistic style associated with the real Fakatsa girls. This was equivalent to the satiric imitation of cross-dressing and linguistic speech adoption of stereotyped groups. These fictitious *Fakatsa* blogs became widespread in the blogosphere during 2005, until most readers could not differentiate between the real and the parodic. Not unlike the fabricated text messages used by journalists in their reporting (see Thurlow, 2006, 2007), the male bloggers who created these spoof blogs would normally exhaust all possible practices and language play conventions in a few lines of text, making the text nearly unreadable. *Fakatsa* girls would never write an entire blog post in playful typography. In addition, girls almost never exhaust all possible replacements in one word, allowing some standard orthography that keeps the word decipherable. It is this that marks girls' practice as creative but also culturally situated; the ultimate goal is to communicate with each other, to be recognized and understood by their in-group peers.

Hackers' language, l33t, evolved as a way of eluding computer search algorithms that are unable to make sense of the orthography if one letter is replaced by a sign (Sherlbom-Woodward, 2002); nevertheless, l33t could be interpreted as a playful performance of the (mostly masculine) hacker identity (Danet, 2001), demonstrating their technological virtuosity and expertise in software decoding through their virtuosity in the coding of language. *Fakatsa* girls, who seemingly applied the same principle of typography and orthography choices to those of hackers and other male-dominated subcultures like graffiti and hip-hop mentioned previously, always made the effort to maintain its orthographic clarity, replacing only a few letters based on aesthetic criteria rather than coding.

Cameron (1997) has argued that discourse is male or female insofar as its style rather than its content is stereotypically recognized as such. In her well-known fraternity house piece, she demonstrates how young men perform heterosexual masculinity through gossip (i.e., considered as feminine style) about "gay" masculinity, thus defining the masculine against the feminine (gender but not necessarily sex) performances of other men. In my work, *Fakatsa* girls take up orthographic/typographic practices often associated with male hacker subcultural style to perform their "glocalized" feminine identities. However, their femininity is not constructed solely through the discursive content of these literations, but also through their "messing with" colloquial "rules" and patterns of literation. In other words, if vernacular literations are a creative performance of youth and (often subversive) subculture, *Fakatsa* style is a creative performance of girlhood, possibly subversive to male-dominated youth subcultures.

Feminist theorists are at odds with contemporary girlhood, often accusing girls of actively adopting the stereotypes their mothers fought to dissolve (Mazarella & Pecora, 2007). Yet postfeminist discourse isn't limited to girls (see Gill, 2006; McRobbie, 2009). For example, Gill (2006) argues that postfeminism isn't a historical turn, an epistemological break, or a backlash, but rather a sensibility defined by free choice and a move from objectification to subjectification. Furthermore, one person's hegemonic mainstream global culture, media, and stereotypes can be another person's empowering alternative or resistive performance. It is no coincidence, I believe, that my findings correspond so well with case studies of Japanese women (Kataoka, 1997; Katsuno & Yano, 2007) where global styles—including new media styles—are indeed sometimes liberating for certain traditionally oppressed groups (see Peuronen, Chapter 8 of this volume). In the case of *Fakatsa* girls, digital discourse is a powerful but also playful resource for (re)negotiating their stereotype as shallow, vain fashion victims and for reframing their social identities in a self-aware performance of a desirable, stylish girlhood.

Acknowledgments

I am very grateful for the help of Yukiko Nishimura and one external reviewer who kindly offered help with improving an earlier version of this chapter, as well as to Crispin Thurlow for his very detailed comments and suggestions.

References

Androutsopoulos, J. (2004). Typography as a resource of media style: Cases from music youth culture. In K. Mastoridis (Ed.), *Proceedings of the 1st International Conference on Typography and Visual Communication*, (pp. 381–392). Thessaloniki: University of Macedonia Press.

Androutsopoulos, J. (2006). Introduction: Sociolinguistics and computer-mediated communication. *Journal of Sociolinguistics*, 10(4), 419–438.

Androutsopoulos, J. (2007). Style online: Doing hip-hop on the German-speaking Web. In Auer, P. (Ed.), *Style and Social Identities: Alternative Approaches to Linguistic Heterogeneity*, (pp. 279–317). Berlin & New York: de Gruyter.

Baron, N.S. (2000). *Alphabet to E-mail: How Written English Evolved and Where It's Heading*. London: Routledge.

Bortree, D.S. (2005). Presentation of self on the Web: An ethnographic study of teenage girls' weblogs. *Education, Communication and Information*, 5(1), 25–39.

Bucholtz, M. (1999). "Why be normal?": Language and identity practices in a community of nerd girls. *Language in Society*, 28, 203–223.

Butler, J. (1990). *Gender Trouble: Feminism and the Subversion of Identity*. New York: Routledge.

Cameron, D. (1997). Performing Gender Identity: Young Men's Talk and the Construction of Heterosexual Masculinity. In S. Johnson & U.H. Meinhof (Eds.), *Language and Masculinity*, (pp. 47–64). Oxford: Basil Blackwell.

Coates, J. (1999). Changing femininities: The talk of teenage girls. In M. Bucholtz, A.C. Liang, & L.A. Sutton (Eds.), *Reinventing Identities: The Gendered Self in Discourse* (pp. 123–144). Oxford: Oxford University Press.

Danet, B. (1998). Text as mask: Gender, play and performance on the internet. In Steven Jones (Ed.), *Cyber Society 2.0. Revisiting Computer-Mediated Communication and Community*, (pp. 129–158). London: Sage.

Danet, B. (2001). *Cyberpl@y: Communicating Online*. Oxford: Berg Publishers.

Danet, B., & Herring, S.C. (Eds.). (2003). Introduction: The multilingual internet. *Journal of Computer-Mediated Communication*, 9(1). Available online at http://jcmc.indiana.edu/vol9/issue1/intro.html

Danet, B., & Herring, S.C. (Eds.) (2007). *The Multilingual Internet: Language, Culture, and Communication Online*. New York: Oxford University Press.

Eckert, P., & McConnell-Ginet, S. (1992). Think practically and look locally: Language and gender as community-based practice. *Annual Review of Anthropology*, 21, 461–490.

Eckert, P., & McConnell-Ginet, S. (2003). *Language and Gender*. New York: Cambridge University Press.

Eckert, P., & Rickford, J.R. (Eds.). (2001). *Style and Sociolinguistic Variation*. Cambridge: Cambridge University Press.

Gilbert, P. (1993). Narrative as gendered social practice: In search of different story lines for language research. *Linguistics and Education*, 5, 211–218.

Gill, R. (2006). *Gender and the Media*. Cambridge: Polity Press.

Goodwin, M.H. (2006). *The Hidden Life of Girls: Games of Stance, Status, and Exclusion*. Oxford: Blackwell.

Hall, K. (1995). Lip service on the fantasy lines. In K. Hall & M. Bucholtz (Eds.), *Gender Articulated: Language and the Socially Constructed Self*, (pp. 183–216). New York: Rutgers.

Herring, S.C. (1993). Gender and democracy in computer-mediated communication. *Electronic Journal of Communication*, 3, 1–17.

Herring, S.C. (2000). Gender differences in CMC: Findings and implications. *Computer Professionals for Social Responsibility Journal*, 18(1). Available online at http://cpsr.org/issues/womenintech/herring/

Herring, S.C., Kouper, I., Scheidt, L.A., & Wright, E. (2004). Women and children last: The discursive construction of Weblogs. In L. Gurak, S. Antonijevic, L. Johnson, C. Ratliff, & J. Reyman (Eds.), *Into the Blogosphere: Rhetoric, Community, and Culture of Weblogs*. St. Paul: University of Minnesota. Retrieved 10 December 2006 from http://blog.lib.umn.edu/blogosphere/women_and_children.html

Herring, S.C., Scheidt, L.A., Bonus, S., & Wright, E. (2005). Weblogs as a bridging genre. *Information, Technology & People* 18(2), 142–171.

Hjorth, L. (2003). Cute@keitai.com. In N. Gottlieb & M.J. McLelland (Eds.), *Japanese Cybercultures*, London & New York: Routledge.

Huffaker, D.A., & Calvert, S.L. (2005). Gender, identity, and language use in teenage blogs. *Journal of Computer-Mediated Communication* 10(2). Available online at http://jcmc.indiana.edu/vol10/issue2/huffaker.html

Kataoka, K. (1997). Affect and letter-writing: Unconventional conventions in casual writing by young Japanese women. *Language in Society* 26, 103–136.

Katsuno, H., & Yano, C. (2007). *Kaomoji* and expressivity in a Japanese housewives' chat room. In B. Danet & S. Herring (Eds.), *The Multilingual Internet: Language, Culture, and Communication Online*, (pp. 278–302). New York: Oxford University Press.

Kearney, M.C. (2006). *Girls Make Media*. New York: Routledge.

Lakoff, R. (1975). *Language and Woman's Place*. New York: Harper & Row.

Langellier, K.M., & Petterson, E. (2004). *Storytelling in Daily Life: Performing Narrative*. Philadelphia: Temple University Press.

Lanham, R.A. (1993). *The Electronic Word*. Chicago: University of Chicago Press.

Mazzarella, S.R. (Ed.). (2005). *Girl Wide Web: Girls, the Internet, and the Negotiation of Identity*. New York: Peter Lang.

Mazzarella, S.R., & Pecora, N. (2007). Revisiting Girls' Studies. *Journal of Children and Media*, 1(2), 105–125.

McRobbie, A. (2009). *The Aftermath of Feminism: Gender, Culture and Social Change*. London: Sage.

Nishimura, Y. (2010, September). Linguistic ideologies of orthography in Japanese: Corpus-Based study of non-standard miniature Hiragana. Poster presented at the 18th Sociolinguistics Symposium, University of Southhampton, UK.

Orellana, M.F. (1999). Good guys and "bad" girls: Identity construction by Latina and Latino student writers. In M. Bucholtz, A.C. Liang, & L.A. Sutton (Eds.), *Reinventing Identities: The Gendered Self in Discourse*, (pp. 64–82). Oxford: Oxford University Press.

Page, R. (2008). Gender and genre revisited: Storyworlds in personal blogs. *Genre: Forms of Discourse and Culture*, XLI (Fall/Winter), 151–177.

Pennycook, A. (2010). *Language as Local Practice*. London: Routledge.

Rampton, B. (2009). Speech community and beyond. In N. Coupland & A. Jaworski (Eds.), *The New Sociolinguistics Reader*, (pp. 694–713). Basingstoke: Palgrave Macmillan.

Raymond, E.S. (Ed.). (1991). *New Hacker's Dictionary*. Cambridge, MA: MIT Press.

Rodino, M. (1997). Breaking out of binaries: Reconceptualizing gender and its relationship to language in computer-mediated communication. *Journal of Computer-Mediated Communication, 3*(3). Available at http://jcmc.indiana.edu/vol3/issue3/rodino.html

Schmidt, J. (2007). Blogging practices: An analytical framework. *Journal of Computer-Mediated Communication 12*(4), 1409–1427.

Sebba, M. (2003). Spelling rebellion. In J. Androutsopoulos & A. Georgakopoulou (Eds.), *Discourse Constructions of Youth Identities*, (pp. 151–172). Amsterdam & Philadelphia: Benjamins.

Sherblom-Woodward, B. (2002). Hackers, gamers and lamers: The use of l33t in the computer sub-culture. Unpublished paper, Swarthmore College, Swarthmore, PA. Retrieved 6 January 2008 from http://www.swarthmore.edu/SocSci/Linguistics/Papers/2003/sherblom-woodward_blake.pdf

Shortis, T. (2007). 'Gr8 Txtpectations': The Creativity of Text spelling. *English Drama Media*, 8: 21–26 (June).

Stern, S.R. (2002). Virtually speaking: Girls' self-disclosure on the WWW. *Women's Studies in Communication*, 25(2), 223–252.

Su, H.Y. (2003). The multilingual and multi-orthographic Taiwan-based Internet: Creative uses of writing systems on college-affiliated BBSs. *Journal of Computer-Mediated Communication 9*(1). Available at http://jcmc.indiana.edu/vol9/issue1/su.html

Thurlow, C. (2003). Generation Txt? The sociolinguistics of young people's text-messaging. *Discourse Analysis Online*, 1(1).

Thurlow, C. (2006). From statistical panic to moral panic: The metadiscursive construction and popular exaggeration of new media language in the print media. *Journal of Computer-Mediated Communication*, 11(3), 667–701.

Thurlow, C. (2007). Fabricating youth: New-media discourse and the technologization of young people. In S. Johnson & A. Ensslin (Eds.), *Language in the Media: Representations, Identities, Ideologies*, (pp. 213–233). London: Continuum.

Thurlow, C. (2011). Determined creativity: Language play, vernacular literacy and new media discourse. In R. Jones (Ed.), *Discourse and Creativity*. London: Pearson.

Turkle, S. (1997). *Life on the Screen: Identity in the Age of the Internet*. New York: Touchstone.

van Leeuwen, T. (2006). Towards a semiotics of typography. *Information Design Journal*, 14(2), 139–155.

Werry, C. (1996). Linguistic and interactional features of Internet Relay Chat. In S. Herring (Ed.), *Computer-Mediated Communication: Linguistic, Social and Cross-Cultural Perspectives*, (pp. 47–63). Amsterdam: John Benjamins.

PART FOUR

Stance: Ideological Position Taking and Social Categorization

Chapter 10

"Stuff White People Like": Stance, Class, Race, and Internet Commentary

Shana Walton and Alexandra Jaffe

STUFF WHITE PEOPLE *Like* is a blog started in January 2008 by Christian Lander, a self-described White person and aspiring comedy writer from Toronto, and his friend Myles Valentin, a half-Filipino and fellow Canadian who inspired the blog with an instant message note to Lander that said to not trust any white person who didn't watch the HBO television series "The Wire" (France, 2009). The blog was a viral success, with more than 23 million hits by April of that year, often more than 300,000 hits a day. Lander, working solo, soon had a book contract with Random House, and the resulting book sat on the *New York Times* bestseller list for more than seven weeks in 2009. SWPL was so popular that within a few months the blogosphere and *Facebook* had an assortment of copycat, opposition, and parody sites, like "Stuff Asian People Like," "Stuff Ghetto People Like," "Stuff Educated Black People Like," and "The Other White Folks." In 2010, Lander continued to post new SWPL blog entries and was on the lecture circuit.

This chapter first explores the particular kind of elite, educated class positionality that Lander constructs through the metaphor of race, simultaneously parodying, inhabiting, embracing, and benefiting from a privileged race/class habitus. But Lander's posts are, of course, not the only texts on the SWPL blog, which also contains thousands of reader commentaries from self-described Whites and non-Whites. The second part of our analysis, then, focuses on the way that this particular new media creates rich, complex, and interactional spaces in which readers actively take up, oppose, and reframe Lander's stances. On the one hand, we argue that this space constitutes an alternative public forum where privileged Whites may have the unfamiliar experience of being confronted with "non-White" perspectives and stereotypes on their class/race habitus, a mild sort of culture shock experience. Because of its use of humor to create a friendly access point for discussing the difficult topic of race, the blog and its comment section offer a site of possibility for social transformation—the Web 2.0 version of Habermas's public sphere (1979) for deliberative democracy hoped for by new media theorists (Benkler, 2006; Shirky, 2008; Young, 2008; see Thurlow & Mroczek, Introduction to this volume). While we do identify instances of discourses and blog commentaries by self-identified White participants that grapple with issues of power and privilege, we also use this chapter to point out the ways in which the site actually confirms White privilege by offering readers the potential to align with a humorous reflexivity that insulates them as potential targets of real critique.

Stance, Medium, and Genre

The notion of stance is central to our analysis and can be defined as "a public act by a social actor, achieved dialogically through overt communicative means (language, gesture, and other symbolic forms), through which social actors simultaneously evaluate objects, position subjects (themselves and others) and align with other subjects, with respect to any salient dimension of the sociocultural field" (Dubois, 2007, p. 163). "Alignment" toward others and their positions can be seen as taking place on a continuum with both positive and negative poles. As the analysis below will show, alignments are accomplished both directly/explicitly and indirectly/implicitly. Readers of Lander's blog, for example, align with him as an author indirectly by imitating his style and voice on new subjects of their own choosing; others align or disalign directly by confirming or challenging the content or presuppositions of his blog. As Jaffe (2009a) points out, the "stance objects" toward which speakers and writers take up positions can also be discursive and ideological; acts of stance thus simultaneously respond to and create their discursive and social objects and formations. This is particularly relevant for our analysis of the SWPL site, where Lander and his readers take up stances toward the practices, values, and models of identity described as part of a "White" habitus, as well as toward the implicit conflation of race and class used to frame the blog. Stancetaking potentialities are shaped both by media in the broadest sense and by genre or "key" of the blog as parody: both affect the participant structures available to speakers and writers. First, the fact that Lander's blog entries are framed as parodic allows him to simultaneously occupy "insider" and "outsider" stances with respect to "Whiteness." Secondly, the format of blog commentaries as an increasingly familiar online genre puts stancetaking at the center of the activity; entering a comment is a priori the taking of a position vis-à-vis both Lander's blog entry (or the site as a whole) and the prior readers and their comments that constitute the textual context for the entry and reading of each new comment. With respect to the original blog, reader-commentators may take up or decline Lander's parodic voice and, under the protection of internet anonymity, choose how to identify themselves with respect to race and/or class. In short, both genre and media in SWPL offer Lander and his readers multiple stance options/flexibility (Thurlow & Jaworski, Chapter 11 of this volume, make this case, too; see also Jones et al., Chapter 2, on *Facebook* as "stance rich").

SWPL: Framing and Background

The fictive frame of Lander's blog is the ethnographic account, in which he writes in the voice of a cultural outsider for other supposed cultural outsiders (non-Whites) to help them "understand, infiltrate and eventually exploit" (Fat American, 2009) the upper-class, elitist White group he portrays. Blog entries are thus often "reports" of activities and preferences of White people. The evaluative subtext of these "neutral" reports is almost always the excessive, extreme, absurd, shallow, or hypocritical nature of White behavior. He especially likes to take aim at actions and costly/exclusive patterns of consumption geared toward projecting "simplicity," "authenticity," and "sincerity"—in short, at people who supposedly can't see or actively deny their positions of privilege. It is this false consciousness that is indexed by the imagined success of the non-White who infiltrates White social circles through flattery or superficial imitation. Lander has emphasized that the blog is "comedy first and foremost" (Wolinsky, 2008), and in the blog itself he does not break frame nor participate in the comments. However, in interviews he also affirms the blog as a form of cultural critique. In particular, he has said that his goal is to give Whites an "ethnic identity"—that is, to take away their unreflexive self-image as "unmarked" in contrast to marked, ethnic others. In an interview with the quintessentially White online newspaper *The Onion* (which has an SWPL entry, of course), Lander acknowledged the use of "race" as a proxy for "class," and that he does not stand outside of his own critique:

> ... people get the joke, and that it is as much about class as it is about race. People who are in this upper-middle class, they relate to it. And the fact is, that class is still overwhelmingly dominated

by white people. As much as we'd like to think it isn't— "No, it's dominated by this perfect coalition." No, it's white people. ... But yeah, there's anger about it, there's a lot of things I'm angry about. One of them is sort of saying, "Look at our generation. What do we have? What's left?" Stuff is all we have. ... It's not a display of wealth. It's about a display of authenticity and taste. And so it's [the blog] just my anger about that competition. And what I'm angry about is, I just can't stop myself from doing it. (Wolinsky, 2008)

Lander's ending statement that "I just can't stop myself from doing it" poignantly shows his recognition that moments of clarity about White privilege are not necessarily transformative for behavior.

Stance in Lander's Blog

In the first 19 months, Lander posted 128 entries. With this wealth of data, Lander's blog entries are a rich source for examining racial commentary in new media. Because our focus is on the interaction between Lander's posts and the reactive positioning in his readers' comments, we offer only a concise overview of his entries. According to Lander, stuff that "White people like," ranges from "Coffee" to "Gifted Children," "Hating Their Parents," "Asian Girls," or "Being Outdoors." The largest category of blogs "document" activities and consumption habits of White people, including entries on yoga, sushi, or television shows like "Arrested Development." The entries make the consumption practice or activity seem silly and, in the guise of directly addressing the habits of a "racial" group, indirectly index class-based practices, showing an investment in the "stuff" of being middle class, which is intimately linked, consciously or unconsciously, with an investment in Whiteness itself (Lipsitz, 1998). The entry on "Moleskine Notebooks," for example, incorporates critiques of visiting "independent" coffee shops and preferences for *Apple* products (which both have separate entries as well), placing the practice in a larger context of an elite lifestyle and written in the voice of an outside cultural observer:

Much like virtually everything else that white people like, these notebooks are considerably more expensive yet provide no additional functionality over regular notebooks that cost a dollar. .... [The] growing popularity of these little journals is not without its own set of problems. One of the strangest side effects has been the puzzling situation whereby a white person will sit in an independent coffee shop with a Moleskine notebook resting on top of an Apple laptop. You might wonder why they need so many devices to write down thoughts? Well, if a white person has a great idea, they write it by hand, if they have a good idea, it goes into the computer. ... So when you see a white person with one of these notebooks, you should always ask them about what sort of projects they are working on their free time. But you should never ask to actually see the notebook lest you ask the question "how are you going to make a novel out of five phone numbers and a grocery list?" (from blog entry #122, Moleskine Notebooks, February 24, 2009)[1]

Lander's conceit of neutrality is belied by evaluative stance markers, like references to high price, conspicuous consumption and display, and low functionality. The use of "puzzling" and "strangest" to characterize the scene aligns Lander with the purported non-White addressee. A limited number of Lander's blog entries directly address forms of racial "crossing" by Whites as a strategy for marking class territories. For example, topics such as "Having Black Friends" or "Black Music That Black Folks Don't Like Anymore" mock the idea that a certain type of class privilege rests on finding hipness and coolness through contact with the racial, non-White other, and showing how the non-White other serves as a resource for hip/cool consumption (hooks, 1992):

Apparently, once a music has lost its relevance with its intended audience, it becomes MORE relevant to white people...Today, white people keep The Blues going strong by taking vacations to Memphis, forming awkward bands, making documentaries, and organizing folk festivals. ... there [also] are literally thousands of white people who are giving their all to keep old school Hip Hop alive. ... Calling this style of music 'old school' is considered an especially apt name since the majority of people who listen to it did so while attending old schools such as Dartmouth, Bard, and Williams College. (from blog entry #116, "Black Music That Black Folks Don't Like Anymore," November 18, 2008)

Clearly, once again, although the trope is "race," class habitus and class-based consumption are prominent. In this post, as in the majority of the entries, Lander draws on specific insider knowledge to index the group, in this case, invoking as objects of ridicule alumni of prestigious but lesser-known elite educational institutions. As we have seen above, he uses evaluative stance markers ("awkward" bands) and hyperbole ("literally thousands") to "other" the practices and attitudes described. Finally, the play on "old school" rhetorically unmasks his White targets' presumption that they can align with non-Whites and "erase" race through practices of consumption and appreciation. His audience—unlike the majority of Americans—knows these schools and knows who, for the most part, attends them.

In a very small number of entries, the blog's artificial conflation of race and class gets reseparated, and Lander "documents" attitudes toward class by talking about "the wrong kind" of White people. In rare cases, such as "Hating People Who Wear Ed Hardy[2] T Shirts," an entire entry is devoted to looking directly across the class divide. More commonly, other Whites are kept in the background, only mentioned as an understood, obvious status to avoid, as in the entry on late-night television comedian Conan O'Brien, which ends with this postscript: "Under no circumstances should you ever mention that you prefer Jay Leno. This might cause white people to think you have the same taste in humor as the wrong kind of white people, or worse, their parents" (from blog entry #131, "Conan O'Brien," January 13, 2010).

Taken as a whole, the SWPL site (and book) constitutes a corpus of stereotypes about White people: broad generalizations about a group as a whole, seen through the critical eyes of cultural outsiders. As a consequence, even attributes deemed "positive" from a liberal White worldview—including appreciation for diversity—are represented as *not* able to be taken at face value. Through juxtaposition, ostensibly progressive ideologies are framed as being like consuming elite coffee and all the other things described: a collective position that indexes privilege and its reproduction. Our analysis builds on earlier examinations of race/class culture and discourse behavior, in which Whites, particularly those of the middle class, are shown able to position themselves as color blind or "beyond race," or to focus their assessments of racism on intent rather than outcomes, allowing them to both participate in racial privilege and eschew being painted as a "racist." Our work, then, reinforces earlier researchers who pointed out that the emphasis on class behavior distinctions among Whites combined with a focus on individual actions and behaviors (rather than institutional structures) permits racism without racists and classism without classes (cf. Bauman & Briggs, 2003; Bonilla-Silva, 2006; Hartigan, 1999; Hill, 2008; Jackson, 2005; Rasmussen et al., 2001; Roediger, 1991).

Reader/Participant Stances in Blog Commentaries

With more than 7,000 comments on the site as a whole (under the tab "About" and under each blog entry), this is a heavily participatory site. Focused on a socially hot-button topic like race, drawing people in through the "safety" of humor and offering unmoderated comments, the site gives us a window on the potentials and limitations of Web 2.0. The interactive dimension of the SWPL blog allows readers/participants to take up, modify, or reject the content, the underlying premises, or the parodic voice of Lander's posts. The body of reader comments does not, however, just respond to Lander; it also introduces new figures/personas/stances. In some cases, these make the implicit explicit: naming reflexivity as social capital and making class visible.

Alignment

There are several forms of stance alignment with Lander's blog entries, including creating new topics, confirming a personal connection to the topic, or displaying "extra" reflexivity about the topic or other commenters. The new topics suggested (wine tasting; Tibet; irony; Portland, OR; hand sanitizer; supporting WalMart employees; organizing a blood drive; claiming Native American heritage) show that the reader "gets" the fact that race is holding proxy for class. This type of alignment takes full form when commenters take up Lander's authorial role and create new extended examples of the blog discourse. The following reader post was supplied by a self-described new mother:

> BREASTFEEDING... White women are all about bonding with their infant and breastfeeding is the only way they can think of to accomplish this goal. 6-months is the minimum, but if a woman does it for at least a year, she gains wide acceptance and admiration...The only way to gain acceptance if a woman does not breastfeed is if the mom has medical issues or isn't producing enough milk or has twins/triplets/etc. But even with that, the woman has to pretend to really be upset about not being able to do it and show her envy of other moms who do breastfeed. Along with breastfeeding, ATTACHMENT PARENTING is popular as well and includes co-sleeping (family bed), wearing your child (there are more and more slings out there versus strollers), and so on. Also, aspects of

attachment parenting are prevalent in third world countries, which allow white people to feel more cultured. (from the "About" section, posted by Erin, March 18, 2008)

In this post, "Erin" borrows Lander's rhetorical practices to "other" White mothers by describing them from an outsider position ("the woman"; "a woman"; "they") and through the negative stance evaluations embedded in "bizarre" characterizations of their practices ("wearing your child"), deprecatory terms for their competencies ("the only way they can think of to accomplish this goal"), and doubting their sincerity (they "pretend" to be upset). In new posts and topic suggestions such as this one, readers also align themselves with Lander through content, displaying similar "ethnographic" knowledge of White practices and values. Many of them also deploy the explicit references to White appropriation and/or exploitation of cultural capital from "exotic" and underprivileged groups. "Breastfeeding" is a perfect illustration of this theme because of its class-aligned performative stance toward motherhood: it makes an ideological virtue of the choices economically privileged White women can make to appropriate pragmatic "third world" practices like lengthy breastfeeding and carrying babies in slings (rebaptized "attachment" parenting in White discourse).

In the most prominent and direct forms of alignment, commenters affirm a personal connection with the practices described, participating in Lander's stance of reflexivity by showing their awareness of Whiteness as a marked category:

Wow. You never feel as white as you do when SWPL really pegs you and cuts you to the bone (response to blog #116, "Black Music That Black People Don't Listen To Anymore," posted by fats, November 18, 2008)

I have a Moleskine notebook and planner...and unfortunately I cannot argue with a single point made in the post. I carry my notebook with my MacBook in a computer bag that's covered in patches of countries I've been to, and yes, I use the journal to jot down ideas for an amateur novel. I never knew how white I was until I saw this website... (response to blog #122, "Moleskine Notebooks," posted by Renard, July 13, 2009)

A variation on this type of alignment comes from those who write in as non-Whites to say that they too participate in "Whiteness," thus displaying reflexivity about their own class positionality and the class positioning of the object or activity. For example, consider another response to the Moleskine notebook entry:

> Hey. I'm not white and I have a Moleskin. OK, my white friend bought it for me. I have written lots of interesting things in it (to me, anyway). (response to blog #122, "Moleskine Notebooks," posted by "The Chick from New York," July 5, 2009)

A third form of alignment can be seen in those comments that make explicit reference to the stance potentials ("extra" Whiteness) of being reflexive, calling out other Whites for their Whiteness and calling out those who call out, and so on. This category of commenters, illustrated in the following two extracts, also "calls out" either Whites who refuse the parodic stance (taking the blogs at face value) or those commenters who assert a genuine authenticity and/or nonracist or non-classist stance toward the activity or object.

> But I do like the white people that comment about how white other white commenters are. What I love is that white people love to call out other white people as white and thus prove that they aren't so white themselves. White people also like to call out other white people that call out white people for being white. And on and on.... (response to blog #116, "Black Music That Black People Don't Listen To Anymore," posted by beb, November 19, 2008)
>
> The only thing better than the people offended by this site are the people that defend themselves by expounding on how "its so true how some people pretend to like jazz but others, like myself, truly appreciate it." It makes the blog even more relevant. (response to blog entry #116, "Black Music That Black People Don't Listen To Anymore," posted by matt, November 22, 2008)

Below is an example of a reader/participant in this category who is aligning by adopting "extra" reflexivity:

> i'm sure someone has said this already, but its ironic that stuffwhitepeoplelike.com is now on the list of stuff white people like. (posted by cody on August 30, 2009)

Reader/participants sometimes don't align with the actual activities, practices, or even the reflexivity of Lander's parodic stance but do align with his implicit antiracist project of exposing White privilege. These comments by self-identifying White readers allow them to claim superior White-person status by virtue of awareness:

> I've never felt so White as when I am reading your blog. I, like many other White people, tend to think that I am somehow different–you know, not as White as my bretheren. Thanks for reminding me of where I come from and for making me ROTFLMAO.

> The truth is that so many people still exist in a world of White privilege where they view their perspective as the norm, not a culturally constructed reality that not everyone shares. The ability to ignore one's privilege, and hence its impact on others, may be the most insidious aspect of privilege. Thank you for illustrating what is so often overlooked. (posted by Aerynn on November 20, 2008)

> In college in the early 2000s, I used to go to a bar where they played Biggies "Juicy" and all the middle class white kids from Ll and Westchester used to go crazy. ... People singing along to a song that they cant relate to in any way. It was the only time in my life I was embarrassed to be white. (response to blog entry #116, "Black Music That Black People Don't Listen To Anymore," posted by Pat, November 19, 2008)

These posts introduce a new figure: the White with a higher-order (serious) consciousness of White privilege, sometimes expressed in an academic register (first post above) that is another manifestation of the overtly expressed stance. This confirms a hierarchy in which reflexivity is the highest form of capital. Lander, of course, occupies the pinnacle of this hierarchy as the initiator of a reflexive Whiteness; readers participate in this position through their acts of alignment.

However, as we have seen in the "calling out" examples above, it is critical to note that in the highly interactive textual world of comments and responses to comments, these superior stances are subject to challenge and refutation: that is, they are granted no more "face-value" status than the liberal White positionality that Lander critiques. Often, these challenges take the form of the original commenter being told to "lighten up," or to remember that the blog is meant to be humorous. In other cases, reader posts are simply ignored in the ensuing comments, thus denying the commenter an explicitly ratified positive status. This is a useful reminder that stances are not monologic but, rather, are constructed dialogically and intertextually, over time, across turns at talk, texts in a sequence, and so forth (Clift, 2006; Goodwin, 2007; Jaffe, 2009b). In this light, we emphasize that a full analysis of the stance outcomes of the blog site would require a detailed, sequential analysis of the interactional co-construction and evaluation of stances that is not possible here.

Nonalignment

There are also several forms of reader nonalignment in the comment sections.

The most common is a literal engagement with the propositional content of the site. Just as readers can confirm the ethnographic truth of the blog, they can also refute it:

> I'm a white uppermiddle class woman, but I can't relate to about half of the stuff that I'm supposed to like... I don't own a single apple product, I like cats and not dogs, and I studied science in college. (from the "About" section, posted by Lisa, February 15, 2008)
>
> I'm white, I've read through your list, and I can barely tolerate any of the things you've listed. I despise most of them.
>
> Stereotypes suck, even when you're trying to be funny.
> (You're not funny.) (from the "About" section, posted by Bull on February 15, 2008)

It's interesting to note that in refuting the blog's claim to ethnographic accuracy, these commenters do not reject Lander's underlying proposition that there *is* stuff middle-class White people like—but just that he didn't get it right. In doing so, they agree that there is a White middle class, and that they belong to it. Implicit in their comments is either that this White middle class is characterized by a different set of preferences and practices from those Lander describes, or it is simply resistant to generalization. In the latter case, these commenters affirm the privilege of being "individuals" who cannot be assimilated into a group.

Another category of such responses is one Lander himself labeled as "offended white people posts." There are a range of these to consider. Here we look at a series of exchanges in the "About" section of the blog in which people are debating the purpose and point of the site. The first interchange is between Kelly, who is "hurt" by the blog's generalizations, and Cart, who trumps Kelly's criticism with reflexivity:

I picked this up and at first i was amused.
"oh haha i get it, i'm white."
but then the comments were hitting a little close to home.
i don't really feel all that original anymore.
it kinda hurts to be generalized and put down the way this book
has put me down. (from the "About" section, posted by Kelly on
November 30, 2008)

Responding from a "consciousness of privilege position," "Cart" replies to
Kelly's post with the following:

White person reaction = getting offended, and thinking that your
feelings should somehow matter.
Oh. And outsmarting someone purporting to be smarter...
(December 8, 2008)

Then a week or so later, White girl disaligns by asserting the site is
"racist:"

My point is that it's suddenly pc to stereotype white people, but god
forbid anyone mentions watermelon and blacks, or mexicans and
beans in the same sentence. Give it a couple more decades, when
whites are actually the minority in the US, then we'll talk – you
intellectually stunted idiot. (from the "About" section, posted by
White girl on December 14, 2008)

White girl's insult is countered with an alignment retort from "Whitish
guy," written from a stance of humorous reflexivity, using classic hip/cool
"Other" voicing ("sister," "girl") to simultaneously invoke an ethnicized
intimacy and to invoke (and critique) her equation of White and non-
White victimhood in a way that echoes Lander's juxtaposition of White
and non-White uses of "old school":

I'm embarassed reading this post from my white, misguided sister.
Girl, we need to talk. First latte's on me. (December 16, 2008)

Another category of readers disaligns with Lander's implicit antiracism
itself, copying the frame of "ethnographic truth" and the parodic freedom to
stereotype and assert/confirm biases against non-White, non-middle-class

people. In the following string of blog excerpts, we see the eruption of a familiar kind of Web 2.0 conversation, in which comments are interspersed with comments about comments. In this string, the first commenter accepts the "stuff" Lander identifies as race/class based and then both rejects and tries to neutralize criticism by "calling out" the people who refuse to acknowledge that some consumption practices, even if they are race/class based, are simply better for society.

> If these are things white people love, then I guess that makes them more dignified than any "minorities" are. I'll take recycling, bicycles, healthy eating, exercise, and books any day over smoking crack, AIDS, mugging, robbery, vandalism, having tons of kids and not paying child support, gun violence, being an overall decadent waste of existence, etc.

> (can't wait until people respond to how "racist", "intolerant" and "insensitive" I am when my post isn't any more deserving of those adjectives than this whole pathetic excuse for a blog is! LOL! you all are a bunch of fucking hypocrites) (from the "About" section, posted by blargyblarg, February 15, 2008)

Again, this post is followed by a critique from a more reflexive stance. "S" writes:

> The main difference between this blog and your comment, which could be called racist, is that the blog is satire, and you're being dead-serious. (May 8, 2008)

In addition to commenters who reject the idea that consumption can be race based, other commenters take a principled individualist stance. That is, they reject the idea of racism as a structural/institutional problem (which is embedded in Lander's blog) and reframe the problem as one of individual action, positing a "colorblind" stance that rejects any generalizations about a group (racialized discourses) as racist.

> Wow, what a stupid thing to say. I am a 52 year old white guy that has listened to and loved rap and hip-hop since its inception, going back to Sugar Hill Gang when it first came out. Before that, I enjoyed Kool and the Gang, Ohio Players, Parliament Funkadelic, De La Soul, Barry White, and all sorts of so-called "black music." I also like classic

rock and bluegrass. I'm a diverse person who loves music. I think it's very racist to believe that when people say they are really into something that they aren't being genuine. (response to blog #116, "Black Music That Black People Don't Like Anymore," posted by Steve Meyers, November 25, 2008)

Have you considered the racial implications of your posting in over-generalizing a group of people? ... Having lived in Africa for 7 years among a nation of people with 42 distinct tribes – yet all being black in color – I have learned to identify and respect different qualities and distinctions among white ethnic lines as well. ... White people, as well, have different histories, ancestral lines and cultures. Please don't group us all together. (from the "About" section, posted by Heather Jamison, March 13, 2008)

In this kind of disalignment, commenters do not identify as a problem the idea that society won't accept public assertions of similar types of stereotypical things about non-White ethnic groups. The problem they identify is lumping or grouping *anybody* (particularly them). In both of the excerpts provided, the commmenters take pains to establish their credibility to reject the blog as "racist." In both cases, they seek the authority to point out that they are not members of some undifferentiated group.

As a whole, nonaligning commenters refuse to accept some or all of the following:

(1) the parodic stance as mitigating the literal or propositional content of the blog
(2) the legitimacy of generalizations about anyone
(3) the legitimacy of generalizations applied to the self ("I'm White and listen to rap music and always have!")
(4) structural differences in group privileges and power, and their differential consequences for the extent to which racial generalizations constitute a threat to identity or self-image, and/or
(5) the indexical connections between patterns of consumption and class habitus/stance.

However, as we have seen, the reflexively aware, ironic White contingent almost always "wins" the posting competition. Its members post more often and assert a more "appropriate" alignment with SWPL. In his interview with *The Onion*, Lander weighed in on the "offended white people posts," saying:

I always find that particularly funny, because it's like, "So you're offended that I've made a generalization about your race that doesn't apply to you? I think every other minority on earth has been through this in the last thousand years, so good. I'm glad you feel that way." And then the other thing is people who get offended by the whole idea of stereotypes in any capacity. I got an e-mail from someone in Canada who reported the site to a hate-crimes commission. Actually submitted it and said that they wanted to get the Canadian government involved to shut it down as a hate crime. (Wolinsky, 2008).

Readers also disalign with Lander's stance by explicitly naming the race–class connection that must remain implicit for the blog to play its role as a humorous cultural critique. These include suggestions for renaming the site as "Stuff Middle-Class People Like," "Stuff LIBERAL White People Like," "Stuff Rich People Like," and so on. Alternatively, comments name the largely invisible "other" White people. "Zack" writes:

White people like trailer parks, ho-downs, tractor pulls and Nascar. Yet they're nowhere in your list. You've taken a sector of so-called 'white' culture (or its implements) which are, like sushi or raggae music, the best pickings from other races and cultures, and reinvented it as white.

You're not talking about 'white' people; you're talking about mon-eyed, educated, young, white Americans.

In a similar vein, "Paul" provides a list of what Lander "left out":

And you left out...
Thanksgiving
Firearms
Hunting
Fishing
Pumpkin Pie
Beer
Pickup Trucks
Heavy Metal

Country Western
Bagpipes
Red meat, preferably cooked on the grill
Bible thumping evangelical churches
Mormon churches
Conservative Catholic churches
and finallly, the Puritan Work Ethic (the results of which are often
falsely called "white privilege")
Where are these freaky white people you're describing on your site?
West Hollywood? Seattle? I don't recognize them at all. (posted
November 22, 2008)

In doing so, he not only names the "other" White people but also takes
up a stance of alignment with "the Puritan Work Ethic" that he attributes
to them. He also disaligns with places (Seattle, West Hollywood) that are
heavily loaded with a number of ideologically specific associations with
particular groups (among them, liberals, actors, homosexuals). In doing
so, he implicitly renames the Whites described on the site as particular
rather than generic and thus *nonrepresentative* of a racialized middle class
he belongs to. Privilege is thus also displaced: "generic" White people are
not privileged; West Coast liberal elites are.

Class, Race, and Risk?

Both class and race are sources of potential risk to liberal, White readers of
SWPL. The blog entry about *Facebook* makes a (rare) reference to underlying class-based insecurity:

.... As noted in earlier posts, white people are obsessed with being
in the right neighborhood and the Internet is no exception. ... For
a brief period of time, MySpace was the site where everyone kept
their profile and managed their friendships. But soon, the service
began to attract fake profiles, the wrong kind of white people, and
struggling musicians. In real world terms, these three developments would be equivalent to a check cashing store, a TGIFridays,
and a housing project. All which strike fear in the hearts of white
people. White people were nervous but had nowhere else to go.
Then *Facebook* came along and offered advanced privacy settings,
closed networks, and a clean interface. In respective real world

terms, these features are analogous to an apartment or house with a security system/doorman, an alumni dinner, and a homeowners association that protects the aesthetics of the neighborhood. ... Within a matter of months, MySpace had gone from a virtual utopia to Digital Detroit, where only minorities and indie bands remain. (Blog #106, *Facebook*, July 31, 2008)

This blog entry reveals the insecurity associated with using race as a place-holder for class, and the resulting constant need to police both the boundaries within the self (will I know enough not to buy an Ed Hardy T-shirt?) and social boundaries (who belongs to my group?).

SWPL also creates potential for race-based insecurity. Consider the figure of the non-White "infiltrator" (the fictional addressee of the blog), whose efforts to ingratiate him or herself expose membership attributes as "learnable" and subject to social manipulation. This could call into question non-White "acceptance" of Whites or of Whites' friendship, puncturing a positive, liberal White self-image. It could also expose Whites' desire for that friendship as hierarchical rather than truly inclusive and, thus, as hypocritical.

This risk is offset, however, by the range of validating stances available to White readers of the blog and, in particular, the insulation provided by the humorous frame that, as one astute commentator put it, "comforts rather than challenges." This early analysis of SWPL characterized the safety of the stances offered, which either: "1) don't reflect you and therefore make you feel superior... 2) ... do reflect your choices and make you feel like you are in on the joke and good humored enough to go along and therefore make you feel superior ... or 3) ... nod at stereotypes ... and because you recognize the stereotype, you feel superior" (Sternbergh, 2008). Lander himself dismisses the risk:

One of my commentators left this; it was the best comment they ever said: "There's a big difference between these stereotypes and other stereotypes. The difference is, white people don't get denied jobs for liking yoga" (Wolinsky, 2008)

The risk differential is apparent when we look at the copycat sites. That is, there is a serious blowback factor for middle-class African Americans who are too dismissive of non-middle-class Black culture, whereas the reader comments on SWPL show that middle-class Whites who align with

SWPL do not hesitate to alienate any of the disaligners (racists or serious/ literal antiracists) or to critique the "other White people" referenced in the comment pages. In contrast, the site "Stuff Educated Black People Like" originally started as a mirror image of SWPL, but its bloggers ultimately changed the site name to "Stuff Educated Black People Talk About," dropped the parodic stance, and embraced a forum of discussion about serious issues facing the group. The example of the site "Stuff Educated Black People Talk About" clearly shows that the new media have not created a new racial politics. The parodic voice remains constrained for a group with less social power—the outside, public audience is too great of a social risk. Such groups are also constrained from the "inside" in the sense that the stance flexibility enjoyed by Lander as both an insider and an outsider may not be readily ratified if group members demand evidence of unconditional group alignment.

Class, Race, and the New Media Context

Race theorists have posited the idea of "racial projects," which historically have redistributed power or resources, resulting in group oppression (Omi & Winant, 1994). In theory, alternative projects could be intentionally created with the goal of redistributing power or resources or, more generally, to further racial understanding or lessen group divides. As discussed earlier, because SWPL has active commenters who identify themselves as both White and non-White and more or less middle/upper-middle class, and because it approaches race/class from a relatively nonthreatening stance rather than head on, the site has the potential to be a new media forum offering space for genuine discussion about racial issues. We do see some examples of posts of this sort—usually very long posts—in which people drop the parodic participation to indicate their sincere engagement in acknowledging White privilege without a safety net. The following are excerpts from some of these posts:

> Observing race is not being racist. People are different, that's just reality. We need more forums like this one (from the "About" section, posted by Banana, November 20, 2008).

> I don't know much about you or the book, but it opens a complicated and sensitive debate about race. ... Still, kudos for getting people talking, thinking – myself included (from the "About" section, posted by Zack, July 21, 2009).

Posts like these, however, are certainly not the dominant discourse, and other commenters only occasionally take up the thread and enter into conversation over these ideas. The posts usually remain as isolated observations (see also Thurlow & Jaworski, Chapter 11 of this volume, on this). Whatever the potential, SWPL does not, in reality, provide a model of engaged discourse about current racial issues as a direct topic. However, the body of comments left by readers on the virtual space of the SWPL website creates a social space in which the critical race/class awareness agenda of SWPL has the *potential* to be realized as an "experience" for people who come to the site. That is, while they are not forced to do so, it is on the web that elite White people may experience a limited kind of "unsafeness" related to group/personal identity: what it is like to respond to stereotypes created by, and in the presence of, an uncomfortable blend of insider–outsider (and invisible) audiences. For example, there are hundreds of direct statements of alignment on the blog that are variations of the following:

> Holy crap. It hurts. Please stop it. Too close to the bone...(from the "About" section, posted by Whitey McWhitester, March 10, 2008)
>
> This is amazing. This defines my life. (from the "About" section, posted by Zach, July 25, 2010)
>
> This makes for cringe-inducing moments (from the "About" section, Anonymous girl)

We read these posts as moments of affect (Stewart, 2007), a moment when "things snap together." In this case, the new media format—the original blogs and resulting comments—combine to provide this mild culture shock in a quasi-public space. However, these small, individualistic moments do not a social movement create. We do not see these comments, for instance, growing into longer posts about personal transformation or other deeper realizations.

For non-Whites, SWPL has some potential as a new public sphere in which they can comment on Whites outside of internal circuits of communication unseen by their targets—that is, on White/mixed, rather than segregated turf, and where they can choose and enjoy reflexive distance from a variety of practices and attitudes associated with privilege.

There are some things about the White experience that the new media context does not change. In particular, we have noted that once reflexivity is posited as the highest form of cultural capital, the elite White consumer of Lander's blog and the elite White participant in reader comment forums can always assume a superior stance. It's important to acknowledge that the site also provides a platform for truly racist voices, as well as for a relatively unreflexive White enjoyment of class privilege.

Finally, the SWPL blog also offers anonymity. While the relative anonymity of responses to blog posts is not unique to the web, it does offer a foil for the trying out of various stances of Whiteness, and for the maintenance of stance ambiguity—being free from the constraint of taking a single, unmodifiable stance. The openness of the space, and the many different kinds of alignments and stances that it gives rise to, also allows for the multiple faces of Whiteness to become apparent. This may also be understood as part of Lander's project, and something that he can only accomplish with the participation of his readers on the blog.

Notes

1. All of the *Stuff White People Like* citations come from the blog and not the book and can be found at www.stuffwhitepeoplelike.com. In most cases, we have included the section of the blog and the date in order to find the sources more easily.

2. Ed Hardy was a famous tattoo artist whose designs were printed on posters and T-shirts, among other products. First popular among White motorcycle enthusiasts, he was also documented as a vocal racist. His politics weren't always as well known as his designs, many of which, ironically, became popular among some African-American rap artists.

References

Bauman, R., & Briggs, C.L. (2003). *Voices of Modernity: Language Ideologies and the Politics of Inequality*. Cambridge: Cambridge University Press.

Benkler, Y. (2006). *The Wealth of Networks: How Social Production Transforms Markets and Freedom*. New Haven: Yale University Press.

Bonilla-Silva, E. (2006). *Racism Without Racists*. New York: Rowman & Littlefield.

Clift, R. (2006) Indexing stance: Reported speech as an interactional evidential. *Journal of Sociolinguistics*, 10(5), 569–595.

DuBois, J. (2007). The stance triangle. In R. Englebretson (Ed.), *Stancetaking in Discourse*, (pp. 139–182). Amsterdam: John Benjamins.

Fat American. (2009). Stuff White People Like Merchandise. http://www.fatamerican.tv/t-shirt-page/stuff-white-people-like/

France, Lisa Respers. (2009). Finding Humor in 'Stuff White People Like.' CNN Entertainment.Available online at http://articles.cnn.com/2009-01-29/entertainment/stuff.white.people.like_1_cnn-christian-lander-white-child?_s=PM:SHOWBIZ

Goodwin, C. (2007). Interactive footing. In E. Holt & R. Clift (Eds.), *Reporting Talk: Reported Speech in Interaction*, (pp. 16–46). Cambridge: Cambridge University Press.

Hartigan, J. (1999). *Racial Situations: Class Predicaments of Whiteness in Detroit.* Princeton: Princeton University Press.

Hill, J. (2008). *The Everyday Language of White Racism.* London: Wiley-Blackwell.

hooks, b. (1992). Eating the other. In *Black Looks: Race and Representation*, (pp. 21–39). Boston: South End Press.

Jackson, J.L., Jr. (2005). *Real Black: Adventures in Racial Sincerity.* Chicago: University of Chicago Press.

Jaffe, A. (2009a). Introduction: The sociolinguistics of stance. In A. Jaffe (Ed.), *Stance: Sociolinguistic Perspectives*, (pp. 3–28). Oxford: Oxford University Press.

Jaffe, A. (2009b). Stance in a Corsican school: Institutional and ideological orders. In A. Jaffe (Ed.), *Stance: Sociolinguistic Perspectives*, (pp. 119–145). Oxford: Oxford University Press.

Lipsitz, G. (1998). *The Possessive Investment in Whiteness: How White People Profit from Identity Politics.* Philadelphia: Temple University Press.

Omi, M., & Winant, H. (1994). *Racial Formation in the United States from the 1960s to the 1990s* (2nd ed.). New York: Routledge.

Rasmussen, B., Nexica, I., Klinenberg, E., & Wray, M. (2001). *The Making and Unmaking of Whiteness.* Durham: Duke University Press.

Roediger, D. (1991). *The Wages of Whiteness: Race and the Making of the American Working Class.* London: Verso.

Shirky, C. (2008). *Here Comes Everybody.* New York: Penguin Press.

Sternbergh, A. (2008). Why White People Like "Stuff White People Like." *The New Republic*, online edition, March 17. Available online at http://www.tnr.com/article/books-and-arts/why-white-people-stuff-white-people

Stewart, K. (2007). *Ordinary Affects.* Durham: Duke University Press.

Wolinsky, D. (2008). Interview: Christian Lander. *A.V. Club, The Onion*, August 21. Retrieved from http://www.avclub.com/articles/christian-lander,14296/

Young, K. (2008). Participatory democracy, Web. 2.0, and the citizen journalists' relationship to political campaigns. *Global Affairs*, 9 (July).

Chapter 11

Banal Globalization? Embodied Actions and Mediated Practices in Tourists' Online Photo Sharing

Crispin Thurlow and Adam Jaworski

ONE HALLMARK OF *good* new media scholarship is work that does not take "new technologies" as its starting point or necessarily make technology its primary object/topic of analysis (see Thurlow and Mroczek, Introduction to this volume). Work like this starts instead from the understanding that technologies are more importantly historical, cultural, and social phenomena. For example, new technologies always emerge within the context of existing, more established technologies; new technologies are also quickly embedded into the patterned frameworks of everyday life; and new technologies are inevitably folded into a wider semiotic field of human communication. Viewed this way, it is impossible to think of new media as wholly new, as overly deterministic, or as isolated, singular modes of interaction. For us, *Flickr* is a perfect case in point. In photo sharing we find a relatively new, technologically enhanced variation on the long-standing practices of personal photography and photo albums. It is also a new media *format* that relies as much on the technological affordances of digital photography as it does on those of the internet. *Flickr* also blends the multimodal communicative practices of message boarding, social networking, and perhaps even blogging. So, even though it is hailed as "something of a poster child for Web 2.0 and user-led content creation" (Burgess, 2010), *Flickr* is in many ways far from extraordinary. In both technological and cultural terms, it is, in fact, really quite ordinary. This does not mean that it is uninteresting or unworthy of study. *Flickr* actually offers some very helpful, new perspectives into some otherwise well-known, old practices.

In this chapter, we examine a particular instance of *Flickr* use: the posting of holiday snapshots taken by tourists at the Leaning Tower of Pisa in Italy. Specifically, we attend to those photos in which tourists are playing

Obligatory Cheesy Pisa Shot

Wow, here's Jayne holding up the Leaning Tower of Pisa!. Yep, it's cheesy, it's bad, it's got to be done.

FIGURE 11.1   A *Flickr* posting: " … It's got to be done."

with—or shown playing with—forced perspective (as in Figure 11.1). We also consider the way these embodied and mediated practices are further framed (i.e., explained and justified) by their posters and by commenters. Neither the taking of holiday photos nor the playful technique of forced perspective is new. Indeed, we are not interested in the "new technology" per se. Our starting point is instead the role of language and communication in tourism as a global cultural industry—what we characterize as "tourism discourse" (Thurlow & Jaworski, 2010) and, specifically, "the sociolinguistics of fleeting relationships" (Jaworski & Thurlow, 2010a). This is what directs us to consider the way words, visual imagery, nonverbal behavior, space, and material culture are used to construct tourist identities, to organize host–tourist relations, to represent and manage tourist sites, and to produce/perpetuate the meanings or ideologies of both tourism and globalization.

And the technologies of travel (e.g., photography and air travel) always have a role to play in shaping the activities and meanings of tourism. With this in mind, we will consider here one specific sociolinguistic phenomenon: *stancetaking*. We examine this very important communicative behavior by using *Flickr* as both a research source and as another technological development now mediating tourism discourse. Before we turn to stancetaking and *Flickr*, however, we begin with a few broad contextualizing comments about tourism discourse and social space.

Setting the Scene: Tourism as a Mediatized and Mediated Activity

Tourism discourse is always simultaneously a *mediatized* and a *mediated* activity. As a service industry, tourism is fundamentally—and, at times, solely—semiotic in nature, and it is necessarily reliant on linguistic/ discursive exchanges between tourists and hosts, and between tourists and other tourists. Much of the significance, the cultural capital, of tourism lies also in the "tourist haze" created as tourists return home with their own travel stories about well-trodden destinations, the souvenirs they bring for the folks back home, and indeed the photos of themselves in exotic locations. More than this, however, the tourist imagination and tourist practices are always heavily (in)formed by—and prefigured in— the *mediatized* representations of television holiday programs, travel brochures, newspaper travelogues, postcards, guidebooks, and so on (see Thurlow & Jaworski, 2010). In this way, as Mike Crang (1997, p. 361) explains, "a structure of expectation is created, where the pictures circulating around sights are more important than the sites themselves ... The signs that mark out what is to be looked at become as, or more, important than the sites themselves." With particular reference to photography, John Urry (2002) calls this search for the-already-seen the *hermeneutic cycle*:

> What is sought for in a holiday is a set of photography images, which have already been seen in tour company brochures or on TV programmes. While the tourist is away, this then moves on to a tracking down and *capturing* of these images for oneself. And it ends up with travellers demonstrating that they really have been there by showing their version of the images that they had seen before they set off (2002, p. 129) (emphasis ours).

In this regard, there can be few touristic destinations as heavily mediatized as the Leaning Tower of Pisa, ranked by one website (see Figure 11.2) as being among the "great wonders" of the world. By the time many people find themselves in Pisa and at the foot of the Tower, they certainly have a pretty clear idea about what to expect and, more than likely, what to do. It is not only through the formal, professional practices of tour company brochures and television programs that tourists are drawn into the hermeneutic circle; equally influential are the informal, amateur practices of tourists' themselves, as is the case in the mediatized spaces of *Flickr*, for example.

While some communication is clearly channeled and filtered through technological and institutional processes (i.e., it is mediatized), this should not mean that communication is otherwise unfiltered or unchanneled. Each and every communicative act, whether verbal or nonverbal, is bounded and reflexively configured or *mediated* by other semiotic structures of the environment (Jaworski & Thurlow, 2009b; Scollon, 1998; see also Jones, 2009, and Chapter 15 of this volume). These include the layout of the space, built environment, various fixed and nonfixed physical

FIGURE 11.2 The mediatized contexts of tourist practice (source: http://www.hillmanwonders.com/italy/).

objects, signage, other people present in the shared space, the sociocultural norms of conduct, and any practices associated with the communicative frame that is believed to be taking place (e.g., photography constitutes a typical activity associated with the frame "sightseeing"). We are thus also concerned with tourism discourse as a form of *mediated* action understood in the sense of Pierre Bourdieu's (1990a) *habitus*, that is, a system of internalized, durable, and transposable dispositions that generate similar practices and perceptions in agents belonging to the same class, and that can be adjusted to specific situations. Regardless of the media used—photography or *Flickr*—all tourist practice is structured, organized, or mediated by this broader framework (or context).

From a sociolinguistic point of view, stancetaking is an ideal concept with which to approach habitus. In his discussion of the overlaps and connections between Bourdieu's habitus and language practice, Hanks (2005, pp. 69–71) overviews three key lines of thought present in the notion of habitus:

(1) Individual disposition (*hexis*) combines or aligns intention (desire) with evaluation or judgment of good and bad, appropriate and inappropriate—this corresponds with stancetaking as a reflexive, metadiscursive, and evaluative practice.

(2) The social actor's momentary grasp of his or her corporeality and communicative practice, an awareness of one's actual postural disposition and all other possible, but not actual, postural arrangements—for Hanks, there is overlap here between habitus and language ideology, and for us, the activating and actualizing of ideology in stancetaking.

(3) Habitus is the necessary, social, generative, unifying, and largely unconscious principle that makes all individual and creative acts intelligible (by analogy to Chomsky's generative grammar)—by analogy to doxa, stancetaking is a force of social, cultural, political, and economic control and class inequality working largely beyond social actors' awareness.

Furthermore, as Hanks explains, Bourdieu's (1993) habitus "emerges specifically in the interaction between individuals and the field, and it has no independent existence apart from the field" (2005, p. 72). It is precisely the discursive, mediated space of *Flickr* where we find the sublimation of the interaction between individual tourists and the field of tourism. Ultimately, it is through a combination of *mediatization* and *mediation* that tourism is made meaningful, that tourist (and host) identities are realized, and that tourist practices are learned and organized. It is also through these combined processes that tourist sites are themselves discursively produced.

Making Space: The Discursive Production of Tourist Sites

It is nowadays a received wisdom in the social sciences that space is as much a social construction as it is a physical phenomenon (e.g., Harvey, 1996; Lefebvre, 1991; see also Jaworski & Thurlow, 2010b). Just as communication is mediated by space, therefore, space is itself communicatively constituted. For example, the meanings of a place are established by the way the place is represented (e.g., written and talked about) and by the nature of social (inter)actions that "take place" within it. For Henri Lefebvre (1991), space is best thought of as being realized in three dimensions: *conceived* space (mental or represented images), *perceived* space (its

FIGURE 11.3 *Holding Up the Leaning Tower of Pisa.* Ok it had to be done!

FIGURE 11.4 *Couldn't resist.* Just had to do the Pisa pushers' pose.

material or physical dimension), and *lived* space, which emerges through
the intersection/interaction of/between both conceived and perceived
space. Places are therefore always in the process of becoming, of being
spatialized, through what Miriam Khan (2003) describes as an "animated
dialogue" between people's ideas or fantasies about the place and its on-
the-ground, material properties. In their postings and commentary on
Flickr, tourists are unavoidably caught in the act of making space, as well
as positioning of Self. As much a production of the tourist imagination
as it is a lopsided construction of stone, the Leaning Tower of Pisa is a
socially and dialogically achieved *lived* space.

We offer one other general comment before turning to our study proper,
and this relates to the matter of *embodiment*. Space, as something conceived,
perceived, and lived, is clearly realized in the ways we represent it: how
we write about it, talk about it, photograph it, advertise it, and design it.

But spaces also emerge in the ways we move through them, interact in them—and interact *with* them. Without wanting to rehearse an already well-rehearsed literature, we also start from the premise that tourist performances in/of space are never simply visual (e.g., Edensor, 2001; Franklin & Crang, 2001; Larsen, 2005). When asked how many of Italy's 51 wonders you have *seen* (Figure 11.2), you are really being asked how many of these iconic sites you have *been* to, you have *moved* through, you have *sat* in front of and, in the case of the Leaning Tower of Pisa, you have actually *climbed* (see Jaworski & Thurlow, 2009a). Besides, the visual itself is never the kind of passive, two-dimensional, reflectional phenomenon that it seems to be written off as; vision, too, is an embodied act, an accomplishment of/with bodies, as we see time and again in Pisa photos (also Figures 11.3 and 11.4). In his ethnographically organized study of tourist photography, Jonas Larsen (2005, p. 417) highlights this important quality:

> The nature of tourist photography is a complex theatrical one of corporeal, expressive actors; scripts and choreographies; staged and enacted "*imaginative geographies*". ... Tourist photography is [thus] made less visual and more embodied, less concerned with spectatorship and "consuming places" than with producing place myths, social relationships.

Photography is always both an embodied/mediated action. Posting photos on *Flickr* is an act not only of recontextualization but also of "reincarnation" and what Jean Burgess (2010) calls *remediation* (see Jones, Chapter 15, and Newon, Chapter 7, this volume). For our purposes, Larsen's added observation about the relational nature of tourist photography is also key. Tourists' ways of seeing and behaving in a place—and their ways of communicating about a place—are clearly powerful in shaping the meanings of the place. They are equally powerful in structuring *relations* between tourists and *relations of power* between tourists and hosts. We see this clearly in the kinds of photos tourists often like to take at/of the Leaning Tower of Pisa and in the complex stances they take toward these "imaginative geographies."

Flickr's *Forced Perspectives: New Media Opportunities*

As we have already begun to show in Figures 11.1, 11.3, and 11.4, tourists often like to take snapshots of themselves or someone else positioned in relation to the Leaning Tower of Pisa in such a way as to create the

FIGURE 11.5

FIGURE 11.6

Figures 11.5 and 11.6 Forced perspective images: top-London, bottom-Agra.

FIGURE 11.7

FIGURE 11.8

Figures 11.7 and 11.8 Forced perspective images: top-Kuala Lumpur, bottom-Paris.

perspectival illusion of either holding/pushing it up or kicking/pushing it down. In fact, thanks to *Flickr* we know that this playful performance or technique (known as forced perspective) is a *very* popular one; we also know that it is used around the world and usually with buildings, monuments, statues, and other features of the built environment.

Immediately—and somewhat selfishly—we see some of the unique opportunities afforded by new technology for us as tourism discourse scholars. First and foremost, *Flickr* provides solid empirical evidence for the circulation and ubiquity of tourist practices—in this case, both the popularity of forced perspective as a style of touristic photography (see Figures 11.5 to 11.8) in a number of different locations, but also its particular and very common deployment at the Leaning Tower of Pisa.[1] There are literally hundreds and hundreds of pictures like those in Figures 11.1, 11.3, and 11.4 (see also below). *Flickr* even enables the formation of dedicated "Pisa Pushers" network (or group).[2] All of which reveals nicely John Urry's "hermeneutic cycle": the touristic impulse to show one's own version of images of a place that one has already seen before setting off for the place. Not only does *Flickr* add, therefore, to the prefigured, mediatized tourist imagination, but it also offers up evidence for the disciplining of tourists (i.e., how they learn what it means to be a tourist) and for the discursive production of tourist spaces (or sites).

There is one other important insight that *Flickr* affords us and that has to do with the reflexivity and "creativity" of tourists themselves. In particular, we find first-hand evidence of what John Urry (2002, after Fiefer, 1985) has famously theorized as the "post-tourist," who is, in turn, characterized by what Ed Bruner (2001) calls the "questioning gaze"—a capacity to recognize themselves as tourists and to see beyond the highly stylized, scripted, staged performances of tourism. As we will show presently, this reflexivity is apparent in the different interpretations of the "classic" Pisa Push that tourists devise and to which we have unprecedented access in *Flickr*. Thanks also to the particular format of *Flickr*, tagging (i.e., titles and descriptions) of photos by posters and the comments of viewers enables us to see how tourists themselves make sense of their own and others' performances. We have evidence, too, that tourists are often—although not always—aware and sometimes critical of their actions. This is revealed most noticeably in the range of explicit and implicit *evaluations* that posters and commenters make of their own and others' photos, and of the embodied tourist practices depicted in the photos—in other words, their stancetaking.

Stancetaking and the (Re)mediation of "Pisa Pushers"

Considered to be "one of the fundamental properties of communication" (Jaffe, 2009, p. 3), stancetaking entails the various ways people position themselves with respect to the things they say or do themselves, or with respect to the things other people say or do. This positioning is typically associated with evaluative comments or behaviors, which may be explicit (e.g., "That shirt looks awful") or implicit (e.g., "Are you really going to wear that?" or simply a raised eyebrow). John Du Bois (2007, p. 173) refers to stance as possibly "the smallest unit of social action" and defines it as

> a <u>public</u> act by a social actor, achieved dialogically through overt communicative means (language, gesture, and other symbolic forms), through which social actors simultaneously evaluate objects, position subjects (themselves and others), and align with other subjects, with respect to any salient dimension of the sociocultural field. (p. 163)

Following Du Bois, we ourselves view stance as an *evaluation* or appraisal of an *object* (whether a thing, a person, an event, a behavior, or an idea) as being somehow desirable/undesirable or good/bad (Jaworski & Thurlow, 2009b). Since it will become relevant in just a moment, we add that *elitist* stancetaking entails evaluations that are made partly on the basis of the evaluated object but always through a claim to both distinction and superiority. So, where a stance might express the judgment "this is good," an elitist stance carries the added or specific implication of "this is better," or even "this is the best." In either case, the object is evaluated in its own right, but primarily as a *vehicle* for expressing a relational (i.e., alignment), identificational (i.e., positioning), and, most importantly for our purposes here, *ideological* orientation (i.e., the sociocultural field).

With this brief account of stance in mind, we want to return to the "Pisa Pushers" photos in Figures 11.1, 11.3, and 11.4 and consider first the collaborative, *embodied* stance taken by the original photographer and poser. The very act of choosing to deploy the forced perspective is itself an evaluation of an object (i.e., the Tower) and a place (i.e., Italy), in which the photographer and poser position themselves, literally and socially, as tourists. The embodied/mediated act also entails a relational alignment between the two of them, as well as a relational alignment (or misalignment) between them and the unknown people to whom the place "belongs." We take this up as a matter of ideology in our general discussion below.

In posting the photo to *Flickr*, at least one of the original participants (we assume) is given an opportunity to *remediate* (Burgess, 2010) both the photo and the original embodied action by giving the posting a title and a short description. These small textual spaces offer themselves as ideal moments for stancetaking, as we see in their descriptions (the extracts here and elsewhere retain original spelling and typography):

Figure 11.1:   Wow, here's Jenny holding up the Leaning Tower of Pisa!. Yep, it's cheesy, it's bad, it's got to be done.

Figure 11.3:   Ok it had to be done!

Figure 11.4:   Just had to do the Pisa pushers' pose

In their titles, Figure 11.1 ("Obligatory Cheesy Pisa Shot") and Figure 11.4 ("Couldn't Resist") also echo the description of one of our very first *Flickr* finds (not reproduced here) described as "The obligatory 'holding up the Leaning Tower of Pisa' photo." It is this repeated sense of feeling forced to participate in an apparently foolish or somehow inappropriate photographic act that strikes us as interesting. Why these evaluative remarks? The need for a performance of duty clearly lies in the underlying recognition and/or judgment that the "Pisa Push" is in some way undesirable, inappropriate, reprehensible, or, as the one poster puts it, "cheesy." Alternatively, the poster perceives this as a possible judgment coming from others. The ambiguity of public/private and in-group/out-group status on *Flickr* merely complicates matters; even when participants are members of a group (e.g., Pisa Pushers), it is not always clear if they are *known* to each other or if they are relative strangers. Either way, the stance taken suggests that there is something suspect with the Pisa Push. In three more examples, this threat of sanction reveals itself a little further in the form of a different series of stances.

Knowing the Script and Knowing Irony

The titles of Figures 11.9 and 11.10 both invoke a deep-seated and often self-deprecating discourse in tourism: that tourists themselves are people worthy of scorn (see McCabe, 2005; for more on this also Jaworski & Thurlow, 2009b). As is implied by these titles, no one should want to be a "Typical Tourist," a visitor usually mythologized as a mindless package or mass tourist with only a shallow regard for local people and with little or no interest in "really" learning about the local culture. The "tourist" is invariably

FIGURE II.9 *Typical Tourist.* Mom didn't position me quite right for me to be holding up the Leaning Tower of Pisa.

FIGURE II.10 *Annoying Leaning Tower Tourists.*

FIGURE II.II *My Turn.* Holding up the Leaning Tower of Pisa. Oh we're so clever!

juxtaposed with the "traveler," who is narrated as an independent visitor with an altogether deeper, more educated commitment to understanding the tourist destination. The pejorative tone of "typical" in the label given to Figure 11.9 works to reinscribe this antitourist discourse; it also expresses a similarly negative evaluation of the Pisa Push. This judgment—along with ones like the "annoying" tourists tag from Figure 11.10—exposes the kind of face threat all Pisa Pushers must manage and explains why some of them adopt the stance of having being "forced" into (taking) the picture. At the very least, what posters perform is their knowledge of the tourist script—there are ways of being tourists, some typical and some not, some acceptable, some less so.

The same position is ultimately taken—albeit even more subtly—in Figure 11.11 where "My turn" expresses a sense of the repetitiveness of the Pisa Push and the habituated practices of tourists. The ironic "Oh we're so clever!" adds a judgement of stupidity to the Pisa Push. In this case, the stance taken is that of knowing irony, which allows the kind of "only joking" *discursive license* often needed for transgressing norms seeking to minimize sanction or loss of face (see Coupland & Jaworski, 2003). Take a look now at the following contested exchanges between commenters (C) and the posters (P) of a Pisa Push photo:

Extract 11.1:

1	C:	I wish I had a dollar...
2	P:	... my original title for this photo was 'being a tourist'
3	C:	I hope you realize it was not a criticism...I did it too. I just
4		really wish I had a dollar for every time it's been done. I'm
5		sure I could split it with you and we'd be filthy rich. :-)
6	P:	When you are there you almost have to do it.
7	C:	... of course I know it wasnt...I filmed people doing it, its
8		amazing how many people you see doing it

Extract 11.2:

1	C:	I can't believe you did that pose!
2	P:	I can't believe anyone wouldn't, doing that pose was the whole reason I went!

No wonder Pisa Pushers feel a little defensive! These opening gambits make clear the generalized stance of disapproval and/or disdain that may accompany the Pisa Push—and the posting of a Pisa Push online. In Extract 11.1, this is expressed indirectly ("I wish I had a dollar ...") and, in Extract 11.2, directly ("I can't believe you did that pose!"). The commentator in Extract 11.1 also acknowledges in Line 3 the *potential* reading of Line 1 as a criticism but mitigates the threat with the positive politeness strategy of claiming common ground ("... I did it too") and further, altruistically, attending to the poster's welfare by offering to share the hypothetical riches (cf. Brown & Levinson, 1987). The poster, too, is seen doing a lot of careful facework, first by distancing him/herself through the idea of ironically titling the photo "...'being a tourist'" and then by the familiar stance of (reluctant) obligation ("...you almost have to do it"). Finally, the commentator shifts the focus of his stancetaking back to other tourists, once again (lines 7–8) reemphasizing the mass nature of the ritual. Confronted with the bald-on-record evaluation of Extract 11.2 ("I can't believe ..."), the poster this time defiantly turns the table in a vivid moment of post-tourist (post hoc) reflexivity: I went to Pisa precisely to get my own version of this well-known image. And do you think I don't know this?

Positioning Oneself above the Masses

Given the kinds of subtle but consistent social judgment they face, Pisa Pushers (as with tourists in general) have a number of other options available to them. In keeping with the stance of knowing irony, many tourists apparently take the moral high ground by not giving in to the obligatory Pisa Push themselves, but choosing to photograph others doing it—"the next best thing" for someone who *promised* themselves they would not succumb to the pull of the Pisa Push (Figure 11.12 caption).

Once again, a stance is achieved in multiple ways—by the original decision to photograph others rather than oneself, by positioning oneself as an onlooker rather than an active participant, and by the remediating

FIGURE 11.12 *Push it, push it real good.* I promised myself I wouldn't do the *hold the tower up* photo. But I did get the next best thing! =)

FIGURE 11.13 *Tourist originality.* Everyone was doing lame poses of either holding up or pushing down the tower of Pisa, so I had to jump on the band wagon and discretely snap a picture with me doing a similar thing.

FIGURE 11.14 *Mass hysteria.* Wish i'd been faster with the camera to get more, but i was laughing too hard.

opportunities of posting the photo to *Flickr*. In this case, we see in the titles of Figures 11.12, 11.13, and 11.14 the implied mockery of "Push it, push it real good" and "Tourist originality" together with more overt disdain in "Mass Hysteria." The mocking stance emerges as somewhat less implied in "I was laughing too hard" (Figure 11.14).[3] All three posters, along with the others above, are clearly aligning themselves with the mythical "traveler" and pointedly distancing themselves from the mindless collectivity of "tourist." The elitist claims to superiority and distinction (i.e., originality) of these posters aim to put them "above the masses."

But not for long. Extract 11.3 shows another commentator–poster exchange, this time in response to an above-the-masses photo like those in Figures 11.12, 11.13, and 11.14.

Extract 11.3

1   C: LOL! There must be thousands every day doing this. :-)

2   P: Yeah, everyone goes there, sees the crowds doing this, and

3   thinks 'these would be funny, original shots.'

4   C: Well, they're certainly funny, and often interesting—but unfortunately, not

5   terribly original. ;) Nice shot!

In his laughter ("LOL"), the commentator shores up his own elitist stance toward the elitist stance taken by the poster (see also "its [sic] amazing" in Extract 11.1, Line 7). The precarious, tiers-within-tiers nature of elite status is thus exposed (Jaworski & Thurlow, 2009b; Thurlow & Jaworski, 2006). As the commentator points out, taking photos of other Pisa Pushers (the "this" in Line 1) is not so original after all. Both as an embodied photographic performance (i.e., taking the photo of others doing the Pisa Push) and in the remediation of the original act, the commentator positions him/herself above the masses ("thousands every day") who stoop to doing the Pisa Push. The bar has now been raised, and not surprisingly, the poster moves to save face by distancing himself—a hasty act of realignment—from not only the "crowds" who do the Pisa Push but now also from the "everyone." His use of reported speech (i.e., "... 'these would be funny, original shots' ") is reminiscent of Bakhtin's (1984) notion of varidirectional double voicing, in which the original voice is ironically and somewhat disingenuously subverted; as such, he puts even further social distance between himself and "everyone" else. By these defensive and elitist processes of aligment/disalignment in stancetaking, *Flickr* participants merely reinscribe the same antitourist ideology. These contested meanings of tourism are also, however, struggles over the meaning of space/place, as we are about to show.

"Creative" Variations on the Theme of Self-Location

The above-the-masses stance directs us to the value placed on "originality"—by tourists in general and by *Flickr* posters in particular. However, what quickly becomes apparent from reviewing *Flickr* is that even attempts by tourists to break with the more familiar cliché of the standard Pisa Push inevitably become hackneyed. In other words, their symbolic capital is very localized and fleeting. Disembedded from the situated creativity of the moment and recontextualized (or remediated) into *Flickr*, each photo is exposed to, and devalued by, hundreds of other unoriginal "original" shots (see Note 2 again). In a different bid for "originality," some photographers/posers play with another variation on the theme of Pisa Push by locating themselves vis-à-vis the Tower with an alternative body part.

In Figures 11.15, 11.16, and 11.17, the intended creativity is expressed with the use of the foot, the finger, and the pregnant belly, respectively. Once again, what *Flickr* enables us to see is that this variation is no more or less creative than the classic Pisa Push. Certainly, their posters take up many of the same positions toward the original embodied actions, as we see in the caption for Figure 11.16 ("everyone," "lame poses," "I <u>had</u> to jump on the bandwagon"). In this case, the poster claims superiority through his discretion ("discreetly snap") and by doing something "similar" but different. For many tourists, of course, so much of their practice is experienced as *singular*, a one-off—perhaps even a "once-in-a-lifetime"—encounter with a place; what this means is that, understandably, they can never be fully aware of the patterned, recurrent, scripted nature of things. In tourism, back-stages unexpectedly reveal themselves to be front-stage after all (cf. Edensor, 2001), and the "genuine" or "authentic" can turn out to be "fakes" manufactured somewhere else (cf. Bruner, 2001; Favero, 2007). We know from *Flickr* that some tourists do recognize this (see also the post-tourist's questioning gaze from above). What *Flickr* also helps us see, however, are some of the limits of this awareness.

This brings us to one last interpretive remark about our *Flickr* data, which also starts to return us to an earlier observation about the ideological implications of Pisa Pushers. A number of complex stances are taken in the final set of (re)mediated actions shown in Figures 11.15, 11.16, and 11.17; for example, a *playful* stance (i.e., "I'm only having fun"), a *victorious* stance (i.e., the self-centered emplacement of posers), and a *subversive* stance (i.e., the mocking of iconic sites of local history/culture). It is unclear, for example, if the title of Figure 11.17 ("What a Pisa crap!") refers to the place or the photographic enactment—or both. We do not want to deny the inherent light-heartedness

FIGURE II.15 *PUSHING. Italy*. My left foot holds up the Leaning Tower of Pisa.

FIGURE II.16 *The tower of Pisa and my finger*. Everyone was doing lame poses of either holding up or pushing down the tower of Pisa, so I had to jump on the band wagon and discretely snap a picture with me doing a similar thing.

FIGURE 11.17 *What a Pisa crap!* Who knew Bren's belly could hold up an entire ancient leaning tower?

and localized reflexivity of all of these embodied actions and mediated practices, nor do we fail to see the sensual and technological pleasures of, say, photography and new media (cf. Jones, 2010, Chapter 15 of this volume). Nonetheless, we cannot help but consider the broader significance of tourists turning local cultural artifacts and heritage spaces into playthings. In much the same way, we have elsewhere discussed how local languages are often framed—and taken up—as ludic resources in tourism (Jaworski et al., 2003; Thurlow & Jaworski, 2010). What does it mean, therefore, when the normative response of tourists to the Leaning Tower of Pisa is to embody, document, and promote it as an object of play and/or of mastery? And especially when *Flickr* affords us such a compelling—and empirical—insight into both the scale and the performative power of these particular touristic practices?

The Bigger Picture: Tourist Practice as Banal Globalization

Symbolic capital, a transformed and thereby disguised form of physical "economic" capital, produces its proper effect inasmuch, and only inasmuch, as it conceals the fact that it originates in "material" forms of capital which are also, in the last analysis, the source of its effects. (Bourdieu, 1977, pp. 6 & 183)

FIGURE 11.18 Posting from "Photo Clichés" on *photobucket* and movie poster for *Deuce Bigalow European Gigolo* (2005, reproduced by permission of Sony Pictures).

Like the airplane, the camera is an iconic feature of tourism. The highly ritualized practices of photography in general and of the Pisa Push in particular are not surprisingly played out by thousands of visitors each day; it is in this way that visitors are able to mark their identities as tourists and achieve the *raison d'être* of their travels by engaging with the act of photography and through an explicit performance of their knowledge of this particular, place-dependent photographic convention. In many respects, it is possible to think of these personalized poses with the Tower as a kind of bodily graffiti in which individual tourists look to "tag" the Tower, to leave their mark, not unlike the (re-)claiming of space by graffiti artists (see Pennycook, 2010). While the physical location of Self in the place is momentary, the representational (i.e., photographic) inscription is enduring and, through its constant repetition, it becomes substantial.

FIGURE 11.19 Posting from "Photo Clichés" on *photobucket* and movie poster for *Deuce Bigalow European Gigolo* (2005, reproduced by permission of Sony Pictures).

These photographic enactments are not just tourist performances, but also performative reenactments of the spectacle itself. For Susan Sontag (1977) and Pierre Bourdieu (1990b), photography is always a mode of appropriation and accumulation, of possession. At the very least, it is about seizing the moment and *capturing* it "for posterity" (see also the quote from John Urry above). What our *Flickr* data confirm is how the tourist "gaze" is both an embodied and a mediated activity; it is not merely an act of production or reception—as framing rather than being framed (Larsen, 2005) or, as Mike Crang (1997, p. 362) puts it, "the world is apprehended as picturable, it is 'enworlded' by being framed." Nor is *Flickr* by any means just a convenient source of data. It is now folded into the "imaginative geographies" of tourism as another powerful technology for documenting and narrating tourism, the world, and the Self.

Pisa Pushing is therefore a quintessential embodiment of a nexus of practice that is predicated on symbolic consumption—of images and sights—and the conspicuous performance of this consumption. As we have argued elsewhere (Jaworski & Thurlow, 2009a), the conceit of holding up or kicking over the tower also enacts a particular sense of mastery and ownership—perhaps even a degree of disrespect? Some of the more reflexive, apparently playful variations on the theme express this even more powerfully: for example, visitors appearing to tower over the Tower, appearing to hold the Tower in their hand, or appearing to topple the Tower with a single finger. And then there is always the possibility of transforming the Tower into a penis as in Figure 11.18.[4] Whatever their intent, these "conventionalized poses of the spectacle" (cf. Scollon, 1998, p. 107) are integral to the styling of the tourist identity (i.e., it's the thing to do in Pisa), the generic organization or *staging* of the Tower, and, indeed, the discursive production of tourism as playful appropriation. Posted to *Flickr*, these embodied and already mediated (by photography) actions are remediated and circulated even further as they resurface in the "old media" cycle of representation (see Figure 11.19).

Just as the new media make possible new insights into some old, well-established practices, so too do they force a re-examination of otherwise tried and tested academic perspectives. In the present case, for example, we see the multimodal, multilayering of stancetaking in a series of staged performances: from striking a particular pose in front of the Tower, to its capture in the digital image, its remediation on *Flickr* together with a title, description, and tag, to the verbal commentary and banter between posters and commenters. Each stage in this discourse trajectory involves a degree of social actors' focusing on their communicative behavior, or what Bauman and Briggs (1990) call performance—an enactment of Jakobsonian poetic function. (Again, compare this with Jones, Chapter 15 of this volume, on "re-embodiment".) In performance, entextualizations of discourse objectify it and make it detachable and hence particularly prone to commentary and evaluation. Each entextualizing moment also exposes the cultural values and ideologies of producers and audiences. For Pisa Pushers, posing for a forced perspective photograph is a reenactment of earlier, similar acts and their visual retellings by others. What is particularly interesting in the context of tourist discourse and its representation on *Flickr* is that the metacultural awareness of tourists and *Flickr* users allows for the stancetaking to be expressed through this series of multimodal performances dynamically negotiated over time.

Another aspect of stancetaking revealed in a photo-sharing website like *Flickr* is its complex footing (see also Walton & Jaffe, Chapter 10 of this volume). In a number of our examples, it is virtually impossible to work out whether the poster is the photographer, the poser, or another third party, and whether the commentator knows the poster (or the poser). Some photograph captions (e.g., "Wow, here's Jenny ..." in Figure 11.8) suggest that at least some of the posts are intended for family and friends of the poser or photographer (poster), but, "Jenny" is certainly not familiar to most people who can access her photo on this public site. With a blurring of private–public domains, *Flickr* provides an interesting example of how explicit, blunt, and bald-on-record stancetaking occurs between people who may be quite familiar with each other or may be total strangers engaging in a fleeting moment of virtual chat framed by the "Comments" window on the site. This kind of open-endedness, the ambiguity of participation framework, and the greatly extended *potential* audience is what lends a broadcast quality to otherwise interpersonal alignments and realignments. As such, these already normative acts of self-presentation and social judgment may reach even further.

Stance is always an act of self-presentation and social judgment by which I say something not only about myself but by which I also make a judgment about you and about others as being like me or unlike me. In doing so, I must unavoidably say something about my view of the world. What gives stances their inherently ideological significance then is that they are less likely—relatively speaking—to draw attention to themselves. Rather, stancetaking *tends* to be subtle and is premised on inference rather than assertion (cf. Du Bois, 2007; Jaworski & Thurlow, 2009a). Indeed, these small (see Du Bois, above) discursive moments partly derive their normative influence precisely through their being unobtrusive and fleeting. Often they are concealed further by being ambiguous, artful, and humorous. Nonetheless, it is through their constant repetition that these momentary evaluations constellate and "solidify" (cf. Butler, 1990; also Giddens, 1984, on *structuration*). In much this way, the fleeting alignments, orientations, and adjustments of *Flickr*'s photographers, posers, posters, and commenters become habituated and taken for granted. Just as a passing alignment or *footing* may over time persist as a *relationship*, and a *style* become an identity or even a *lifestyle*, innocuous moments of stancetaking endure as personal *stands* and, eventually, as collective ideologies or "regimes of truth" (Foucault, 1980).

What is the ideological force realized in—or generated by—the collective actions of Pisa Pushers and their online agents? For us, part of the answer lies in what we have called *banal globalization* (Thurlow & Jaworski, 2010) in parallel to Szerszynski and Urry's (2002, 2006) term "banal globalism," and following the ideas of Mike Billig (1995, on "banal nationalism") and Ulrich Beck (2006, on "banal cosmopolitanism"). We choose to invoke the banal ourselves for framing and understanding tourism discourse as being rooted in everyday communicative actions and textual practices. By "everyday" we do not mean to say that these actions/practices are either foolish or inconsequential: on the contrary. It is, we suggest, at the level of "innocent" texts and "harmless" (inter)actions that globalization is actually realized. For example, Szerszynski and Urry (2002) find examples of "globalizing" imagery in everyday, recurring TV imagery which includes globes, bird's-eye views of generic "global" environments, images of the "exotic" Others consuming global brands and products, children standing for the globe in charitable appeals, and so on. These discursive practices may well be trite (for example, forced perspective snapshots of the Leaning Tower of Pisa), but they are far from trivial. Just as "small talk" is always, pragmatically speaking, "big talk" (cf. Coupland, 2000), and just as reiterative performances of gender solidify and naturalize the "heteronormative matrix" (Butler, 1990), so, too, do the mundane practices—embodied and mediated—of tourism turn out to be global in their reach and possibly also in their impact.

Tourism discourse, it seems, invariably finds itself caught between, on the one hand, a deep-seated mythology of cosmopolitanism as intercultural contact and understanding and, on the other hand, the kind of "aesthetic" cosmopolitanism Mike Featherstone (2002, p. 1) caricatures as voyeuristic, parasitic, and dabbling. All travel by choice is, of course, inherently privileged (see Bauman, 1998) and unavoidably mapped onto histories of travel and conquest. In these terms, tourism discourse is to global inequality as color blindness is to racism; where the one hinges on its mythology of interculturality, the other relies on its rhetoric of multiculturalism. Yet both are neoliberal, neocolonial sleights of hand conveniently serving the interests of the privileged (those who *choose* to travel and those who pass as "unraced") by typically concealing their historical origins and material consequences (see Bourdieu quoted previously) and by "containing" difference under an earnest guise of celebration and respect (hooks, 1992). What better way to alleviate our intercultural discomforts, our fears of the unknown and of difference, than to turn it into a destination, a playground, a spectacle.

Notes

1. We have done our best to disguise the people in these *Flickr* photos by marking out their faces and by changing names where relevant. (Also see our acknowledgments below.) As far as we can judge, all our examples come from predominantly White, relatively young, L1 English speakers. We make here no claims to the universality of photo- and stancetaking among tourists from diverse cultural backgrounds. We do not assume that all tourists visiting the Leaning Tower of Pisa (or any other site) take photographs playing with forced perspective and we do not know what proportion of tourists post their photographs of any kind on the internet. We do not normally take forced perspective photos when we are ourselves involved in any form of tourism, including academic. However, after this chapter was presented as a paper at the "Language in the (New) Media: Technologies and Ideologies" conference held at the University of Washington (September 3–6, 2009), one of the author's had a forced perspective image taken by several conference participants on campus. One of these has been displayed and/or discussed in subsequent presentations of this material in relation to our own stance vis-à-vis forced perspective tourist images.

2. In another photo-sharing site, *photobucket*, we find a group similar to *Flickr's* "Pisa Pushers"; this one, called "Photo Clichés," collects "pictures of people being uniquely hilarious, just like all the other people who took the same photo."

3. In a personal note, Keith Walters asks whether part of the humor expressed by the poster isn't his realization of the possibility of infinite regress? We think not, but Keith's following anecdote is worth citing here: "We were visiting a friend in a local hospital a few weeks back where there was a photography exhibit of photos from around the world by a single photographer, each image being of tourists taking photos of other tourists whom, it appeared, they did not know taking photos. (And we might guess what this photographer's next exhibit might be of...)."

4. In one comment on a "Pisa Pusher" posting someone talked about having visited Pisa in the 1960s while at college; he and his friends crafted a forced perspective image to show the tower being pushed over by one of their exposed penises. We were unable to track this picture down.

Acknowledgments

We are grateful to Elaine Chun and Keith Walters for their detailed comments on the penultimate draft. Special thanks are due to Jocelyn Maher at the University of Washington for her help with collecting our *Flickr* texts. We made every reasonable effort to get people's permission to reproduce their photos (many of which are posted under a Creative Commons agreement); in particular, we would like to thank, in no particular order: Ahmed Ashour, Vincent Lock, Claude Farden, Christopher Empson, Justin Adams, Buz Carter, Jonathan Hawkins, Regina Sellers, and Darren Langlands.

References

Bakhtin, M.M. (1984). *Problems in Dostoyevsky's Poetics* (C. Emerson, Trans.). Minneapolis: University of Minnesota Press.

Bauman, R., & Briggs, C. (1990). Poetics and performance as critical perspectives on language and social life. *Annual Review of Anthropology*, 19, 59–88.

Bauman, Z. (1998). *Globalization: The Human Consequences*. Cambridge: Polity.

Beck, U. (2006). *The Cosmopolitan Vision*. Cambridge: Polity.

Billig, M. (1995). *Banal Nationalism*. London: Sage.

Bourdieu, P. (1977). *Outline of a Theory of Practice* (R. Nice, Trans.). Cambridge: Cambridge University Press.

Bourdieu, P. (1990a). *The Logic of Practice* (R. Nice, Trans.). Cambridge: Polity Press.

Bourdieu, P. (1990b). *Photography: A Middlebrow Art*. London: Polity.

Bourdieu, P. (1993). *The Field of Cultural Production: Essays on Art and Literature*. New York: Columbia University Press.

Brown, P., & Levinson, S. (1987). *Politeness: Some Universals in Language Usage*. Cambridge: Cambridge University Press.

Bruner, E.M. (2001). The Maasai and the Lion King: Authenticity, nationalism, and globalization in African tourism. *American Ethnologist*, 28(4), 881–908.

Burgess, J. (2010). Remediating vernacular creativity: Photography and cultural citizenship in the Flickr photo-sharing network. In T. Edensor et al. (Eds.), *Spaces of Vernacular Creativity: Rethinking the Cultural Economy*, (pp. 116–125) London: Routledge.

Butler, J. (1990). *Gender Trouble: Feminism and the Subversion of Identity*. New York: Routledge.

Coupland, J. (Ed.). (2000). *Small Talk*. London: Longman.

Coupland, J., & Jaworski, A. (2003). Transgression and intimacy in recreational talk narratives. *Research on Language and Social Interaction*, 36(1), 85–106.

Crang, M. (1997). Picturing practices: Research through the tourist gaze. *Progress in Human Geography*, 21, 359–373.

Du Bois, J.W. (2007). The stance triangle. In R. Englebreston (Ed.), *Stancetaking in Discourse: Subjectivity, Evaluation, Interaction*, (pp. 139–182). Amsterdam: John Benjamins.

Edensor, T. (2001). Performing tourism, staging tourism: (Re)producing tourist space and practice. *Tourist Studies*, 1(1), 59–81.

Favero, P. (2007). "What a wonderful world!": On the "touristic ways of see-ing", the knowledge and the politics of the "culture industries of otherness" (extract). *Tourist Studies*, 7(1), 51–81.

Featherstone, M. (2002). Cosmopolis: An introduction. *Theory, Culture and Society*, 19, 1–16.

Fiefer, M. (1985). *Going Places: The Ways of the Tourist from Imperial Rome to the Present Day*. London: Macmillan.

Foucault, M. (1980). *Power/knowledge*. New York: Pantheon.

Franklin, A., & Crang, M. (2001). The trouble with tourism and travel theory. *Tourist Studies*, 1, 5–22.

Giddens, A. (1984). *The Constitution of Society: Outline of the Theory of Structuration*. Cambridge: Polity.

Hanks, W.F. (2005). Pierre Bourdieu and the practices of language. *Annual Review of Anthropology*, 34, 67–83.

Harvey, D. (1996). The social construction of space and time. In *Justice, Nature and the Geography of Difference*, (pp. 210–247). Oxford: Blackwell.

hooks, b. (1992). Eating the other: Desire and resistance. In *Black Looks: Race and Representation*, (pp. 21–39). Boston: South End Press.

Jaffe, A. (Ed.). (2009). *Stance: Sociolinguistic Perspectives*. New York: OUP.

Jaworski, A., & Thurlow, C. (2009a). Gesture and movement in tourist spaces. In C. Jewitt (Ed.), *Handbook of Multimodal Discourse Analysis*, (pp. 253–262). London: Routledge.

Jaworski, A., & Thurlow, C. (2009b). Talking an elitist stance: Ideology and the discursive production of social distinction. In A. Jaffe (Ed.), *Perspectives on Stance*, (pp. 195–226). New York: OUP.

Jaworski, A., & Thurlow, C. (2010a). Language and the globalizing habitus of tourism: A sociolinguistics of fleeting relationships. In N. Coupland (Ed.), *The Handbook of Language and Globalization*, (pp. 255–286). Oxford: Wiley-Blackwell.

Jaworski, A., & Thurlow, C. (Eds). (2010b). *Semiotic Landscapes: Language, Image, Space*. London: Continuum.

Jaworski, A., Thurlow, C., Ylänne-McEwen, V., & Lawson, S. (2003). The uses and representations of local languages in tourist destinations: A view from British television holiday programmes. *Language Awareness*, 12, 5–29.

Jones, R. (2009). Dancing, skating and sex: Action and text in the digital age. *Journal of Applied Linguistics*, 6(3), 283–302.

Kahn, M. (2003). Tahiti: The ripples of a myth on the shores of the imagination. *History and Anthropology*, 14(4), 307–326.

Larsen, J. (2005). Families seen sightseeing: Performativity of tourist photogra-phy. *Space and Culture*, 8, 416–434.

Lefebvre, H. (1991 [1974]). *The Production of Space* (Translated by D. Nicholson-Smith, Trans.). Oxford: Blackwell.

McCabe, S. (2005). "Who is a tourist?" A critical review. *Tourist Studies*, 5(1), 85–106.

Pennycook, A. (2010). Spatial narrations: Graffscapes and city souls. In A. Jaworski & C. Thurlow (Eds.), *Semiotic Landscapes: Language, Image, Space* (137–150). London: Continuum.

Said, E. (1993). *Culture and Imperialism*. New York: Knopf.

Scollon, R. (1998). *Mediated Discourse as Social Interaction: A Study of News Discourse*. London: Longman.

Sontag, S. (1977). *On Photography*. New York: Farrar, Straus & Giroux.

Szerszynski, B., & Urry, J. (2002). Cultures of cosmopolitanism. *Sociological Review*, 50(4), 461–481.

Szerszynski, B., & Urry, J. (2006). Visuality, mobility and the cosmopolitan: Inhabiting the world from afar. *The British Journal of Sociology*, 57(1), 113–131.

Thurlow, C., & Jaworski, A. (2006). The alchemy of the upwardly mobile: Symbolic capital and the stylization of elites in frequent-flyer programmes. *Discourse & Society*, 17(1), 131–167.

Thurlow, C., & Jaworski, A. (2010). *Tourism Discourse: Language and Global Mobility*. London: Palgrave MacMillan.

Urry, J. (2002). *The Tourist Gaze*. 2nd ed. London: Sage.

Chapter 12

Orienting to Arab Orientalisms: Language, Race, and Humor in a YouTube *Video*

Elaine Chun and Keith Walters

IT LIKELY TOOK some by surprise when stand-up comedian Wonho Chung joined the *Axis of Evil Comedy Tour* (AECT) during their 2007 performances in Jordan, Egypt, Kuwait, Lebanon, and Dubai. Chung was of Korean and Vietnamese descent, and his fellow comedians Ahmed Ahmed, Aron Kader, and Maz Jobrani were, respectively, of Egyptian, Palestinian, and Iranian descent. Yet Chung was arguably more "at home" than his U.S.-raised counterparts; as his official website (www.wonhochung.com) states, "[he] was born in Jeddah, Saudi Arabia [...,] brought up in Amman, Jordan [..., and] in 2004 ... moved to Dubai."

The next year, video clips of Chung's Arabic-English bilingual performance in Dubai, filmed by *Showtime Arabia* and subtitled into English, were posted by two of his fans on *YouTube*, and during the two years that followed, viewers residing in over fifty countries and identifying largely as Arab posted over five hundred comments in response to these clips. Chung's appeal to this geographically dispersed audience hinged on his incongruous racial and cultural positioning: phenotypically he looked East Asian, but linguistically and culturally he was an "authentic" Arab.

In his performances, Chung frequently capitalizes on this particular racial and cultural positioning to humorously comment on ideologies of language, race, and nation in the Arab world. In this chapter, we explore the sociocultural significance of his humor by examining three moments in the *YouTube* video clips that were posted. Specifically, we focus on how Chung humorously invokes stereotypes of the Oriental, a figure indexing Eastern inferiority and otherness, and how his *YouTube* audience negotiates sociocultural meanings through their responses. The first moment occurs when MC Ahmed introduces Chung as a suitable addition to the tour in light of George W. Bush's having labeled not only Iran and Iraq but also North Korea as part of an "axis of evil." The second moment occurs when Chung enters the stage embodying the stereotypical persona of a bumbling Oriental. Finally, in a third moment of Orientalism, Chung performs an extensive parody of Filipino English and implicitly comments on relevant ideologies of language and race that circulate within and beyond the Arab Gulf.

In our discussion of these three moments, we draw on the notion of stance, as a useful tool for understanding the meaning of these figures. In particular, we focus on Chung's performance as one of humor and parody, necessarily playing on culturally salient tensions between stances toward the modern-day Oriental. We also explore how the increasingly popular new media space of *YouTube*, a site of cultural negotiation, invites collaborative stancetaking acts by participants in disparate locations. Our analysis thus highlights the significance of the Oriental figure as stances toward it are humorously juxtaposed and their tensions exposed, permitting ideological alignments among a largely Arab-identifying viewership. On the one hand, we note the potential for humor as a valuable tool for critiquing certain forms of Orientalism, and we examine the potential for *YouTube* spaces to encourage linguistically and geographically diverse individuals to collaboratively take positive stances toward Arabic and Arab culture. Yet we also identify ways in which Chung's performance and his audience's responses ultimately reinscribed essentialist notions of Arabness and racist ideologies of Orientalism.

Theoretical Background: Orientalism, Parody, and YouTube

Our theoretical concerns lie at the intersection of sociolinguistic understandings of stance and three cultural phenomena relevant to our analysis: Orientalism, parody, and *YouTube* as an exemplar of the new media. Drawing on perspectives that privilege *stance* as a key sociolinguistic phenomenon and a useful analytical tool (see Du Bois, 2007; Jaffe, 2009), we use this term to refer to the evaluative positioning a speaker achieves in relation to some object or action (see also Walton & Jaffe, Chapter 10, and Thurlow & Jaworski, Chapter 11, this volume). Though we define stance simply in terms of a two-place relation (subject, object/action), stancetaking acts are necessarily complex because of their inherent dialogism, as they articulate with other acts (Bakhtin, 1984). At an interactional level, these acts respond to prior acts, as instances of alignment or disalignment (Du Bois, 2007) as well as constructing intended and invoked audiences (Ede & Lunsford, 1984). Thus, acts of stancetaking are by definition instances of argument in the sense that rhetorical theorists use the term: even when speakers are not "arguing" in any traditional sense, they are putting forward a view of the world, asking that it be ratified by an audience. On a broader sociocultural scale, stances accumulate for individuals, helping construct enduring personas (e.g., an authoritative type) (Johnstone, 2009) as well as across a community, often reproducing yet also fractionalizing community ideologies (see Thurlow & Jaworski's discussion of this in Chapter 11). In our analysis, we are particularly interested in highlighting the dynamic aspects of stancetaking practices permitted by *YouTube*, as these practices intersect with widely circulating ideologies of race, nation, and language.

Orientalisms

Our analysis examines how stances emerge in relation to forms of Orientalism. Originally theorized by Edward Said (1978), this concept critiques a set of related European and American practices and ideas: the academic study of the Orient, a European style of colonizing this area, and an ideology that divides the East and West by constructing the former as a foil for the latter. As Yu (2001) explains, similar discourses about East, Southeast, and South Asians have emerged in popular and academic contexts in the United States. Robert Lee (1999), for example, identifies six Oriental figures—the pollutant, coolie, deviant, yellow peril, model minority, and gook—that arose during the past two centuries in response to U.S. wars in East and Southeast Asia and to Asian immigrant labor in the United States. Much like the discourses described by Said, such Orientalizing discourses in the United States have framed the Other in terms of contradictory and binary moralities, for example, an admirable capitalist work ethic yet a nonmaterialistic spirituality (Maira, 2000). Such discourses about the Other often serve as reminders of the West's own moral failings. In this chapter, we examine how, in an interesting twist of global flows of labor and capital, East and Southeast Asians have emerged as objects of Orientalism not in the West but in the Middle East, particularly the Arab Gulf.

We suggest that Orientalism can be usefully conceptualized in terms of stance and that examining Orientalizing acts as instances of stancetaking sheds light on the nature of both stance and Orientalism. In simple relief, Orientalism may be considered a set of stance acts taken by a subject toward an Eastern object. The subject, however, holds an ambivalent relationship with its object, as seen in Hollywood representations of Eastern (South Asian, East Asian, Southeast Asian, and Middle Eastern) caricatures of business owners, servants, and nerds (Hamamoto, 1994). The linguistic and cultural incompetence of Eastern bodies may delight with their puerility, but their presence sometimes signals a threat to racial purity, moral codes, and economic security (R.G. Lee, 1999). In terms of affective and epistemic stances then, Orientalism is best viewed as an inherent ambivalence of both emotion and knowledge: the subject feels and knows something about its object but likely does not embrace or understand it to any serious degree. Engaging in Orientalism, particularly when "styling" the Oriental, necessarily conveys such ambivalence of stance, much like other forms of linguistic and cultural appropriation (see Hill, 1998). Like stance acts more generally, Orientalism constructs the stancetaker's identity as much as, if not more than, it constructs its object.

Particularly relevant to our own analysis are two more contemporary forms of Orientalism. The first is the implicit and explicit vilifications of Arabs, Muslims, and the Middle East in Western and particularly American political discourses after the events of September 11, 2001 (Hodges & Nilep, 2009). The second, ironically, is the images that Gulf Arabs (in the "Middle East") construct of East and Southeast Asians (in the "Far East"). Such imagery has emerged in response to the formers' importation of cheap Asian laborers, where the "foreign" presence, including that of other nonlocal workers, is often understood as threatening the local moral or cultural fabric while encouraging dependence on foreign expertise.

Parody

Like Orientalism, parody plays on dualities of stance. Yet in parody, a speaker implicitly distances herself from the parodied figure or persona while embodying it, such that her voice "collides in a hostile fashion with the original owner and forces him to serve purposes diametrically opposed to [her] own" (Bakhtin, 1984, p. 160). Although parody, a form of varidirectional double voicing (Bakhtin, 1984; cf. Thurlow & Jaworski, Chapter 11 of this volume), most obviously conveys distance from its parodied object, the embodiment entailed may result in leakages of voice (Hill & Irvine, 1993) and ambivalences of stance.

The parodies described in this chapter are often interpreted as humorous through the heightened tensions of stance. At one level, parodies involve a tension between speakers' stances of voice, or their multiple footings with respect to their words. They enter a play frame (Goffman, 1974) in order to speak *as if* they owned the words they utter though still making clear a primary frame in which it is understood that they, in fact, do not own those words—or at least do not want to take full responsibility for them. At another level, parodies represent two figures at odds—parodist and parodied—with respect to their stances of ideology. Here, we examine tensions of ideological stance between *Axis of Evil* comedians and President George Bush, between those constructed as belonging to the Arab community ("Arabs") and those constructed as not ("Koreans" and "Filipinos"), and between Filipinos in the Gulf and a comedian of Korean and Vietnamese descent who has access to social capital they likely do not. Finally, humor emerges in tensions between stances of acceptability. Audience members, both *YouTube* viewers and commenters, appear to find these acts of parodic aggression acceptable yet take pleasure in them, at least partly because they appreciate an alternative reading: a stance defining these acts as taboo because of their potentially rude and racist interpretations.

YouTube

YouTube constitutes a space not only where performances of Orientalism and parody are displayed but also where stances are invited and shared. Since its inception in 2005, this video-sharing and social-networking site, like other web-hosted spaces, has introduced a culturally significant mode of sharing information and experiences, thus providing its users a space for moving beyond traditional "locational" communities (cf. Baym, 1998). Even those separated by physical distance and language but sharing stances of ideology may engage in interactions that display their mutual alignments.

In theory, *YouTube* provides an ideal space for dominant ideologies of language to be contested (e.g., Jones & Schieffelin, 2009; see also Walton & Jaffe, Chapter 10 of this volume). For example, it provides opportunities for encountering those in culturally distant places, potentially laying to rest stereotypes giving rise to Orientalizing practices. At the same time, the idealism with which some scholars depict online communities must be balanced with an understanding of their limits (see also Thurlow & Mroczek, Introduction to this volume). *YouTube*, in its present form, frequently functions as a site of exoticization and voyeurism (Collins, 2010), showcasing "amazing feats" posted for consumption and encouraging collusive acts of Orientalism. Additionally, as a space that is exclusive to particular subsets of users (Neumayer & Raffl, 2008), *YouTube* discourses may encourage simplistic readings of social others. Finally, these discourses are limited by the website's architectural constraints (Burgess & Green, 2008), such that objectifications and simplifications are normative (e.g., comments are limited to five hundred characters).

Three Orientalisms: Reappropriation, Passing, and Parody

Our chapter analyzes two video postings[1] of the same performance and 530 text comments that *YouTube* viewers posted in response to the videos between September 2008 and February 2010; these videos were uploaded by two different posters in May and September of 2008 after their extraction from the same *Showtime Arabia* broadcast. The earlier posting (9 minutes, 59 seconds) included all three moments of Orientalism analyzed here: MC Ahmed's explanation of how the comedy group had acquired its name, Chung's passing as a native Korean, and his parody of Filipino immigrants in the Gulf. The later posting (5 minutes, 26 seconds) included only the segment in which Chung passes as an Oriental; *YouTube* commenters seemed to view this segment as the centerpiece of both videos.

Strategic Reappropriations of Bush's Orientalism

The first form of Orientalism relevant to our analysis involves the comedy tour's name, a playful reappropriation of and stance toward President Bush's 2002 Orientalizing act of labeling the countries of Iraq, Iran, and North Korea as the "axis of evil." Ahmed explains the significance of the group's act of naming at the opening of the longer video:

Extract 12.1:
AHMED: We call ourselves The *Axis of Evil Comedy Tour*, because President Bush put this ridiculous term on countries in the Middle East, and we thought it was so funny we decided to take the term and put comedy tour at the end, and so we have an Egyptian, a Palestinian, an Iranian.

In a further act of critiquing Bush by playfully legitimizing his ascription, Ahmed cites Bush's inclusion of North Korea as part of the "axis" when he introduces Chung: "We couldn't find any funny North Koreans, but we found the next best thing. We found a funny South Korean." The AECT's revoicing of Bush's words, like all revoicings, dialogically presupposed and responded to a prior stance, in this case one that had Orientalized the Middle East and North Korea by constructing them as dangerous and morally deficient. Their satirical self-Orientalizing, which transformed Arabs and Middle Easterners into speaking subjects rather than Orientalized objects, also represented a stance of "strategic essentialism" (Spivak, 1988), drawing on a common experience of marginalization. Importantly, in addition to displaying a political stance, the act of reappropriation was a strategic act of marketing that potentially appealed to critics of an increasingly unpopular president, both in the United States and later in countries of the Middle East where English is widely understood. These actions demonstrate how objects of stances, (here, people of Middle Eastern origin) can reclaim agency by reprojecting themselves as stancetakers. The AECT thereby made explicit the objectification represented by Bush's prior stance, holding it up to derisive critique.

Passing as an Oriental

A second form of Orientalism in both videos occurs when Chung plays the role of a bumbling South Korean, passing as an Oriental before dramatically revealing his Arabic language skills and knowledge of Arab culture. As Chung explains in this performance as well as others, his father is Korean, and his mother is Vietnamese, yet he embodies a linguistic and cultural Arabness because of his life history. In fact, the language he displays indexes his access to local symbolic capital (Bourdieu, 1991); a few Jordanians we know who have watched the videos stated they have no trouble placing him by his accent as someone from a privileged background. (Chung's website notes that his father is a "prominent physiotherapist.") Yet Chung is presented at first simply and unproblematically as a "South Korean."

In his performance as an Oriental, Chung actively constructs his own outsiderness in various ways, encouraging audience members' Orientalizing stances toward him. In addition to the obvious physical markers of his East Asianness, he signals that he is culturally "out of his element." On entering the stage, he grasps Ahmed's hand firmly, bows to him deeply three times, and then turns to bow to the audience. Awkwardly placing his hands behind his back, he smiles broadly throughout Ahmed's opening words, silently nodding at Ahmed and the audience several times. When asked in English to introduce himself, Chung replies in Korean (see Extract 12.2), a language that presumably neither Ahmed nor audience members understand.

While his audience may have been convinced of his Koreanness, most speakers of Korean would identify Chung as a not fully native Korean speaker: he includes uncharacteristic prosodic breaks and rises, misuses case markers, mispronounces a verbal suffix, inverts the canonical ordering of personal names, includes three superfluous middle names, and inappropriately uses a nondeferential pronoun. Such details are lost on Ahmed and the audience, and what is important in Chung's Korean performance is his convincing portrait of otherness. Ahmed reiterates Chung's linguistic otherness by commenting, "I have no idea what he said" (line 15).

Extract 12.2:

			Researchers' English gloss of Korean
1	AHMED:	Why don't you go ahead and	
2		introduce yourself to the	
3		beautiful people of Dubai	
4	CHUNG:	Annyunghaseyo	How are you?
5		Na-nun ilum	I name
6		uh	uh
7		Nan hankwuk salam-i(e)yo	I'm a Korean person?
8		Na-nun ilum	I name [sic]
9		Wonho	((personal name))
10		Inswuk	((personal name))
11		Ilbong	((personal name))
12		Youngwon	((personal name))
13		Chung	((family name))
14	AUDIENCE:	((cheers and some laughs))	
15	AHMED	I have no idea what he said	

Chung continues smiling broadly and nodding as Ahmed talks. However, when he is handed Chung the microphone, Chung's expression changes to one of abject fear. After whispering with Ahmed a few times, Chung is left alone on the stage, and he moves nervously as if he might run off. Maintaining this Oriental persona for a minute and 40 seconds, he suddenly breaks frame, revealing that he has been playfully "passing" as an Oriental foreigner. A trained vocalist, Chung performs a well-known song from the Egyptian repertoire and then comments in Jordanian Arabic on the audience's expectation that he could not speak Arabic.

Extract 12.3:

	Chung	English video subtitle	Researchers' English gloss of Arabic[2]
1	WOO:		
2	tha:ktʕaliku:m	*I surprised you*	I+fooled (to)+you (pl.)
3	u lɛʔlɛ:ʔ	*didn't I*	or not?
4	((Audience laughs))		
5	ɪs-sədmɛ: ɪlli	*Your shock is not*	the+shock (f.) that
6	ɛntufihɛ:	*new to me...*	you (pl.) [are] in+it (f.)
7	bətsi:rmaʕi:	*It happens*	it+happens with+me,
8	ʕa:dyʒɪddɛn	*all the time.*	normally very
9	ku:lyu:m, uh,		every day, uh,
10	ku:lyu:mmɪn hayɛti		every day from life+my
11	an-na:s	*People always*	the+people
12	bɪnsudmu: ki:f	*wonder how*	(they)+wonder how
13	waħad ku:ribhaki	*an Asian guy*	a Korean is+speaking
14	bɪ-l-ʕrabi,	*like me can speak*	(with)+(the)+Arabic,
15	maʔu:l?	*fluent Arabic*	[is it] possible?

Chung's revelation necessarily questions ideologies of race and cultural/linguistic practice, and his comments implicitly critique the general Orientalizing assumption by "you" (his audience) and "people" generally (lines 2, 6, and 11 of Extract 12.3) that phenotypically East Asian bodies cannot be authentically Arab. Through his skillful performance of a much-loved song by a much-beloved Arab singer, Chung lays claim to an authentic Arab habitus (Bourdieu, 1977).

Legitimized Parody: Performing Another Oriental

The final set of stances examined involves Chung's stylization (Bakhtin, 1984; Coupland, 2001) of a Filipino/Tagalog accent in English—that is, a parodic revoicing of Asian immigrants to the Gulf (cf. Chun, 2004)—which appeared at the end of the longer video. While similar to the previous example in its performance of a stereotypical Asian other, his voicing of Tagalog-accented English in this context rests on the assumption that Chung has the stance of an insider: a native-like knowledge of the local sociopolitical economy of language and race. Specifically, an important aspect of local knowledge that Chung presupposes is that, in the Arab Gulf, the Arabic word *filibini* refers to a complex set of racialized categories and evaluations. Its narrow denotation is someone from the Philippines, while its broad and more common denotation is anyone who is phenotypically East Asian. Both denotations, however, frequently call on decidedly negative connotations reflecting the relatively low social status Filipinos are seen as occupying in local racialized hierarchies,

Extract 12.4:

	Chung	English video subtitle	Researchers' English gloss of Arabic and Tagalog
1	People mistake me		
2	for many things.		
3	B- Arab		
4	is not one of them.		
5	kti:r nɛ: s	*A lot of people*	*((Arabic))* A lot [of] people
6	bfəkru:ni	*mistake me for*	(they)+think+[of]+me
7	filibi:ni	*Filipino*	[as] Filipino
8	Which I don't mind		
9	I love Filipinos		
10	They're great		
11	*((Audience member yells "woo"))*		
12	Whoa		
13	one Filipino in the house		
14	Yes		
15	*((Audience laughter))*		
16	Hello		
17	Salamat		*((Tagalog))* Thank you
18	*((Audience laughter))*		

even among "foreigners." Drawing on this local knowledge, Chung plays the role of a Filipino service provider, a coffee shop barista.

The humor of Chung's performance highlights local tensions of race and the tensions of stance regarding the acceptability of engaging in explicitly racist discourse. He signals his awareness of his performance as potentially unacceptable when he carefully prefaces it with stance claims that align him strategically with the Filipinos he prepares to mock. After noting that he is never taken for an Arab (lines 3–4 of Extract 12.4), he continues, "A lot of people mistake me for Filipino, which I don't mind. I love Filipinos. They're great" (lines 5–8). By doing so, he may construct himself as legitimately positioned to parody a community in which he can claim membership by dominant ascription (cf. Chun, 2004). Continuing to construct alignment with an out-group, at least at an overt level of meaning (cf. Hill, 1998), he responds to a cheer in the audience with a Tagalog phatic expression ("Salamat"; 'thank you,' line 17).

Yet after presenting a stance of alignment with Filipinos, he goes on to critique a cultural practice he identifies as Filipino: "They love singing like in the most inappropriate places." His explicit critiques are then also merged with stylized illustrations of how Filipinos pronounce the names of pop singers and the lyrics of songs and, finally, how they speak in service encounters familiar to audience members. Throughout, Chung employs marked phonological features that index and stylize a Filipino Oriental whose English contrasts with his own otherwise "unaccented" English and Arabic.

By navigating tensions of acceptability through acts of adequation (Bucholtz & Hall, 2004) with the target of his parody, Chung (2004) may minimize the likelihood of being judged as racist. Yet the framing of his performance as "acceptable" belies the racialized hierarchies of power he reproduces. Employing a strategy of condescension (Bourdieu, 1991; Hill, 1998), Chung benefits from his stylized Filipino English precisely because of his audience's awareness that he could, if needed, use locally unstigmatized varieties of Arabic or English while the Filipino baristas he mocks could presumably never do the same. Although humor sometimes opens up avenues for social critique by questioning dominant, naturalized ideologies of various sorts, Chung's parody reinscribed a local Orientalism linked to racialized hierarchies of accent. In the rest of this chapter, we offer a brief analysis of 530 *YouTube* comments about the videos to illustrate how these stances of Orientalism were taken up by Chung's *YouTube* audience.

Negotiating Orientalizing Humor on YouTube

In examining the uptake of Chung's performance among *YouTube* users, we explore how this specific new media served as both a window to understand and a vehicle to recirculate discourses of Orientalism. In particular, we explore how *YouTube* provided a space where Orientalizing discourses were countered, primarily through cultural alignments among commenters who aligned positively with Arab culture and identity. Yet we also show how these largely Arab-identifying commenters simultaneously reinscribed certain Orientalisms through the stances they took toward Chung's skillful linguistic embodiments.

Constructing a Transnational Multilingual Arab Intersubjectivity

As described earlier, the comedy tour's name presented a direct critique of discourses linking the Middle East with terrorism, primarily as they circulated in the United States. At the same time, comments responding to the *YouTube* videos of the AECT performance were hardly suggestive of political defiance against such Orientalizing stances. In fact, only one of the analyzed comments alluded to the problematic nature of an Arab stereotype ("nice show // but still the world won't believe that we are not dangers," kingofdeath2008, Bahrain). In addition, no comments specifically referred to Bush's definition of the "axis of evil," while one commenter in fact admitted a lack of awareness of how the tour had acquired its name ("Why is the title (Axis of evil) :S," yotobia). These facts suggest that the political critique intended by AECT performers may not have been appreciated as such by all audience members.

However, the comedy tour's subversion of an Orientalizing stance was successful to the extent that *YouTube* commenters constructed a shared Arab subjectivity through alignments of affective stance. In particular, *YouTube* commenters who responded to Chung's performance presented stances that mutually and positively oriented to his performance and other AECT comedians. Among the 530 *YouTube* comments posted in response to the two videos and analyzed for this paper, 69.6% had positive valences (e.g., "lolz lolz aah my stomach hurts // i'm a big fan of him," MrsoNamikaze) and only 7.7% had negative valences (e.g., "not funny :$," mnmsgirl, Kuwait), while the remaining comments were neither clearly negative nor positive.

The videos and their circulation around the world provided an opportunity for Arab-identifying individuals to coconstruct positive stances toward not only Chung's performance but also Arab culture, politics, and language more generally. Among the comments, 38 referred to Chung's opening Egyptian song, whether as inquiries about its title (e.g., "does anybody know what song he's singing?" Shorty324lyfe, United States) or as responses to these inquiries (e.g., "Hes singing 'Gana el hawa' by abdl haleem hafiz," sultan7, Bouvet Island). Fifty-five comments specifically named the Arabic language (e.g., "Yay for him for talking in Arabic :D," ShadowyChan, United Arab Emirates). Commenters also constructed themselves as aligning with Arab culture by drawing on diverse indexical strategies (cf. Bucholtz & Hall, 2005). At times, they made explicit claims ("A Syrian here. // That guy's Arabic is awesome," SnowKid32, United States), while at other times, they used Arabic in either Arabic script (e.g., "لهم الصراحه ههه ههههه سوى" "Hahaha. He was telling the truth," Thrbalm3ani, United Arab Emirates) or transliterated Roman script, often referred to as Arabizi (Johnson, 2010) (e.g., "wala ishiiii el 333 o el 7777 !!!! mish tabi333333iiiiiiiii" 'I swear, this is something funny. ????? Amazing,' chocolatecake250, Serbia). Arab subjectivities were constructed not only in the content and form of comments, but also through participants' *YouTube* names displayed above their comments (e.g., khalidfakiha, saudi0barbie).

It should be noted that commenters constructed an Arab intersubjectivity not so much through a shared Arab identity or Arabic language but rather through a shared stance toward Arabness. Commenters' profile pages suggested an immense geographic, linguistic, and cultural diversity: 194 claimed to be from North America with the United States representing the largest group (n = 145); 187 comments were identified as being from 21 countries in the Middle East and North Africa, nearly all from the Gulf region; 57 listed a European location; and 21 stated that they were in South or Southeast Asia. Likewise, although Arabic was a linguistic resource used to index Arabness (97 comments contained some Arabic), English was the primary lingua franca among commenters (433 comments were completely in English) (cf. Danet & Herring, 2003; Durham, 2003).

Showtime Arabia's English subtitling of the Arabic portions of Chung's performance also facilitated a shared positive orientation toward Arabic by allowing the bilingual and multidialectal performance to be accessible even to viewers who did not understand Arabic or fully understand the varieties of Arabic that Chung used. (During his performance, Chung generally spoke Jordanian Arabic but also used Modern Standard Arabic and Saudi Arabic.)

Even if the subtitling was poorly done (e.g., "every arab that understood English that watched this with me noticed the bad subtitles. ;D," SnowKid32, United States), evidence for which can be seen by comparing the English subtitles with the English glosses in Extracts 12.3 and 12.4 above, the technology of subtitling was critical to bringing into alignment an otherwise linguistically and geographically dispersed set of individuals. Thus, new media technologies, coupled with the AECT's stance toward the marginalizing discourses of contemporary Orientalism, evoked and encouraged positive stances toward Arabness in this multilingual and transnational *YouTube* space.

Authenticating Arabness through Surprise

We now turn to a discussion of how other forms of Orientalism remained intact in the discourses circulated by Chung's *YouTube* audience. Specifically, we consider how commenters displayed strong affective stances toward Chung's revelation of his linguistic and cultural competence and examine what these stances suggested about commenters' understandings of their own Arabness and Chung's. As noted, part of the humor of Chung's performance lay in the assumed disjuncture between his physiognomy and his cultural practices. Reifying this incongruence, 37 participants expressed overt surprise (e.g., "Wow!") and thus presented a layered act of stance taking: a sudden shift between epistemic stances (from not knowing to knowing) as well as a strong affective stance toward this epistemic shift. Nearly all such comments employed capitalized or reduplicated letters and exclamation points to encode the increased volume, pitch, and lengthening typically found in spoken expressions of

Example 12.1: Constructions of high affect and surprise

YouTube Name	Country	Comment
evolutionHA	Brunei	NO WAY! // HE SOUNDS SOO NICE! // i would never have guessed he was arab // lol
OmaRex	Italy	HEE just SHOOOKKEED MEE !!!XD
Swamp666heaD	Saudi Arabia	LoooooooooooooooooL my brain's gone n twisted for today !! truly UNEXPECTED ?????????????????
8ssamm8	Korea	OMG!!!!!!!!! // big shock // he is talk Lebanon // hehe

surprise. Through orthographic choices such as those shown in Example 12.1, commenters manipulated visible linguistic form to index stances of high affect and to situate Chung as an Oriental spectacle.

These examples suggest that a large number of commenters assumed an Orientalizing stance toward Chung. Likewise, only three of the commenters referred to Chung as an Arab (*arab comedian sensation, asian arabi, he [is] arab*); most others either labeled him as Korean, Asian, or not Arab by using phrases such as *sounds arab, like ourselves, an Asian, that Korean guy*, and *the South Korean-Vietnamese*. These commenters recognized that Chung spoke Arabic fluently, treating him as an exception to their ideologies of race and language, yet positioned him as an outsider to—and at best an honorary member of—the Arab community constructed in this *YouTube* space.

In their Orientalizing acts, commenters also understood Chung as an "other" against which to measure themselves, recalling Said's description of Orientals as serving as Western mirrors of morality. Although evaluations of his performance were largely positive, Chung's skills were frequently compared with those of commenters, several of whom appeared to be ethnic Arabs in diaspora, according to their profile information. In many cases, some of which are shown in Example 12.2, commenters bemoaned their own Arabic language skills because of their supposed inferiority relative to the skills of Chung.

Example 12.2: Metalinguistic self-deprecating comments

YouTube Name	Country	Comment
xPsYcHoSyS	Canada	SPEAKS BETTER ARABIC THAN ME!!!!! // for those of you who dont speak arabic, trust me hes perfectly fluent, no accent either
xx3xotiicxx	Canada	HOLYYY SHITTTTTT. i was not expectin that at ALL he speaks better than my parents :
L45	United Kingdom	Wow This guy is inspiring..to be able to speak all those languages is something special. He speaks better Arabic than me! :)
stlais1094	United States	oooooo god . an asian speaks arab more than me and im full lebanese, and has a better accent

In so doing, these commenters employed a common genre of compliment across the Arab world in which a speaker praises an outsider for more skillfully engaging in a culturally "Arab" practice (e.g., speaking Arabic, dancing in the *sharqi* "Eastern" fashion, bargaining) than herself. Such a compliment simultaneously authenticates the complimenter's own Arabness while marking the object of praise as non-Arab, that is, inauthentic. It likewise constructs the person paying the compliment as having the authority to offer such evaluations (cf. E. Lee, 2007). Thus, *YouTube* commenters' stances, when highlighting Chung's "amazing" feats of language, appeared to be acts of self-critique, but they also presupposed an Arab authority and authenticity that Chung, by contrast, did not possess.

Trajectories of Parody on *YouTube*

Much like Chung's performance of Arabic, his performance of a Tagalog-accent was positively evaluated by his *YouTube* audience as both humorous and accurate (Example 12.3). Among the 11 commenters who specifically addressed his parody of Filipino English, two commenters, both of whom claimed affiliation with the Philippines on their profile pages, legitimated Chung's performance and accepted his critique:

Example 12.3: Evaluations of Chung's Filipino performance

YouTube Name	Country	Comment
mahdogzbite	Philippines	This guy HAS to be Filipino. The way he could do the Filipino-English accent was just too accurate for a non Filipino.
shewolf1983	Philippines	ahahahaha! i'm filipino... still found this so funny!!! 'coz it's true... some of us do need to work on pronunciation... :))

In a similar display of appreciation, seven commenters directly quoted Chung's stylization, drawing on nonstandard English orthography to indicate his accented speech. A few cases are presented in Example 12.4.

Example 12.4: Quotations of Chung's stylizations

YouTube **Name**	Country	Comment
khalidfakiha	Saudi Arabia	hahahahah chocolate cake on the side plz...hehe
plastof	India	MARRIAH CURRY......LOOL
pilotman24	United States	LMAO i luv the ending when he goes...u want a black coffe chocolate cale...and so onnn.... THAT WAS TOO FUNNY
Dark-Crow200	Qatar (Palestine)	OMG! he is so funny, I thought he said I pee you! And when he went to the coffee shop LOL!

The humor for Chung's audience depended on a metalinguistic awareness of a locally circulating typification of Filipino speech that was linked
to salient cultural tensions regarding racialized hierarchies in the Gulf
as well as the acceptability of engaging in racist discourse. Despite their
likely recognition that performing Filipino stereotypes reproduced racialized hierarchies, both Chung and his audience sought to frame their racialized performances as culturally acceptable. As noted in our discussion
of Extract 12.4 above, Chung licensed his discourse by framing it as an
act of adequation through his repeated references to his Filipino alignments. On the other hand, *YouTube* commenters framed their words as
direct quotations, repeating Chung's exact words. By doing so, they constructed Chung as both "principal" and "author" of the Filipino mimicry
and presented themselves as its mere "animators" (Goffman, 1981). While
Chung used strategic stances of ideology to frame his racist performance
as acceptable, his audience drew on strategic stances of voice to relinquish
ownership and responsibility.

Importantly, such stance strategies did not make these Filipino parodies less racist, but they did permit a racist discourse to be understood as
relatively acceptable. We also note the consequences of the distribution
and acceptability of such parodies, particularly when circulated widely.
The potential consequences were clear in one case as Chung's performance was transformed into a hostile commentary on a Filipino problem
("OMG .....That was hilarious ..I'm half Saudi and half Jordanian and I
have a big problem dealing with philippino accent in Saudi Arabia ,,,and
won Ho got it right ,,,.......heheheh," shooshoosharon, Saudi Arabia).

The Potential and Limits of Social Critique in Parody and on YouTube

In this chapter, we have examined the multiple stances that performers and audiences negotiated in relation to an AECT performance featuring comedian Wonho Chung and posted on *YouTube.* Specifically, we noted that the parody used in this performance relied on the tension between simultaneous stances that were claimed by the parodist and ratified by the audience. (Those who are not aware of the tension because they lack necessary background knowledge or disapprove of the stances for ideological reasons likely miss the humor.) We have likewise analyzed Orientalism as a particular historicized act of stancetaking that continues to be negotiated in present-day discourses.

Our analysis speaks to the potential of *YouTube* parody, circulating in a particular new media space, to engage in ideological commentary while encouraging sociocultural participation. On the one hand, we suggested that Orientalizing stances that have marginalized Arabs in discourses within and beyond the United States are potentially subverted through the satirical self-Orientalizing name that the AECT adopted and the positive orientations toward Arabness that commenters expressed. As the largely Arab-identifying viewership became speaking/writing subjects, rather than Orientalism's objects, they revoiced and recontextualized prior Orientalizing stances, imbuing them with new meanings. In this regard, *YouTube* provides a site where those who share stances can connect and interact in ways created and constrained by available media.

On the other hand, we also suggested that other aspects of Chung's performance and his audiences' evaluations ultimately reinscribed Orientalizing stances. Although Chung's revelation of his Arab habitus seemed potentially to denaturalize local ideologies of race, language, and culture, his performance of Arab authenticity precisely *as humor* necessarily legitimated a local Orientalism that treats phenotypical East Asians like Chung as outsiders; that is, humor was achieved precisely because of the tension of stances that lay between his own claim to Arabness and the widely circulating assumption of its impossibility. This tension must be understood in the current context of the Arab Gulf, where growing numbers of East Asians now live and work. (Chung's revelation as a fluent speaker of English would hardly be humorous or surprising in San Francisco or Honolulu.) As demonstrated, *YouTube* commenters responded by expressing a clear appreciation for Chung's verbal and vocal skills, but they drew on a variety of resources to reproduce the assumption of

Chung's inauthenticity as an Arab and their authority to offer such evaluations. We have shown how both Chung and his audience drew on strategies that navigated tensions arising from performing and appreciating racial parodies: Chung's acts of adequation, aligning himself with Filipinos, and his audience members' acts of quotation, assigning responsibility for the parody to Chung rather than themselves. While these careful acts of footing may have constructed these performers/speakers/commenters as engaging in "acceptable" forms of humor, racialized hierarchies of accent were necessarily reproduced through every act of performance, circulation, and appreciation.

Importantly, our own critical stance regarding the racist potential of Chung's performance, especially as it was taken up by his viewers, should be qualified. On the one hand, we note that not all parodic or satirical acts of subversion by marginalized groups are read as such by all audiences, particularly those whose worldviews are being parodied (cf. Walters, 1999). As suggested, parody by definition is driven by a tension between ideological stances—at least a temporary ambiguity of "whose side the parodist is really on"—even if some forms of humor ultimately function as social critique. Yet we are not suggesting that parodies of race are doomed in their attempts to subvert racist ideologies. Certain parodies succeed in encouraging direct reflection and introspection regarding the racist logic that underlies the value we assign to languages, accents, and skin colors. Racial caricatures performed by some comedians can parody not merely Orientals but, more importantly, popular racist representations of Orientals, disrupting the Orientalizing gaze by parodying the parodist (Chun, 2004). In fairness, Chung also achieves such ideological disruptions in other performances, inviting viewers to reflexively examine their own racist assumptions, though space does not permit us to address these performances here.[3]

We hesitate to suggest that *YouTube* inherently magnifies stances of Orientalism, though we contend that hegemonic ideologies may be reproduced because of the limits of purpose and form characterizing *YouTube* commenting as a genre. Primarily, comments serve as a communal "rating system" that tends not to presume "conversations" beyond paired sequences (e.g., question–answer or comment–agreement)[4]; commenters also value pithiness and spontaneity as they draw from readily available, widely circulating discourses. Certainly, this space has potential to engender alternative stances contesting hegemonic ideologies, such as if a video were posted in order to frame a racist act as clearly problematic. In fact, in the data we analyzed, we observed the contestation of dominant Arabic language ideologies through *YouTube* commenters' predominant postings in dialectal rather than Modern Standard Arabic, contributing to a renegotiation of Arabic diglossia (cf. Walters, 2003).[5] Yet ultimately, *YouTube* may be a space that inherently Orientalizes difference; objects of videos, whether an Oriental figure or a racist figure who Orientalizes, tend to be appreciated for embodying precisely what viewers likely never can.

Finally, we acknowledge that while we have attempted to understand the complex layers of stancetaking involved in the videos analyzed here, our readings are necessarily products of our own understandings of race and language. Elaine, a Korean American, has written on issues of Asian-American identity and mocking, while Keith, a White American, has written about the limits of parody as social critique and language in the Arab world. In the course of reflecting and writing, our understandings of Chung's performance have shifted considerably. But like Chung and his audiences, we offer our stances as part of a dynamic dialogue and negotiation—a particular interpretation that we trust will meet with both alignment and critique.

Authors' Note and Acknowledgments

Thanks to Suad Alazzam-Alwidyan, a Jordanian, as well as Hamad AlShammari and Tasneem Al Sultan, both Saudis, for discussion of the data used in this paper and of racial attitudes in the Gulf. We also thank Julia McKinney for assistance in transcribing the English-language sections of Chung's performance. Finally, we thank Crispin Thurlow, Shana Walton, and an anonymous reviewer whose insightful comments helped shape key ideas in our analysis.

Notes

1. The URLs for the videos we are analyzing here are http://www.youtube.com/watch?v=EmUsOUvrk6o and http://www.youtube.com/watch?v=6xzuKzUEFJE
2. The English glosses are fairly literal. Parenthetical information represents Arabic elements not found in English; information in square brackets represents English elements not required in Arabic. Elements of what are Arabic morphologically derived words (e.g., conjugated verb forms) are indicated with the symbol +s in the English glosses
3. See http://www.youtube.com/watch?v=-Ccdm-1Xdq8
4. We thank Shana Walton for this observation.

5. Indeed, a topic beyond the scope of this paper but meriting careful attention is how Arabs reading these postings assume they can assess sociodemographic aspects of a commenter's identity on the basis of the particular dialect written and then use this information in computing the commenter's stance.

References

Bakhtin, M.M. (1984). *Problems of Dostoevsky's Poetics*. Minneapolis: University of Minnesota Press.

Baym, N. (1998). The emergence of on-line community. In S.C. Jones (Ed.), *Cybersociety 2.0: Revisiting Computer-Mediated Communication and Community*, (pp. 35–66). Thousand Oaks, CA: Sage.

Bourdieu, P. (1977). *Outline of a Theory of Practice*. Cambridge: Cambridge University Press.

Bourdieu, P. (1991). *Language and Symbolic Power*. Cambridge: Harvard University Press.

Bucholtz, M., & Hall, K. (2004). Language and identity. In A. Duranti (Ed.), *A Companion to Linguistic Anthropology*, (pp. 369–394). Oxford: Blackwell.

Bucholtz, M., & Hall, K. (2005). Identity and interaction: A sociocultural linguistic approach. *Discourse Studies*, 7, 585–614.

Burgess, J. E., & Green, J. B. (2008, October). Agency and controversy in the YouTube community. Paper presented at the Association of Internet Researchers (AoIR) Conference. Copenhagen, Denmark. Retrieved from http://eprints.qut.edu.au/15383/

Chun, E. (2004). Ideologies of legitimate mockery: Margaret Cho's revoicings of Mock Asian. *Pragmatics*, 14, 263–289.

Collins, P.H. (2010). The new politics of community. *American Sociological Review*, 75, 7–30.

Coupland, N. (2001). Stylization, authenticity and TV news review. *Discourse Studies*, 3, 413–442.

Danet, B., & Herring, S.C. (2003). Introduction: The multilingual internet. *Journal of Computer-Mediated Communication*, 9, 0. doi: 10.1111/j.1083-6101.2003.tb00354.x. Available at http://jcmc.indiana.edu/vol9/issue1/intro.html

Du Bois, J. (2007). The stance triangle. In R. Englebretson (Ed.), *Stancetaking in Discourse: Subjectivity, Evaluation, Interaction*, (pp. 139–182). Amsterdam & Philadelphia: John Benjamins.

Durham, M. (2003). Language choice on a Swiss mailing list. *Journal of Computer-Mediated Communication*, 9, 0. doi: 10.1111/j.1083-6101.2003.tb00359.x. Available at http://jcmc.indiana.edu/vol9/issue1/durham.html

Ede, L., & Lunsford, A. (1984). Audience addressed/audience invoked: The role of audience in composition theory and pedagogy. *College Composition and Communication, 35,* 155–171.

Goffman, E. (1974). *Frame analysis: An Essay on the Organization of Experience.* Boston: Northeastern University Press.

Goffman, E. (1981). *Forms of Talk.* Philadelphia: University of Pennsylvania Press.

Hamamoto, D.Y. (1994). *Monitored Peril: Asian Americans and the Politics of TV Representation.* Minneapolis: University of Minnesota Press.

Hill, J.H. (1998). Language, race, and White public space. *American Anthropologist, 100,* 680–689.

Hill, J.H., & Irvine, J.T. (1993). Introduction. In *Responsibility and Evidence in Oral Discourse,* 1–23. Cambridge: Cambridge University Press.

Hodges, A., & Nilep, C. (2009). *Discourse, War and Terrorism.* Amsterdam: John Benjamins.

Jaffe, A. (2009). *Stance: Sociolinguistic Perspectives*. New York: Oxford University Press.

Johnson, A. (2010, March). *il7mdella good ;)* : *Code Choice & Arabizi in a Meebo Chatroom.* Paper presented at Georgetown University Roundtable on Language and Linguistics, Washington, DC.

Johnstone, B. (2009). Stance, style, and the linguistic individual. In A.M. Jaffe (Ed.), *Stance: Sociolinguistic Perspectives,* (pp. 29–52). New York: Oxford University Press.

Jones, G.M., & Schieffelin, B.B. (2009). Talking text and talking back: "My BFF Jill" from Boob Tube to YouTube. *Journal of Computer-Mediated Communication, 14,* 1050–1079.

Lee, E. (2007). *Chinese Nationals among "Overseas Chinese" in Singapore: The Sociolinguistic Authentication of Mainland Chinese Identities.* Unpublished dissertation, Austin: University of Texas at Austin.

Lee, R.G. (1999). *Orientals: Asian Americans in Popular Culture.* Philadelphia: Temple University Press.

Maira, S. (2000). Henna and hip hop: The politics of cultural production and the work of cultural studies. *Journal of Asian American Studies, 3,* 329–369.

Neumayer, C., & Raffl, C. (2008). Facebook for global protest: The potential and limits of social software for grassroots activism. In L. Stillman & G. Johanson (Eds.), *5th Prato Community Informatics & Development Informatics Conference 2008: ICTs for Social Inclusion: What Is the Reality? Conference CD,* (pp. 1–14). Caulfield, Victoria, Australia: Caulfield School of Information Technology.

Rampton, B. (1995). *Crossing: Language and Ethnicity among Adolescents.* London: Longman.

Said, E.W. (1978). *Orientalism.* New York: Pantheon Books.

Spivak, G.C. (1988). Subaltern studies: Deconstructing historiography. *Selected Subaltern Studies,* 3–34. Oxford: Oxford University Press.

Walters, K. (1999). "He can read my writing but he sho' can't read my mind": Zora Neale Hurston's revenge in *Mules and Men*. *Journal of American Folklore*, 112, 343–371.

Walters, K. (2003). Fergie's prescience: The changing nature of diglossia in Tunisia. *International Journal of the Sociology of Language*, 163, 77–109.

Yu, H. (2001). *Thinking Orientals: Migration, Contact, and Exoticism in Modern America*. New York: Oxford University Press.

PART FIVE

New Practices, Emerging Methodologies

Chapter 13

From Variation to Heteroglossia in the Study of Computer-Mediated Discourse

Jannis Androutsopoulos

DESPITE THE NOVELTY that labels such as "internet linguistics" (Crystal, 2006) seem to imply, most language-focused research on new media tends to situate itself within established approaches in socially oriented linguistics. As a consequence, the state of the art in new media discourse studies is characterized by attempts to adapt established methods of data collection and analysis to new environments of discourse, and new techniques in internet research tend to supplement rather than replace concepts and methods from linguistic scholarship (Androutsopoulos & Beißwenger, 2008; Herring, 2004). Variation is one such key concept. As any search across classic publications in the field shows, *variation* is a ubiquitous keyword understood in a number of ways. In terms of linguistic structure, it is usually viewed as variation between "speech" and "writing" or standard and vernacular linguistic forms. In terms of contextual factors, language variation online has been associated with the effect of digital communications technologies on written language, or with the absence of institutional regulation, or with people's opportunities to realize digital modes and genres in ways that are much more diverse than their apparent technological standardization.

Within the broader context of "coding-and-counting" approaches in computer-mediated discourse analysis (Herring, 2004), the study of linguistic variation is delimited from other quantitative studies of language online (such as Tagliamonte & Denis, 2008; Yates, 1996) by using the linguistic variable as a structural unit of analysis. This involves the identification of linguistic variables and the calculation of the frequency of their variants in correlation to linguistic or nonlinguistic independent variables (Androutsopoulos, 2006, pp. 424–426). Based on that premise, researchers have examined linguistic variables from various languages in different new media modes and in relation to different independent variables. Let us briefly review these aspects. First, researchers mostly focus on modes of synchronous interactive written discourse such as Internet Relay Chat and Instant Messaging (see Androutsopoulos & Ziegler, 2004; Christen & Ziegler, 2006; Franke, 2006; Paolillo, 2001; Siebenhaar, 2006; Squires, 2011), though forums, blogs, newsgroups, and personal ads have been studied as well (Androutsopoulos, 2007; Hering & Paolillo, 2006; van Compernolle, 2008). The traditional variationist focus on phonology is replaced by the analysis of written representations of phonological variation between standard and dialect or formal and casual style (see work by Androutsopoulos & Ziegler, 2004; Christen & Ziegler, 2006; Franke, 2006; Siebenhaar, 2006). Cases of grammatical variation have also been studied (Herring & Paolillo, 2006; Siebenhaar, 2006; van Compernolle, 2008), but only a few studies have examined variation that is specific to written language, such as spelling substitutions and apostrophe usage (Paolillo, 2001; Squires, 2011, forthcoming). Mixed-method studies that combine quantitative and qualitative analysis of style shifting have also been conducted (Androutsopoulos, 2007; Androutsopoulos & Ziegler, 2004; Franke, 2006), and Paolillo's (2001) social network analysis of language variation in an IRC (Internet Relay Chat) channel is a combined study of five linguistic variables (three spelling substitutions, use of obscenity, and code switching into Hindi). The relevant dimensions of variation are between standard and dialect as well as spoken and written style, even though concerns are sporadically raised as to what actually constitutes a "standard" in online settings that lack institutional control (Paolillo, 2001; Squires, 2011, forthcoming). Independent variables examined include gender, region, age, genre (Androutsopoulos, 2007; Herring & Paolillo, 2006), type of chat channel (Siebenhaar, 2006), and network structure (Paolillo, 2001).

Despite its fairly limited empirical coverage in terms of languages (especially English, German, and French), this work has established that language variation online is socially and generically patterned. It has thereby contributed to a differentiated and deexoticized understanding of new media discourse. However, in the remainder of this chapter I am concerned less with the achievements of variation analysis and more with its "blind spots," its limits in exploring and theorizing language online. I therefore use this work as a backdrop against which to ask: What else? And what next?

Limits of a Language Variation Approach to Language Online

In particular, five "limits" of a language variation approach will be briefly discussed: its unimodal and monolingual focus, and its reliance on the linguistic variable, on predefined independent variables, and on quantification. These "limits" echo, in part, a broader critique of variationism within sociolinguistics, which must remain implicit in this chapter (see Auer, 2007; Coupland, 2007). At the same time, they reflect a gap between the state of art in new media language research and our experience of contemporary popular, yet still poorly researched, digital environments such as social networks and content-sharing websites, which are of central importance to my argument (see, however, Chapters 2, 3, 6, 9, 10, 11, & 12 in the current volume). The contrast between these and "older," but much better researched, computer-mediated communication (CMC modes (such as e-mail, mailing lists, IRC, and IM) is central to the following discussion.

First, as the literature review suggests, a language variation approach to language online seems most efficient with modes that enable users to approximate conversational interaction, are available in large and easily extractable volumes, and rely on written language as the main resource for the construction of meaning. However, in contemporary Web 2.0 environments (discussed further in this chapter) language comes integrated in visually organized environments, verbal exchanges tend to be more fragmented and dependent on multimodal context, and meaning is constructed through the interplay of language and other semiotic means. Second, a language variation approach seems best suited for the analysis of relations within the same linguistic system, and therefore less well equipped to address multilingual discourse and code switching, whose importance to new media discourse is by now well attested.[1] Third, a language variation approach tends to exclude features that are not easily operationalized as linguistic variables. This may affect single semiotic features such as emoticons as well as discourse phenomena such as language or script choice. Fourth, the quantitative premise of variation studies implies that features that are scarce in frequency may be excluded, even though they might be pragmatically and socially meaningful in the data. Finally, the reliance on independent, nonlinguistic variables may lead to a preference for data in which such variables can be construed. This in turn may marginalize new media contexts whose classification in sociodemographic terms is less obvious (see discussion in Androutsopoulos, 2006, pp. 424–425). The preference for clear-cut social variables such as gender and age may reflect scholarly convention rather than the categories that are relevant to participants in online communication.

Awareness of such limitations is probably as old as language-centered new media research, and it is not news that new media data is often more messy and unpredictable than a language variation approach can handle. One 1998 monograph concludes with the observation that the new media are characterized by linguistic elements and fragments from different discourse worlds, which are put together to a specific "style-mix" (Runkehl et al., 1998, p. 209).[2] Five years later, Georgakopoulou (2003) suggests that the new media are "by no means a homogeneous and centralized site: in contrast, [they] encourage hybridity, diversity of voices and ideologies, and expression of difference." Another five years later, Tagliamonte & Denis (2008, p. 26) view a "quintessential characteristic of IM discourse" in the "consistent juxtaposition of 'forms of a different feather.'" While to some researchers this is no more than a footnote, others have used ideas from pragmatics, conversation analysis, stylistics, and interactional sociolinguistics in order to study new media not primarily as technological containers of speech, but as sites of users' social activities with language. In such approaches, the classification of language use on dimensions of variation is complemented by an attention to the situated exploitation of linguistic difference, which doesn't shy away from the importance of singular, unrepeated instances of linguistic difference as used in a strategic, yet nonquantifiable way. Likewise, the correlation with predefined social categories is replaced by a focus on identities as discursive constructions that participants claim and negotiate by drawing on a variety of semiotic means (e.g., Danet, Ruedenberg-Wright, & Rosenbaum-Tamari, 1997; Tsiplakou, 2009). This and other work offers examples for the code-centered stylistic choices that Georgakopoulou (2003) views as characteristic of informal new media. It suggests that what characterizes language and discourse online is neither a specific new pattern of variation between two predetermined poles nor a new language variety, but rather a heightened attention to all aspects of written language as a key mode of signification.

As far as language use online is concerned, then, variation analysis leaves a number of "blind spots," which have been partially circumvented by focusing on specific CMC modes at the expense of others. Interactional and ethnographic research has acted to some extent as a complement and corrective to variation studies, and its insights resonate with the heteroglossia approach outlined below. However, its focus still being on "classic" CMC modes, neither its research questions not its data take the sociotechnological evolution of digital communication into account.

Web 2.0: Participation, Convergence, and Discourse

Out of the overwhelming array of digital communication modes available today, typical Web 2.0 environments such as social networking and content-sharing websites dominate popular practice and imagination. Even though there is no easy and straightforward distinction between an "old" and a "new" web, these environments share technological, sociological, and structural features that clearly separate them both from earlier stages of the web as well as from the pre-web applications linguists are so familiar with (Cormode & Krishnamurthy, 2008; although see Thurlow & Mroczek, Introduction to this volume). Some of these differences are captured by the concepts of convergence and participation, which, even though not directly referring to language, have important, yet not well-understood implications for language online (Androutsopoulos, 2010). Simply put, participation relates to the accessibility of localized, bottom-up production and distribution of online content, while convergence refers to the fusion of formerly distinct technologies and modes of communication in integrated digital environments (Jenkins, 2006).

An implication of participation from the perspective of new media studies is related to the types of role relationships and repertoires of digital media practice it enables. Web 2.0 is different from earlier stages of the web in the modes of production and consumption it facilitates. Instead of a clear-cut role distribution between professional content production and read-only consumption, Web 2.0 sites of social networking and content sharing feature a greater "co-mingling of commentators and creators, and every visitor has the opportunity to click, comment, create, etc." (Cormode & Krishnamurthy, 2008). In this context, one effect of convergence is a dramatic increase in the range of available semiotics and resources and their combinatory potential.

Drawing on concepts more familiar to sociolinguistics and discourse analysis, we might say that participatory and convergent digital environments are characterized by processes of multimodality and multiauthorship: their content is produced by multiple participants, simultaneously and in part independently of each other; and they host and integrate complex combinations of media and semiotic modes, including written text (and, increasingly, speech), standing image, moving image, color, and graphic design. (Compare with, for example, Jones et al., Chapter 2; Newon, Chapter 7; Thurlow & Jaworski, Chapter 11, this volume.)

These dimensions of media and semiotic complexity, I argue, exhaust the potential of variation analysis and call for analytical and theoretical attention to current web environments.

Introducing Heteroglossia

Heteroglossia sets in at this point, as one concept that, I argue, might offer an alternative perspective of linguistic heterogeneity online. However, heteroglossia is an elusive and slippery concept, and in this section I indicate its complexities besides discussing some of its definitions and analytical applications (see also Squires, Chapter 1, this volume).

Originally introduced by Mikhail Bakhtin in his 1935 essay "Discourse in the Novel," the notion of heteroglossia has been embraced by literary studies and sociolinguistics (see Lähteenmäki, 2010; Vice, 1997, pp. 18–21). Bakhtin originally speaks of "the co-existence of socio-ideological contradictions between the present and the past, between differing epochs of the past, between different socio-ideological groups in the present, between tendencies, schools, circles and so forth" (1981, p. 291). From the range of available scholarly definitions, two I find particularly insightful are by Ivanov (2001, p. 95) who defines heteroglossia as "the simultaneous use of different kinds of speech or other signs, the tension between them, and their conflicting relationship within one text," and Bailey (2007, p. 257), who suggests that "Heteroglossia addresses (a) the simultaneous use of different kinds of forms or signs, and (b) the tension and conflicts among those signs, based on the sociohistorical associations they carry with them."[3]

Compared with sociolinguistic concepts like variation and code switching (Bailey, 2007), the notion of heteroglossia entails a number of differences. Bakhtin locates it at a double level: in the novel, which uses language to articulate tensions between voices of different social origin and standing, and at the same time in the social reality a novel reflects or draws on (see also Lähteenmäki, 2010, p. 23). Therefore, heteroglossia does not *occur*, as one might say with regard to language variation, but is *made*: it is fabricated by social actors who have woven voices of society into their discourses, contrasting these voices and the social viewpoints they stand for. Such an understanding of heteroglossia as the outcome of purposeful, and often artful, semiotic activity ties in well with the concept's use to study relationships between linguistic diversity, social difference, and power in media discourse.[4] As Bailey points out in his study of bilingual interaction, heteroglossia is more inclusive than variation in that it can address both mono- and multilingual discourse (2007, p. 258). Indeed, any kind of linguistic difference at different levels of linguistic structure can be potentially viewed as heteroglossic, to the extent it produces ideological oppositions that are meaningful to participants in a communicative encounter. Because heteroglossia "takes as its starting point the social and pragmatic functioning of language" (Bailey, 2007, p. 262) rather than linguistic form as such, it enables analysts to contextualize locally contrastive patterns of usage within larger social, historical, and ideological processes. Thus, heteroglossia goes beyond the co-occurrence of and shift between languages or language varieties, and focuses on "the coexistence of different competing ideological points of view" (Lähteenmäki, 2010, p. 25) that are indexed by language in specific communicative situations.

However, the literature reviewed here has not produced an agreed methodology on how to identify instances of heteroglossia in discourse, which units of analysis to work with, and which levels of linguistic structure to consider. On the contrary, researchers have located heteroglossia in widely different discourse domains and processes, and while one might argue that such a breadth of application is made possible by the fluidity of the concept, it arguably makes its application more complex and runs the risk of subjectivity and lack of transparency. Especially when contrasted with the clear-cut operationalizations of variation analysis, heteroglossia appears very difficult to operationalize (Bailey, 2007, p. 263). However, bearing in mind the critique of variationism discussed in this chapter, this openness and flexibility should be thought of as an advantage. It allows us to "think big," offering space to envisage heteroglossic relations between signs of various kinds and structural properties, whose coexistence and dialogue may be established at different levels of discourse.

Locating Heteroglossia in Digital Discourse Environments

Summing up the previous discussion, heteroglossia invites us to examine contemporary new media environments as sites of tension and contrast between linguistic resources, social identities, and ideologies. However, the discussion also makes clear that heteroglossia is not a ready-made concept; it needs to be tailored to the conditions of discourse under investigation. A crucial issue is therefore how to locate its spaces of articulation: Is digital heteroglossia, one might heuristically ask, text- or practice-based? In other words, does it emerge in the eye of the beholder, or can it also be pinpointed in a configuration of textual/semiotic resources? What is its level of articulation? Is it the entire web? An entire website or just one full web page? A thread of posts or just a single post within a thread? A single text within a web page or just some constituents of that text?

The quick answer is—all of the above. Heteroglossic relations can manifest at different levels of linguistic and textual organization, and such relations can coexist, owing to the convergent, multimodal, and multiauthored structure of Web 2.0 environments. However, any text-based analysis of heteroglossia requires an "anchor," a pivotal point in discourse structure. With regard to social network and content-sharing websites, the anchor I propose in this research is the web page, including personal profile pages or those that host a photo or video and viewers' comments. Two caveats seem important here. First, we focus specifically on dynamically generated Web 2.0 pages (Cormode & Krishnamurthy, 2008) with all their textual components. Second, an emic justification for that anchor is the observation that Web 2.0 pages are functional units tied to social actors or media items—in other words, they "belong" to someone (such as a profile page or blog) or host a particular semiotic artifact (a video, photo, or other media item). Web 2.0 pages constitute a mesolevel of discourse structure, providing rich context for the analysis of microlevel elements (such as posts and the linguistic utterances they contain) and constraining the overwhelming mass of content that is experienced at the macrolevel of entire websites. Using Web 2.0 pages as units of analysis is not an obstacle for an ethnographic approach to new media discourse because the ownership of blogs and profile pages may motivate contact and communication with content creators.

Against that backdrop, I now identify potential locations of heteroglossic contrasts, moving between the level of an entire web page and its textual constituents. It is especially at a microlevel of analysis, zooming in on single utterances by the same speaker/author, that my observations resonate with previous findings on synchronous or asynchronous new media. Consider an example (Excerpt 13.1) from a prototypical Web 2.0 environment:

Excerpt 13.1: *YouTube* comment

xXxCroatiaStylexXx (2 months ago)
des is doch echt so geil zefix oida^^
so sama hoit mia bayern :D^^

This comment refers to an amateur video, which appropriates a global pop song to stylize local identity in Bavaria, Southern Germany (discussed in Androutsopoulos, 2010). Like most comments in this thread, it gives praise to the video (the first line reads: "this is really great, mate") and asserts a collective local identity (second line: "that's how we are, we Bavarians"). Both sentences are cast in Bavarian dialect, as evidenced in the orthographic representation of dialect features and the use of dialect lexis (such as the interjection *zefix*, a Bavarian malediction derived from *Kruzifix* ["crucifix"]). What strikes me here is less the comment's alignment to the language style of the target video than the contrast between the comment proper and the screen name. While the former uses dialect to praise the video and claim (jocularly, perhaps) local identity, the latter is cast in English and signifies at the propositional level a different identity (namely, Croatian). I interpret this as heteroglossic: two different languages explicitly indexing two different identities, molded together into one post yet at the same time differentiated in terms of its functional components. Here, as elsewhere, the elements participating in a heteroglossic contrast belong to different parts of a genre, and previous research suggests that the difference between a post proper and accompanying emblematic elements, such as names and mottos, is consequential to style and language choices. At the same time, the example makes transparent the inevitable (it seems) subjectivity of such an analysis, and the tension between a screen-based and a user-based approach to new media discourse: that contrast is salient to me as an analyst on sociolinguistic grounds, but not necessarily to other posters or viewers of that thread or, indeed, its author, at least as far as we can tell without asking them. I return to this point in the "Conclusions" section.

Such tensions of language and identity, viewpoint, or participation role have of course been reported from older new media modes as well, for example, chat channels, forum discussions, or e-mail exchanges among friends or colleagues (e.g., Hinrichs, 2006, and Tsiplakou, 2009, in part with disparate labels). Heteroglossic contrasts of this sort manifest not just within single utterances but in the dialogic and sequential relation among utterances, such as threads of comments or posts, in which different participants draw on linguistic heterogeneity to contextualize specific readings of their contributions or to position themselves toward others (Androutsopoulos 2007; see also Peuronen, Chapter 8, this volume).

Moving "upward" to the level of an entire web page, we find that user-contributed content may contrast to the linguistic design of the surrounding web interface. More specifically, heteroglossic effects can be located at the relation between components of a web page that are designed and authored by different individuals and institutions: user interface, institutional and participatory content, and advertisement space. These components can all come in one single language but often don't, thereby reflecting relations of inequality between languages as much as user-specific conditions of participation. In my own experience with social network and content-sharing sites, which I'd like to draw on here by means of an example, users' language choices often part ways from those of the website frame and those of advertisements. For example, as a speaker of Greek, my own *YouTube* experience is always framed by a language other than Greek, as that language is not (yet) included into the site's language localization options. These are restricted to a handful of languages, including fairly small ones in terms of speaker numbers (such as *Suomi* and *Svenska*, but not Ukrainian, Punjabi, or Arabic). As with other corporative websites (Kelly-Holmes, 2006), decisions on linguistic localization are based on the power of languages in the digital economy rather than their mere number of speakers. Another example is *Facebook*, where the linguistic activities on my own profile "wall" are usually trilingual (in English, German, and Greek), while entries on my "home page" involve a larger number of languages as selected by my "friends." In addition, there is by now quite an extensive choice of "primary languages" for the website's user interface (see Lenihan, Chapter 3, this volume). However, setting my interface to English or Greek will not stop Google ads targeting me in German, based on the automatic recognition of my Internet Protocol address. Similar tensions may emerge wherever contributions of different social origin or participation role coexist: "consumers" reviews and professionally authored copy in online shops, user reviews and promotional copy on web-mapping applications, and so on. In all these cases, the composition of digital spaces can be thought of as heteroglossic, as the linguistic choices of various components reflect and reinforce boundaries between actual user activity and its multiple corporate framings.

An Example: Heteroglossic Relations, on a Profile Page

The previous section identified potential locations of heteroglossic contrasts in Web 2.0 environments, from the microlevel of a single utterance to the configuration of entire web pages, and from processes already familiar from earlier new media to those that seem specific to the participatory and convergent structure of Web 2.0. Against that backdrop, this section illustrates how an analysis of heteroglossia on the web might proceed. The example comes from *MySpace*, one of the most popular social networking websites worldwide (boyd, 2008). It is the profile page of *Mantoinette*, a German musician in her twenties, which has been online since 2006. The version I analyzed (by now modified) is from spring and early summer of 2009. Based on procedures of discourse-centered online ethnography (Androutsopoulos, 2008), my analysis is based on repeated visits to the profile page, selection of textual data for linguistic analysis, and an interview with the producer, all of which contributes to the interpretation offered in what follows.⁵

The analysis reconstructs *Mantoinette*'s profile page as a multipurpose discursive space where different types of social relationships and discourse activities are acted out. Following the profile's linear order, it shows how M's own contributions and those by her "friends" come together to form a semiotic collage that is reminiscent of 1990s personal home pages, albeit with a higher density of multimodality and multiauthorship. That collage is framed in a twofold way that lies beyond M's control: by the viewer's choice of the language of interface, which determines the automatically generated headings of various text boxes (e.g., *X's Friends Space*), and by the advert banners at the top of the page whose language follows the viewer's location. Against that backdrop, heteroglossic relations will be identified in the ways different representations, activities, and relationships constructed on the profile page are realized through distinct, and possibly conflictual, choices of semiotic resources.

MySpace offers its users different opportunities to select and arrange page elements in individual ways (boyd, 2008). *Mantoinette*'s profile is customized in some respects, such as color design and embedded media, but rather standardized in others, especially sequential structure. A schematic representation of its components and their sequential order is given in Figure 13.1. One aspect this scheme does not capture is M's customized use of background color: the page background is a red floral wallpaper, and the various text boxes are given a dark red background, framed by a golden hairline. M's "contact box," an automatically generated list of contact options, is given the background photo of a stylus, thereby indexing, as M explains in the interview, her commitment to music. Another standardized text box is the "calling card" with information about the profile owner, including her name, a photo, a tagline with her music style, her

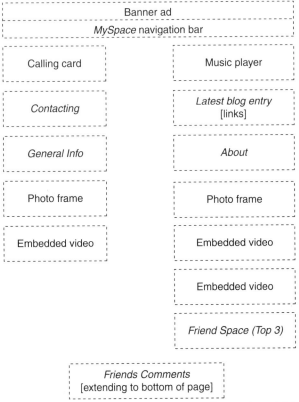

FIGURE 13.1 Schematic representation of *Mantoinette's MySpace* page in June 2009. Not to scale. Profile's own descriptors are set in *italics*.

location (*Germany*), and a slogan (**thevoiceisthesisterofthesoul**). M's music player, to the right of the calling card, is a standard feature of musician profiles on *MySpace*. It offers at the time of observation four songs sung by M, all in English.

The longest pieces of verbal text on the page are M's self-presentation blurb (*General Info*) and the testimonial placed to its right (*About*). The former is quite short and fully in English (Excerpt 13.2); the latter is longer and comes in a German and an English version (Excerpts 13.3 and 13.4, with two sentences from each version).

Excerpt 13.2: *General Info*

Contemporary soultunes move and influence me the most, I think. In some ways I feel kinda „at home" within rap, but soul defines it wonderfully concrete for me according to the attribute „feeling".(shouldn't mean rap has no feeling for me =))**

Excerpt 13.3: *About*, German version

Marie-Antoinette ist eine Künstlerin, die schon sehr früh ihren Lebensweg im Singen, in der Performance, in der Musik gesehen hat. [...] Die Jahre, die ich mit ihr arbeiten durfte, waren eine große Bereicherung, denn sie sucht unermüdlich den Kern in allen Dingen und bringt ihn dann stimmlich ausdrucksstark ans Licht. [...]

Excerpt 13.4: *About*, English version

Marie-Antoinette is an artist, who saw it's way in singing, performing and music very early in her life. [...] The years I worked with her were a great pleasure because she's straight looking for the source in everything and brings it to life with her voice very expressive. [...]

Written from a first-person perspective throughout, M's English usage indexes familiarity with music and computer-mediated discourse (cf. *soultunes*, *kinda*, ellipses, emoticons, and the decorative use of asterisks). The bilingual testimonial is signed off with first name + last name + professional title of its author, a voice therapist and M's former singing teacher. Its style approximates that of a reference, with long sentences, complex syntax, characterizing and evaluating modifiers, learned vocabulary. The English version is equivalent to the German one in terms of propositional content, but rich in nonnative features in English such as missing adverbial suffixes and errors in gender congruence. The two authors use not just different languages, but different genres and language styles in order to convey different, but spatially adjacent, perspectives on one individual.

Just below these texts, the embedded photo frames show M in singing poses, and the embedded videos show her perform her songs in English, some preceded by German addressing the audience. The music player and the embedded videos can be operated sequentially or simultaneously, offering a "sound carpet" that turns the profile page consumption into a rich multimodal experience. Just below the videos, we see a small box with three "Top Friends" and her total number of "friends" (1,020 as per June 22, 2009), followed by a comments list, which extends over two thirds of the visible page. Each comment consists of screen name, photo, date, and the comment proper, sometimes accompanied by visual material; some comments are longer and more colorful than others.

Two types of comments that are common in the context of *MySpace* are advertising entries (Excerpt 13.5) and "thanks for adding" messages (Excerpt 13.6). The former are generally informal, sometimes intentionally heteroglossic (see Excerpt 13.10 below), and make frequent use of English, which is quite expected in youth-cultural contexts, even though German is clearly the base language in M's comments space; but they usually lack a personal term of address, indexing their orientation to a public audience. "Thanks for adding" messages are posted after a request to befriend has been accepted by the page owner. They are conventionally brief, consisting of a greeting + thanksgiving + politeness formula, again indexing the absence of an established personal relationship. By contrast, other comments on M's page (Excerpts 13.7–13.9) rely on and evoke such personal relationships. Their discourse functions and stylistic choices index a longer communication history between writer and profile host that is not restricted to *MySpace*, for instance, catching up or arranging meetings, referring to past or future events, and so on. In Excerpt 13.7, note how the "thanks for befriending me" wording is joined by an emoticon to contextualize irony, since this online befriending follows up on an existing offline friendship. In Excerpts 13.7 and 13.8, the choice of leave-taking formula (*liebe grüße* and its acronym, *Lg*, "loving greetings") comes from the informal end of the greetings repertoire in current German new media. In Excerpts 13.7 and 13.9, reference is made to places presumably known to both interlocutors, and Excerpt 13.9 simulates a dialogue whose interpretation by the analyst is supported by ethnographic knowledge (e.g., *gospel* is one style of M's singing). Typical spoken-like and "netspeak" features such as informal greetings, contractions and assimilations, and lack of normative capitalization and emoticons occur regularly in this type of comment. Put differently, we see here relations between the discourse activity carried out in a comment, the social relation between commenter and page host, and the selection of stylistic resources, leading to considerable heterogeneity as one scrolls down the list.

Excerpt 13.5: User A on June 10, 2009 12:54
neuer Track online! "Folge dem Licht" mit Manic und RasRic ab jetzt im player!!!!
Über ein Feedback würde ich mich sehr freuen

"New track online! 'Follow the light' with Manic und RasRic now in the player.
I'd greatly appreciate any feedback"

Excerpt 13.6: User B on May 9, 2009 14:13
Hallo!
Grüße und
Danke für die Freundschaft!
Der IndividualPerformer

"Hello!

Greetings and
Thanks for the friendship!
The IndividualPerformer"

Excerpt 13.7: User C on May 6, 2009 16:55

hey danke fürs freunde sein! :)
hab mich eben fürs fieber angemeldet! *jihaaa*
bis dann also hoffentlich im riff!
Lg E

"hey thanks for being friends! :)
I just registered for fever
Well then hopefully see you at riff
Love E"

Excerpt 13.8: User D April 1, 2009 16:14

hi [M], bist du über Ostern vielleicht in Berlin? liebe grüße!
"Hi [M], are you over Easter maybe in Berlin? Love!"

Excerpt 13.9: User E November 18, 2008 16:24

wie jetzt?! du? gestern? g-town? ich? keine ahnung gehabt?! versteh ich nich, weil ich hab eigentlich ahnung. gospel?! doll!

"what now?! You? Yesterday? G-town? Me? Not knowing? I don't get it, because I usually do know. Gospel!?! Great!"

Other instances of heteroglossia are located within single entries and identified by salient style contrasts. One example are promotional entries such as Excerpt 13.10, whose wording articulates two distinct discourses of music and culture: the African-American tradition of soul/funk music and that of German "contemporary adult" music called *Schlager*. Both the propositional content and the wording of this entry reinforce that hybrid meeting, and the phrase *weird stuff aus deutschen Landen*—the nominal phrase indexing music youth culture, the prepositional phrase being typical for agricultural produce—is iconic to that articulation.

Excerpt 13.10: Dynamite Soul on December 17, 2008 19:04

Are you ready for some Super Dynamite Soul?
Plug und Mr. Edd droppen auf Krauty Schlager und German Freak Beats im wesentlichen Weird Stuff aus deutschen Landen. Musik zu der unsere Eltern gerne getanzt hätten, wenn sie ihnen so gekonnt serviert worden ware, wie es die Leipziger Funksoulbrothers auf diesem Mixtape tun. Damenwahl!

"Are you ready for some Super Dynamite Soul?
Plug and Mr. Edd drop on Krauty Schlager und German Freak
Beats essential weird stuff from German soil. Music our parents
would have danced to if it only was as well served as Leipzig's own
Funksoulbrothers do now on this mixtape.
Ladies' choice!"

Excerpt 13.11: User F on January 31, 2009 16:47

*und so saß er da... auf den monitor starrend, der ihn vor kurzem noch
mit freude erfüllte.*
was war mit ihr geschehen, warum antwortete sie nicht?
*zu gerne hätte er diese frage beantwortet bekommen, doch der raum
verblieb stumm...*
wassup girl, why you ain..t answering my mail?? ;-)

"and so he sat there... staring at the computer screen that filled him
with joy just a while ago.
what had happened to her, why didn't she respond?
all too much did he wish an answer to this question, but the room
remained silent...
wassup girl, why you ain..t answering my mail?? ;-)"

A second type of micro-heteroglossia is in comments that initiate social
contact to the page host. While these are similar to promotional entries in
their poetic use of language, their pragmatics is oriented to interpersonal
relationships rather than commercial marketing. My example is a stretch
of comments by one writer, which were posted in a very short period of
time, three messages within twelve hours and a fourth one (reproduced
as Excerpt 13.11) ten days later. Their common pattern of composition is
that the concluding line comes in English—the informal, internet sav-
vy style of English that M herself uses in her blurb (Excerpt 13.2). The
last message in this series, displayed here, comes after an apparent communication breakdown of several days. What is remarkable is the way it
seams together a rather "literary" style of German with a concluding line
of stylized vernacular English. This entire post is shaped as a multiple
contrast between languages (German/English), styles (literate/vernacu-
lar), perspectives (third/second person), and speech acts (wondering/in-
quiring), and the outcome is arguably a resource for politeness as much
as a display of communicative skills on the part of the writer. Here, as
elsewhere in new media discourse, working with linguistic heterogeneity
allows participants to achieve a higher level of quick-wittedness, humor,

and skillful playfulness, all of which may increase their communicative attractiveness to others.

Mantoinette's profile is not exceptional. Quite the contrary, just about every *MySpace* profile page has a certain heteroglossic potential. Even though "owned" by a particular user, its participative and convergent properties give rise to a variety of coexisting discourse activities and textual components, each with their specific linguistic choices. A variation analysis of such profile pages in terms of spoken/written style, vernacular/standard varieties, or German/English language choice is, of course, possible. However, it would probably miss the subtle style differences and indexical tensions that heteroglossia makes us aware of. This echoes Bailey's (2007) suggestion that heteroglossia, with its social and historic grounding, offers a breadth of perspective that formally defined concepts (in his case, code switching) seem to lack. Metaphorically speaking, the visual association prompted by heteroglossia is viewing a profile page not as a single a point in variational space but rather as a patchwork of speech styles related to discourse activities, interpersonal relations, ideological positions, and identity claims.

This analysis attempted to present Mantoinette's profile page as a space of heteroglossic relations articulated across and within its distinct components through the juxtaposition of linguistic resources. Discourse on this page is shaped by a constant contrast between German and English, which can be identified across a number of genres. M chooses English as her emblematic language in her "calling card" and as her language of self-presentation in her "General Info" box, but the testimonial ("About") is both in German and English. She sings in English, but addresses her audience in German, most friends' comments also being in German. This bilingual contrast is reinstantiated within some textual units, as in the embedded videos (performance in English, intro words in German) and the bilingual testimonial. However, caution is needed in order not to decontextualize the two languages from their situated usage. If heteroglossic contrasts may be identified here, these are not between German and English as a whole, but between more specifically contextualized instantiations thereof: between spoken and written material (the former in English throughout, the latter in both English and German); between the language of M's performance (English) and that of her audience (predominantly German); and between resources selected for distinct modes of identity construction, such as musical performance (sung, in English) as opposed to self-narrative (*General Info* authored by M, in English) as opposed to others' utterances on the profile page (written, predominantly in German). As we saw with Excerpts 13.2–13.3, this is not just a contrast of languages but rather language styles selected for different kinds of identity work. We see here once again how the notion of heteroglossia enables us to move beyond binary oppositions of "whole" languages and toward situated uses of linguistic resources.

Conclusions

I conclude with four points, which attempt to capture some specifics of Web 2.0 heteroglossia as analyzed in this chapter. First, heteroglossia seems particularly useful with respect to the layered composition of web pages out of different elements because it allows us to interrelate phenomena on different levels of analysis, from single semiotic forms to larger textual units, such as posts or videos to sequences of such units on a web page. Second, one aspect of Web 2.0 heteroglossia is its dual nature as both intentional and emergent. In line with its traditional understanding, heteroglossic discourse is an outcome of intentional semiotic action, in which linguistic resources are juxtaposed in ways that index social, historical, and ideological tensions and conflicts. However, Web 2.0 heteroglossia also appears as a by-product, or side effect, of the composite structure of contemporary dynamic web pages, which are not composed in their entirety by one single author.

Third, such use of the concept needs to be wary of the pitfalls of technological determinism. I argued that the convergent and participatory composition of Web 2.0 sites gives rise to social and ideological contrasts, which, depending on the linguistic resources they are given, can find heteroglossic expressions. However, it is not technology that creates heteroglossia. Web 2.0 may well be experienced in monoglot terms—but it often isn't, and, one might add, it almost certainly isn't to speakers of smaller or "weaker" languages. Web 2.0 environments open a range of possibilities for heteroglossic "hot spots," but their exploitation ultimately depends on institutional and situational context and discourse dynamics. Fourth, heteroglossia in this chapter goes beyond the type of class-based social tension that shapes its original understanding and some of its applications to media discourse (e.g., by Georgakopoulou, 2000, on film). While classic Bakhtinian heteroglossia revolves around the expression of social conflict and carnivalesque subversion "from below" (White, 1993), this chapter also focuses on global/national and global/local relations as new domains of heteroglossic tension. We also saw a stylized usage of linguistic heterogeneity (Excerpts 13.10–13.11), which ties in well with the insight that in the absence of visual cues or a face-to-face encounter, a playful and creative use of language becomes a key resource for interpersonal communication and identity management in digital media.

Future work on and with the concept of heteroglossia will need to refine its operationalization and diagnostic criteria, and to spell out its conceptual relation to sociolinguistic notions such as style and style shifting. It will also need to engage with issues of interpretation and perspective, in particular with questions such as: Heteroglossic to whom? And is heteroglossia on the web a property of textual surfaces or rather their situated reception by users? Stronger online ethnography would probably rebalance the dominance of a text-based over a user-based perspective in this chapter, and that, in turn, would help to enhance the robustness of the interpretations offered here. At the same time, we need to acknowledge that heteroglossia is a notion that is sensitive to perspective and time, and therefore to researchers' social positions and their understandings of social change. The issue therefore will not be to construct an "objectively valid" interpretation of heteroglossia, which would seem an illusory undertaking, but to lay bare the perspectives from and criteria on which given linguistic practices on the web may be viewed as heteroglossic.

Acknowledgments

First presented to the 5th International Conference on Language Variation in Europe (ICLaVE#5), June 25–27, 2009, Copenhagen. Thanks are due to *Mantoinette* for permission to use data from her profile page.

Notes

1. See papers in Danet & Herring (2007) and in the special issue of *Journal of Sociolinguistics* (10:4, 2006) on computer-mediated communication. A rare quantitative study of code switching online is Paolillo (2001).

2. In the original German wording, "daß sprachliche Elemente und Versatzstücke aus diversen Diskurswelten zu einem spezifischen Stilmix zusammengebastelt werden."

3. Other useful definitions are "the different kinds and uses of speech that struggle within a speech community" (Stivale, 1997, p. 134) and "the diversity of social meaning making practices in a particular community" (Thibault, 2004, p. 41). The definition by Leppänen et al. (2009)—"the

coexistence, combination, alternation and juxtaposition of ways of using the communicative and expressive resources language/s offer us"—seems to downplay the aspect of socioideological tension that is central to my use of the concept here.

4. Heteroglossia has been used to study advertising discourse (Cook, 2001, pp. 187–88), multilingual media in minority contexts (Busch, 2006), popular film (Georgakopoulou, 2000), and new media (Stivale, 1997; Leppänen et al., 2009).

5. Permission has been obtained by the page owner to publish her screen name and extracts from her profile page.

References

Androutsopoulos, J. (2006). Introduction: Sociolinguistics and computer-mediated communication. *Journal of Sociolinguistics*, 10(4), 419–438.

Androutsopoulos, J. (2007). Style online: Doing hip-hop on the German-speaking Web. In P. Auer (Ed.), *Style and Social Identities*, (pp. 279–317). Berlin & New York: de Gruyter.

Androutsopoulos, J. (2008). Potentials and limitations of discourse-centered online ethnography. *Language@Internet*, 5, article 8. Available at http://www.languageatinternet.de/articles/2008

Androutsopoulos, J. (2010). Localising the global on the participatory web. In N. Coupland (Ed.), *Handbook of Language and Globalization*, (pp. 203–231). Oxford: Blackwell.

Androutsopoulos, J., & Beißwenger, M. (2008). Introduction: Data and methods in computer-mediated discourse analysis. *Language@Internet*, 5, article 2. Available at http://www.languageatinternet.de/articles/2008

Androutsopoulos, J., & Ziegler, E. (2004). Exploring language variation on the internet: Regional speech in a chat community. In B. Gunnarsson et al. (Eds.), *Language Variation in Europe*, (pp. 99–111). Uppsala, Sweden: Uppsala University Press.

Auer, P. (Ed.). (2007). Introduction. In P. Auer (Ed.), *Style and Social Identities: Alternative Approaches to Linguistic Heterogeneity*, (pp. 1–21). Berlin & New York: de Gruyter.

Bailey, B. (2007). Heteroglossia and boundaries. In M. Heller (Ed.), *Bilingualism: A Social Approach*, (pp. 257–274). New York: Palgrave.

Bakhtin, M. (1981). Discourse in the novel. In M. Bakhtin (C. Emerson & M. Holquist, Trans.), *The Dialogic Imagination*, (pp. 259–422). Austin: University of Texas Press.

boyd, d. (2008). Why youth (heart) social network sites: The role of networked publics in teenage social life. In D. Buckingham (Ed.), *Youth, Identity, and Digital Media*, (pp. 119–142). Cambridge, MA: MIT Press.

Busch, B. (2006). Changing media spaces: The transformative power of heteroglossic practices. In C. Mar-Molinero & P. Stevenson (Eds.), *Language Ideologies, Policies and Practices* (pp. 206–219). Basingstoke: Palgrave Macmillan.

Christen, H., & Ziegler, E. (2006). Können Promis variieren? Beobachtungen zur Sprachformenwahl in schweizerischen und deutschen Prominentenchats. *Germanistische Linguistik*, (pp. 186–187), 11–42.

Cormode, G., & Krishnamurthy, B. (2008). Key differences between Web1.0 and Web2.0. *First Monday*, 13(6), June 2. Available at http://firstmonday.org/

Cook, G. (2001). *The Discourse of Advertising*, 2nd ed. London: Routledge.

Coupland, N. (2007). *Style. Language Variation and Identity*. Cambridge: Cambridge University Press.

Crystal, D. (2001). *Language and the Internet* (2nd ed.). Cambridge: Cambridge University Press.

Danet, B., & Herring, S.C. (Eds.). (2007). *The Multilingual Internet*. Oxford: Oxford University Press.

Danet, B., Ruedenberg-Wright, L., & Rosenbaum-Tamari, Y. (1997). "Hmmm... Where's that smoke coming from?" Writing, play and performance on Internet Relay Chat. *Journal of Computer-Mediated Communication*, 2(4). Available at http://jcmc.indiana.edu/vol2/issue4/danet.html

Franke, K. (2006). Language variation in #berlin. *Networx*, 48. Available at http://www.mediensprache.net/networx/networx-48.pdf.

Georgakopoulou, A. (2000). On the sociolinguistics of popular films: Funny characters, funny voices. *Journal of Modern Greek Studies*, 18(1), 119–133.

Georgakopoulou, A. (2003). Computer-mediated communication. In J. Verschueren, J. Östman, J. Blommaert, & C. Bulcaen (Eds.), *Handbook of Pragmatics* (2001 Installment), (pp. 1–20). Amsterdam & Philadelphia: Benjamins.

Herring, S.C. (2004). Computer-mediated discourse analysis: An approach to researching online communities. In S.A. Barab, et al. (Eds.), *Designing for Virtual Communities in the Service of Learning*, (pp. 338–376). Cambridge: Cambridge University Press.

Herring S.C., & Paolillo, J.C. (2006). Gender and genre variation in weblogs. *Journal of Sociolinguistics*, 10(4), 439–459.

Hinrichs, L. (2006). *Codeswitching on the Web. English and Jamaican Creole in e-mail communication*. Amsterdam & Philadelphia: Benjamins.

Ivanov, V. (2001). Heteroglossia. In A. Duranti (Ed.), *Key Terms in Language and Culture*, (pp. 95–97). Malden, MA: Blackwell.

Jenkins, H. (2006). *Convergence Culture: Where Old and New Media Collide*. New York. University Press.

Kelly-Holmes, H. (2006). Multilingualism and commercial language practices on the internet. *Journal of Sociolinguistics*, 10(4), 510–523.

Lähteenmäki, M. (2010). Heteroglossia and voice: Conceptualising linguistic diversity from a Bakhtinian perspective. In M. Lähteenmäki & M. Vanhala-Aniszewski (Eds.), *Language Ideologies in Transition: Multilingualism in Russia and Finland*, (pp. 15–29). Frankfurt/Main: Peter Lang.

Leppänen, S., Pitkännen-Huhta, A., Piirainen-Marsh, A., Nikula, T., & Peuronen, S. (2009). Young people's translocal new media uses: A multiperspective analysis of language choice and heteroglossia. *Journal of Computer-Mediated Communication*, 14, 1080–1107.

Paolillo, J.C. (2001). Language variation on Internet Relay Chat: A social network approach. *Journal of Sociolinguistics*, 5(2), 180–213.

Runkehl, J., Schlobinski, P., & Siever, T. (1998). *Sprache und Kommunikation im Internet*. Opladen, Germany: Westdeutscher Verlag.

Siebenhaar, B. (2006). Code choice and code-switching in Swiss-German Internet Relay Chat rooms. *Journal of Sociolinguistics*, 10(4), 481–509.

Squires, L. (2011, forthcoming). Whos punctuating what? Sociolinguistic variation in instant messaging. In A. Jaffe, J. Androutsopoulos, & M. Sebba (Eds.), *Orthography as Social Action*. Berlin & New York: Mouton de Gruyter.

Stivale, C.J. (1997). Spam: Heteroglossia and harassment in cyberspace. In D. Porter (Ed.), *Internet Culture*, (pp. 133–44). New York: Routledge.

Tagliamonte, S.A., & Denis, D. (2008). Linguistic ruin? LOL! Instant messaging and teen language. *American Speech*, 83(1), 3–34.

Thibault P.J. (2004). *Agency and Consciousness in Discourse: Self-Other Dynamics as a Complex System*. London: Continuum

Tsiplakou, S. (2009). Doing (bi)lingualism: Language alternation as performative construction of online identities. *Pragmatics* 19(3), 361–391.

van Compernolle, R.A. (2008). Language variation in online personal ads from Quebec: The case of *ne*. *Language@Internet*, 5, article 1. Available at http://www.languageatinternet.de/articles/2008/

Vice, S. (1997). *Introducing Bakhtin*. Manchester, UK: Manchester University Press.

White, A. (1993). *Carnival, Hysteria, and Writing: Collected Essays and Autobiography*. Oxford: Clarendon Press.

Yates, S.J. (1996). Oral and written linguistic aspects of computer conferencing. In S.C. Herring (Ed.). (1996). *Computer-mediated communication*. (pp. 29–46). Amsterdam & Philadelphia: Benjamins.

Chapter 14

sms4science: An International Corpus-Based Texting Project and the Specific Challenges for Multilingual Switzerland

Christa Dürscheid and Elisabeth Stark

Introduction

FREED OF ANY restrictions imposed by grammar and spelling, cell phone users in Switzerland enjoy texting. Dialect is used alongside Standard German or French, words are omitted, shortened or creatively modified; English short-forms like *cu* (= see you) are being used, languages get intermingled. [...] Not all texters use these (and other) strategies, and those who do, abandon them depending on the situation. Our research group investigates which means of expression are actually used in SMS, which varieties of spelling are being used for one and the same concept (e.g. *bisous, bizous, bizoux, bx, b* for *bisous*, 'kisses' in French) and also the strategies used for typing fewer characters [...].

This statement is part of an announcement (translated into English) we published in Swiss newspapers, via broadcast and on advertising folders in September 2009 in order to invite Swiss people to send us their text messages.[1] The text makes allusions to features often assumed to be typical for text messaging. But how can we know whether these features are really applied, whether and how languages in Swiss text messages are intermingled, whether words are omitted and abbreviated forms are actually used? Maybe the use of certain writing strategies mentioned here (such as *cu*) depends on the age of the texters, maybe they do not appear at all?

Corpus-based research is capable of answering these questions, since it not only offers the possibility of checking hypotheses on writing strategies empirically but also allows for corpus-driven research, that is, finding patterns that have not yet been taken into consideration as special features of text messages within SMS ("short message service" or text messaging) communication. As we will show shortly, some corpus-based SMS studies already exist, but up until now the databases used were very small and the findings therefore not statistically significant.

This is why we launched the project *sms4science.ch*, a subproject of the international project *sms4science* (coordinated in Belgium), which brings together researchers from various countries in order to conduct corpus-based research on text messaging. Our approach will be presented in detail below; first, we will give a brief overview of different types of new media corpora and the classification criteria used to distinguish them. Then, we will introduce some projected research work based on our corpus, which will give answers to linguistic and sociolinguistic questions about the text messages and the texters. Finally, we will finish by briefly discussing the future of text messaging and of text messaging research.

Reviewing Corpus-Based SMS Research

In order to position our own corpus and explain what is innovative about it, we start by introducing a number of corpora used in the past together with their classification criteria. This enables us to identify the typical features of these corpora, such as the type of data included, the data's origin, and the availability/accessibility of the data.

As we mentioned above, our project was not the first to carry out corpus-based research on new media data. The website http://www.cmc-corpora.de, a supplement to an article by Beißwenger and Storrer (2008), provides a selected list of corpora (e-mail, chat, newsgroups, mailing lists) and offers a typology that we will follow for our classification. First, the authors differentiate between *project-related corpora* and *corpora for general use*. They note: "The former are compiled as an empirical basis for questions in a particular project, the latter do not directly pertain to a particular research project" (cf. Beißwenger and Storrer, 2008, p. 294). Second, they make a distinction between *corpora of raw data* and *annotated corpora*. The *Enron Email Dataset* (cf. http://www-2.cs.cmu.edu/~enron/), for instance, contains over half a million business-related e-mail messages but is not annotated, while the *Dortmund Chat Corpus* (cf. http://www.chatkorpus.

uni-dortmund.de/), which comprises 511 protocols of chat communication, contains annotations for emoticons, nicknames, gender as given by the informant, and more. Parts of this corpus are freely available for research work on the internet while the main corpus is password protected and not for general use.

Applying these criteria further to the classification of SMS corpora, we observe that most SMS corpora discussed in the literature do not comprise data for open access. Exceptions are the *NUS SMS Corpus* collected by students at the University of Singapore,[2] which consists of about 10,000 messages, or a corpus collected for a study by Schlobinski et al. (2001), with "about 1,500 messages" sent by texters aged "younger than 12 years" up until "older than 30."[3] The latter was compiled for a specific study, but its form and accessibility make it available for other studies, too. The main Belgian *sms4science* corpus (cf. Fairon et al., 2006a, 2006b) and our own sister corpus are for general use as well. Unlike our own corpora, many existing SMS corpora are also project specific; that is, they were created for the restricted research goals of a particular researcher. Examples of this type of limited or restricted corpora include a 544-message corpus from Great Britain (Thurlow, 2003; Thurlow & Poff, 2011), one with 882 messages in Norway (Ling, 2005), and a South African corpus with 312 messages (Deumert & Masyniana, 2008). A relatively large project-specific corpus, consisting of 10,626 English messages from friends and family (aged 19 to 68), was compiled by Tagg (2009) for her doctoral research.

From a technical point of view, one more important distinction between existing corpora and our own corpus is that in all other SMS studies (except Fairon et al., 2006a, 2006b) text messages were transcribed by participants. In this regard, the *sms4science* corpus is quite unique: We asked participants to forward their text messages directly to a designated, free mobile number, thereby avoiding any transcription errors or deliberate modifications. Another important difference to most other corpora is the availability of our data. At the beginning of her thesis, Tagg (2009, pp. 10–18) presents a comprehensive overview of previous sociocultural studies of text messaging and describes the respective corpus specifications, which shows that most of the mentioned SMS corpora (including her own) are not accessible on the internet. This is most likely due to privacy issues. Data created on the internet such as online chat are freely available and can therefore be used and redistributed. SMS data on the other hand are normally not publicly available because they are stored on the users' cell phone only. If users agree to share their text messages for scientific research, it is the researchers' responsibility to protect the texters' privacy, and the easiest way of achieving this aim is by not making the corpus public. Furthermore, the data are often of a very confidential nature and thus have to be dealt with in an extremely responsible way. Absolute confidentiality and anonymity must be assured, and the texters have to agree to having their messages, rendered anonymous, made available for publication. However, collecting text messages in cooperation with the texters also represents a major advantage over data publicly available on the internet such as chat protocols because once the texters are willing to cooperate, they will also very likely provide personal demographical information such as age, sex, or education.

Finally, we would like to mention one last distinctive linguistic feature of our corpus. Typically, data in SMS corpora are based on a single language depending on the country.[4] The *sms4science* corpus was intended to be multilingual from the outset. In Switzerland, there are four official languages (German, French, Italian, and Romansh) and—at least for the German, the Romansh, and partially the Italian speaking part of Switzerland—there are also different regional dialects, which are used in almost every situation of daily life (cf. Rash, 1998; Siebenhaar, 2006). Accordingly, any text messaging data collected in Switzerland are likely to show a considerable degree of language variation (official languages, Romance dialects, and Swiss-German[5]). A project such as ours therefore offers not only insight into the specific practices of a particular mode of communication (i.e., text messaging) but also an array of new information about the contemporary nature and status of language use in a multilingual country (compare this with, for example, Peuronen, Chapter 8, this volume).

To sum up, different types of existing corpora can be classified as in Table 14.1 (with an example for each type), which we base on the classification scheme in the study by Beißwenger and Storrer (2008), but supplemented with further criteria in order to characterize the corpora in more detail. As can be seen, none of the corpora presented here contain in-depth demographic data, even though for some the nicknames and the given age of the informants are known. As for the data source, some corpora offer data obtained directly from the informants, manually or automatically, and others consist of data taken from the internet. Concerning data availability, there is a difference between data accessible on the internet in a browser and data that must first be downloaded in order to be used. Having the data available for direct access on the internet not only guarantees it to be

Table 14.1: The corpus *sms4science.ch* in comparison with other corpora

Type of data	sms4science.ch SMS (cell phone)	Schlobinski et al. (2001) SMS Corpus SMS (cell phone)	Enron e-mail dataset E-mail	COSMA[6] e-mail corpus E-mail	Dortmund chat corpus Chat
For general use	X	X	X	-	X
Annotated	X	-	-	X	X
Multilingual	X	-	-	-	-
Anonymous	X	X	-	-	X
Laid out for linguistic purposes	X	-	-	-	X
Data source					
Obtained from users	X	X	-	X	
Acquired from the internet	-	-	-	-	X
Availability of the data					
Download	-	X	X	-	X
Browser	X	-	-	-	X
Password protected	X	-	-	-	(X)
Special features					
Search for "Regular Expressions"	X	-	-	-	X
Demographics	X	-	-	-	-

available to any type of computer with any type of operating system but also makes sure that it is presented in a form ready for research and not in a raw format. Thus, the researcher can focus on her project and does not have to struggle with setting up a computer-based working environment. On a similar note, retrieval tools such as "regular expressions"—a formal language based in computer programming allowing search for text patterns—are built right into the online research environment. This feature allows, for instance, the identification of different spellings (e.g., *hello, helo, hallo, hallooooo*), collocations, and more.

Building an International SMS Corpus Network: sms4science

In 2004, Cédrick Fairon and his research group at the Institute for Computational Linguistics CENTAL of the Catholic University of Louvain (UC Louvain, Belgium) launched a scheme called "Faites don de vos sms à la science" ("Donate your text messages to science!").[7] The motivation for this enterprise, described in more detail below, was that—in spite of the ever increasing public and linguistic interest in the topic—no corpora of a significant size and comprising authentic cell phone text messages were available at the time. The resulting first step toward establishing a large corpus of electronically and automatically gathered (i.e., not transcribed) text messages was initially restricted to the French-speaking part of Belgium (cf. Fairon et al., 2006a, 2006b) but enabled the group to develop a general methodology for message collection and establish protocols for the preparation of SMS corpora (e.g., anonymization, transcription, annotation). The corporate partners of the project, the most important national telecommunication companies, managed the technical aspects of data collection. The Belgium media spread the news, which enabled the project to reach a large part of the French-speaking population. After only two months, the results were impressive: more than 75,000 text messages gathered from about 3,200 persons (aged between 12 and 73, with 76% of them under 25), with 2,775 participants also having answered a biographical questionnaire.

This successful start encouraged the Belgian group to contact researchers interested in corpus linguistics, sociolinguistics, and language variation in order to build an international network and to establish more and mutually comparative corpora of text messages stemming from different countries and languages. Currently, this research network comprises fifteen universities in nine countries (Belgium, Canada/Québec,

France, Great Britain, Greece, Italy, Romania, Spain, Switzerland), and an array of commercial partners. The network makes possible a wide range of sociolinguistic studies on topics such as variation in pluricentric languages (e.g., French in four different regions in France, La Réunion, Belgium, Canada, and in Switzerland) or multilingualism within countries (e.g., in Spain with universities from Catalonia and the Basque Country; in Switzerland with the University of Zurich from the German-speaking and the University of Neuchâtel from the French-speaking parts of the country).

Closer to Home: The sms4science.ch *Corpus*

In 2008, a collaborative agreement was signed between the Belgian group, the University of Zurich (Elisabeth Stark for French and Italian, Christa Dürscheid for German, later Matthias Grünert for Romansh) and the University of Neuchâtel (Marie-José Béguelin, later also Simona Pekarek-Döhler, both for French), marking the beginning of the subproject *sms4science.ch*. The Swiss researchers then contacted a corporate partner, *Swisscom*, to help with the technical part of the data collection. *Swisscom* provided a central mobile number connected to an automatic collection tool, where potential participants could send their original messages for free or for a small fee, depending on their service provider. The decision of whether or not to make a specific text message available would thereby always remain with the informants. Most people either forwarded their text messages or added the project's phone number as a second recipient of the original message. Participants thus sent individual messages that they selected themselves to the designated mobile number to then be included in the corpus. Finally, before launching the data collection itself (from November 2009 to January 2010 with one previous call in September 2009), the University of Zurich set up a quadrilingual website (www.sms4science.ch) and made contact with the media, resulting in a broad coverage across Switzerland.

At the time of writing, the results of our data collection have been promising. We have collected a total of 23,988 text messages sent by 2,627 different people (see Table 14.2). 18% of the messages originate in the French-speaking part of Switzerland (the *Romandie*). Most participants have had between 1 and 5 messages forwarded to the project, with 80 people sending more than 50 text messages each and one even sending 413 messages. About half of the participants also completed the

Table 14.2: Some raw facts about the corpus *sms4science.ch*

	Text messages	Words	Participants	Questionnaires	Sex M	F
Total Number	23,987	About 480,000	2,627	1,308	477	831

Table 14.3: Age of the participants (of those who answered this question)

10–19	20–29	30–39	40–49	50–59	60–69	70+
245	599	190	152	80	38	5

Table 14.4: Mother tongues of the participants (more than one possible)

	Swiss-German	Standard German	French	Italian	Romansh	Others
Total number	889	161	256	54	26	125

biographical questionnaire, anonymously indicating their sex, age, profession, education, mother tongue, language competence, and specific SMS habits (e.g., frequency of use, language mixing, preferred addressees, use of other new communication forms like e-mail, online chat, etc.) as well as their general reading and writing habits (e.g., whether and how often they read and write in a week, what they read [newspapers, books, etc.], what they write, how they write [by hand, etc.]). Given this biographical information, we know that 831 participants are women (60%), that more than two thirds of those who filled in the questionnaire have Swiss-German as their mother tongue, 12% Standard German, 20% French, 4% Italian, 2% Romansh, and 10% other languages (more than one option was possible). These figures reflect quite accurately the percentages of the Swiss population in general. About 45% of our participants are between 21 and 30 years old, but we also have many teenagers and people over 50. (Seven people are older than 70.) Altogether, about 75% of our text messages can be linked to sociodemographic information (see Tables 14.3 and 14.4). This rate is higher than the 50% of the informants who submitted biographical details because of those people who sent in more than one text message.

With regard to the content and the form of the text messages, our initial impression is that they mostly comprise personal communication about romantic dates, problems, love affairs, and jokes, but we have also noticed messages of a more official character such as exchanges between business partners or between pupils and teachers (mostly apologies for absences). Even at first sight, their linguistic form and orthography shows several interesting features such as a high level of multilingualism and an overall preference for Swiss-German dialects as opposed to Standard German. It is even possible, from phonetic spelling, to recognize the different dialect regions of Switzerland. By *phonetic spelling* we mean that texters try to approximate the pronunciation of the word (cf. Frehner, 2008, p. 104; also Thurlow, 2003). Since the pronunciation (and many other linguistic features) may differ from dialect to dialect, the spelling may sometimes reveal the dialectal zone the texters are coming from, without having to consider the zip code in the sociodemographic information of the questionnaire.

Moving from Raw Data Toward a Linguistic Corpus

From the very beginning, our research group wanted the *sms4science* corpus to be open to other academics for different types of studies. This was not only a fundamental aim when collecting the data, but also when processing and presenting it. Unlike its Belgian counterpart, which is distributed as Microsoft Access® database on a CD-ROM, our Swiss corpus will be made available as an online database accessible with any major web browser (after having received a password form our research group, a security feature that allows us to restrict the access to researchers and students). In its current state, the corpus is already capable of processing "regular expressions" (see above), which will be greatly enhanced once the planned annotations (discussed further in this section) are added to the corpus.

The data, consisting of both text messages and biographical information, were collected by *Swisscom* and made available to the research project in the form of two independent mySQL dumps (SQL = *Structured Query Language*), the standardized export/import format of the open source database system MySQL.[8] Biographical data and text messages were linked by a hexadecimal code derived from the phone number but generated by SWISSCOM in order to keep the texters' privacy while still providing us with information about sex, age, and other demographics for each participant who filled in the biographical form. This cooperation with the provider also ensured that text messages longer than 160 characters were kept together as one text. In the final version of the corpus, personal data are still stored in a mySQL database while the text messages are retrieved from an XML file.

Turning to the SMS database, four problematic aspects for the future usability of the corpus were immediately apparent. First, not all messages could be retained for the future corpus. There were a number of doublets (i.e., exactly repeated messages), which had to be removed, as well as some of the initial messages sent by participants in order to sign up for the project, all of which reduced the number of messages by about 7,000 to the quoted number of 23,988. All other marginal cases (i.e., automatic messages sent by computers such as information about incoming e-mail or else reminders for administrative actions, and so forth; messages not written but forwarded by the participants; messages written on a computer keyboard and not on a cell phone) were kept in order to give a complete and authentic picture of the data collection. The very first were exported into a separate list; the last ones, wherever recognizable, were marked in the corpus in order to identify them when working with the corpus, assuming that the different condition of production influences their linguistic and formal appearance. This was a slight deviation from the procedures of the Belgian group (cf. Fairon et al., 2006a, p. 19f.).

A second challenge we have faced is that messages contain a lot of confidential information such as names or phone numbers. This was first of all a legal problem and required that all confidential information in the text messages be eliminated systematically and, wherever possible, automatically (cf. for the Belgian corpus, Fairon et al., 2006a, p. 21).[9] So all types of numbers, that is, telephone numbers as well as street names and e-mail addresses were substituted. Numbers consisting of three or more digits were replaced by NNN, where every N stands for one digit. Also for e-mail addresses, the number of characters was kept while replacing them with xxx@yyy.ch. Street names were replaced as a whole by [StreetAddress]. We decided not to substitute toponyms, website addresses, and names of public institutions, economic enterprises, or brands since they are unlikely to reveal confidential information.

Personal names represented a special problem with regard to future research on our corpus, particularly in terms of sociolinguistic and communicative questions, such as who communicates how with whom. Around 95% of the (few) surnames in the corpus could be found manually and then automatically substituted by [LastName]. A different approach was chosen for first names, thereby deviating from the approach of the Belgian team (cf. Fairon et al., 2006a, p. 21). Because dialogic sequences are easily retrievable through repeating first names, we decided to rotate the first names found within the corpus so as to detach names from content rather than to replace them by a label, for example [FirstName], so *Paul* would become *Ted, Fred* would become *Peter*, and so on. In cases of potential homonymy, items remained unsubstituted (e.g., the name *Hans* is homonymous with dialect quite frequently; e.g., *I hans gseh*, "I have seen it"). We consider the probability of a person being identified based on these very common first names to be close to zero. Additionally, because we did not replace first names but rotated them, the researcher working on the corpus will never know whether a first name he comes across has actually been rotated or not and will therefore not even attempt to match it to real persons.

As a result of all these anonymizations, we obtained messages such as the following one (in Standard German):

Extract 14.1:

Zur Erinnerung: diese Woche Mittwoch, 0.8:15 Berufsberatung [StreetAddress], Bottmingen, Tel: NNNNNNNNNN, Brief vorweisen. Und am Freitag, dem NNNNNNNNN. um 12.50 zu Dr. [Lastname], Birshofklinik neben MFP Münchenstein. GlG! Mama

"As a reminder: this week Wednesday: 0.8:15 career counseling [StreetAddress], Bottmingen (= place name), Tel: NNNNNNNNNN, present letter. And Friday, NNNNNNNNNN. at 12.50 at Dr. [Lastname], Birshof-clinic, next to MFP (= public building), Münchenstein (= place name). GlG! (= very kind regards) Mama"

In this way, our corpus data were anonymized to a standard that complies with both Swiss legislation and the promises made to potential participants.

Third, our text messages contain different languages and language varieties, especially different forms of Swiss-German, with which we are not necessarily familiar and which have to be identified in order to permit a sufficiently accurate language tagging (e.g., only French text messages, only Swiss-German messages, etc.). Our intention was from the very beginning to preserve the corpus' multilingual character because multilingualism is an essential sociolinguistic fact of life in Switzerland. Given that a considerable number of text messages have already shown signs of code mixing, we considered two possible forms of language tagging: (a) marking the whole SMS with the languages used in this SMS, and (b) marking the individual text parts in the respective languages. In Extract 14.2, we show the complexity of some multilingual text messages:

Extract 14.2:
<Spanish>**Olla fratello!!!**</Spanish> <Italian>**Come stai?**</Italian> <Standard German>**Wie geht's dir so? Immer noch so lange am arbeiten wie früher? Ich hab endlich mein eigenes Restaurant und**</Standard German> </Spanish>**mucho travajo**</Spanish> **...;-)** </Standard German>**aber macht mir extrem spass**</Standard German> **...;-)** <Italian>**allora amore, buona giornata**</Italian> <German Dialect>**und luegsch uf di, gäll**</German Dialect> **...;-)** <English>**peace**</English>

"Hello brother!!! How are you? Still working as long hours as before? I finally have my own Restaurant and a lot of work ...;-) but it's extreme fun... ;-) so my love, have a nice day and take care, yeah...;-) peace"

We opted for the solution of attributing multiple language tags to individual messages, allowing users of the corpus to search for, for example, all messages containing French, including those that are multilingual, with French being one language among two or more. As a first step, a trained coder applied a tagging system for the main language in every SMS. For Standard German, French, Italian, and English, existing word lists were used to compare words in the corpus with words on the lists and thereby recognize the respective language. However, for Romansh and especially Swiss-German, no data were available. A former student of ours came to help. She had, in fact, created her own corpus of Swiss-German text messages for her Master's thesis and kindly made it available to us to be used as a word list. Additionally, our specialist for Romansh provided us with electronic newspapers containing texts in all the Romansh dialects and also texts in the standard variety *Rumantsch Grischun*.

This first automated tagging resulted in a language tag for each individual SMS, which is fairly accurate. In a next step, the aforementioned tagging with all languages contained in individual text messages will have to be tackled. For this step, classes will be offered to students of German and Romance philology and computational linguistics. In the course of these classes, students will be asked to tag all the messages for all the languages they contain; at the same time, they will also be asked to verify the

automatically applied main language. A special challenge in this procedure will be the assignment of loan words (e.g., French *merci*: "thank you"
in, for example, Swiss-German). So the students will have to be guided by
strict rules defined by the team.

Finally, many messages also show a considerable number of graphical
variations. This remains an open problem for the moment and will be
addressed in classes at the University of Zurich in the near future, too.
The transcription of the original graphical representation (in at least four
languages) in a standard orthographic form cannot be done automatically
and comprises a multitude of decisions (cf. Fairon et al., 2006a, pp. 21–24
and pp. 100–110, for the Belgian corpus). There are several reasons for
this. One is the very high level of graphical variation found in text messages. Compare the different graphic variants of *soirée* ("evening") or *bisous*
("kisses") in Extract 14.3:

Extract 14.3
a. Merci. Bisous, bonne soirée...
b. Bonne swarée et a+??? Bisouxx
c. Bizzøux bone soiré
d. G pase bon soire. Now g mal tet (Fairon et al., 2006a, p. 23)

Examples of the same phenomena, here based on the special writing
strategy of using the phonic value of letters and numbers for homopho-
nic syllables or words ("letter/ number homophones"), are very frequent
in English (cf. the examples listed by Thurlow, 2003) and can be found
in our corpus as well, for example, for *guet nacht* (Swiss-German "good
night" using the phonic value in German of the number *acht* "eight") in
guetn8, guet n8, g n8, or *gutN8*. In fact, only very few (French) items that
deviate from standard spelling show regularities that point toward a form
of typical "SMS spelling" (e.g., in the Belgian corpus this holds for <pcq>
for *parce que*, "because," or <tt> for *tout*, "everything," never amounting to
more than 70% of all occurrences, cf. Zimmermann, 2009, p. 130).

Another obstacle for an automated standard transcription (or coding system) is the fact that at least French text messages show some innovative structural phenomena like new conversions (denominal verbs without any markers). These are not easily understandable and recognizable by corpus users
unfamiliar with specific linguistic phenomena of SMS and certainly not by
the sorts of analytic tools used by computational linguistics. Take a look at the
following extracts, for example (the first from Fairon et al., 2006a, p. 23):

Extract 14.4:

Mon prochain sms, li le qd tu **dodo** stp (= mon prochain sms, lis-le quand tu dors, s'il te plait)

"**my** next SMS, please read it when you are asleep/in bed"

Extract 14.5:

Je quitte la répét + tot.Ouf.Vais 1 peu mieux.Ai essayé de te **tel** mais pas de réponse.Bonne soirée cartes mon adorable amour. Moi **repas** puis **dodo** dès 22h. TQA (= Je quitte la répétition plus tôt. Ouf. Je vais un peu mieux. J'ai essayé de te téléphoner, mais il n'y a pas de réponse. Bonne soirée ??? mon adorable amour. Moi je vais man- ger/dîner et ensuite dormir à partir de 22 heures. TQA)

"I leave the rehearsal earlier. Ouf. I am a bit better. I have tried to call you, but there was no answer. Goodnight ??? my beloved one. I will have dinner and then go to sleep at about 22 o'clock. TQA"

In Extract 14.4, *dodo*, part of the phrasal verb *faire dodo*, "sleep," is used as a verb alone, which does not exist in this form in Standard or even col- loquial French. Likewise, the abbreviation *tel* for (numéro de) *téléphone*, "telephone (number)," appears in Extract 14.5 as the abbreviation for *télé- phoner*, "to call." And the elliptical *moi repas puis dodo* in Extract 14.5 has to be understood and/or transcribed as *moi je vais prendre un repas et ensuite faire dodo*, "I will have dinner and then go to sleep," thus omitting at least the verbs *prendre* and *faire* or converting the nominals *repas* and *dodo* into verbs. Finally, some quite regular omissions in French text messaging can be indicators of a certain informal style or code (like the omission of the first negation particle *ne* of standard French bipartite sentential negation *ne...pas*), while the omission of articles in front of nouns (similar to tele- grams) are ungrammatical in every variety of French, just like in English. Accordingly, the former should be left out in a transcription, too, while the latter should be added. In the following example, *ne* in front of *oublie* ("forget") has to be left out also in the transcribed version of the SMS, as it would never appear there in spoken French:

Extract 14.6:

1h juste 1h après tu rentre s'il te plais et oublie **pas** le carton (= Une heure, juste une heure, et après tu rentres, s'il te plaît, et n'oublie pas le carton)

"one hour, just one hour and then you'll come home, please and don't forget the carton"

What becomes clear from all this is that any standardized transcription of original text messages must inevitably be subject to some interpretation by the transcriber, and clear reasons must be given for choosing one or the other variant.

The last step in the constitution of our corpus is the implementation of *Corpus Navigator*, a corpus-browsing tool developed at the English Department of the University of Zurich.

In addition to the main corpus, some smaller corpora will be available through the same website. One will be the corpus of machine-generated messages (as previously mentioned), and another one a private collection of some 1,200 dialogical messages we received. These messages cannot be included in the main corpus, first due to their different production/transmission conditions, and second because of a potential overrepresentation of certain ideolectal features, given the high number of single text messages written by only two individuals compared with the rest of our corpus. Yet, they may be considered ideal for studies on a dialogical level, so we still want to make them available.

In the final version of *Corpus Navigator*, the software should allow for searches for single items, including emoticons, different strings of graphic characters, sociodemographic properties of the respective texters, and possibly also parts of speech (which of course presupposes as an additional step a part-of-speech-tagging; cf. for the Belgian corpus, Fairon et al., 2006a, pp. 25–30).

Taking sms4science *Forward: Looking to the Future*

In the next few years, a series of different graduate student research projects (e.g., master's and Ph.D. theses) will be conducted through third-party funded research on the basis of our corpus. In bringing this chapter to a close, therefore we want to highlight a few of the kinds of possible research questions we envisage. These concern (a) language choice and code switching; (b) structural features of text messages; and (c) pragmatic issues. Thanks to the demographic data submitted by the participants in our study, we have a solid empirical foundation for investigating these types of topics.

(a) Investigating Language Choice and Code Switching

Given the fact that Switzerland is a quadrilingual country, there are at least three main research fields concerning the messages at hand. The first of these is the degree of code switching different to that in monolingual countries, and this question: What are the communicative reasons for code switching when it does take place?[10] One respective hypothesis might be that code switching is particularly frequent in the Swiss corpus and much less so in officially monolingual countries. On the other hand, Swiss speakers themselves are mostly not multilingual, their main language usually is the language of the region/the canton in which they live. It will therefore be worthwhile to compare our data with the text messages gathered in other countries participating in the *sms4science* project to investigate the influence of a multilingual environment on the individual monolingual texter. The second research field we can identify is this question: Which varieties of the four national languages in Switzerland are actually used in the Swiss SMS corpus? Is it true, for instance, that speakers of Swiss-German mainly draft their messages in dialect and not in Standard German (cf. the investigation of Braun, 2006)? By the same token, one might ask if there is a correlation between the age of texters and their choice of Standard German or Swiss-German. As Siebenhaar (2006, p. 492) has shown for Swiss internet chat rooms, younger chatters use more dialect, while the middle-age generation prefers Standard German. Does this apply for SMS communication in the German-speaking part of Switzerland as well? Lastly, our third research field concerns the following: And what about messages submitted in Romansh? Are they usually monolingual, or do we always find two languages within these messages given the fact that there are no monolingual Romansh speakers? One may, for instance, assume that typical abbreviations of a second language (such as *hdl* in German, "hab dich lieb," "I love you") are used in the text messages even if the dominant language is Romansh.

(b) Investigating Structural Features of Text Messages

On a structural level, future research projects will examine the persistent issue of orthography, for example, the use of abbreviations, spelling practices in general, strategies of phonetic writing (searching for occurrences of *cu* for *see you*, *kul* for *cool*, emoticons, etc.), letter–number homophones, non-standard spelling, and the use of uppercase lettering (such as *SUUUPER*). Furthermore, two kinds of ellipses will be analyzed, especially in relation to the morphosyntactic and dialogical structure of the messages at hand. In the first type of ellipses, functional elements (such as articles) are omitted; in the second one, content words are dropped. The latter typically occurs in responses to previous messages.[11] Both are features commonly assumed to be typical for text messaging and ones that can be empirically

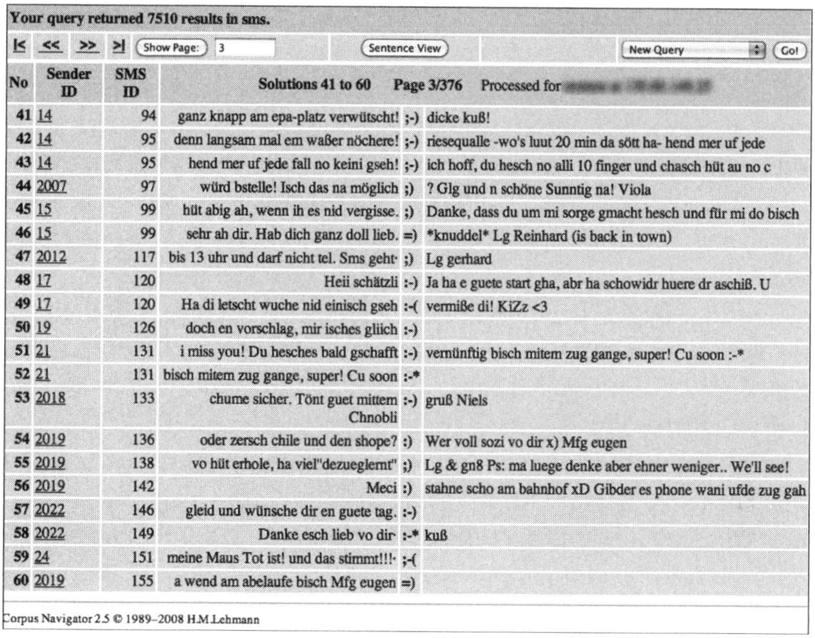

Your query returned 7510 results in sms.

|< << >> >| (Show Page:) 3   (Sentence View)   (New Query) ⬍ (Go!)

No	Sender ID	SMS ID	Solutions 41 to 60 Page 3/376 Processed for ...
41	14	94	ganz knapp am epa-platz verwütscht! ;-) dicke kuß!
42	14	95	denn langsam mal em waßer nöchere! ;-) riesequalle -wo's luut 20 min da sött ha- hend mer uf jede
43	14	95	hend mer uf jede fall no keini gseh! ;-) ich hoff, du hesch no alli 10 finger und chasch hüt au no c
44	2007	97	würd bstelle! Isch das na möglich ;) ? Glg und n schöne Sunntig na! Viola
45	15	99	hüt abig ah, wenn ih es nid vergisse. ;) Danke, dass du um mi sorge gmacht hesch und für mi do bisch
46	15	99	sehr ah dir. Hab dich ganz doll lieb. =) *knuddel* Lg Reinhard (is back in town)
47	2012	117	bis 13 uhr und darf nicht tel. Sms geht ;) Lg gerhard
48	17	120	Heii schätzli :-) Ja ha e guete start gha, abr ha schowidr huere dr aschiß. U
49	17	120	Ha di letscht wuche nid einisch gseh :-(vermiße di! KiZz <3
50	19	126	doch en vorschlag, mir isches gliich :-)
51	21	131	i miss you! Du hesches bald gschafft :-) vernünftig bisch mitem zug gange, super! Cu soon :-*
52	21	131	bisch mitem zug gange, super! Cu soon :-*
53	2018	133	chume sicher. Tönt guet mittem :-) gruß Niels Chnobli
54	2019	136	oder zersch chile und den shope? :) Wer voll sozi vo dir x) Mfg eugen
55	2019	138	vo hüt erhole, ha viel"dezueglernt' ;) Lg & gn8 Ps: ma luege denke aber ehner weniger.. We'll see!
56	2019	142	Meci :) stahne scho am bahnhof xD Gibder es phone wani ufde zug gah
57	2022	146	gleid und wünsche dir en guete tag. :-)
58	2022	149	Danke esch lieb vo dir :-* kuß
59	24	151	meine Maus Tot ist! und das stimmt!!! ;-(
60	2019	155	a wend am abelaufe bisch Mfg eugen =)

Corpus Navigator 2.5 © 1989–2008 H.M.Lehmann

FIGURE 14.1 Emoticons in a KWIC view representation in Corpus Navigator.

investigated in our SMS corpus, but also framed theoretically. Due to the retrieval tools in *Corpus Navigator*, it is also possible, for instance, to find all the orthographic variations of one word and to gain an idea about the frequency of specific items.

Here is an example of what the results of a search for emoticons in *Corpus Navigator* might look like (Figure 14.1). The illustrations show in which context emoticons appear and how often they can be found all together (i.e., 7,510 times).

By examining these types of features, it will be possible to verify popular stereotypes (cf. Thurlow, 2006, for an overview) about texting in a well-grounded, empirical manner. It will also be possible to reveal underlying regularities in the messages, showing that the morphosyntax of texting does not diverge from language-specific or maybe even universal rules (cf. Stark, 2011). Finally, thanks to the sociodemographic data, it will be possible to examine correlations between stylistic choices and age, sex, or the educational background of the texters.

(c) Investigating Pragmatic Issues

As we have already mentioned, within *sms4science.ch* some dialogically oriented corpora will be available as well. These subcorpora can serve as a basis for the study of text messaging conversations, the study of the relationship between the interlocutors, or the study of the similarities and differences between texting and face-to-face communications. However, this type of discourse-analytic research may not only be examined in the subcorpora. Some of the questions can also be answered by the main corpus because the texters can partially be recognized by their identifiers and first names as being one and the same person, thus making it possible to retrace the respective messages.

Another pragmatic research field is the use of salutation formulas at the beginning and the end of the messages (see Spilioti, Chapter 4, this volume). Is it correct that they are often missing, in other words, that "the most significant characteristic of salutations is their absence" (cf. Frehner, 2008, p. 91)? And are there any differences between individual languages in using or omitting these formulas? Additionally, the main communicative functions in the text messages may be investigated. Regarding this research field, several possible questions spring to mind: Does the thematic content (personal matters, business) correspond with the degree of informal or formal style used in the messages? Are the particular strategies applied to maintain a social relationship (such as sending good night messages) the same in all languages in our corpus, and are they the same in the international SMS corpus, which will be established on the basis of the individual national ones?

The Future of SMS—A Guessing Game?

No one can predict whether text messaging will remain as frequently used as it is at the moment, especially given the fact that there are other communication tools that can be used on cell phones as well (such as social networking sites, instant messaging, and microblogging such as *Twitter*). This question clearly has implications for future research. What, for example, are the differences between text messaging and microblogging? Are they substantially different communication practices, or is this just old wine (i.e., text messaging) in new bottles (i.e. *Twitter*), since in both cases we are faced with messages limited to a certain number of characters and since one-to-one messages are possible within *Twitter* as well? (See Lee, Chapter 6, this volume.) If the internet can be accessed from a mobile device, *Twitter*, *Facebook*, instant messaging, and others may be used on the cell phone as well, so the differences seem to minimize even more. And like *Twitter* or other modes of communication, text messaging is not necessarily text based, as other modalities (such as images and video clips) may appear in text messages as well.[12]

As for the frequency of use of texting compared with other modes of communication, a *Pew Internet & American Life* study from April 2010 revealed that the use of text messaging had continuously been gaining ground in the USA with one in three teens sending more than 100 text messages a day (Lenhart et al., 2010).[13] Given this development in one of the richest countries on the planet, we can assume that there will remain a huge interest in all kind of research work around SMS communication. However, it is imperative that the scientific exchange between scholars in different countries be intensified in order to carry out better-informed research on text messaging. As we have already seen, different SMS corpora exist, which were compiled for different purposes. Furthermore, studies in SMS communication other than in English should be brought closer to the research community. Perhaps *sms4science* will achieve the goal of bringing together SMS researchers from all over the world.

Acknowledgments

We would like to thank the research group of Cédrick Fairon, especially Louise-Amélie Cougnon, for their continuous support of the Swiss subproject; our Swiss colleagues from the University of Neuchâtel, Marie-José Béguelin and Simona Pekarek-Döhler, for their always pleasant and most effective cooperation; *Swisscom*, and especially Peter Schüpbach, for the perfect technical support of our data collection; and, finally, all our collaborators at the University of Zurich, particularly Charlotte Meisner, Andi Gredig, Beni Ruef, and Hans Martin Lehmann. We also thank our two reviewers and Crispin Thurlow for their very helpful comments. A special thanks goes to Simone Ueberwasser for her fruitful ideas, technical support, proofreading, and correction, and for always keeping a clear view whenever we were lost in technical or administrative trouble. All remaining errors and shortcomings are, of course, ours.

Notes

1. Note that in Switzerland, according to *Swisscom* (one of the major Swiss telecommunication companies), on their network alone 10 million text messages are being sent per day. This is an impressive number for such a small country with around seven million inhabitants only, and the use of SMS is still on the rise.

2. Cf. http://www.comp.nus.edu.sg/~rpnlpir/downloads/corpora/smsCorpus/

3. The demographic information on the texters as well as the total number of text messages is only given in a very general way (cf. http://www.medien-sprache.net/archiv/corpora/sms_os_h.pdf).

4. Cf. Fairon et al. (2006a, p. 100), who decided to erase all non-French data from their Belgian corpus, even though Belgium is a bilingual country.

5. Swiss-German is the "umbrella term applied to all German dialects spoken in Switzerland" (Rash, 1998, p. 21).

6. COSMA (= Cooperative Schedule Management Agent) is a German e-mail corpus containing 160 messages, cf. ftp://lt-ftp.dfki.uni-sb.de/pub/papers/local/klein97_dgfs.ps.gz

7. Cf. the website of the project at the time of data collection: http://www.sms-pourlascience.be.

8. This format was considered to be superior to the most obvious format for such a task, a text file in which the fields are separated by one or several defined characters, because basically any combination of characters must be expected in a text message, and therefore no combination of any characters at all can be used as a separator.

9. For ethical considerations and the principles of anonymization, cf. also Tagg (2009, pp. 80–93).

10. Siebenhaar (2006) discusses code switching between Standard German and Swiss-German, that is, between two varieties of the same language. For a broader view on code switching, we refer the reader to Chapter IV in the volume "Multilingual Internet" (2007), edited by Brenda Danet and Susan C. Herring.

11. For this type of adjacency ellipsis, cf. Klein (1993).

12. Although this is not the case in our SMS corpus.

13. When the study was published, a Swiss newspaper referring to this data was titled: "US-Teenager sind süchtig nach SMS" ("US-Teens are addicted to SMS", cf. Tages-Anzeiger, April 22, 2010).

References

Beißwenger, M., & Storrer, A. (2008). Corpora of computer-mediated communication. In A. Lüdeling & M. Kytö (Eds.), *Corpus Linguistics. An International Handbook*, vol. 1, (pp. 292–308). Berlin & New York: de Gruyter.

Braun, B. (2006). Jugendliche Identitäten in SMS-Texten. In C. Dürscheid & J. Spitzmüller (Eds.), *Zwischentöne. Zur Sprache der Jugend in der Deutschschweiz*, (pp. 101–114). Zürich: Verlag Neue Zürcher Zeitung.

Danet, B., & Herring, S.C. (Eds.). (2007). *The Multilingual Internet: Language, Culture, and Communication Online*. New York: Oxford University Press.

Deumert, A., & Masinyana, S.O. (2008). Mobile language choices – The use of English and isiXhosa in text messages (SMS). *English World-Wide*, 29(2), 117–147. Amsterdam: Benjamin.

Fairon, C., Klein, J.R., & Paumier, S. (2006a). *Le langage SMS. Etude d'un corpus informatisé à partir de l'enquête 'Faites don de vos SMS à la science.'* Louvain-la-Neuve, Belgium: Presses universitaires de Louvain.

Fairon, C., Klein, J.R., & Paumier, S. (2006b). *Le Corpus SMS pour la science. Base de données de 30.000 SMS et logiciels de consultation.* CD-ROM. Louvain-la-Neuve, Belgium: Presses universitaires.

Frehner, C. (2008). *E-mail – SMS – MMS. The Linguistic Creativity of Asynchronous Discourse in the New Media Age.* Bern: Peter Lang.

Klein, W. (1993): Ellipse. In J. Jacobs, A. von Stechow, W. Sternefeld, & T. Vennemann (Eds.), *Syntax. Ein internationales Handbuch zeitgenössischer Forschung /An International Handbook of Contemporary Research,* (pp. 763–799). Berlin: de Gruyter.

Lenhart, A., Ling, R., Campbell, S., & Purcell, K. (2010). *Teens and Mobile Phones.* Pew Research Center's Internet & American Life Project, April 20, 2010. Retrieved July 13, 2010, from http://www.pewinternet.org/~/media//Files/Reports/2010/PIP-Teens-and-Mobile-2010.pdf

Ling, R. (2005): The socio-linguistics of SMS: An analysis of SMS use by a random sample of Norwegians. In R. Ling, & P. E. Pedersen (Eds.), *Mobile Communications: Re-negotiation of the Social Sphere* (pp. 335–349). London: Springer.

Rash, F.J. (1998). *The German Language in Switzerland: Multilingualism, Diglossia and Variation.* Bern: Peter Lang.

Schlobinski, P., et al. (2001). Simsen. Eine Pilotstudie zu sprachlichen und kommunikativen. Aspekten in der SMS-Kommunikation. *Networx*, 22. Retrieved July 13, 2010 from http://www.mediensprache.net/de/networx/docs/networx-22.asp

Siebenhaar, B. (2006). Code choice and code-switching in Swiss-German Internet Relay Chat rooms. *Journal of Sociolinguistics*, 10(4), 481–506.

Stark, E. (2011). La morphosyntaxe des SMS suisses français: Le marquage de l'accord sujet-verbe conjugué. *Linguistic Online.*

Tagg, C. (2009). *A Corpus Linguistics Study of SMS Text Messaging.* Unpublished Ph.D. dissertation at the Department of English, University of Birmingham, UK. Retrieved July 13, 2010, from http://etheses.bham.ac.uk/253/1/Tagg09PhD.pdf

Thurlow, C. (2003). Generation Txt? The sociolinguistics of young people's text messaging. *Discourse Analysis Online*, 1(1). Retrieved July 13, 2010 from http://faculty.washington.edu/thurlow/papers/Thurlow%282003%29-DAOL.pdf

Thurlow, C. (2006). From statistical panic to moral panic: The metadiscursive construction and popular exaggeration of new media language in the print media. *Journal of Computer Mediated Communication*, 11(3) article 1. Retrieved July 13, 2010 from http://jcmc.indiana.edu/vol11/issue3/thurlow.html

Thurlow, C., & Poff, M. (2011). Text messaging. In S.C. Herring, D. Stein, & T. Virtanen (Eds.), *Handbook of the Pragmatics of CMC*. Berlin & New York: Mouton de Gruyter. Retrieved July 13, 2010, from http://faculty.washington. edu/thurlow/papers/thurlow&poff%282009%29.pdf

Zimmermann, T. (2009). Le 'langage SMS' – une nouvelle varieté écrite de la langue française? Une analyse empirique basée sur un corpus de 30'000 SMS sous considération particulière de la relation phonie-graphie. Unpublished master's thesis, directed by Elisabeth Stark, University of Zurich.

Chapter 15

C me Sk8: Discourse, Technology, and "Bodies without Organs"

Rodney H. Jones

FIND YOUR BODY *without organs. Find out how to make it. It's a question of life and death, youth and old age, sadness and joy. It is where everything is played out.*
(Deleuze & Guattari, 1988, p. 151)

It's two a.m. and Gary and his crew are out at a twelve set with a bitchin' rail at a new housing estate in Kowloon. Chun Jai is there, and Johnny, and Arrow, and Owen with his funny hat. Simon's brought the camera and his portable halogen lights that reflect off the concrete making everything seem flat and unreal. They start out messing around, laying down some lines on the pavement,

doing kickflips and half cabs on the smooth, pop ground, while Simon is setting up the camera and Owen's sliding a dirty block of wax along the rail. Gary's the first to go and bails. He hardly gets his board up on the rail before tumbling backward down the stairs to the groans and laughter of his friends. This set is seriously sick. Owen's hard core crazy and doesn't even bother with the rail, just tries to ollie the set and of course slams hard against the pavement at the bottom, his board racing out from under him. Then comes Arrow who stupidly tries to nose grind the rail and falls, his arms flailing in the air before he lands. Then Chun Jai, and Simon, and Johnny, and it begins again, each of them bailing in their own way until finally Chun Jai lands a gnarly backside flip down the rail. Gnarly, but at least he lands it. And after a few more attempts, Owen gets it too, touching down sweetly at the foot of the set and rolling into the darkness beyond the halo of the halogen lamp. Then Gary does it too, to howls of mad respect. That's the way it goes. They skate. They bail. Sometimes they land it, but most times not. Afterward they go to the 7-11 for beers, which they drink while watching the footage on the tiny LCD screen of Simon's camera.

A week later they're in Simon's bedroom stitching together footage from that and other nights using a pirated copy of Final Cut Pro on Simon's battered white Macbook, weaving Chun Jai's gnarly backside with a fakie kickflip and 50–50 along a park bench in Sha Tin and an impossible that he landed at some other place on some other night, making it all seem like one line, which isn't hard since he always wears that same ripped up Hesh Kings tee shirt, synchronizing the rhythm of the board rolling and grinding and flipping with the beat of a Lynyrd Skynyrd song, all of them crowded around the screen, attending to each frame pasted and trimmed, each note of the song, each movement of Chun Jai's amazing body.

In this chapter I will consider the relationship between technology and the human body. In particular, I will be asking how the process of turning our bodies into texts affects what we can do with them, and who we can *be* with them.

The theoretical framework I will be using comes from "mediated discourse analysis" (Norris & Jones, 2005; Scollon 2001), a perspective on discourse that focuses on how texts and other cultural tools *mediate* human activities and social identities. The concept of *mediation* has its roots in the work of Soviet psychologist Lev Vygotsky. For Vygotsky, all thoughts and actions are *mediated* through artifacts or "cultural tools." Since different kinds of tools make different kinds of thoughts or actions either more or less possible, *mediation* has a profound effect on limiting and focusing human activity. "The inclusion of a tool in the process of behavior," writes Vygotsky (1981, pp. 139–140), "alters the course... of all the mental processes that enter into the composition of the instrumental act (and) re-creates and reorganizes the whole structure of behavior." (See also Thurlow & Jaworski, Chapter 11 of this volume, on mediation versus mediatization.)

Cultural tools can be either physical (hammers, screwdrivers, computers, skateboards) or psychological (language, gestures, reading and writing, counting systems, mnemonic techniques, works of visual art). All cultural tools, however, have both physical and psychological dimensions (Jones, 2001; Wertsch, 1998). Even psychological tools are essentially material since, in order to be used to perform actions, they must undergo some kind of physical instantiation: ideas and languages must be transformed into spoken utterances or written texts. At the same time, all tools are also psychological or *semiotic*, that is, they exist simultaneously as objects in the world and in the minds of users as mental representations imbued with meaning.

One cultural tool that has received relatively little attention in this model is the human body itself, although some, like Randolph (2000) and Nelson (2002), have pointed out how people make use of other social actors as meditational means to accomplish actions: a bank robber uses the body of a hostage to shield himself from gunfire, crowds are used by politicians at rallies to create an ambiance of excitement, medical students regularly use the bodies of the dead to study anatomy, and physicians use the live bodies of their patients as meditational means to practice their profession. The kinds of bodily cultural tools I am concerned with here, however, are not the bodies of others, but representations of our own bodies, which, through various processes of technologization (Jones, 2001; Scollon, 2001), we are able to separate from our physical bodies and appropriate into social actions. I have in mind things like passport pictures, portraits, the photos of we post on *Facebook*, and the videos Gary and his friends upload to *YouTube* (see also Newon, Chapter 7 of this volume, on avatars). The position I will be taking is that representations of the human body (whether printed, painted, photographed, or pixilated) represent a unique and powerful class of meditational means with their own special set of affordances and constraints, and their own set of consequences on social behavior and interaction.

To refer to this particular class of meditational means, I will rather shamelessly appropriate from the French philosophers Gille Deleuze and Felix Guattari (1988) the term "bodies without organs." Deleuze and Guattari use the term to refer to the "virtual" dimension of the body, the body freed from the "organization of the organism," the body outside any determinate state, torn from the here and now, exemplified, for them, in

the body of the masochist, the drug addict, the lover, and the schizophren-
ic. The subject that I will be drawing upon to illustrate my analysis may
in fact have some similarities to these figures, for the bodies I would like
to consider are the bodies of urban skateboarders—not their physical bodies, but the representations of their bodies they produce and consume in
amateur skateboarding videos.

Bodies without Organs: Reification versus Virtualization

EXT. NEAR THE ENTRANCE TO A SHOPPING ARCADE
*Arrow is arguing with a security guard who has told him he can't skate there
and wants to see his ID card. What right does he have to see his ID card? He's
not a cop. And what are they doing wrong away way? They're not taking drugs
or robbing old ladies. Arrow screams at the guard and jabs his finger in the air.
The guard screams back calling Arrow names and using language he probably
wouldn't use if he knew he were being secretly filmed.*

SOUNDTRACK STARTS: *"I Need Some Fine Wine And You, You Need To Be Nicer,"* The Cardigans
CUT TO
Arrow in front of a poster for a topless bar in Wan Chai advertising models from all over the world. Russia, Japan, the Philippines. Arrow turns around and starts stroking the pictures on the poster lovingly.
CUT TO
Arrow sailing over a railing in Tsim Sha Tsui, the tiger stripes on the bottom of his
board visible to the camera.
CUT TO
Arrow doing a 360 flip in Sha Tin.
CUT TO
Arrow doing a nollie nose grind against a park bench with group a surprised secondary school girls in uniform watching.
CUT TO:
Arrow sliding down the railing of a set of stairs near the cultural center.
CUT TO:
Arrow holding his skateboard and looking out into the harbor.
SOUNDTRACK:
Well it's been a long slow collision,
I'm a pitbull, you're a dog,
Baby you're foul in clear conditions
But you're handsome in the fog

I say I am appropriating the term "bodies without organs" shamelessly because much of what I mean by it is not really part of Deleuze and Guattari's definition, and much of what they mean I am not including in mine. By "bodies without organs," I simply mean all representations of our bodies that we or others make use of to take actions in the world. "Bodies without organs" defined in this way are always the result of what Bauman and Briggs (1990) call *entextualization*, the process by which discourse (insofar as the body is inherently discursive) is rendered "extractable," able to be lifted out of its immediate spatial and temporal materiality and inserted into another (Jones, 2009).

"Bodies without organs" are characterized by five main features, which both distinguish them from and connect them to their physical antecedents. The first is *deterritorialization*; "bodies without organs" can be separated from the physical space that the body occupies and transported into different spaces. The second is *desynchronization*: moments in the existence of the physical body can be captured and lifted out of time and used in future moments, and these bodily representations are often not subject to the same laws of time and space that physical bodies are. The third is *reproducibility*: "bodies without organs" can be reproduced and duplicated so that multiple instances of the same body can exist simultaneously. Fourth is *mutability*: "bodies without organs," like other texts, can be revised, edited, altered, and realtered in ways that are not possible with physical bodies; "bodies without organs" always have some degree of plasticity, depending on the media in which they are rendered and the technologies that are employed in this rendering. Finally, the fifth and perhaps the most important feature of "bodies without organs" is *mimesis*; "bodies without organs" are above all representations, and their sole utility as cultural tools is based on there existing some kind of resemblance to or connection with some actual physical body existing (or supposedly existing) somewhere. "Bodies without organs" qualify as a special class of cultural tools precisely because of the reflexive relationship they have to the particular, concrete human bodies that they represent.

One example of such a "body without organs" is Arrow's Hong Kong ID card, which includes a photograph of him taken when he was sixteen. This photograph, however, is not the only representation of his body that appears on the card. It also contains a textual "body without organs" in the form of his full Chinese name (which, by the way, is not "Arrow") and various other information, like his date of birth, and, in the corner of the card, an electronic chip that contains an image of his thumbprint. With this tool he can perform a whole host of actions that would be physically or legally impossible without it. He can carry it in his pocket. He can use it to open a bank account, to vote in District Council Elections. He can use it to gain entry to topless bars in Wan Chai if they ever bothered to check IDs, which they don't. He can use it at the border to mainland China to enter or leave the Special Administrative Region of Hong Kong through a special turnstile that collects an image of his actual thumbprint and compares it to the image embedded in the electronic chip.

This example illustrates a number of other important aspects of "bodies without organs," in particular the fact that they are always partial, that a "body without organs" can never be a "copy" of the original body and often represents the body through synecdoche, with a part of the body like the face or the fingerprint signifying entire body. Furthermore, bodies without organs are often deployed in "semiotic aggregates" (Scollon & Scollon, 2003), with several different representations working together to complement or verify one another. Finally, despite the potential for deterritorialization (or despatialization) inherent in "bodies without organs," many ways in which they are used require the physical body and its representation to be copresent, as when Arrow uses his ID card to cross a border or to buy alcohol in a bar.

There are, however, a number of very important things Arrow cannot do with this body without organs. He cannot, for example, alter it in any way, even though the picture of him as a sixteen-year-old with a crew cut looks nothing like he looks now. He cannot legally reproduce it, at least not in the same form, or easily embed it into or combine it with other representations. He cannot use it to imagine himself as anything else but what it says he is: male, Chinese, born on a particular date, in a particular year. He cannot even access much of the information on the card such as that encoded onto the electronic chip. Most importantly, he has no choice about whether or not to use this body without organs. He is required by law, as are all Hong Kong residents, to carry it with him when he goes out in public.

Here is where Deleuze and Guattari and their followers would no doubt cringe, for nothing could be farther from their conception of the "body without organs" as a "field of intensities" than the example I have just given. In fact, they have another term for such objects as passports and identity cards and mug shots and other socially orchestrated "captures" of the body, especially those based on categorizations like gender, race, and citizenship. These they call "incorporeal transformations," and their function is not to facilitate flows of desire, but to control it, to fix it into various assemblages as determined by institutions (the state, the church, the prison). They are operations of discipline that aim to enforce particular regimes of representation and economies of meaning (Foucault, 1979).

Closer to what Deleuze and Guattari had in mind with their notion of "bodies without organs" would be Arrow's pixilated form sailing through the air in the video described previously, him snaking down sidewalks and grinding against ledges and olleiing down stairs as if totally free of gravity.

The reason I have chosen to use the same term to describe both of these things is that they really do not describe different phenomena, but rather aspects of the same phenomenon. The field of possibilities which Deleuze and Guattari imagine to be "the body without organs" and the disciplinary regimes of "incorporeal transformations" are simply two different sides of *entextualization*, two different potentials present in all representations of the body. I will refer to these as the potential for *virtualization* and the potential for *reification*. Reification is based on disembodiment and alienation. Its aim is to transform a dynamic process into a fixed object: an identity, a document, a piece of evidence. Virtualization, on the other hand, has the opposite effect: rather than close down possibilities, it opens them up. It is a kind of problematization of the body. In the words of Pierre Lévy (1998, p. 44):

> virtualization involves a change of identity, a transition from a particular solution to a general problematic, the transformation of a specific and circumscribed activity into a delocalized, desynchronized, and collectivized functioning. The virtualization of the body is therefore not a form of disembodiment but a recreation, a reincarnation, a multiplication, vectorization, and heterogenesis of the human. However, the boundary between heterogenesis and alienation, actualization and commodity reification, virtualization and amputation, is never clearly defined. This uncertain boundary must constantly be estimated and evaluated.

"Bodies without organs" are used in all sorts of different ways, each of these ways exploiting, to various degrees, the potential for reification or virtualization inherent in all representations. One of the most important functions of bodies without organs is their *evidentiary* function—their use as records of identities or actions for the purpose of verification. I put into this category photographs on passports and drivers' licenses, medical drawings, and the bodies that appear in footage from surveillance cameras. Another popular function of "bodies without organs" is their *memorial* or *retrospective* function. Here we think of family photos, for example, or the portraits of ancestors, representations whose function is not so much to verify past bodies as to aid us in remembering them. "Bodies without organs" can also serve a *surrogate* function, acting as replacements for our physical bodies that we deploy into the present moment to perform actions. Examples of these include pornographic pictures, objects of worship, voodoo dolls, and the images of ourselves we transmit in real time over webcams. And finally, there is what I will be calling the *anticipatory* function of bodies without organs. This is the function by which representations are used not to recall past bodies, nor to control present bodies, but to imagine future ones, in the way plastic surgeons create computer-generated mock-ups of what patients might look like with a nip here and a tuck there, or Tibetan Buddhist meditators make use of images of deities on *tankas* to imagine themselves as enlightened beings. Bodies without organs, then, have the potential to link us to the past, to fix us in the present, or to propel us into the future.

C me Sk8

When I first started skating my friend had a camera and we started to film some short videos. The camera was very low-tech. The quality of the clips was really bad and shaky. But we couldn't wait to add some songs to it. Later we finally got a DV camera. We were determined to buy a DV camera no matter how poor we were. Then we started to put our clips up online. Sometimes you feel so happy when people compliment your work. And if it sucked, then next time we would do better.

On Jai, 20

Ever since the early days of the sport, "bodies without organs" have played a central role in skateboarding (Weyland, 2002), although the technologies of entextualization and the uses to which these representations have been put have changed. In the sixties and seventies, skaters used

analog photography to capture the ephemeral moments of their performances in durable documents, which they would send to skateboarding magazines for possible publication. In fact, what made early pictorial publications like *Skateboarder* magazine unique was that they depended so much on photographs taken by readers. These photographic "bodies without organs" primarily served evidentiary and memorial functions: they were used first and foremost to document the accomplishments of particular skaters, and the reputations of many of the early heroes of the sport were built on these often blurred and grainy amateur photos. These pictures also, however, served to build social cohesion, which contributed significantly to the early growth of the sport. As skateboarding historian Jacko Weyland (2002, p. 162) writes, "It wasn't about self aggrandizement or fame; it was about your far-flung tribe recognizing your will to exist and skate under the toughest of circumstances."

There has also been a long tradition of self-publication in skateboarding, as skaters early on took control of distributing their "bodies without organs" though photocopied "zines" with titles like *Body Slam* and *Curbsnot*. This early adoption of DIY media underlines a fundamental ideological construction of skateboarding as a sport created and controlled by participants themselves.

When video technology came on the scene in the early eighties, skateboarders were among its earliest adopters, although then most skateboarding videos were commercially produced by sporting goods companies to market their products. The fist widely distributed skateboarding video made by skaters themselves was *The Bones Brigade Video Show* produced by George Powell and Stacey Peralta in 1984, which featured such legendary skaters as Tony Hawk and Rodney Mullen. It was in these early videos that Powell and Peralta developed the techniques and generic conventions that informed later amateur videos.

As video cameras became increasingly affordable, and with advances in digital technology that made sophisticated editing and special effects more and more accessible to nonprofessionals, video became a central part of the activity of skateboarding. Learning how to shoot, perform in, and edit video to some extent became part of learning to be a skater. Skaters began to bring video equipment with them when they skated, to spend hours meticulously editing these videos and setting them to music, and then to post them to sites like *You Tube* and *My Space*, creating online digital archives of their personal accomplishments, the histories of the social groups they were part of, and of the locales in which they skated.

Everybody films these videos and shows them to everyone around, ask-
ing, 'Am I getting better? Am I good?' To tell you the truth, I don't know
about this stuff because I'm not a pro. We just set up the camera, ask
someone to follow us on their board and film our lines. Where did we
learn this? We learned from professional videos. We look at the kinds
of shots they use, the angles. If the trick I do looks like a particular shot
in a particular video, I shoot it the way they shot it. For the music we
pick the songs we love. It's like giving a theme song to follow your own
rhythm, your own skill, your own speed. And the music can create a per-
fect match. I can review my skateboarding skills from the first tape to the
last. If I keep filming, there must be some improvement.

Johnny, 17

The skate video is not just a random collection of shots of people skating. It is a genre with clear conventions that have particular meaning and
currency within this discourse community. Typically these videos open
with an initial narrative frame in which the characters are introduced, characters that often include not only the skaters themselves but also various
bystanders, passersby, and antagonists (usually in the form of policemen
and security guards). The bulk, of course, consists of skating, a series of
successive beautifully executed lines that give the viewer the impression
that the skater is traveling seamlessly through the environment, weaving
a geographic narrative, a journey in which successive architectural objects
present obstacles for the hero to overcome, rather like traditional hero narratives. Music, of course, is an important feature, and soundtracks range
from hip-hop to punk to Billie Holiday, but whatever track is chosen, the
footage is edited so that the rhythms of the skating are carefully entrained
with the rhythms of the music. As with all hero narratives, there are inevitable setbacks, represented by what skaters call "bail footage," shots of falling down. And as with more traditional hero narratives, there are scenes of
comic relief represented through episodes of ritual insulting or horseplay.

The "bodies without organs" that these videos constitute continue to
fulfill the evidentiary functions previously performed by photographs.
Within the subculture of skateboarding, in fact, these videoed documents of individual accomplishments are extremely important tools for
the ongoing and cyclical process of verifying membership and earning
cultural capital within the group (Donnelly & Young, 2001). With each
new video posted online, a skater renews this membership and revises the
status associated with it.

And, of course, as with any home videos, the retrospective or memorial function is quite important: to have a chance to relive the good times of past skate sessions, to recall past skate spots that have since been re-appropriated by the authorities, and to create a digital record of the history of the group and its members. For skaters, however, this retrospective function has an important cognitive dimension as well. These practices of retrospection are, in fact, integral to the process of learning to be a skater, allowing them to reflect on past successes and dissect past failures, and to understand the motions and timing that go into performing particular tricks by attending to what Ferrell et al. (2001, p. 182) and his colleagues call the "microphysics of representability" aided by their ability to freeze, slow down, and speed up their movements. Over time, these videos constitute visual records of particular skaters' learning trajectories, allowing them to understand how they have improved and what they still need to work on, encouraging them to view their learning from a broader temporal perspective. After the videos have been posted online, groups of skaters engage in collective recollection through posted comments and feedback, which facilitate not just individual learning but also group cohesion.

The most important function of these "bodies without organs," I would argue, however, is not documentary or retrospective, but *anticipatory*: their ability to help skateboarders *imagine futures* and to contribute to their ongoing symbolic projects of self-formation. The selves in these videos are not just representations of past bodies, they are rehearsals of future ones.

Even when I first started out and I would like film myself and put it up on a website so that people could like talk about it. In a way it's kind of like... we like to film because we like to show people what we've done. It's not showing off. It's just like, hey, look what I did. Skateboarders want to film either for themselves to see what it looks like, or like to say that they've done it, or it's like another way to push yourself. You might try something not that hard down something or on something, but then if you're filming, you want to try something even harder, to push yourself to like go to the next level, because you know you did it, the feeling like oh I did this!

Jason, 18

To really understand these "bodies without organs" one must consider the plight of bodies *with* organs from the perspective of skaters. Anyone

who has watched a lot of skateboarding videos but has not gone out skating would be surprised at how different the real procedure is from what one sees on the screen. Far from the unbroken lines of successful tricks that make it seem as if the skateboarder is traveling effortlessly through the city, what actually occurs is a lot of falling down. Skateboarders do *not* land tricks far more often than they do, and a successful *line*, an unbroken series of tricks across sequential obstacles, is even more rare. The lived experience of an actual skateboarding session is a tedious and painful process of trial and error in which error is the rule.

And so what occurs in the editing process of these videos is not just a reliving of the experience but a *re-creation* of it. The lines documented in skating videos, and the chains of lines that give the impression of seamlessly traveling through the urban landscape, in a sense portray skating not as it is but as it "ought to be,"; they are at once documents of serendipitous moments and the compression of many hours and days of failed attempts, at once documents of what really happened, and idealized versions of what could happen or should happen, produced through careful selection and editing. This is where these "bodies without organs" function in particularly powerful ways for skaters, allowing them to string together their successes into idealized portrayals that reveal not only their past glory but also their future potential. "I'm really not that good, you know," one skater admitted to me, "but if I'm good at editing, I can make myself look like a pro."

One important feature of digital editing that facilitates this function is the way it amplifies the potential for *desynchronization* inherent in all processes of entextualization. Digital media makes the relationship between time and space more fluid and contingent, allowing time to be slowed down so that the brief, visceral, adrenalin intensity of a trick can be elongated into a slow, balletic dance and speeded up, so that the tedious and painful processes of learning, and the experiences and accomplishments of weeks of skating, can be collapsed into a single document. On the one hand, this manipulation of time helps to mediate the objective observable time of the stationary observer with the relative psychological time of the skater in motion. "That's really the way it feels when you're doing it," said one of my participants, "like time is slowed down and you're aware ... aware of everything around you and everything you do." On the other hand, it helps skaters to reconstruct past experiences occurring on multiple timescales (Lemke, 2000) into coherent narratives—from the level of the micro move that skaters study to understand intricate aspects of timing, to the discrete trick, to the line, to the session, to their skating careers, to the various local and global histories of skateboarding, fashion, and popular music within which they situate their lives, the rhythms of all of these timescales are carefully synchronized so that the sounds of the skateboard along the surface of the ground are entrained to the beats of the skater's favorite song, and to trajectories of learning that have brought him to this moment and will carry him into the future.

> *Sometimes it's in the skating, but sometimes it's completely in the filming. Sometimes it's completely in the editing. Sometimes it's in the music. And in the way the edit's put together to fit with the music ... sometimes there's no meaning in it at all. It just looks pretty ... You go through phases. Sometimes you skate a lot, and then sometimes it drops off and you don't see each other for a few weeks and you've got all of this footage on your computer and you want to get it out there. The older your footage gets the less interesting it gets because the trick progression gets even better.*
>
> Piet, 19

Skate videos, and skateboarding itself, are examples of what Lemke (2001) calls "traversals"—defined as "temporal-experiential linkings, sequences, and catenations of meaningful elements that deliberately or accidentally, but radically, cross boundaries or standardized genres, themes, types, practices, or activities" (p. 86). What characterizes a traversal, writes Lemke, "is precisely that some kind of coherent meaning is made in the unpredictable sequencing over "text-scales" that are longer than the scales of the standardized elements which are strung together along the traversal" (p. 89). Examples of traversals include hypertexts, channel surfing, mall cruising, Djing and Mcing, and skateboarding, a practice in which skaters construct coherent *lines* through navigating across disparate and seemingly unrelated features of urban architecture, and then reedit these lines into videos that are later embedded into other genres like web pages. "Bodies without organs" become figures in a mobile, reconfigurable textual field, incorporated into the structure of other texts, pretexts, cotexts, and contexts and various instrumentalities of entextualization and interpretation, infinitely multiplying opportunities for producing meaning.

And these connections ultimately extend back out to the physical body itself. Just because these narratives of future successes are virtual and, in some respects, highly idealized, it does not mean that they have no connection to the "real world." The anticipatory qualities of the videos skaters have made in the past infiltrate their future skate sessions, creating dynamic feedback loops. One of the most memorable lessons I received during my fieldwork came when I asked a skater who was practicing at a local skate park while listening to his iPod if he tried to skate to the rhythm of the music he was listening to, rather naively assuming a linear relationship between one mode and activity type and another on a single, linear timescale. "No," he said, "it doesn't really work that way. When I listen to the music, what the songs remind me of are the videos I made and the times I landed the trick and like how it felt ... and so I'm thinking about the next video and the music and the editing and stuff."

> *It's such good fun to see our own footage, to see whether or not we had the style that we thought was good. And it was also just to see other people's reactions. I made a video once. I made it in two hours because I was just too excited to like not make it, which I thought was amazing, but it turned out a year later it was complete crap.*
>
> *Ben, 16*

> *It's like to capture like that day. If you film for a whole day, that day is forever digitally preserved. Like a history book of your life and your friend's lives. It's like, it's always going to be there. It'll always be there.*
>
> *Jason, 18*

Technologies of Entextualization

Different kinds of technologies of entextualization involve different sets of affordances and constraints regarding the processes of deterritorialization, despatializtion, reproducibility, mutability, and mimesis that I discussed previously, and these configurations of affordances and constraints have consequences on how the resulting "bodies without organs" can be used. The degree of deterritorialization enabled by digital technology, for example, which can send representations of the body instantaneously across the globe, is very different from that enabled by drawing or print technology, and the degree of mimesis afforded by photography differs radically from that of drawing or painting.

Perhaps the most significant advance in technologies for representing the human body in the past two hundred years came with the development of photography, which facilitated more than ever before the *documentary* and *evidentiary* functions of "bodies without organs." No technology, perhaps, is more emblematic of the modern era, what Benjamin (1969) calls "the age mechanical reproduction," than analog photography, and with its introduction, entextualizations of the body became increasingly associated with discipline and surveillance. Photography became a central tool for journalists, police officers, hospitals, schools, insane asylums, prisons, and departments of immigration and public health, and photographs themselves began to take on a truth value that paintings never had; they could be used, for example, to prove or disprove one's identity or to convict one of a crime (Tagg, 1999).

At the turn of the 20th century, however, a development occurred in photography that irreversibly altered the disciplinary nature of the technology: the invention and marketing by Eastman Kodak of the small personal camera. Suddenly for the first time in history people had at their command means to produce highly accurate representations of their own and others bodies for their personal use. This change in control over the means of production of "bodies without organs" gave to photographs a more reflective function: photography became not just about being looked at by the other, but about looking at and reflecting upon oneself.

The rise of digital photography and video and of computers and the internet has further increased individuals' potential to create and control their own bodily representations, to alter these representations, to combine them with other representations, to make them more immediate and interactive, and to disseminate them at an unprecedented speed to an unprecedented number of people. The increased *mutability* of "bodies without organs" brought on by digital technology has seriously undermined the *evidentiary* function of such objects as the truth value of photographs became compromised (Mitchell, 1992). At the same time, it has opened up possibilities for other functions.

The effect of digital technologies on practices of entextualization seems primarily to be to amplify those processes that I discussed at the beginning of this chapter. The body becomes more deterritorialized, more desynchronized, and more able to be copied and multiplied. But the most important effect is that is that digital technologies make the body more mutable, more editable, more susceptible to the imagination, and so more resistant to the *reification*. They problematize the body rather than stabilize it, and this might be in part what people find so threatening about them. Digital technologies do not so much capture the body as set into motion new processes of pursuing it. They facilitate what I have been calling the *anticipatory* function of "bodies without organs."

This has created for people new opportunities to engage in self-fashioning through narrative projects using digital tools—projects that allow them to articulate important moments in their lives, to reflect on life's trajectories, and to reposition themselves as agents in and authors of their own stories. Like Tibetan meditators, skaters use their "bodies without organs" to visualize themselves not as they are, but as they'd like to be, not just to recount to themselves the narratives of how they got to where they are, but to write the narratives of where they are going from here.

A number of scholars have seen extreme sports like skateboarding and snowboarding as metaphors for the new affordances of digital virtualization. (See Peuronen, Chapter 8 of this volume, on extreme sports.) Rushkoff (2006), for example, compares skateboarders surfing the city streets to "screenagers" surfing the internet, and Lévy sees extreme sports as physical manifestations of virtualization, attempts to exceed physical limits, to explore other velocities as ways of intensifying our physical presence and lifting us momentarily out of the here and now. Like an avatar, the skater is "never entirely there. Leaving the soil and its support he rises into the air, slides along interfaces, follows vanishing lines, is deterritorialized and vectorized" (p. 43). And the body escapes itself, acquires new velocities, conquers new spaces, and overflows itself.

The entextualization of the body using digital technology, for skateboarders at least, rather than resulting in disembodiment, results in *reembodiment* (cf. Thurlow & Jaworski, Chapter 11 of this volume). Far from alienating these young people from their bodies, these technologies have in many cases created for them opportunities to experience their bodies in completely new ways, ways that approach what Deleuze and Guattari might

have had in mind when they spoke of "bodies without organs" as presenting us opportunities to "find potential movements of deterritorialization,
possible lines of flight, experience them, produce flow conjunctions here
and there, try out continuums of intensities segment by segment."

References

Bauman, R., & Briggs, C.L. (1990). Poetics and performance as critical perspectives on language and social life. *Annual Review of Anthropology*, 19, 59–88.

Benjamin, W. (1969). The work of art in the age of mechanical reproduction. In
H. Arendt (Ed.) & H. Zohn (Trans.), *Illuminations*, (pp. 217–252). New York:
Schocken Books.

Deleuze, G., & Guattari, F. (1988). *A thousand plateaus: Capitalism and schizo-
phrenia*, B. Massumi (Trans.). Minneapolis: University of Minnesota Press.

Donnelly, P., & Young, K. (2001). The construction and confirmation of identity in sport subcultures. In A. Yiannakis & M. Melnick (Eds.), *Contemporary
Issues in Sociology of Sport*, (pp. 299–411). Champaign, IL: Human Kinetics.

Ferrell, J., Milovanovic, D., & Lyng, S. (2001). Edgework, media practices, and the elongation of meaning: A theoretical ethnography of the Bridge Day Event. *Theoretical Criminology*, 5(2), 177–202.

Foucault, M. (1979). *Discipline and Punish: The Birth of the Prison*, A. Sheridan (Trans.). Harmondsworth: Penguin.

Jones, R. (2001). Mediated action and sexual risk: Discourses of AIDS and sexuality in the People's Republic of China. Unpublished Ph.D. dissertation, Macquarie University, Sydney, Australia.

Jones, R. (2009). Dancing, skating and sex: Action and text in the digital age. *Journal of Applied Linguistics*, 6(3) 283–302.

Lemke, J.L. (2000). Across the scales of time: Artifacts, activities, and meanings in ecosocial systems. *Mind, Culture, and Activity*, 7(4), 273–290.

Lemke, J.L. (2001). Discursive technologies and the social organization of meaning. *Folia Linguistica*, 35(1–2), 79–96.

Lévy, P. (1998). *Becoming Virtual: Reality in the Digital Age*, R. Bononno (Trans.). New York: Plenum.

Mitchell, W. (1992). *The Reconfigured Eye: Visual Truth in the Post-Photographic Era*. Cambridge, MA: MIT Press.

Nelson, M. (2002). On the border of humanity: A mediated discourse analysis of four medical students and one cadaver in gross anatomy lab. Master's Research paper, Department of Linguistics, Georgetown University, Washington, DC.

Norris, S., & Jones, R. (Eds.). (2005). *Discourse in Action: Introducing Mediated Discourse Analysis*. London: Routledge.

Randolph, T. (2000). Mediated discourse analysis: The social actor as mediational means in agents' habitus. Paper presented in the colloquium *Mediated Discourse: An Integrated Theory of Sociolinguistic Action* at Sociolinguistics Symposium, April 21– 29, Bristol, UK.

Rushkoff. D. (2006). *Screenagers: Lessons in Chaos from Digital Kids*. Cresskill, NJ: Hampton Press.

Scollon, R. (2001). *Mediated Discourse: The Nexus of Practice*. London: Routledge.

Scollon, R., & Scollon, S.W. (2003). *Discourses in Place: Language in the Material World*. London: Routledge.

Tagg, J. (1999). *The Disciplinary Frame*. Minneapolis: University of Minnesota Press.

Vygotsky, L.S. (1981). The instrumental method in psychology. In J.V. Wertsch (Ed.), *The concept of activity in Soviet psychology*, (pp. 134–143). Armonk, NY: M.E. Sharpe.

Wertsch, J.V. (1998). *Mind as Action*. New York: Oxford University Press.

Weyland, J. (2002). *The Answer Is Never: A Skateboarder's History of the World*. New York: Grove Press.

Commentary

Susan C. Herring

MORE THAN FIFTEEN years ago, I invented an approach to the study of computer-mediated language that I called computer-mediated discourse analysis (CMDA—see Thurlow & Mroczek, Introduction). It was an ambitious act on the part of a junior scholar frustrated by the indifference with which the discipline of linguistics, at the time, seemed to regard the new kinds of communication taking place on the internet. Having staked a claim to the territory in the name of discourse studies early on, I am immensely gratified to see how the study of digital discourse has grown in the intervening years. This volume is a testament, in more ways than one, to just how far it has come.

I should note first that I read the entire volume practically in one sitting, and I enjoyed it immensely. It is a veritable feast for the intellect, on a range of topics that I consider important and interesting. While the volume's contributions are numerous, and different readers will take away from it different ideas, I see it as making especially important (and in some cases, groundbreaking) contributions in five areas: structural features of computer-mediated language, internet multilingualism and language choice, Web 2.0 (especially user-generated content and collaborative authorship), convergence in relation to new media, and methodology. I elaborate on each briefly below, following which I advance some criticisms in light of where I think future digital discourse research (or, in my terms, CMDA) should be headed.

At first blush, structural features of computer-mediated language might not seem like a groundbreaking topic, especially since casual observers and the popular media for years have fretted over the characteristics of "Netspeak" (see Naomi Baron's Foreword). Indeed, throughout the present volume one finds recommendations to move "beyond" a focus on lower-level grammatical features of new media language such as typography and orthography. Ironically, however, one of the most consistent contributions of the chapters in this volume is to knowledge about structural features of computer-mediated language, or what, for the sake of convenience and as an alternative to the problematic term "Netspeak," I call "e-grammar" (Herring, in press). For example, at the level of typography, Vaisman's comparison of Israeli girl bloggers' *Fakatsa* style to that of Leetspeak in Western hacker culture is a fascinating analysis, all the more so in that the symbols substituted for (Hebrew) letters are characters from another language (English). Chun and Walters provide evidence that nonstandard spoken language varieties—Arabic dialects and comedic representations of Filipino English—are typed in *YouTube* comments, and Androutsopoulos identifies English nonstandard orthography as one of the style varieties strategically manipulated in the "heteroglossic" discourse of a German musician's *MySpace* profile. I also noted with interest Jones et al.'s rare attestation of the use of "lolspeak," and their description of the use of a new lexical item, *meh*, in teens' IM gossip about *Facebook*.

E-grammar is not limited to typography and orthography, however. Peuronen's data show Finnish morphology on English loanwords, indicating the extent to which English and Finnish are mixed in the online communication of the Christian extreme sports enthusiasts she studied, while Dürscheid and Stark note the presence of French deverbal nouns in their corpus of Swiss text messages—a morphological innovation not found in either written or spoken French! At the level of syntax, Lee's chapter reports the effects on her Hong Kong subjects of *Facebook* removing the (username) "is" prompt: the incidence of utterances in Cantonese increased, as did interactive utterances. This suggests, intriguingly, that online discourse behavior can be "engineered" to some extent through the choice of linguistic features of the interface. Newon's chapter about MMORPG discourse includes a substantial, contextualized analysis of a syntactic phenomenon that is particular to e-grammar but has received little attention from language scholars: third-person emotes (another technologically facilitated behavior), and Nishimura analyzes sentence fragments in Japanese *keitai* novels. The latter analysis is reminiscent of Baron's (2010) analysis of structural fragmentation in American students' IM—both are attributable to properties of the medium. Thus, although "technological determinism" in the strong sense is out of fashion in new media research, there is evidence in these chapters that the properties of the media do influence some aspects of language use. The challenge is to identify the what, where, when, and how of such influence (Herring,

2007); the situated analyses in this volume help address these questions. Finally, Squires reports on how journalists selectively edited the text messages of Detroit politicians caught in a recent scandal, thereby reflecting the attitudes of mass media toward e-grammar and its users. Far from showing the need to move beyond structural features, these chapters demonstrate the need to examine them seriously (rather than anecdotally) in their sociocultural contexts. This is a major contribution, in my view.

It is also gratifying to see that the rapid growth of multilingualism on the internet since the mid-1990s (see Danet & Herring, 2007) is well reflected in the contexts of digital discourse analyzed in this volume; in this respect, its coverage is very contemporary. Beyond presenting data from other languages and analyzing them in their cultural contexts, several chapters—for example, Peuronen for Finnish and English; Androutsopoulos for German and English—shed welcome empirical light on the forms and functions of online language alternation and mixing. Also of great interest is the multilingual nature of the SMS corpus compiled by Dürscheid and Stark, reflecting the linguistic diversity of Switzerland (cf. Durham's 2003 analysis of a pan-Swiss discussion forum, in which speakers of different languages chose English as their lingua franca), and Lenihan's report on how *Facebook* is having its services translated into all the languages of the world (as of May 2010, 180 language versions were available). Lenihan characterizes *Facebook*'s vision as one of "parallel monolingualism"; in that regard, it resembles *Wikipedia* with its different language "editions" but differs from *LiveJournal*, where bloggers in different languages share a single hosting site and can "friend" one another easily (see Herring et al., 2007). It will be interesting to observe the long-term consequences of these organizational decisions, especially in light of contradictory evidence of interlanguage contact and integration taking place in many online contexts, as described in other chapters in this volume. Finally, the chapter by Chun and Walters illustrates yet another aspect of internet multilingualism: a multilingual (Korean-Arabic-English) performance by a comedian broadcast on *YouTube*. These studies are valuable because they attest to the spread and diversity of multilingualism in new media, while at the same time pointing to tensions within it. One tension in a number of studies is the use of English as a lingua franca, second language, or marker of (elite) social identities. One might say that this is the "elephant in the room," however, in that while its influence is pervasive, none of the chapters address its broader implications (cf. Danet & Herring, 2007).

Another important set of contributions center around the collaborative and/or co-constructed nature of discourse in Web 2.0 contexts. The creation and editing of *Wikipedia* articles is perhaps the paradigm case of this phenomenon, and indeed, the user-generated content and the process through which it is vetted in creating *Facebook* translations, as described by Lenihan, raise similar issues of "zero cost" labor and peer editing. Co-construction in other chapters is more asymmetrical: *keitai* novels, for example, are authored by single individuals, whose names are attached to the final products, yet feedback provided by readers and fans through comments and e-mail shapes the novels' contents (Nishimura). And in Walton and Jaffe's analysis of the satirical blog *Stuff White People Like*, it is stances toward race and class that are co-constructed through the blogger's posts and reader comments on them. In contrast, Rodney Jones characterizes skateboarding videos produced by teens in Hong Kong as individual, highly edited products, albeit shared in a community of skateboarders through posting on *YouTube*. This may be a limitation of current technology, however—no easily accessible tools yet exist for collaborative online video editing—more than a counterexample to the trend toward collaborative co-construction.

Related to Web 2.0 are the contributions that a number of chapters in this volume make to the study of discourse in convergent media platforms, or what I call convergent media computer-mediated communication (e.g., Zelenkauskaite & Herring, 2008). This is of utmost importance because digital discourse increasingly coexists on a single platform with other activities and applications, including other new media applications. *Facebook* is a prime example of the latter, in that it offers private in-box messages, private chat, semipublic "notes" that resemble blog entries, and several types of semipublic "wall" communication: status updates, posting of links, videos, and images, posts on others' walls, and comments on all of the above. Newon's *World of Warcraft* research site is also especially rich, but in communicative media of different types (voice+text+emotes+avatar actions), all of which, as she shows, may be used simultaneously. Moreover, the combination of media sharing and text comments—on *Flickr*, as analyzed in the case of "Pisa pose" photographs by Thurlow and Jaworski; on *YouTube*, as analyzed for reactions to a multilingual comic video by Chun and Walters; and on the *MySpace* page of a young German musician as analyzed by Androutsopoulos—is by now a widespread multimedia phenomenon, yet it has been little studied; these chapters are welcome empirical contributions. New to me was the situation of *keitai* novels, yet it clearly represents another convergence phenomenon. All of these contexts raise interesting issues: of polyvocality, multiple layers of addressees, conversational (in)coherence, and allotment of attentional resources, to mention but a few.

Methodological contributions are perhaps the least glamorous, but important nonetheless, especially to those of us who train others to analyze digital discourse. One hoary problem in computer-mediated discourse analysis has been how to collect a large corpus of authentic (not transcribed by users) SMS text messages. Both Spilioti, in making use of infrared technology to transfer Greek SMSs directly from mobile phones to a laptop computer, and Dürscheid and Stark, who collected a large corpus of Swiss SMSs by asking participants to forward their text messages directly to a designated, free mobile number, innovate in this regard. Useful, too, are the coding scheme for *Facebook* message content presented by Lee (adapted from an earlier scheme of Baron's for coding IM "away" messages) and Newon's transcription technique, which represents multiple channels of communication in a single transcript. I also read with interest Lee's methods for obtaining informed consent from her subjects in a context (*Facebook*) that has been difficult to study up to now for privacy reasons. These innovations might well serve as models for future researchers to adopt. Moreover, media convergence, multimodality, and linguistic heteroglossia all raise major methodological challenges, which the chapters in this volume grapple with in various ways, mostly through qualitative (descriptive) and ethnographic analysis. While I appreciate the necessity of such approaches to gain an overall initial sense of what is going on in a complex environment, I admit feeling a need for more rigorous empirical approaches, as well—methods that direct the researcher's attention to phenomena in systematic and principled ways, and that are informed by theory and research about the interactions of multiple semiotic systems (cf., e.g., Norris, 2004), whether the methods allow for ready quantification or not. As a field we are not there yet, I believe, but the approaches adopted in the chapters in this volume nonetheless constitute important advances.

Having described some of the volume's numerous contributions, I will now add a few cautionary observations. There is a focus in the volume overall on the new and unusual. This is necessary to update the field of digital discourse studies, and it is one of the strengths—and appeals—of the book. But it could give a distorted impression of digital discourse as a whole, by "exoticizing" it (some past research did this as well, by focusing on, e.g., typographic creativity). The bulk of digital discourse is rather less creative, as the chapter by Thurlow and Jaworski on "Pisa pose" photos on *Flickr* illustrates. Related to this is the fact that phenomena that fascinate new media scholars may be banal to younger users, who have known these media all their lives. Yet the theoretical and interpretive lenses through which their online discourses are analyzed in those chapters that deal with youth contexts are *adult* lenses, rather than the perspectives of the youth themselves (Jones' inclusion of quotes from interviews with Hong Kong skateboarders helps to offset this). For a critique of this tendency as a broader problem in studies of computer-mediated communication, see Herring (2008) and Thurlow (2009).

My last two critiques are aimed not so much at the chapters in this volume as at the field of digital discourse studies as a whole. The incorporation of theory is an important advance over earlier studies that were mostly descriptive; it represents an evolution of the research domain. However, there is a tendency in scholarship in the discourse-critical tradition for the theoretical framing to serve as a foregone conclusion, rather than for the conclusion to be an original discovery made by the researcher. Conclusions such as "language use is socially situated," "social identities are constructed through discourse," and "different language varieties intermingle (when multiple languages come in contact)" are not new ideas. Although such tenets serve to frame some of the studies in this volume in useful ways, my recommendation is that digital discourse researchers in general strive to develop original interpretations and conclusions, as a way to move thinking about language in new media forward.

Finally, there is a tendency in Western academic scholarship as a whole, reflected in a few of the chapters in this collection, to be dismissive of past research in an effort to motivate one's own approach. Critique is valuable, but in a young field such as computer-mediated discourse studies, which has yet to achieve a widely recognized critical mass, it should build upon, rather than seek to replace, what has already been done. By all means let us adapt and create new methodologies and new analytical lenses, as new phenomena require. But let us also recall that the early work is our foundation; it, too, was groundbreaking in its time, as the present volume breaks further new ground.

The seeds of the future can generally be discerned in the present, if one knows where to look. The combination of new data, new methods, and new analytical lenses applied to digital discourse situates this volume on the cutting edge of this historical moment, and I anticipate that its contributions will remain relevant for some time to come. Still, modes and media of computer-mediated communication arise, combine, and fall in and out of favor with various cultures, and new generations of users access mediated communication technologies with potentially radically different expectations every few years. What kinds of approaches—in addition to conducting further studies—might new media researchers adopt in order to produce scholarship that has lasting relevance? At the conclusion of a 2004 article, I wrote that: "[computer-mediated communication] researchers would do well to take a step back from the parade of passing technologies and consider more deeply the question of what determines people's use of mediated communication. In addition to technological determinism, the effects of time, familiarity, and mass popularization [...] need to be theorized and investigated" (Herring, 2004, p. 34). To this list I would add the desideratum of learning from the past, now that the field has reached a level of maturity at which this can meaningfully be done: synthesizing, distilling, and extracting core insights from the available corpus of empirical digital discourse discourse studies. The studies published in this volume enhance the size and quality of that corpus considerably and, as such, stand to shape the future of digital discourse research.

References

Baron, N.S. (2010). Discourse structures in instant messaging: The case of utterance breaks. *Language@Internet*, 7, article 4. Special issue on *Computer-Mediated Conversation*, part 1. Available at http://www.languageatinternet.de/articles/2010/2651/index_html/

Danet, B., & Herring, S.C. (Eds.) (2007). *The Multilingual Internet: Language, Culture, and Communication Online*. New York: Oxford University Press.

Durham, M. (2003). Language choice on a Swiss mailing list. *Journal of Computer-Mediated Communication*, 9(1). Available at http://jcmc.indiana.edu/vol9/issue1/durham.html

Herring, S.C. (2004). Slouching towards the ordinary: Current trends in computer-mediated communication. *New Media & Society*, 6(1), 26–36.

Herring, S.C. (2007). A faceted classification scheme for computer-mediated discourse. *Language@Internet*, 4, article 1. Available at http://www.languageatinternet.de/articles/2007/761

Herring, S.C. (2008). Questioning the generational divide: Technological exoticism and adult construction of online youth identity. In D. Buckingham (Ed.), *Youth, Identity, and Digital Media*, (pp. 71–94). Cambridge, MA: MIT Press.

Herring, S.C. (in press). Grammar and electronic communication. In C. Chapelle (Ed.), *Encyclopedia of Applied Linguistics*. Wiley-Blackwell Publishers.

Herring, S.C., Paolillo, J.C., Ramos Vielba, I., Kouper, I., Wright, E., Stoerger, S., Scheidt, L.A., & Clark, B. (2007). Language networks on LiveJournal. *Proceedings of the Fortieth Hawaii International Conference on System Sciences.* Los Alamitos, CA: IEEE Press.

Norris, S. (2004). *Analyzing Multimodal Interaction: A Methodological Framework.* London: Routledge.

Thurlow, C. (Ed.). (2009). Young people, mediated discourse and communication technologies. Special issue of the *Journal of Computer Mediated Communication,* 14(4), 1038–1282.

Zelenkauskaite, A., & Herring, S.C. (2008). Television-mediated conversation: Coherence in Italian iTV SMS chat. *Proceedings of the Forty-First Hawai'i International Conference on System Sciences (HICSS-41).* Los Alamitos, CA: IEEE Press.

Index

Italicized page numbers indicate a figure
Page numbers followed by t indicate a table
Page numbers follwed by e indicate an extract